LINGUISTIC SURVEYS OF AFRICA

Volume 14

THE LANGUAGES OF WEST AFRICA

THE LANGUAGES OF WEST AFRICA
Handbook of African Languages Part 2

DIEDRICH WESTERMANN AND M. A. BRYAN

LONDON AND NEW YORK

First published in 1970 by Dawsons of Pall Mall

This edition first published in 2018
by Routledge
2 Park Square, Milton Park, Abingdon, Oxon OX14 4RN

and by Routledge
711 Third Avenue, New York, NY 10017

Routledge is an imprint of the Taylor & Francis Group, an informa business

© 1970 International African Institute

All rights reserved. No part of this book may be reprinted or reproduced or utilised in any form or by any electronic, mechanical, or other means, now known or hereafter invented, including photocopying and recording, or in any information storage or retrieval system, without permission in writing from the publishers.

Trademark notice: Product or corporate names may be trademarks or registered trademarks, and are used only for identification and explanation without intent to infringe.

British Library Cataloguing in Publication Data
A catalogue record for this book is available from the British Library

ISBN: 978-1-138-08975-4 (Set)
ISBN: 978-1-315-10381-5 (Set) (ebk)
ISBN: 978-1-138-09658-5 (Volume 14) (hbk)
ISBN: 978-1-138-09668-4 (Volume 14) (pbk)
ISBN: 978-1-315-10523-9 (Volume 14) (ebk)

Publisher's Note
The publisher has gone to great lengths to ensure the quality of this reprint but points out that some imperfections in the original copies may be apparent.

Disclaimer
The publisher has made every effort to trace copyright holders and would welcome correspondence from those they have been unable to trace.

Due to modern production methods, it has not been possible to reproduce the fold-out maps within the book. Please visit www.routledge.com to view them.

THE LANGUAGES OF WEST AFRICA

BY

DIEDRICH WESTERMANN

AND

M. A. BRYAN

With a supplementary bibliography
compiled by

Professor D. W. Arnott

Published for the
INTERNATIONAL AFRICAN INSTITUTE
by
Dawsons of Pall Mall
Folkestone & London
1970

First published for the
International African Institute
by the Oxford University Press in 1952

New edition 1970

Dawsons of Pall Mall
Cannon House
Folkestone, Kent, England

ISBN: 0 7129 0462 X

© International African Institute 1970

Unwin Brothers Limited
The Gresham Press, Old Woking Surrey England
A member of the Staples Printing Group

FOREWORD

THIS volume presents a survey of the languages of West Africa, that is to say, the languages spoken in an area extending from the Atlantic coast at the Senegal River eastward to the Lake Chad region. The eastern limit of the area has been more or less arbitrarily determined,[1] since available information is not adequate for a strictly linguistic boundary to be drawn. The area covered by this volume being thus a geographical one, it follows that not all the languages included are related to one another, though a certain degree of homogeneity appears.

The languages of West Africa have been the subject of much study and research, and numerous classifications have been made by, e.g. Delafosse, Drexel, Cust, and Greenberg; the basis of classification adopted in this volume is in the main that of my *Westliche Sudansprachen*. Nevertheless there are areas where, on the basis of existing information, classification is far from easy, and there are languages whose place within the system here set forth may be disputed (see p. 95). Moreover, although the importance of tone in certain West African languages has long been recognized, tonality has not hitherto been used as a basis of classification; the possibility of its use is being explored (see *Africa*, **19,** 3, pp. 213–19).

Every effort has been made to take account of all available information, both published and unpublished, but it is highly probable that much more material exists, or may become available as a result of current researches. The International African Institute, therefore, will welcome any comments, criticisms, or additional data which readers of this volume are able to furnish. This is the more to be desired since the preparation of this volume has revealed many lacunae in the existing material, and many cases where information is clearly unreliable, and should be checked and supplemented.

I wish in the first place to express my debt to the late Professor Ida Ward, who revised the first draft, though her death most tragically prevented her from seeing the completion of the work. Thanks are specially due to my collaborator Miss M. A. Bryan, who analysed, classified, and arranged the greater part of the material; to Professor Lukas, for most generous assistance, not only in supplying material and advising on arrangement, but also in drafting several sections of the present text; to Mr. I. Richardson and Dr. Emmi Meyer, who supplied material for the Cameroons area; to the Director of IFAN, who provided data for French West Africa; to the Rev. Professor G. van Bulck, S.J., for much valuable information, especially on the Chad area; and to numerous others who generously and patiently answered inquiries and otherwise placed their knowledge and experience at our disposal.

D. WESTERMANN

March 1952

[1] e.g. KANURI and some languages in the Chad area are dealt with in another volume of the Handbook.

TABLE OF CONTENTS

FOREWORD	3
INTRODUCTORY NOTES	7
I. WEST ATLANTIC LANGUAGES	11
II. MANDE LANGUAGES	31
III. SONGHAI	46
IV. KRU LANGUAGE GROUP	48
V. GUR LANGUAGES	55
VI. KWA LANGUAGES	76
VII. ISOLATED GROUPS OR UNITS (Class Languages)	95
VIII. ISOLATED GROUPS OR UNITS (non-Class Languages)	133
IX. CHADIC LANGUAGES	153
X. CHADO-HAMITIC LANGUAGES	162
BIBLIOGRAPHY	178
SUPPLEMENTARY BIBLIOGRAPHY	203
INDEX	265

INTRODUCTORY NOTES

THE method of classification used in the Handbook of African languages is based on a technique devised for the purpose by the Linguistic Advisory Committee of the International African Institute.[1]

1. *The BASIC UNIT of classification*

The starting-point for the classification is not the large area but the individual language. Since the individual language is the basic unit of classification, it is necessary to determine exactly what this unit is. In some cases this proves difficult, particularly where several dialects have been recognized of one 'language'. Thus it is necessary to distinguish different types of basic unit:

(a) a language, without recognized dialectal variations;
(b) a language, with which are associated dialects of lesser importance.
   Both these types of unit are termed LANGUAGE.
(c) a number of dialects, no one of which appears to dominate.
   This type of unit is termed DIALECT CLUSTER.

For purposes of classification, however, they are all regarded as basic units at the same level of classification.

In the case of the simple LANGUAGE, i.e. type (a), no subdivision is necessary; the other units, however, may be subdivided into dialects, that is, into something smaller than a unit. Useful or even necessary though this subdivision may be for purposes of reference, it must be emphasized that this is a kind of fragmentation, since the dialect is smaller than the basic unit.

2. *The LANGUAGE GROUP*

Basic units known to be related are grouped together into larger sections which have a linguistic significance, since the principal criteria of grouping are linguistic. These are termed LANGUAGE GROUPS; the term 'Group' being used exclusively to denote a number of related languages or dialect clusters, any loose use of the word becomes undesirable, in view of the precise linguistic significance given to it. The criteria governing the establishment of Groups are linguistic; in certain cases, where these criteria are indecisive, it may become necessary to take other factors into consideration.

3. *The LARGER UNIT*

In some cases, however, it can be seen that several Language Groups and/or Single Units (see par. 4 below) show an over-all relationship. Thus the classification of Language Groups into some larger unit may be necessary. This is shown in the linguistic notes, where the characteristics of a larger unit consisting of several language groups can be comprehensively described. No attempt is, however, made to attach any label (such as 'family') to these larger units, which are limited in number. Thus, in the West African geographical area, the Larger Units are: the KWA languages, the GUR languages, the West Atlantic languages, the MANDE languages, the Chado-Hamitic languages, and the Chadic languages (?).

4. *The SINGLE UNIT*

In some cases a Language or Dialect Cluster can be seen to belong to one of the Larger

[1] *Africa*, 16, 3, 1946.

Units, while yet not sufficiently closely related to any other to form part of a Language Group. This is termed a SINGLE UNIT, e.g. WOLOF.

5. *The ISOLATED GROUP*

On the other hand, a Language Group may be found to display inter-relationship between its constituent basic units without forming part of any Larger Unit. This is termed an ISOLATED GROUP, e.g. the 'Togo Remnant' Languages.

6. *The ISOLATED UNIT*

Finally, there are many basic units which cannot be considered to have any relationship with any other. These are termed ISOLATED UNITS.

Isolated units may be of two kinds:

(*a*) those of which enough is known for it to be reasonably certain that they are unrelated to any other unit, e.g. SONGHAI Dialect Cluster;
(*b*) those which cannot be classified owing to lack of linguistic evidence, e.g. many of the 'Class Languages' of Nigeria.

Although the same term is used to designate both kinds, the latter is indicated by the use of a question mark.

The use of question marks is, in fact, fundamental to the scope of the Handbook at its present stage, and the presence or absence of a query should be taken throughout as an indication of the reliability of the information available.

Note on typography

NAMES of languages and tribes are given as follows:

1. Roman Capitals: (*a*) name of language or dialect by which it is known to Europeans—alternative spellings in brackets, including French (Fr.) and Portuguese (Port.); (*b*) names by which known to other tribes.

2. Italic Capitals: (*a*) name of tribe or section by which known to Europeans (variants as above under (1)); (*b*) names by which known to other tribes.

3. Heavy type lower case: name of language or tribe in the 'Africa' orthography, with tone marks where known.

4. Ordinary type in inverted commas: name of locality when used as the name of language or tribe.

Abbreviations used

TP = Tax-payers.   C = Consonant.   V = Vowel

INTRODUCTORY NOTES

Notes on phonetic symbols used

FOR the spelling of vernacular names, and in the linguistic notes, the 'Africa' alphabet is used, with the following additional symbols:

ɪ, ʊ	open i and u;
ḭ, ṵ	(p. 128) used by Prof. Guthrie for close i and u;
æ	(p. 142) as in English 'hat';
ɑ	(p. 130) back a;
ɯ	unrounded u;
ʌ	central vowel as in English 'but';
ö, ä, ü	central vowels;
'y	(p. 170) implosive y;
ɥ	semi-vowel as in French 'huit';
pˈ, tˈ, kˈ	unexploded plosives;
ɢ	uvular voiced plosive;
ħ	(p. 130) pharyngal fricative;
kp, gb	labio-velar plosives;
kɓ, gɓ	labio-velar implosives;
ṭ, ṛ, ẓ	retroflex t, r, z;
m̥	(p. 129) unvoiced m;
ɬ, ɮ	(pp. 108, 159) lateral fricatives.

Section I
THE WEST ATLANTIC LANGUAGES
(LARGER UNIT)

The West Atlantic languages are spoken in the coastal area of West Africa from Senegal to River Loffa (Liberia), with *ADYUKRU* far to the south-east on the Ivory Coast.

Single Unit: ADYUKRU

ADYUKRU. Language.

Spoken by: ADYUKRU (*AJUKRU, ADJUKRU,* Fr. *ADYOUKROU, A-DJOUKROU*), call themselves **adyukru** or **adiukru** (Sing. **odiukru**),[1] called 'Dabu' by the *ANYI*, also known as *BUBURI*.

Where spoken: In the southern Ivory Coast, Cercle Lagunes, north of Ebrié lagoon around Dabou (Dabu) and Toupa.

Number of speakers: 30,000 (Labouret);[2] 21,000.[1]

Parts of the New Testament have been translated.

Single Unit: GOLA

GOLA, own name **eǵola mie**. Language (or Dialect Cluster?).

Spoken by: *GOLA*, call themselves **ǵola**, called *GULA* by the *MENDE*.

Where spoken: Western Liberia, between Rivers Moa and St. Paul; also on the left bank of the St. Paul.

Number of speakers: 150,000 (about 8,500 in Sierra Leone[3]).

The *GOLA* consist of several sections, calling themselves:

deŋ ǵola (from the GOLA name for the St. Paul river);
toldil (toodii), south of the deŋ ǵola on the left bank of the river;
tɛ́gɛ ǵola, on the right bank of the river, adjoining the deŋ ǵola on the west, the *KPELLE* on the east;
sɛ̀nyɛ ǵola, north of the tɛ́gɛ;
mána gɔ̀bla (gɔbla ǵola), on the right bank of the St. Paul as far as River Loffa;
kɔŋbaa ǵola, on the right bank of the St. Paul;
pio ǵola, also on the right bank.

Nothing is known of dialectal differences within GOLA.

---

[1] Bertho, 'La place du dialecte adiukru par rapport aux autres dialectes de la Côte d'Ivoire' (*Bull. IFAN*, 1950). Note that he considers ADYUKRU to have vocabulary affinities with the KWA languages, but this is due to recent borrowing.

[2] Figures cited 'Labouret' are taken from his contributions to *Afrika: Handbuch der angewandten Völkerkunde* (ed. H. A. Bernatzik), Innsbruck, 1947.

[3] 1931 Census.

THE WEST ATLANTIC LANGUAGES
Language Group? KISSI-LANDOMA

Consists of: KISSI   Language.
BULOM   Dialect Cluster?
MMANI   Language?

LIMBA   Language.

TEMNE   Language.
BAGA   Dialect Cluster?
LANDOMA   Language?

Where spoken: French Guinea and Sierra Leone.

KISSI, BULOM, and perhaps MMANI are closely interrelated, as are TEMNE, BAGA, and LANDOMA. LIMBA differs somewhat from the other units in this Group.

KISSI. Language.

Spoken by: KISSI (*KISI*), call themselves **kisi** or **gisi**, called **gizi**, **gihi**, **gii** by neighbouring tribes, *GIZI*, *GIZIMA* by the Liberians, **dɛi** by the *GOLA*.

Where spoken: Mainly in French Guinea, Cercles Macenta, Guékédou, Kissidougou, and Dabola; also in a strip of territory on both sides of the Liberia–Sierra Leone border.

Number of speakers: about 240,000 (French Guinea 164,346,[1] Sierra Leone c. 35,000,[2] Liberia 25,000).

In the Sierra Leone–Liberia border area three sections of the *KISSI* have been distinguished: *KAMA*, *TENG*, *TUNG*.

IFAN[3] names a dialect LIARO spoken in Cercle Macenta.

Two Gospels have been published (multigraphed).

BULOM. Dialect Cluster?

Spoken by: BULOM (*BOLOM*, *BULLOM*, *BULLUN*), also known as *SHERBRO*, call themselves **bulǝm**, called *MAMPA*, *AMAMPA* by the *TEMNE* and *VAI*.

Where spoken: Sierra Leone, Sherbro District, and in coastal villages of Sierra Leone peninsula.

Number of speakers: BULOM and SHERBRO 167,200, KRIM 44,600.[4]

There appear to be several sections of the *BULOM*; those living in the Bome River area are known as *BOME* (*BUM*, *BOMO*); those in the Krim River area call themselves *KIM*, *KIMI*, and are known as *KRIM* (*KIRIM*, *KITTIM*); the name *MAMPA* (*MAMPWA*) is used to denote in particular the *BULOM* of Sherbro, who are called *SHIBA* (a corruption of the English 'sea-bar') by the *VAI*.

---

[1] *La Guinée Française* (published in connexion with the Exposition coloniale internationale, Paris, 1931).   [2] 1931 Census.
[3] Information marked IFAN in this and other sections of the Handbook was supplied by the Institut Français d'Afrique Noire.   [4] From recent (1945) Government sources.

THE WEST ATLANTIC LANGUAGES

Dialects: The 'BULOM' and 'MAMPA' of Koelle appear to differ; the dialect of the *BUM* is closely akin to that of the *MAMPA*. There may be other dialects, as the class system of *BULOM*, according to Koelle, differs from that given by Sumner, as does the vocabulary to some extent.[1]

A Gospel has been translated into BULOM; there is also a Prayer Book.

MMANI. Language?[2]

Spoken by: *MMANI*, call themselves *MMANI*, called *MANDENYI* (*MENDENYI*) by the *SUSU*.

Where spoken: On the coast of French Guinea between Rivers Grand Scarcie (Kolente) and Morebaya.

LIMBA. Language.

Spoken by: *LIMBA*, call themselves **limba** (variant **yimbɛ**).

Where spoken: Sierra Leone, between Rivers Rokel and Scarcie, north of the *TEMNE*; according to IFAN, also in French Guinea, Cercle Mamou.

Number of speakers: 174,400 in Sierra Leone.[3]

Thomas[4] gives vocabularies from the following localities: Sella, Safroko, Biriwa, Tonko, Warawara. Dialectal differences do not appear to be significant.

A Gospel has been translated; another is in the press (1950).

TEMNE. Language.

Spoken by: *TEMNE* (*TIMNE, TIMENE, TIMMANNEE*), call themselves **a-temnɛ** (Sing. **ɔ-temnɛ**).

Where spoken: Sierra Leone, north and north-west of the *MENDE*, between Rivers Little Scarcie and Sewa; according to IFAN, also in Mellacorée (Mellakori) on the coast of French Guinea in Cercle Forecariah.

Number of speakers: Sierra Leone 505,600.[3]

The TEMNE are in two sections (it is not known whether they speak different dialects):
SANDA TEMNE in the north;
YONNI TEMNE in the south.

There is a small amount of vernacular literature, including the New Testament and parts of the Old Testament. The Sierra Leone Protectorate Literature Bureau is encouraging the production of literature.

BAGA. Dialect Cluster?

Spoken by: *BAGA* (*BARKA*), call themselves **baga**.

[1] Koelle, *Polyglotta Africana*; Sumner, *A handbook of the Sherbro language*.
[2] M. Houis, 'Les minorités ethniques de la Guinée côtière. Situation linguistique' (*Et. Guinéennes*, 1950), from an unpublished study of the MMANI language by Moity.
[3] From recent (1948) Government figures.   [4] Specimens of languages from Sierra Leone.

Where spoken: Scattered along the coast of French Guinea, from Conakry to River Compony.

Number of speakers: 4,000 (Labouret); 23,436;[1] 50,000.[2]

The various *BAGA* sections are designated by names of localities. They include:[3]

BAGA 'Kalum', in Kalum (Kaloum) peninsula. They are almost completely assimilated to the *SUSU* (see p. 37) and only the old people still speak *BAGA*.
BAGA 'Koba', in Cercle Boffa. They are in process of assimilation to the *SUSU*.
BAGA 'Sobane'.
BAGA 'Sitemu' ('Sitémou'), on Rio Nunez.
BAGA 'Madure' ('Mandouré'), on islands in the Rio Nunez delta (very few in number).
Note: For BAGA FORE see below, under NALU.

Arcin[4] suggests that the *WAELE* in Futa Djallon may be a *BAGA* remnant, and perhaps speak a BAGA dialect.

LANDOMA (LANDUMA). LANGUAGE?

Spoken by: *LANDOMA* (*LANDUMA*, Fr. *LANDOUMAN*), call themselves **landoma** or **landuma**.

Where spoken: French Guinea, between the upper Rio Nunez and upper Rio Pongas (Pongo), inland from the *NALU*.

Number of speakers: uncertain: Méo gives 28,000 in Cercle Rio Nunez,[5] Labouret a total of 12,500.

A dialect of LANDOMA is said to be spoken by the *TIAPI* (*TYAPI*, *TAPESSI*) in Cercles Gaoual and Boké; they appear to be a section of the *LANDOMA*.

Number: 10,000 (Labouret); 8,179.[6]

SINGLE UNIT? NALU

NALU. LANGUAGE?

Spoken by: *NALU* (Fr. *NALOU*).

Where spoken: On the coast between Rio Nunez in the south and Rio Tombati in the north, on both sides of the French Guinea–Portuguese Guinea border.

Number of speakers: 10,000 (Labouret).

According to Houis,[7] the so-called *BAGA FORE* ('Black *BAGA*') of Monchon speak a dialect which differs markedly from the BAGA dialects, but is very closely akin to NALU, and may be a NALU dialect.

[1] *La Guinée Française*, 1931.
[2] France d'outre-mer leaflet.
[3] Houis, loc. cit. [4] *Guinée Française* (1907).
[5] 'Études sur le Rio Nunez' (*Bull. Com. Et. hist. et scient. de l'A.O.F.*, 1919).
[6] M. M. Kéita, 'La famille et le mariage chez les Tyapi' (*Et. Guinéennes*, 1947).
[7] Loc. cit.

THE WEST ATLANTIC LANGUAGES

LANGUAGE GROUP OR SINGLE UNIT? BANYUN

Little is known about the languages or dialects spoken by the following tribes, except that they are said to be related to each other:

BANYUN (Fr. *BAÏNOUK*, Port. *BANHUN*), call themselves *BANYUN* (Sing. *ANYUN*),[1] *BANYUNG* or *BANYUK*, called **banyuŋka** by MANDE-speakers; also known as *ELOMAY, ELUNAY*; in Portuguese Guinea, between Rivers Casamance and Cacheo, and in Senegal, in the Sedhiou–Bignona–Ziguinchor area.

Number: 18,000 (Labouret).

KOBIANA (about 300); and *KASANGA* (Port. *CASSANGA*, Fr. *CASSANGUE*) (420)[2] who call themselves *IHAJA* (*IHAGE*); both in the same area as the *BANYUN*.

LANGUAGE GROUP OR SINGLE UNIT? BALANTE[3]

The languages or dialects spoken by the following tribes are closely interrelated:

BALANTE (*BALANT, BALANTA, BULANDA*), call themselves *BALANT* or *BELANTE* (Sing. *ALANTE*), also known as *BRASSA*; in Portuguese Guinea, between Rivers Casamance and Geba; also in Senegal, around Ziguinchor and Sedhiou.

There are two sections of the tribe (northern and southern), with some dialectal differences.[3]

Number: 154,246,[2] including the *BALANTA MANE*, who are much mixed with *MANDINKA*.

The *NAGA* north-west of the *BALANTE* are closely related to them, and probably speak a related dialect.

KUNANTE, call themselves *KUNANTE* or *KUNÃT*; in Portuguese Guinea, on the borders of the administrative districts of Bafata and Mansoa.
Number: 6,050.[2]

LANGUAGE GROUP OR SINGLE UNIT? MANDYAK

The languages or dialects spoken by the following are closely related both in vocabulary and structure:

MANDYAK (Fr. *MANDJAQUE*, Port. *MANJACO*), call themselves *MANDYAK, MÃDYAK*, or *MANDYAKO*, also known as *KANYOP*; in Portuguese Guinea, on the coast between Rivers Cacheo and Mansoa, and on Pecixe Island; also in Senegal, in the Ziguinchor–Sedhiou area.

Number: 12,000 in Senegal (Labouret); 71,712 in Portuguese Guinea.[2]

---

[1] **ba-** (BANYUN, BALANTE) and **ma-** (MANDYAK, MANKANYA) are plural prefixes. See Tastevin, 'Vocabulaires inédits de 7 dialectes . . .' (*J. Soc. Afric.*, 1936).
[2] 1950 Census.
[3] Information on the location of *BALANTE, MANDYAK*, and related tribes from L. Brierley (personal communication).

PEPEL (*PAPEL*, Port. *PAPEI*), call themselves *PAPEL* or *PEPEL* (pɛpɛl); in Portuguese Guinea, mainly on Bissao Island; also in French Guinea.

Number: 36,341.[1]

MANKANYA (Fr. *MANCAGNE*, Port. *MANCANHA*); also known as *BOLA*, *BRAME*, called *BURAMA*, *BURAM*, *BULAMA* by the *BALANTE*; in Portuguese Guinea, between Rivers Cacheo and Mansoa; west of the *MANJAKO*, east of the *BALANTE*; also on Bolama Island.

Number: 16,300.[1]

There appear to be two dialects, SHADAL or SADAR, spoken on the mainland, and BURAMA, spoken on the island. The names *MANKANYA* and *BOLO* or *BRAME*, supposed by some writers to denote different tribes, are, however, as pointed out by Carreira,[2] two names for one tribe.

The languages or dialects spoken by the following may also be related to the above:

BIAFADA (*BIAFAR*, *FADA*, Port. *BEAFADA*), also known as *BIDYOLA*; in Portuguese Guinea, on both banks of the Geba estuary.

Number: 11,851.[1]

According to Nogueira[3] they call themselves *BEDJOLA* (Sing. *DJOLA*); Richard-Mollard[4] calls them '*DJOLA* de Boké'; the *YOLA* (2,000–3,000) on River Company are said to be a section of the *BIAFADA*. There may, however, be some confusion with the *DYOLA* (see p. 17); linguistic material available is insufficient to show the affiliations of their language or dialect.

BIDYOGO (*BUDJAGO*, *BUGAGO*, Fr. *BIJOUGOT*, Port. *BIJAGO*), call themselves *BIDYOGO* (**bidyogo, bidoyo,** or **biʒagɔ**); on Bijago (Bissagos) archipelago.

Number: 10,332.[1]

The dialect spoken on Roxa (Canhabaque) Island differs from that of the other islands; the people of Roxa call themselves (Port.) *ANHAQUI* (**anyaki**).[5]

Single Unit? TENDA

TENDA is a general name comprising a number of tribes or tribal sections, and the languages or dialects spoken by them, on the Senegal–French Guinea border. Little is known about them. The following names are given by various writers as those of *TENDA* sections:

BADYARA (*PAJADE*, Fr. *BADYARANKE*, Port. *PAJADINCA*), call themselves *BADYAR* or *BADYARE*, called **badyaraŋkɛ** by MANDE-speakers, also known as *GOLA*, *AGOLA*, *BIGOLA*, *AXUS*; around the point where French Guinea, Portuguese Guinea, and Senegal adjoin.

Number: 10,000 (Labouret).

---

[1] 1950 Census.   [2] *Vida social dos Manjacos*.   [3] (Note in *Bol. cult. Guiné Port.*, 1946.)
[4] Map of populations of West Africa prepared for IFAN (unpublished).
[5] D. A. G. Alves (note in *Bol. cult. Guiné Port.*, 1947).

THE WEST ATLANTIC LANGUAGES

KONYAGI (KONYAKI, Fr. *COGNIAGUI*, Port. *CONHAGUE*), called **awõhẽ, azɛn** by neighbouring tribes; in French Guinea, east of Youkounkoun, extending to the border of Senegal.

Number: 85,000 (Labouret).

BASARI, call themselves *BASAR*, also known as *AYAN, BIYAN, WO*; on the borders of French Guinea, Senegal and Gambia, around Youkounkoun.

Number: 11,500 (Labouret).

Note: Arcin[1] divides the TENDA into:
TENDA;
TENDA BOENI on the lower Miti and middle Tomino rivers (included in BASARI by Richard-Mollard[2] and described by him as '*TENDA* foulisés');
BADYARANKE;
KONYAGI;
BASARI.

Single Unit? DYOLA

DYOLA. Dialect Cluster?

Spoken by: *DYOLA (DIOLA, JOLA, YOLA).*[3]

Where spoken: Between Rivers Gambia and Cacheo, in Senegal and Gambia.

Number of speakers: 125,000 (Labouret); 19,467 in the Gambia,[4] 115,000 in Senegal.[5]

The *DYOLA* consist of a number of sections (15 according to Labouret), mostly known by place-names. They include:

'Karones', also known as 'Dyembaren (Dyembering) Karones', on the rivers of the same names;
BLISS, in much the same area as the above;
'Carabane', on Carabane Island;
DYAMATE, call themselves *KUDAMATA* (Sing. *ADAMAT*); on the right bank of River Casamance;
FONY (FOGNY), between Bignona and River Sangrogrou (according to IFAN, extending as far as Sedhiou); also in the Gambia, and south of Carabane. The dialect of the *FONY* is the most widely understood of the Cluster.
BAYOT (BAIOT, Fr. *BAYOTTE)*, south of Ziguinchor, mainly in Portuguese Guinea (4,373[6]);
FLUP (FELUPE, FULUP, FILHAM, Fr. *FLOUP, FELOUP)*, call themselves **u-luf**;[7] between Rivers Casamance and Cacheo (8,167[6]).

Single Unit? SERER

SERER. Dialect Cluster.

Spoken by: *SERER (SERRER*, Fr. *SERÈRE*, &c.).

Where spoken: Mainly in Senegal, south of Cayor; also in the Gambia.

Number of speakers: 300,000 (Labouret).

[1] Op. cit.
[2] Loc. cit.
[3] Not to be confused with *DYULA* (see p. 35).
[4] Report of the Senior Commissioner on the Annual Census of the Protectorate of Gambia, 1945.
[5] France d'outre-mer leaflet.
[6] 1950 Census.
[7] Tastevin, loc. cit.

Dialects: There are two main dialects, spoken by:

SERER NON (*NONE*), also called *DYOBA*; on the coast in the region of Thiès;

SERER SIN (*SINE-SINE*), also called KEGEM ('Ndyegem', 'Dyéguèmé'—a place-name); in the Saloum valley, around Joal. (These are the *BARRACIN* of old Portuguese writers.)

IFAN further mentions dialects:

NYOMINKA, spoken around Kaolack and Foundiougne;
SEGUM, spoken at M'Bour;
NDOUTE, spoken in the Thiès area.

SINGLE UNIT: WOLOF

WOLOF (Fr. VOLOF, OUOLOF, &c.). LANGUAGE OR DIALECT CLUSTER.

Spoken by: *WOLOF*, call themselves **wɔlɔf**; they call their country **dyɔlɔf**, and this name (*JOLOF, DYOLOF*) is also used by Europeans to denote both the people and their language.

Where spoken: Mainly in Senegal, from the left bank of River Senegal to Cape Vert, but also in *SERER* country as far south as the Gambia, and (according to IFAN) extending in the north into Mauretania.

Number of speakers: 640,000 (Labouret); 28,510 in the Gambia.[1]

Dialectal differences have been noted, especially in the speech of St. Louis, Cayor (Kayor), Walo, Saloum, and Lébou.

WOLOF is an important trade language spoken or understood throughout Senegambia. Parts of the Bible have been translated, and there are some religious and educational books.

SINGLE UNIT: FULANI

FULANI (FUL, FULA, PEUL, POULAR, &c.), own name **fulfulde**. DIALECT CLUSTER.

Spoken by: *FULANI*, call themselves **fulɓe** (Sing. **pulo**), called *FULANI* (*FUL, FULA*, &c.) by many Europeans, *FILANI* by the *HAUSA, FULATA, FELATA* by the *KANURI, PEUL* (*PEULH, POULAR*, &c.) by the French. In the north-west (i.e. mainly in Senegal) they are called *TOUCOULEUR* (*TUKULOR*, &c.) by the French.

Where spoken: Scattered over a vast area of West Africa from Senegal and Mauretania to Sierra Leone in the west, and extending as far east as Bagirmi and Wadai. The main *FULANI* concentrations are in Senegambia, Macina in the French Sudan, and Adamawa in Nigeria.

Number of speakers: The total number of FULANI-speakers cannot be estimated, in view of the enormous distribution of the *FULANI* and the great number of people who have adopted FULANI or who speak it as a second language. The following figures give some indication of approximate numbers of *FULANI*:

[1] Report of the Senior Commissioner . . ., 1945.

French West Africa:[1] Mauretania 12,000; Senegal 250,000; French Sudan 600,000; Ivory Coast and Haute-Volta 52,000; Dahomey 54,000; Niger 269,000; plus *TUKULOR* in Senegal, French Sudan and a few in Mauretania 240,000, and '*FULA*' in Futa Djallon 720,000;
Gambia 50,000;[2]
Portuguese Guinea 108,400;[3]
Nigeria (Northern Provinces) 2,025,200;[4]
French Cameroons 257,680;[5]
giving a total of well over 4 millions.

Dialects: No detailed study of the dialects of FULANI has yet been made. The following main geographical areas where different dialects are spoken have been distinguished:[6]

Futa Sénégalais (dialect PULAR, Fr. POULAR, according to Cremer);
Futa Djallon (dialect FULA);
Macina, Haute-Volta, and the Niger bend;
Northern Nigeria, with main centres Kano and Katsina;
Nigeria: Adamawa Province and adjacent territory;
Nigeria: Bauchi Province and part of Plateau Province;
Bagirmi (dialect FOULBÉRÉ according to Cremer).

In Nigeria the dialect of Kano and Katsina may be considered as the most widely understood. The name 'Western FULANI' is applied in Nigeria to dialects of FULANI other than that of Adamawa.

Parts of the Bible have been published in the dialects of Adamawa, Futa Djallon, and Macina. There is little other vernacular literature.

Linguistic notes on the West Atlantic Languages

The West Atlantic languages do not form nearly so close a unit as, for example, the GUR languages. There is great diversity in vocabulary and in the Noun Class system, also in many grammatical details. Their common features are: (*a*) Noun Classes formed mostly by Prefixes; (*b*) *nomen rectum* following *nomen regens* in the Genitive construction (for exceptions to (*a*) and (*b*) see below); (*c*) a common vocabulary containing words not occurring in other West African languages.

The linguistic position of FULANI has long been in doubt, largely owing to the fact that Meinhof classed it as HAMITIC.[7] The possibility of some relationship between FULANI and languages of the West Atlantic Larger Unit (notably SERER, WOLOF, and BIAFADA) has been pointed out by various writers,[8] and it now appears certain that FULANI belongs to this Larger Unit.

[1] Labouret; figures in France d'outre-mer publications differ considerably with regard to distribution, but add up to approximately the same total.
[2] Report of the Senior Commissioner . . ., 1945.
[3] 1950 Census.
[4] 1931 Census.
[5] 'Inventaire ethnique et linguistique du Cameroun sous mandat français' (*J. Soc. Afric.*, 1934).
[6] Cremer, *Dictionnaire français-peul*; information on Nigerian dialects from F. de Ste-Croix.
[7] *Die Sprachen der Hamiten*.
[8] e.g. Faidherbe, 'Essai sur la langue poul . . .' (*Rev. de linguistique*, 1875); Klingenheben, 'Die Permutationen des Biafada und des Ful' (*Z. Eingeb. Spr.*, 1914–15); Delafosse, 'Classes nominales en wolof' (*Festschrift Meinhof*, 1927); Homburger, 'Le sérère-peul' (*J. Soc. Afr.*, 1939); Greenberg, 'Studies in African linguistic classification. 2. The classification of Fulani' (*Southwestern J. of Anthrop.*, 1949).

A. *Languages other than* FULANI

Only a limited number of these languages has been sufficiently investigated, so that in most cases it is not possible to make definitive statements on the nature of their sounds or on grammatical structure. Further research is badly needed.

1. Many languages appear to have a nine-vowel system. Thomas[1] distinguishes thirteen vowels in TEMNE, Sumner[2] nine, while in BULOM there are, according to Sumner,[3] seven.

Nasalized vowels are rare.

2. The labio-velar sounds **kp, gb** are of frequent occurrence in the eastern languages (ADYUKRU, GOLA, TEMNE, BULOM), while in the western languages they are rare or absent.

ADYUKRU has unusual consonant combinations such as **kl, bm, gŋ**.

Nasal compounds exist.

3. Tone is important in at least a number of languages, but little is known about it.

Examples from GOLA: **dìi** ground; **díí** maize.

4. The majority of Word Roots consist of CVC(V). Roots consisting of CV are far less common. The second consonant of a Root may be preceded by a nasal:

    GOLA   **ò-kándâ**   chief   **ké-kómbò**   smoke
    TEMNE   **kombila**   shell

5. Apart from the Class Affixes there are few Noun Formatives, while Compound Nouns are frequent:

    GOLA   **daa-gwɛ**   'Lord of the Sun' (a proper name for men)

6. Noun Classes are formed mostly by Prefixes, in some languages by Prefixes and Suffixes. These Affixes may also be used for forming a Definite and Indefinite Form of the Noun.

Examples from GOLA (the Indefinite Form of the Noun has no Affix in the Singular):

kándâ	chief	Plur.	**a-kándâ (nyā)**
fɛ	eye		**ma-fɛ**
saa	house		**ma-saa**
kul	tree		**ma-kul**

The **ma-** Class also denotes liquids:

    ma-mal water   **ma-gwala** rain   **ma-han** salt

---

[1] *Temne grammar and stories.*
[2] *A handbook of the Temne language.*
[3] *A handbook of the Sherbro language.*

The Definite Form of the Noun in GOLA:

kándâ	chief	Definite:	o-kándâ, kándâ-ɔ, o-kándâ-ɔ		
fὲ	eye		e-fὲ		
dî	head		e-dî	dî-lὲ	e-dî-lὲ
kul	tree		ke-kul	kul-ɛ	ke-kul-ɛ
ma-mal	water				ma-mal-ma

Note also **e-gola** crying<**gola** to cry.

Examples of Class Concord in GOLA:

  e-ǵwa fua-lɛ white bone; Plur. **ma-ǵwa fua-ma**
  ke-kul yɛ this tree
  ma-mal mɛ this water

Noun Classes in BULOM:

li-pal	sun	li-kin	knife	li-wu	death (<**wu** die)
la	house	Plur. **i-la**			
kulu	goat	si-kulu			
mende-nɔ	Mende man	a-mende			
bik	mat	i-bik; i-sim	standing (<**sim** stand)		
i-tu	pot	n-tu			

The Nasal Class also denotes liquids:

  ŋ-kusi oil **n-da-kɔ** nut oil

The Definite Form of the Noun in BULOM:

na	cow	Plur. **si-na**	na-lɛ	the cow	Plur. **na-si-lɛ**
kɛ	snake	si-kɛ	kɛ-lɛ	the snake	kɛ-si-lɛ

KISSI has no Noun Classes. The Plural of Nouns is formed by Suffix, a frequent Plural Suffix being **-ɔ, -o**.

ADYUKRU appears to have only remnants of Noun Classes:[1]

ob	thing	Plur. **m-ob**
l-ab	knife	m-ab
li-gbileb	yam	i-gbileb
lo-kleb	banana	o-kleb
nyaman	eye	a-nyaman
ɛ-ǵŋ	man	a-ǵŋ
mi-ji	water	mi-jei oil

Plural of persons may also be formed by suffixing the 3rd Person Plural Pronoun **lɛ (ɛl)**:

us-labm-eb-s-ɛl 'land-money-taking-person-they' (tax collectors).

WOLOF has a system of Noun Classes expressed in the Qualificatives[2] of the Noun

---

[1] But see Bertho, 'La place de l'adiukru.'
[2] For definition of 'Qualificative' see Doke, *Bantu linguistic terminology.*

(in the following examples the Particles following each Noun are Demonstratives denoting different degrees of distance from the speaker):

bai bi	bai bu	bai ba	father
fas vi	fas vu	fas va	horse
safara si	safara su	safara sa	fire
ker ɡi	ker ɡu	ker ɡa	house
nit ki	nit ku	nit ka	man
ndei dyi	ndei dyu	ndei dya	mother
ndox mi	ndox mu	ndox ma	water
ŋgelao li	ŋgelao lu	ŋgelao la	wind

The same alliteration takes place in Numerals, Adjectives, and in Relative, Interrogative, and Indefinite Pronouns.

In the Singular of most Nouns there is a definite relation between the initial consonant of the Noun and the Qualificative. Note, however, that **nit** (man) has the Concord **k-**, while in **ŋgelao** (wind) the Concord is with the second consonant (**ŋg** being regarded as one). For the **m-** Concord with **ndox** (water) cp. **m-, ma-** Prefix for Nouns denoting liquids in other languages.

The Concord for the Plural of Nouns of all Classes is **y-**. This **y-** is identical with the **i-** Prefix which forms the Plural of the indeterminate Noun without regard to Classes:

ɡarap	tree	Plur.	i-ɡarap
paka	knife		i-paka

while in Determinate Nouns the Plural is expressed in the Qualificative only:

bai yi	bai yu	bai ya	fathers
fas yi	fas yu	fas ya	horses
safara yi	safara yu	safara ya	fires

7. There is no grammatical gender.

8. In GOLA the Verb undergoes vocalic changes, e.g.

Perfect	*Imperfect*	*Infinitive*	
na	ne	niie	come
ɡwa	ɡwe	ɡwiie	wash
yɛlɛ	yɛlɛ	yilie	cut
ɡola	ɡolɔ	ɡulie	cry
wawa	wɔwɔ	wuwie	prepare

9. Verbal Derivatives[1] are formed by means of Suffixes.

Examples from BULOM:

-a assimilated to the Root Vowel:

ɡbal	write	ɡbal-a	be writing
sɛm	stand	sɛm-ɛ	be standing
kul	drink	kul-ɔ	be drinking

[1] For definition of 'Verbal Derivatives' see Doke, *Bantu linguistic terminology*.

-i	duk	fall	duk-i	throw down
	piθ	be black	piθ-i	blacken
-ni	fɔɔ	beat	fɔɔ-ni	beat repeatedly
	fɔɔ-i-ni	beat each other repeatedly, fight		
-ma	kɔ	go	kɔ-ma	go with
-il	sɛm	stand	sɛm-il	stand close by
-l	sɛk	be dry	sɛk-ɛl-i	make dry
-k	jo	eat	jo-k	eat from
	cɔ	fight	cɔ-k	fight with

TEMNE has a Causative Suffix -əs, -s:

bak	be heavy	bak-əs	make heavy
dira	sleep	dir-əs	cause to sleep

Examples from WOLOF:

-lo	sopa	love	sopa-lo	cause to love
-le	liġei	work	liġei-le	help work
-i	ub	close	ub-i	open
-an	binda	write	bind-an	write habitually
-ul	sopa	love	sop-ul	not to love

10. In most of the languages there is no Passive Voice, but there is a Passive-Reflexive in WOLOF, with Suffix -u:

    sopa love sop-u be loved

and in LIMBA, with Suffix -o.

11. Word order in the simple sentence is Subject–Verb–Object:

ADYUKRU s ij ob we eat thing

    aġŋ ana eke bo m ɛl eci ġbugŋ ɛm people are (there) who will take me their house in (Luke xvi. 4)

GOLA o na kĩi okanda bawa he then gave the chief (a) sheep

12. In the Genitive construction the *nomen rectum* follows the *nomen regens* in most languages:

GOLA fɔ̃ ġola country of the Gola

Note, however, that in Compound Nouns and in the Intimate Genitive the *nomen rectum* precedes the *nomen regens*:

    kul-koma tree-fruit oġola fela Gola man
    eġola mie Gola language

WOLOF fas u bur ba horse of chief Plur. **fas i bur ba**

In ADYUKRU the *nomen rectum* precedes the *nomen regens*, sometimes with Linking Particle **eci**:

    nyam eci odad God's word
    eġb bɛb ɛi ejaġb kpakp (of) seed some fell road's surface

THE WEST ATLANTIC LANGUAGES

The Possessive Pronoun follows the Noun in GOLA:

  o-di me-ɔ my cow Plur. **a-di me-nyã**

but precedes it in ADYUKRU:

  ŋ eci odad your (Sing.) speech
  in eci ob his thing
  ɛm ɛs my father

and in WOLOF:

  suma fas my horse
  sa ndei your (Sing.) mother

13. The Demonstrative Pronoun follows the Noun:

 GOLA **o-fola wê** this man Plur. **a-fola nyê (nyênyã)**
    o-fola wé[1] that man Plur. **a-fola nyé (nyényã)**
    ma-mal mê this water
    ma-mal mé that water

 ADYUKRU **ɛgŋ i** this man

In WOLOF it may follow or precede the Noun:

  fas vi or **vi fas** this horse

14. The Numeral follows the Noun in GOLA, but precedes it in WOLOF.

B. FULANI

1. There are five vowel phonemes: **i, e, a, o, u**. Vowel length is significant, both in Roots and in Suffixes.

2. Characteristic consonants are: **ɓ, ɗ, 'y** (implosive y), **'** (glottal stop).
Consonants (including glottal stop) may be long.
There are true nasal compounds, the oral part of which is a voiced plosive or affricate, e.g. **goo-ŋga** truth.
Nasal and voiced plosive may also stand together as parts of different syllables (heterosyllabic nasal combination), e.g. **'in-de** name.

3. All syllables begin with a consonant or nasal compound. The vowel of a syllable may be short or long. A closed syllable can never be closed by more than one consonant.

  'o he **naa-ŋge** sun **min** we

4. An outstanding feature of the language is initial consonantal change for grammatical reasons. This change is known as Permutation, according to which the consonants concerned appear in three Stages as:

(1) Fricatives and semi-vowels
(2) Plosives
(3) Nasal compounds

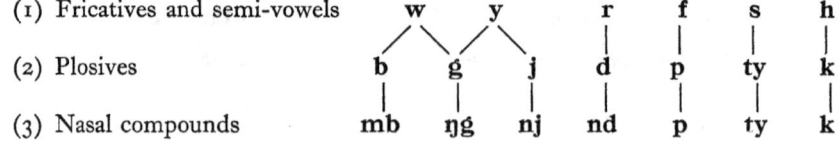

[1] Note change of vowel and tone.

5. Tone does not appear to have the same significance that it has in many West African languages. Stress is important.

6. The Root consists of CVC or CVCC (rarely CV). The vowel of the Root may be short or long. The Root very rarely appears as a complete word (e.g. **mi** I, **be** with, **war** come (Imperative)). In most cases it is enlarged by Suffixes.

7. Compound Nouns and Verbs are rare (but see § 11, under 2*k*).

8. Noun or Adjective Formatives are Suffixes (to which the Class Suffix is attached; see § 10):

-ak (Abstract Nouns)   **kefer-ak-u**   heathendom
-ow- (Noun Agent)   **dem-ow-o**   farmer (<**rem-** cultivate)
-aw- or -aɓ- (Ordinal)   **ɗiɗ'-aɓ-o**   the second
-ir- or -or- (Instrument)   **fe'-ir-ɗe**   axe (<**fe'** cut)
-ee (Adjectives denoting colour)   **ran-ee**   white

9. Nouns are divided into Classes. There are twenty-two Classes in the dialect of Adamawa, but for the FULANI dialects as a whole twenty-eight Classes have been noted. The Classes are characterized by:

(1) Class Suffixes, each of which appears in four forms (Suffix-form). Rules for the use of Suffix-form with Nouns have not yet been discovered. Such rules do, however, exist for Adjectives (see § 12).
(2) A special form of certain initial consonants listed in § 4 (Permutation Stage) and dependent on the Class Suffix.

It is important to state that Permutation Stage and Suffix-class[1] depend on each other, as each Suffix-class corresponds to one of the three possible Permutation Stages only.[2]

The Noun Classes are usually referred to by the shortest form of the Class Pronoun (**nde**-Class, **o**-Class, &c.).

10. Class Pronouns, Permutation Stage, and Class Suffixes in all the dialects studied so far are as follows:[3]

		Class Pron.	Permutation Stage	Suffix-forms				Content
				I	II	III	IV	
S.		(m)ba	3	-a,	-wa,	-ba,	-ba	animals (W.F.).
„	A	nde	1	-re,	-re,	-de,	-nde	animals, things, abstracts.
„	A	ndi	3	-ri,	-ri,	-di,	-ndi	animals, things, abstracts.
„	A	ndu	1	-ru,	-ru,	-du,	-ndu	animals, things, Verbal Nouns.
„	A	ŋga	3	-a,	-wa,	-ga,	-ŋga	animals, things, abstracts; (E.F.) also augmentatives.

[1] The term Suffix-class is used to comprise the four Suffix-forms proper to any one Class.
[2] Note that the term Prefix Classes has been used in the past instead of Permutation Stage to indicate hypothetical Class Prefixes which must have been dropped but whose influence is seen in the change of the initial consonant.
[3] A = dialect of Adamawa (as well as other dialects); W.F. = Western FULANI; E.F. = Eastern FULANI; P. = PULAR.

	Class Pron.	Permutation Stage	Suffix-forms I	II	III	IV	Content
S.	A ŋge	1	-e,	-ye,	-ge,	-ŋge	sun, fire, cow, abstracts.
,,	A ŋgo	1	-o,	-wo,	-go,	-ŋgo	animals, things, abstracts.
,,	A ŋgu	3	-u,	-wu,	-gu,	-ŋgu	animals, things, abstracts.
,,	A ŋgal	2	-al,	-wal,	-gal,	-ŋgal	animals, things, instruments, abstracts; (P.) also augmentatives.
,,	A ŋgel	2	-el,	-yel,	-gel,	-ŋgel	diminutives.
,,	A ŋgol	2	-ol,	-wol,	-gol,	-ŋgol	animals, things, Nouns of action.
,,	A ka	3	-a,	-ha,	-ka,	-ka	things, abstracts.
,,	A ki	2	-i,	-hi,	-ki,	-ki	trees, things, instruments, Nouns of action and other abstracts.
,,	A ko	1	-o,	-ho,	-ko,	-ko	plants, things.
,,	kal	2	-al,	-hal,	-kal,	-kal	diminutives (P., FULA, Nigeria).
,,	kol	2	-ol,	-hol,	-kol,	-kol	calf (Nigeria).
,,	kuŋ	2	-uŋ,	-huŋ,	-kuŋ,	-kuŋ	diminutives (FULA).
,,	A 'o	2	-o,	-jo,	-ɗo,	-ɗo	men.
,,	A ɗam	3	-am,	-jam,	-ɗam,	-ɗam	liquids, &c.
,,	A ɗum	2	-um,	-jum,	-ɗum,	-ɗum	neutral Class.
,,	ŋgii	2	-ii,	-wii,	-gii,	-ŋgii	(FULA).
,,	A ŋgum	?	*-um,	*-wum,	*-gum,	*-ŋgum	biŋgum little child
Pl.	A ɓe	1	-ɓe,	-ɓe,	-ɓe,	-ɓe	men.
,,	A ɗe	2	-e,	-je,	-ɗe,	-ɗe	animals, things.
,,	A ɗi	2	-i,	-ji,	-ɗi,	-ɗi	animals, things.
,,	kol	3	-ol,	-hol,	-kol,	-kol	diminutives (Upper Niger).
,,	A ko	1, 2, 3	-o,	-ho,	-ko,	-ko	augmentatives (E.F.).
,,	kony	3	-ony,	-hony,	-kony,	-kony,	diminutives.
,,	A koi	3	-oi,	-hoi,	-koi,	-koi	diminutives.

11. Adjectives follow the Noun they qualify. There is always some Concord between them and their Noun and therefore the choice of formative changes is much greater than with the latter. The following kinds of Adjectives may be distinguished:

(1) Simple Adjectives, having an Adjectival Root (e.g. **has** new) and including (*a*) **wor** male; (*b*) the indefinite **woɗ** one; (*c*) the Cardinals 2–9 in PULAR and 2–5 and 7–9 in other dialects;

(2) Derived Adjectives:
  (*a*) by reduplication;
  (*b*) by **-ar**;
  (*c*) by **-ee** (Adjectives denoting colour);
  (*d*) Ordinals derived by Suffix **-aɓ** from Cardinals;
  (*e*) **wo'o-t** one;
  (*f*) Deverbative Adjectives:
    Noun Agents (see § 8);
    Verbal Adjectives (see § 22);
    Participles (see § 23);
  (*g*) Nominal Adjectives, i.e. the Stem of which is a complete Noun;
  (*h*) Pronominal Adjectives;
  (*i*) Ordinals 1st, 6th, 10th, 20th, 100th, 1,000th, 1,000,000th in Eastern FULANI;
  (*k*) Phrase Adjectives, the Stem of which is a phrase, e.g. **wilwil-du mauna-noppi-ru** bat with big ears.

12. Adjectives can be divided into groups according to their Suffix-forms (see I–IV, § 10). Thus, following the scheme already set out in § 11:

I includes 1, 1c, 2a, 2b, 2d, 2e;
II includes 2c, 2f (Noun Agents), 2g, 2h, 2i, 2k;
III includes 1a only;
IV includes 1b, 2f (Verbal Adjectives and Participles).

13. There is a Concord between the Noun and Adjectivals of all kinds, and between the Noun and the Verb. The Concord between Noun and Adjective is not the same for all the kinds of Adjectives. Some of them concord with the Noun in so far as they have the same Suffix-class (but not always the same Suffix-form), and a Permutation Stage corresponding to it and therefore to the Permutation Stage of the Noun. As, however, the permutable consonants of Nouns and Adjectives are frequently different, the Concord of concordant words is not always evident at first sight. This kind of Concord may be termed Total Concord.

Other Adjectives are not subject to Permutation; Concord in these cases is Concord of the Suffix-class only. This may be termed Partial Concord.

According to the Concord system the Adjectives are therefore divided into two groups:

Total Concord: Adjectives of types 1, 1c, 2a, 2b, 2c, 2d, 2e;
Partial Concord: Adjectives of types 2f, 2g, 2h, 2i, 2k.

14. The Concord between Noun and Cardinals is irregular. While some Numerals, e.g. **ɡo'o** one, **sappo** ten, **temerre** hundred, are Nouns, and are juxtaposed unchanged, others, i.e. **wo'ot** (**woot** in Adamawa) and 2 to 5 and 7 to 9 (2 to 9 in PULAR), are true Adjectives and appear in three sets (four in Macina), used with Nouns denoting persons, things, diminutives, and (in Macina) augmentatives respectively.

15. The Concord between Noun and Verb is seen from the Permutation Stage of the Verb in the Plural. In the dialect of Futa Djallon the Permutation appears to be lost in this case.

16. There is no grammatical gender.

The idea of the existence of some kind of gender expressed by initial Permutation (see § 4) was introduced into the literature of FULANI by Faidherbe[1] (*genre hominin* and *genre brute*), accepted by others (e.g. Guiraudon,[2] *genre commun* and *genre neutre*, Westermann[3] (differentiation between person and non-person)) and developed by Meinhof[4] into a four-class gender consisting of a Personal Class (Sing. plosive, Plur. fricative), an Object Class (Sing. fricative, Plur. plosive), an Augmentative Class (Sing. nasal compound, Plur. plosive), and a Diminutive Class (Sing. plosive, Plur. nasal compound). Klingenheben[5] has shown the existence of a fifth Class (Neutral: Sing. and Plur. plosive). But following analysis and comparison with Noun Class division in BIAFADA the idea of an independent Prefix system dividing Nouns into genders

---

[1] *Grammaire et vocabulaire de la langue poul.*   [2] *Manuel de la langue foule.*
[3] *Handbuch der Ful-Sprache.*   [4] *Die Sprachen der Hamiten.*   [5] 'Die Präfixklassen des Ful.'

or Classes according to meaning has been abandoned (cp. especially § 9 on the interdependence of Permutation and Suffix-class).

17. No observations on special Case-forms have been made so far. Case is expressed by position in the sentence and by Prepositions.

18. The Personal Pronoun as Subject Pronoun before the Verb exists in different sets according to whether it (*a*) stands before non-Durative or Durative Forms, (*b*) is prefixed or suffixed. The Pronouns for Durative Forms are enlargements of the short Pronouns for non-Durative Forms. In the case of suffixation, forms for the 1st and 2nd Singular and 1st Inclusive and 2nd Plural only exist.

Note the existence of Inclusive and Exclusive Forms for the 1st Person Plural.

The Object Pronoun is suffixed.

Personal Pronouns in PULAR and the Adamawa dialect (where not specified they are common to both):

		Short	Prefixed	Long	Suffixed	Object
			(P.)	(A.)		(A.)
Sing. 1.		mi	miɗe	miɗon	-mi	-am, mi
2.		'a	'aɗa	'aɗon	-ɗaa (-aa); (A.) -ɗa (-a)	-ma, -o
3.		'o	'omo	'oɗon		-mo
Plur. 1.	Excl.	min	'emin	minɗon		-min
	Incl.	'en		'enɗon	-ɗen (-en)	-'en
2.		'on	'oɗon	'onɗon	-ɗon (-on)	-'on
3.		ɓe	eɓe	ɓeɗon		-ɓe

19. The Verb Root is subject to Permutation of its initial consonant and elision of its final consonant, according to fixed grammatical rules.

20. A striking feature of FULANI is the existence of three Voices: Active, Reflexive, and Passive. Some Verbs have all three Voices, some two, and some one only. There are separate sets of Tense Suffixes for Voice distinction.

21. Verbal Derivatives are formed by means of Suffixes. Examples from the dialect of Adamawa:

-(i)d wi' to say, **wi'id** to discuss (Associative);
-(i)t **malf** to put on hat, **malfit** to take off hat (Reversive);
-**in woi** to cry, **woin** to cause to cry, proclaim (Causative);
-**ir yah** to go, **yaar** to go with, lead to (Instrumental).

22. There are three Verbal Nouns for the three Voices, formed by Suffixes:

	Active	Reflexive	Passive
Adamawa	-(u)go	-aago	-eego
PULAR	-de	-aade	-eede

23. Participial Stems are formed by Suffix, e.g.

'and-u- knowing< 'and- to know

Verbal Adjectives can be formed from Verbal Roots by adding Class Suffixes:

ġar-ɗo one who comes

ġar-ai-ɗo one who will come (from a Stem expressing a kind of Future).

24. Verbs are conjugated either by putting after the Subject a Verbal Form composed of Root (or Derived Stem) and Tense Suffix, or by suffixing the Subject Pronoun to that Verbal Form and using Permutation. (On the use of short or long forms of Subject Pronouns see § 18.) If the Subject is a Noun, however, the Pronoun is not expressed except in the Tenses called Duratives by Gaden.[1]

In PULAR the suffixation of the Subject Pronoun appears to have syntactical rather than Tense value, i.e. the Verbal Forms with suffixed Subject Pronoun express subordination (e.g. a Temporal Clause).

25. The Tense system is well developed. Tenses—Positive and Negative—are expressed by Suffixes. These Tenses would appear to be capable of grouping under the headings Perfective and Imperfective. Note that the idea of Past time is expressed in several Tenses by the Suffix -noo (PULAR), -no (Adamawa).

In the following table the Tense Suffixes of PULAR and of the dialect of Adamawa are given. No attempt is here made to create new and definitive names for the Tenses. These are labelled by numbers. Roman numbers represent Perfective Tenses, Arabic numbers Imperfective.[2]

		Active		Reflexive		Passive	
		(P.)	(A.)	(P.)	(A.)	(P.)	(A.)
I	Short	(-zero)		-i		-a	
II	Short	-ii		-iima		-aama	-aama
III	Short	-i	-i	-ii	-ake	-aa	-aa
IV	Suffix	(-zero-)[3]	(-zero-)[3]	-ii-[3]		-aa-[3]	
Ia	Short	-noo		-inoo		-anoo	
IIa	Short	-iino		-inooma		-anooma	-aanooma
IIIa	Short		-ino		-akeno		-aano
IVa	Suffix	-noo-[3]		-inoo-[3]		-anoo-[3]	
Ib	Long	(-zero)		-i		-a	
IIIb	Long	-i		-ii		-aa	
III	Neg.	-aa(-aani)	-aai	-aaki	-aaki	-aaka	-aaka
Ia	Neg.	-aano	-aaino	-anooki	-akino	-anooka	-aakano
1	Short	-a		-oo		-ee	
1	Long	-a	-a	-oo	-o	-ee	-e
2	Short	-ata	-ata	-otoo		-etee	
3	Short	-at	-an	-oto	-oto	-ete	-ete
4	Suffix	-at-[3]	-an	-otoo-[3]		-etee-[3]	
2, 3a	Short	-annoo	-anno	-otonoo	-otono	-etenoo	-eteeno
1–3	Neg.	-ataa	-ataa	-otaako	-ataako	-etaake	-ataake
1–3	Neg.	-ataano	-ataano	-otonooka	-atakono	-etenooka,	-ataakeno
2, 3a	Neg.	-aanoo-[3]		-otonoo-[3]		-etenoo-[3]	

[1] See especially the introduction to his *Proverbes et maximes peuls et toucouleurs.*
[2] The names used by Gaden for PULAR are: I. Parfait indéterminé, II. Parfait déterminé, III. Passé narratif, IV. Participiel suffixé, Ia, IIa, IIIa, IVa. Prétérits, Ib. Duratif Prétérit, IIIb. Duratif Présent, 1 (Short). Imparfait Momentané, 1 (Long). Imparfait Duratif, 2. Imparfait d'habitude, 3. Imparfait d'obligation, 4. Imparfait suffixé, 2, 3a. Imparfait Prétérit.
[3] The hyphen at right represents the Suffix Pronoun.

26. For Verbal Negation see table above. Tense I and the Imperative are negated by the Particle **ta** preceding them. 'Not to be' is expressed by **walaa** (in the dialect of Futa Senegalais **'alaa**).

27. Word-order in the simple sentence is: Subject–Verb–Object.

28. In the Genitive construction the *nomen rectum* follows the *nomen regens*. The short form of the Class Pronoun may stand between, but this is not necessary, e.g.

        pucu lamɗo   horse of the chief.
        pucu ŋgu lamɗo horse (that) of the chief.

For the position of the Adjective see § 11.

29. The short form of the Class Pronoun serves as Copula, if this is not expressed by the Verb **woni**.

Section II
THE MANDE LANGUAGES
(LARGER UNIT)

THE MANDE languages are spoken over a vast area extending from the Atlantic coast to the Black Volta (with an outlier in the north-western corner of Nigeria). In the north they are bounded by the Sahara; in the north-east and east by the GUR languages (with considerable overlapping); in the south-west and south by West Atlantic languages, the coast, and the KRU dialects; in the south-east by the KWA languages.

The name *MANDE* or *MANDINGO* is a general term applied by Europeans and others to all the tribes speaking MANDE languages. The name (other versions of which are *MANDI, MALE, MALI, MELE* (**mɛlɛ**), *MANDING*) is properly applied only to the people commonly known as *MALINKE* and to their speech; each tribe has its own name.

The *MANDE* people as a whole are called **mali, mɛli, malel** by the *FULANI*, **mel, melit** by the *BERBERS*, **melel, malel** by the *ARABS*, **waŋkɔre** by the *SONGHAI*, **nsɔya** by the *GONJA*; in the north-eastern part of the language area they are known as *WANGARA* (**waŋgara**), a name used by the *HAUSA* and others, and semi-officially recognized in the Gold Coast and Nigeria.

MANDE languages consist of two Groups, known to Europeans as MANDE TAN and MANDE FU, after the word for 'ten': **tan, tã (tam, tamu)** or **fu (pu, bu)**.[1] Speakers of MANDE TAN languages form the northern and larger section, while speakers of MANDE FU languages mostly inhabit the southern forest belt.

On account of the trade carried on by the *MANDE* peoples throughout a large part of West Africa, a lingua franca form of the language, known as KANGBE (**kãgbe**), has evolved, which is spoken or at least understood by a number of other peoples.

LANGUAGE GROUP: MANDE TAN

Consists of: SONINKE — Dialect Cluster.
MALINKE-BAMBARA-DYULA — Dialect Cluster.
KHASONKE — Language?
VAI — Language, with associated dialects.

Where spoken: In the northern and eastern part of the MANDE language area, from Senegal in the north to the Ivory Coast in the south, and from the west coast to Haute-Volta.

SONINKE. DIALECT CLUSTER.

Spoken by: *SONINKE* (**soniŋkɛ**). This is a name covering several tribes speaking one dialect, by which name they are known to Europeans and which they themselves

[1] This terminology was first used by Delafosse, *Essai de manuel pratique de la langue mandé* (1901).

recognize. Other names by which they (or a part of them) are known are: *MARKA* (**marka, markaŋka**), originally the name of one *SONINKE* tribe, now widely used in the French Sudan; *SARAKOLE* (*SARAKOLLE, SARACOLE*, &c.), in the north-western part of the *SONINKE* area; *SARAWULE* (*SERAHULI*); *WAKORE*; *GADYAGA*; *DYAKANKE*; (Fr.) *TOUBAKAÏ*; *ASWANIK* (the latter name being that used by the *MOORS*).

Where spoken:[1] Senegal (extending into Mauretania in the north); Cercles Podor, Louga, Matam, Sine Saloum, part of Tambacounda, Ziguinchor; French Sudan: Cercles Kayes, Bafoulabé, Nioro, Nara, Ségou; Haute-Volta:[2] Cercles Bobo Dioulasso and Tougan. There are also colonies of *SONINKE* scattered in many other parts, e.g. on the Niger between Lamorde and Say (called *SILABE* by the *FULANI*) and at Tishit in the western Sahara.

Number of speakers: Mauretania 22,000, Senegal 30,000; French Sudan 283,000; Haute-Volta 100,000;[3] Gambia 9,434.[4] Portuguese Guinea 2,049.[5]

Tribes or tribal sections constituting the *SONINKE* include:

DYARISSO, in Nioro and near Bamako;[6]
DYAWARA, between Nioro and Nara (possibly, however, a section of the *BAMBARA*), and north-east of Bougouni;[6]
PANA (a section of the *MARKA SONINKE*), in the neighbourhood of Tougan; also among the *BAMBARA* in the Bandiagara area;
SAMOGHO, between Sikasso and River Bago (but see *SAMO*, p. 41).

Note: Some of the *SONINKE* in Dédougou, Kurumari and in the Bamako area, and the so-called *NONO* at Djenné, have lost, or are losing, their own language in favour of BAMBARA or ARABIC.

Closely related dialects are spoken by:

BOZO, call themselves **bozo**; also known as **sɔrkɔ, sɔrɔgɔ**; on the banks of the Niger and Bani around Ségou, San, Mopti, &c.
Number: 30,000.
Note: Some of the *BOZO*, however, have adopted SONGHAI.

AZER (*AJER, AZJER*), call themselves **masiin,** called **azer, ajer** by neighbouring tribes, *TAGHDAUSH* by the *MOORS* (the name *GIRGA* or *GIRGANKE*, sometimes applied to the AZER, is really the name of one section of them); in French Sudan, Cercles Nioro, Néma and Nara.[6]

Note: The dialect of the *AZER* was formerly spoken over a much wider area, but is now being replaced by ARABIC.

[1] Information on the distribution of the *SONINKE* contributed by IFAN.
[2] The territory of Haute-Volta was abolished in 1932 and distributed among neighbouring territories, but reinstated in 1947 within approximately the original boundaries.
[3] 'Populations du Soudan central et de la Nigéria' (*Bull. Com. Études hist. et scient. de l'A.O.F.*, 1936); and France d'outre-mer publications.
[4] Report of the Senior Commissioner on the Annual Census of the Protectorate of Gambia, 1945.
[5] 1950 Census.
[6] Urvoy, *Petit atlas ethno-démographique du Soudan entre Sénégal et Tchad* (Mém. IFAN No. 5, 1942).
[7] Part of Cercle Néma has recently been transferred to Mauretania.

THE MANDE LANGUAGES

MALINKE-BAMBARA-DYULA. Dialect Cluster.

Note: MALINKE, BAMBARA, and DYULA, with other dialects, are so closely interrelated that they must be considered, on a linguistic basis, as dialects of one Cluster, in spite of the vast area over which they are spoken and the great number of people speaking them, in spite, also, of the various dialectal subdivisions made by different authors.

Dialect or dialects: MALINKE (MANDINKA, MANDINGO), own name **maliŋka, maliŋkɛ ka**.

Spoken by: MALINKE (*MANDINKA*, &c.), call themselves **maliŋkɛ, maliŋka, maneŋka, mandeŋka, mandeŋga, màndíŋkɔ̀ká** (Sing. **mándìŋkɔ́**) (local variants).

Where spoken: Senegal: Thiès, M'Bour, Ziguinchor, Sedhiou, Vélingara, Tambacounda; French Guinea: Gaoual, Mamou, Dabola, Kissidougou, Guékédou, Macenta, Beyla; French Sudan: Kayes and Bafoulabé; Ivory Coast: Man, Odienné, Seguéla, Bondoukou; also in the Gambia and parts of Portuguese Guinea.

Number: French West Africa:[1] Senegal 135,000, French Guinea 450,000 French Sudan 135,000, Ivory Coast 250,000; Gambia 96,196;[2] Portuguese Guinea 63,750.[3]

Three 'dialects' of MALINKE are generally recognized, spoken in the west, north, and south of the MALINKE language area.[4]

There is some vernacular literature, including Gospels in 'MENINKA' and MANDINGO (Gambia).

Closely related dialects are spoken by the following:

KORANKO (*KURANKO, KURANKE*, Fr. *KOURANKO, KOURANKE*), in French Guinea, Cercles Kankan, Dabola, Kissidougou and Guékédou; also in Sierra Leone.

Number: French Guinea 36,567;[5] Sierra Leone 73,500.[6]

Note: LELE is given by IFAN as the name of a dialect spoken in Kissidougou and Guékédou, and described as 'altération du KOURANKE'.

Two Gospels have been published in KORANKO.

MAU (*MAUKA*), call themselves **mauka** (Sing. **mau**), in the western part of the Ivory Coast, south of Odienné.

The same dialect is said to be spoken by the *MANINYAKA, WODYENEKA* (cp. place-name Odienné?), and *DYOMANDE* (Fr. *GUIOMANDE*), perhaps another name for the *MAU* (but see also under *KONYA*).

WASULU (Fr. *OUASSOULOUNKÉ*), call themselves **wasuluŋka** (Sing. **wasulu**) and their dialect **wasuluŋka ka**; French Guinea, Cercles Kankan and Siguiri; also in Cercles Nioro, Bafoulabé, and Bougouni.

Number: 3,600.

The dialect of the *WASULU* very closely resembles southern MALINKE, according to Delafosse.[7]

---

[1] From France d'outre-mer publications. [2] Report of the Senior Commissioner ..., 1945.
[3] 1950 Census.
[4] Delafosse, *Essai de manuel pratique de la langue mandé*; Hamlyn, *A short study of the Western Mandinka language*. [5] *La Guinée Française*, 1931.
[6] From recent (1948) Government sources. [7] *Essai de manuel* ....

MINYA, call themselves **minyaŋka** (Sing. **minya**), also call themselves *FOLO* (but see also *MINIANKA* under *SENUFO*, p. 55); west of Koutiala, between Rivers Bani and Banifing, among the *SENUFO*.

MANYA, call themselves **manyaŋka** (Sing. **manya**), called **manimo** by the *VAI*; also known as *KOMENDI (COMMENDI)*, a general term used by the *LOMA*, *BANDI*, and others for speakers of MANDE languages living among them as traders and settlers; in western Liberia north of the *VAI*, also among the *KPELLE*, *GOLA*, and *LOMA*.

SIDYA (SIDYANKA, SIDIANKA), call themselves **sidyaŋka**; in French Guinea, Futa Djallon, and in Portuguese Guinea, Pakessi, and Rio Grande.

KONYA, call themselves **konyaŋka**, also known as *DYOMANDE* (but see *MAU*); south of the *WASULU*, extending to Kérouané and Sanankoro; also in northern Liberia among the *KPELLE*, *LOMA*, and *WEIMA*.

Dialect: *BAMBARA*, own name **bamana koma**.

Spoken by: *BAMBARA*, call themselves **bamanaŋkɛ** (Sing. **bamana**), called *BAMBARA* by Europeans and by many neighbouring peoples.[1]

Where spoken: Senegal: Sine Saloum, Matam, Kolda, Tambacounda; French Sudan: Néma, Kayes, Nioro, Nara, Macina, Kita, Ségou, Sikasso, Koutiala, San, Mopti, Bamako, Bafoulabé, Niafounké; Haute-Volta: Tougan.

Number: French Sudan 835,000,[2] French Guinea 19,000,[3] Senegal 12,000.

BAMBARA is also spoken or understood by many other tribes living within the BAMBARA language area. There is some vernacular literature, including the New Testament in Roman characters, and some books of the New Testament in Arabic characters.

Closely related dialects are spoken by the following, some of whom may be *BAMBARA* sections:

DYANGIRTE, in Cercle Nioro.

KAGORO (mixed *BAMBARA* and *FULANI*), in the neighbourhood of Kolokani, also Mourdiah and Nioro.
   Number: 17,000.

KALONGO (KALUNKA), in Mourdiah.

MASASI (BAMBARA MASASI), in and south of Nioro.

NYAMASA, in Nioro.

SOMONO, a tribe of fishermen on the banks of the Niger and Bani, around Ségou and San.
   Number: 13,000 in and around Ségou.

TORO, call themselves **toroŋga** or **toroŋkɛ**, among the *WASULU* north-east of Bissandougou in Cercle Kankan, French Guinea.

The dialect of the *TORO* is almost identical with that of the *BAMBARA* of

---

[1] Not to be confused with the *BAMANA SENUFO*, who are also known as *BAMBARA* (see p. 55). [2] From a pamphlet published by France d'outre-mer (no date).
[3] *La Guinée Française*, 1931.

THE MANDE LANGUAGES 35

Ségou, with some phonetic peculiarities; many of the *TORO* speak the dialect of the *WASULU*.

Dialect: DYULA, own name **dyula kã**.

Spoken by: *DYULA* (*JULA*, Fr. *DYOULA, DIOULA*),[1] call themselves **dyulaŋkɛ,** called *WANKARA, WANGARA* in the Gold Coast and adjoining areas, called *VA* by the *GURO, FEBE* by the *GAGU, NDYURA* by the *BRONG, KAGA* by the *NZIMA* and *BAULE, SOGHA* by the *KULANGO, DYOKEREU* by the *GOUIN*.

Where spoken: The *DYULA* live widely scattered throughout the northern part of the Ivory Coast and in Haute-Volta, among other tribes whom they dominate and many of whom speak DYULA—e.g. in Sikasso among the *SENUFO*, Bobo Dioulasso among the *BOBO* and others, Bondoukou, Kong, and Seguéla among the *SENUFO*. Colonies of *DYULA*, who are active traders, are also to be found in various areas farther east (see *YARSE* under *MOSSI*, p. 64).

Number: 140,000 (Labouret).

Closely related dialects are spoken by the following:

DAFING, known as *DAFE* in the Gold Coast; in Dafina, Haute-Volta, and in the north-western part of the Gold Coast, in Dafena region.

BLE, in Haute-Volta, Cercle Bobo Dioulasso, among the *SONINKE* north of Banfora.

Number: 200 (Tauxier);[2] 500 (Labouret).

DYAKANKA (*DYAKA*, Fr. *DIAKANKE*) (**dyaɣa**), in the French Sudan, in the western part of Cercle Macina (but see also under *SONINKE*, p. 31).

KHASONKE. LANGUAGE?

Spoken by KHASONKE (*KASSONKE, KASSO*), call themselves **xasoŋkɛ**.

Where spoken: French Sudan, Cercles Kayes and Bafoulabé, also in Cercle Nioro.

Number of speakers: 53,000 (Labouret).

VAI. LANGUAGE, with associated dialects.

Spoken by: *VAI* (*VEI, VY*), called **vai** or **vɛi** by the *GOLA* and *KPELLE,* **kɔndɔ, kɔno, karo** by the *MENDE* (but cf. *KONO* below), *TEREBENDYULA* ('Western *DYULA*') by the *DYULA*; also known to Europeans as *GALLINAS*.

Where spoken: In the south-western corner of Liberia and across the border into Sierra Leone, between Rivers Loffa (Liberia) and Sulima (Sierra Leone); also on the banks of River Gallinas and on the lower St. Paul and Mesourado rivers.

Number of speakers: 40,000 (Labouret); Sierra Leone 35,660.[3]

The *VAI* have invented a script of their own, which was discovered by Europeans about a hundred years ago; it has, however, hardly been used for literary or educational purposes.

[1] Not to be confused with *DYOLA* (see p. 17).
[2] 'Les Gouin et les Tourouka' (*J. Soc. Afric.*, 1933).   [3] From recent (1948) Government sources.

Closely associated dialects are spoken by the following:

KONO, call themselves **kɔno** or **kɔndo**; in eastern Sierra Leone, north of the *MENDE*, south of the *KISSI*; also in French Guinea, Cercle Man, and in Liberia.

Number: 112,000 (Labouret); Sierra Leone 79,900.[1]

Parts of the New Testament have been translated into KONO.

LIGBI (LIGWI, NIGBI, NIGWI), also known as *TUBA*,[2] and sometimes called *BANDA* by Europeans (this being the name of part of their country); in the Ivory Coast, near Bondoukou, and north of Séguela at Koradougou. They call their dialect **liɡbi kpira**.

HWELA (HUELA), called *VUELA, VWELA* by the *DYULA*; in the Ivory Coast, in the Bondoukou area. They call their dialect **huela kã**.

NUMU (Fr. *NOUMOU*), call themselves **numu** and their dialect **numu kpera**; in the Ivory Coast, Cercle Bondoukou.

Note: The *NUMU* are not a tribe, but a caste of blacksmiths, or of artisans in general; they have, however, a dialect of their own, which is closely related to those of the *LIGBI* and *HUELA*.

Language Group: MANDE FU

Consists of: SUSU   Dialect Cluster.
              MENDE   Dialect Cluster.
              LOKO   Language.
              KPELLE   Language.
              LOMA   Dialect Cluster.
              BANDI   Language.
              BUSA   Language.
and other languages or dialects.

Where spoken: Mainly in the southern part of the MANDE language area (French Guinea, Sierra Leone, and Liberia).

SUSU. Dialect Cluster.

Spoken by: *SUSU* (*SOSSO, SUSSU*, Fr. *SOUSSOU*, Port. *SOSSO*, &c.), call themselves **soso** (with very close o).

Where spoken: French Guinea: Conakry, Forecariah, Kindia, Mamou, Dabola; also in the extreme north-west of Sierra Leone; French Sudan: Kita and Bafoulabé.

Number of speakers: French Guinea 238,148 *SUSU*, 73,425 *DYALONKE*;[3] Sierra Leone 49,000 *SUSU*, 30,520 '*YALUNKE*'.[1]

Dialects: The *SUSU* are divided into two sections, with slight dialectal variations:

SUSU, on the coast;

DYALONKE (YALONKA, JALONKE, YALUNKE, Fr. *DJALLONKE,* Port. *JALONCA)*, in Futa Djallon and Sierra Leone, in two sections, *LANGA* (**lãɡã**) and *SAKO*.

[1] From recent (1948) Government sources.
[2] Arcin, *Guinée Française*.
[3] *La Guinée Française* (1931).

THE MANDE LANGUAGES

The *SUSU* on the coast are much mixed with *BAGA* and *LANDOMA*, who have largely adopted their language; it is also spoken by *MALINKE, TEMNE*, and others living in the SUSU language area.

SUSU is to some extent intermediate between MANDE TAN and MANDE FU, but its closest affiliations are with the MANDE FU Group.

There is slight vernacular literature in SUSU and DYALONKE, including a Gospel in each dialect.

MENDE, own name **mɛnde yia.** DIALECT CLUSTER.

Spoken by: *MENDE* (*MENDI* in older writings) call themselves **mɛnde**, called **hulɔ, hurɔ** by the *VAI* and *GOLA*, **kɔsɔ** by the *TEMNE*; also referred to by Arcin[1] as '*BOUMPÉ*', and known to Europeans in the past as *KOSSA, KOSSO* (cp. **kɔsɔ**).

Where spoken: The whole of the south-eastern part of Sierra Leone.

Number of speakers: 586,000.[2]

Dialects: Dialectal differences are very slight; four dialects are, however, recognized, in two main divisions:

kɔ mɛnde (**kɔ** = east or north);
komboya mɛnde, spoken in the north-eastern part of the MENDE area;
kpa mɛnde, spoken in the west of Southern Province;
'Sherbro' MENDE, spoken in the Sherbro area.

MENDE is used in primary education by most missions (English being the language of higher education), and is used in religious teaching and worship. There is a strong movement (with Government backing) for mass education and literacy, and the Sierra Leone Protectorate Literature Bureau has been formed for the production of vernacular literature in MENDE and other languages. There is as yet no standard literary form of MENDE, but the Methodists, who have been most active in the production of literature, use **kɔ mɛnde**. A considerable part of the Bible has been translated, and religious and school books have been published.

LOKO (LANDOGO). LANGUAGE.

Spoken by: *LOKO* (*LANDOGO, LANDOGHO*), call themselves **lɔkɔ**, called **landɔyɔ** by the *SUSU*.

Where spoken: Sierra Leone, in a narrow strip along the right bank of River Mabole and in the bend of River Bali as far as its confluence with the Mabole; also extending into French Guinea.

Number of speakers: Sierra Leone 76,400.[2]

LOKO is closely related to MENDE.

KPELLE, own name **kpɛlɛɛ-woo** (speech of the *KPELLE*). LANGUAGE.

Spoken by: *KPELLE*, call themselves **kpɛlɛŋa** (Sing. **kpɛlɛ**), called **akpɛdɛ** by the *GOLA*, **kpɛlɛsɛ** by the *GBUNDE*, **kpɛlɛsɛtini** by the *BANDI*, **kpɛrɛsɛ** or

---

[1] *Guinée Française*.   [2] From recent (1948) Government sources.

gbɛrɛsɛ by the *MANYA* (this name is applied particularly to those in French Guinea, and from it is derived the French name *GERZE (GUERZÉ)* used in French Guinea to denote the *KPELLE*), kpɛsɛ by the *VAI*, kpɛlɛma by the *BASSA*, gbɛizɛ by the *LOMA*, kpɛjɛsia by the *MENDE*, *PESSI, PESSY, PESSA* by the Liberians.

Where spoken: In central Liberia, on both banks of River St. Paul, mainly on the left bank; extending into French Guinea, Cercle Nzérekoré.

Number of speakers: 250,000 (Rev. G. D. Mellish);[1] according to W. E. Welmers[1] 500,000 may be considered a rough estimate for Liberia and French Guinea together; French Guinea 172,546.[2]

The language appears to be more or less uniform. According to Welmers there are local dialectal differences, mainly phonetic, but the various sections of the tribe cannot be said to speak different dialects.

KPELLE is not used in education. A beginning has been made at the production of vernacular literature, in connexion with adult literacy campaigns.

LOMA. DIALECT CLUSTER.

Spoken by: *LOMA* (*TOMA, LOGHOMA, LOOMAGO*), call themselves lɔ́ɔmà in the west (Liberia), tɔ́ɔmà in the east (French Guinea);[3] called tɔma by the *MA-NYA*, tɔa, tɔalɛ, tɔali by the *KPELLE* and others, *BALU* by the *BANDI*, *KUMBA JOKOI* by the *KISSI*, *BUZI* by the Liberians (this name is also used by the *LOMA* themselves when speaking English), also *DOMAR BUZI*. The *MANO* also call them by the nickname *TWA MIA*.

Where spoken: Northern Liberia, north-west of the *KPELLE*; also in French Guinea, Cercles Macenta, Kissidougou, and Guékédou.

Number of speakers: 260,000 (French Guinea 77,641).[2]

Dialect: *GBUNDE*, own name gboode.[3]

Spoken by: *GBUNDE*, call themselves gbundɛ,[4] called *KIMBUZI* by the Liberians, bɔɔ by the *GOLA*; west of the *LOMA* in Liberia.

Dialect spoken by: *WEIMA* (possibly a section of the *GBUNDE*), call themselves wɛima, called kɔimaka by the *KONYA*, *WEIMA BUZI* (*WYMAR BOUZIE*) by the Liberians; in French Guinea, south of the *KONYA* between Beyla and Nzo.

Other sections of the *GBUNDE*, of whose speech nothing is known, are:

BRIAMA (*BULYAMA*), south of River Lauwa;
GISIMA, called *GIZIMA* by the Liberians, farther to the east;
SIAMA (*WEIMA*?), on the upper Lauwa and We rivers;
'Wuboma', south of Bamai.[5]

A Gospel is being translated (1950). In recent years the LOMA have invented a syllabic script of their own.

[1] In reply to a questionnaire.   [2] *La Guinée Française* (1931).
[3] W. E. Welmers, in reply to a questionnaire.   [4] Schwab, *Tribes of the Liberian hinterland*.
[5] Germann, *Die Völkerstämme in Norden von Liberia*.

BANDI. LANGUAGE.

Spoken by: *BANDI* (*GBANDI*), call themselves **bandi** (**gbandɛ** according to Schwab),[1] called *GBANDI*, *GBANDE* by the *MENDE* and *KPELLE*, also called **mamboŋa** by the *KPELLE*, **mamboma** by the *BASSA*.

Where spoken: North-western Liberia, between the *KISSI* on the north-west and the *LOMA* on the north-east, separated from the *GOLA* to the south by an uninhabited forest belt.

Number of speakers: 35,000.

Heydorn[2] mentions YAWAZIRU as the name of a BANDI dialect.

The following languages or dialects are not sufficiently well known for a detailed classification to be made. It is certain that they belong to the MANDE FU Group, but whether they are separate languages or dialects belonging to one or more Clusters has not been established.

MANO, own name **mã-wi**. DIALECT CLUSTER?[3]

Spoken by: *MANO* (Fr. *MANON*), call themselves **maa** (Mellish),[4] **ma mia** (Schwab),[1] called *MANO* by the Liberians.

Where spoken: East of the *KPELLE* in Liberia and French Guinea.

Number of speakers: 45,000 (Labouret); 150,000 (Mellish).

Dialects: Mellish mentions two dialects, spoken in the Teppi area, Liberia:
ya win;
mɛsona.

The GE (**gɛ̃**) possibly speak a dialect of MANO (but see GIO below).

MANO is used in religious teaching; one Gospel has been translated. It is closely related to DAN.

DAN (GIO). LANGUAGE or DIALECT CLUSTER?[3]

Spoken by: *DAN* (*DÃ*), also known as *GIO* (*GYO*, *GE*), *YAKUBA*, **mɛbe**, called **sa-mia** by the MANO. Schwab states that they call themselves *NGERE*, **gɛ**, **gɛma**, and in the Ivory Coast **dã**. On his map, however, he marks *DÃ* (Ivory Coast) and *NGERE* (*GIO*) (Liberia) separately.

Where spoken: North-eastern Liberia (*GIO*) and the adjoining part of the Ivory Coast (*DÃ*), Cercle Man, adjacent to and intermingled with the *KONO*.

Number of speakers: 100,000 (Labouret); Ivory Coast 266,000 with the *GURO* (see below).[5]

There is some confusion of nomenclature, for the GE, called *SAMIA* by the *MANO*, **sã** or **dã** by the *GIO*, are said to live south of the *MANO*, west of the *GIO*, and the *NGERE* (Fr. *GUERE*), also known as *WOBE*, *GON*, *ZAGE*, *ZADYE*,

[1] Op. cit.   [2] 'Die Sprache der Bandi' (*Z. Eingeb. Spr.*, 1940/1).
[3] According to Prost (*La Langue Bisa*) MANA [MANO] and DÃ [DAN] are more closely related to MALINKE than to the MANDE FU Group.
[4] In reply to a questionnaire.   [5] France d'outre-mer leaflet.

BA, BANGWA (baŋwa) to live in Cercle Man; according to IFAN, GUERE and OUBI are two dialects. According to Bertho,[1] however, WOBE and GERE are not MANDE-FU dialects, but belong to the KRU Group (see p. 49). IFAN gives DAHO, BLOHO, and KAHO as names of other dialects related to WOBE and GERE.

Parts of the New Testament have been translated into GIO.

KWENI (GURO). DIALECT CLUSTER?[2]

Closely related dialects are said to be spoken by:

KWENI (GURO, Fr. *GOURO),* call themselves *KWENI,* called *GURO* by the *ANYI, DIPO* by the *GAGU, GURUMBO* by the *DYULA* and others. Delafosse[3] gives *LO* as another name for the *KWENI.* They live in the Ivory Coast, mainly in Cercle Gouros between Rivers Sassandra and Red Bandama, also on the left bank of the Bandama and to the south; also, according to IFAN, farther to the north.

Number: 83,000; 90,000 including the *GAGU* (Labouret); see also under *DAN*.

GAN, call themselves **ganne**, also known as **gbɛŋu** (*GBEINNGN*), called *BIRIFO* by the *BRONG* (but see p. 66); a section of the *KWENI* in the Ivory Coast, on the left bank of River Comoë.

SUAMLE and *MEMNE,* sections of the *KWENI* on the right bank of the White Bandama river.

KANGA BONO (only the name is known).

The dialect (or language?) spoken by the *GAGU (GBAN)* (call themselves **gbã**), in Cercle Gouros, around Oumé, is said to be closely related to the language or dialect of the *KWENI.*

MWA (Fr. *MOUIN*), call themselves **mwɛ̃**, called *MONA* by the *DYULA, MONI, MORU* by the *ANYI*; in the Ivory Coast, between Red and White Bandama rivers, north of the *BAULE.*

NWA (Fr. *NOUA*) (**nwã, ŋarã**), mentioned by Delafosse, and marked on his map on the White Bandama river adjacent to the *MOUIN.* No further information is available.

SYA (SIA), in and around Bobo Dioulasso.
  Note: According to Cremer[4] the dialect spoken by the *BOBO FING* (see p. 60) is related to SIA rather than to the other BOBO dialects.
  Number: 4,000 (Labouret).

TURA, in the hills of Cercle Haut Sassandra.
  Number: 20,000 (Labouret).

[1] 'La place du dialecte adiukru . . .' (*Bull. IFAN*, 1950).
[2] According to Prost (op. cit.) GURO, BẼ [GAN], GBAN, MWA, NWÃ, and SÃ [SYA] are more closely related to MALINKE than to the MANDE FU Group; likewise BOBO FĨ.
[3] *Carte ethnographique de l'Afrique Occidentale Française.*   [4] *Les Bobo. La vie sociale.*

SAMO, SAMOGO. LANGUAGE OR DIALECT CLUSTER? (but see p. 32).

Spoken by: *SAMO* (*SAMOGO, SAMOGHO, SANO,* Fr. *SAMORHO*), call themselves **sanu** (Sing. **sane**), called **ninisi** by the *MOSSI*, **samoxo, samoyo, samo** by the *BAMBARA* and others; also known as *NANERGE*.

Where spoken: Scattered in Haute-Volta, in Cercles Dédougou, Sikasso, Tougan, Ouahigouya, Bobo Dioulasso.

Number of speakers: 120,000 (Labouret).

Dialects: There appear to be two main dialects, corresponding roughly with the main sections of the tribe:

    North-eastern (the larger section), Dédougou, Tougan, and Ouahigouya;
    South-western, Sikasso and Bobo Dioulasso.

IFAN mentions a dialect MAKIA or MAYA, spoken in the north-western part of *SAMO* territory.

The *SEMBLA*, called *SAMBILA* by the *TURUKA*, in Bobo Dioulasso, appear to be a section of the *SAMO*.

Number: 8,000 (Labouret).

The *SEMU* (Fr. *SÉMOU*) of Bobo Dioulasso are probably the same as the SAMO.

BUSA. LANGUAGE.

Spoken by: *BUSA*—see below on nomenclature.

Where spoken: (*a*) Haute-Volta, Cercle Tenkodogo, extending into the Gold Coast; (*b*) Nigeria, Bussa Emirate in Ilorin Province and Illo District in Sokoto Province; also in Dahomey, in the Nikki-Kande area.

Number of speakers: Nigeria about 11,000;[1] Dahomey 16,000 in Cercle Nikki; Haute-Volta about 100,000;[2] Gold Coast 27,228.[3]

There is some confusion of nomenclature. The *BUSA* in Nigeria appear to consist of a fusion of peoples who now all speak the same language (known as ZUGWEYA, and called BUSANCHI by the *HAUSA*):

    BOKO (bɔkɔ), called *BOKOLAWA, BOKO BUSSAWA, BOKOBERU* by the *HAUSA*;
    BUSAGWE (*BISAGWE, BISA*);
    '*KAMBERI BERI-BERI*' (cp. *BERI-BERI*, the name of the *KANURI* in Bornu?).

The *BUSA* of Dahomey are said to call themselves **busano** (Sing. **busa**), and those of Haute-Volta (called *BUSANSE* by some of their neighbours, Fr. *BOUSSANCÉ*) to call themselves **bisano** (Sing. **bisa**).[2]

BUSA is also said to be spoken in Nigeria by the *KYENGA* (*KYENGAWA, KENGA, TYENGA*), north of the *BUSA* in Illo, and the *SHANGA* (*SHANGAWA*), north of the *BUSA* of Bussa.

---
[1] 1931 Census; separate figures are given for the various BUSA-speaking people.
[2] A. Prost, 'Notes sur les Boussancé' (*Bull. IFAN*, 1945); *La Langue Bisa*.   [3] 1948 Census.

Linguistic notes on the MANDE Languages

1. Some languages distinguish seven vowels, some nine.

2. The labio-velar consonants **kp, ɡ̆b** occur in most languages.
Note also the occurrence of velar fricatives **x** and **ɣ**. In some cases these can be seen to occur in the MANDE FU languages where a plosive occurs in the MANDE TAN languages:

TAN:	BAMBARA	kari	to break	kalo	moon
	MALINKE	kati		karu	
FU:	KPELLE	ɣali		ɣalo	
	MENDE	ɣali (ŋɡ̆ali in the Objective form)		ɣalu (ŋɡ̆alu in the Definite form)	

Nasalized consonants (i.e. voiced plosive preceded by a very slight homorganic nasal) are a characteristic feature of the MANDE languages (see below).

An initial consonantal change with grammatical function has been noted, e.g. in KPELLE, MENDE, and BANDI.

In KPELLE it occurs

(a) when the Indefinite Form of the Noun is changed into the Definite Form:

(i) Change of voiceless to voiced plosive:

kɔlɔ	skin	Definite:	ɡ̆ɔlɔ-i
kpana	gun		ɡ̆bana-i
taa	town		daa-i
su	inside		zu-i
pɛlɛ	house		bɛlɛ-i
folo	sun		volo-i

(ii) Change of voiceless to nasalized plosive:

loo, doo	child	ndoo-i, noo-i
wulu	tree	ŋɡulu-i, ŋulu-i
ɣila	dog	ŋɡila-i, ŋila-i

(b) in the Objective Form of the Verb:[1]

ɣɛɛ	gather	di ŋɡɛɛ	they gathered (it)
kaa	see	di ɡ̆aa	they saw (it)
		(cp. e ŋa kaa	he saw me)
toli	call	di doli	they called (him)
		(cp. ŋa di toli	I called them)

In MENDE the same type of consonantal changes takes place, but in different grammatical contexts.

[1] i.e. when the Object of the Verb is known but not named, e.g.

MENDE	i ŋɡ̆àli yá	he has broken (it)
but	i kɔ̀wí yáli yá	he has broken the wood

THE MANDE LANGUAGES

3. Tone is of great importance in the MANDE FU languages. It occurs, for example, in MENDE and VAI as etymological and grammatical tone. There are thus many tonal doublets, e.g.:

MENDE **pú** put **pù** England **pû** cave **pǔ** ten

and certain grammatical categories are distinguished by tone only:

MENDE **tólí** to call **tólì** a call
VAI **kì** to sleep **kí** sleep

Sentence intonation has also been noted in VAI, where special tone-patterns can replace those of an isolated word, at the end of a sentence or question. A special question-intonation has also been observed in MENDE.

In the MANDE TAN languages tone appears to have broken down to a considerable extent. Further research is, however, needed to show to what extent it is still in use.

4. The most common form of the Root (Noun or Verb) appears to be disyllabic: CVCV, CV+syllabic nasal, or CVV.

VAI **kila** way **kuŋ** head **faa** die

Monosyllabic Roots consisting of CV exist, but they are less numerous and in some cases can be shown to be derived from disyllables.

5. Compound Nouns are much in use, e.g.:

MALINKE **da-ji** mouth-water (spittle) **nyɛ-ji** eye-water (tear) **nyɛ-ma** eye-surface (front)

MENDE **nyíní-ya** breast-water (milk) **nyǎ -lò** woman-child (daughter)

6. Derivative Nouns and Adjectives are formed by Suffixes, some of which may perhaps originally have been independent words, e.g.:

MALINKE	**di**	give	**di-la**	giver
	buga	vain	**buga-ya**	vanity
	tege	cut	**tege-na**	cutting tool
	bori	run	**bori-li**	running
	dibi	darkness	**dibi-niŋ**	dark
	di	be fine	**di-ma**	fine
	ga	illness	**ga-to**	ill
VAI	**manja**	chief	**manja-ja**	chieftainship
	kai	man	**kai-ma**	male
	fa	fill	**fa-le**	full
MENDE	**màhã**	chief	**màhà-ya**	chiefdom
	mìní	heavy	**mìnì-gi**	heaviness

7. There are no Noun Classes (but see § 9 for kinds of Plural in MENDE).

8. There is no grammatical gender, nor is a distinction made between persons and things in the Pronoun.

9. In the MANDE TAN languages the Plural is formed by suffixing **-lu** or **-u**. This Suffix can also be attached to the Plural Pronoun (1st, 2nd, or 3rd Person) in certain circumstances.

In the MANDE FU languages various Suffixes are used to form the Plural of Nouns. In some MANDE FU languages there is a separate form of the Plural for persons, e.g. in KPELLE the general Plural Suffix is **-ŋa,** while for persons **-ni** is sometimes used.

In MENDE the following kinds of Plural exist: Indefinite Plural, Definite Plural, Plural of masses, Plural of 'somebody and the people with him', Plural of Nouns signifying agent or doer.

10. Denominative Verbs are formed by a Suffix (MALINKE **-ya**, VAI **-a**):

MALINKE	**foro**	free	**foro-ya**	to free
VAI	**tusa**	question	**tusa-a**	to ask

In a similar way Verbs can be formed by the Verb **kɛ**, to do, in conjunction with a preceding Noun Object, e.g.:

VAI	**ki kɛ**	sleep	**di kɛ**	cry

Many new verbal expressions arise from the compounding of Noun and Verb, or Noun, Postposition, and Verb, e.g.:

MALINKE **da-bo** to wean<**da** mouth, **bo** to take away (take away child's mouth from mother's breast).
da ja to feel weary<**da** mouth, **ja** dry (have a dry mouth).
kũ-ma-bo to redeem<**kũ** head, **ma** surface, **bo** take away (take away head's surface out of bondage).

11. As an example of Tense Formation, some forms are given from MALINKE. According to Abiven,[1] the Tenses of the Verb are formed by Particles and Auxiliaries standing between the Pronoun and the Verb Stem. The following Tenses exist:

m bɛ mita	I was taking
n tun bɛ mita	I was then taking
n ti mita	I have taken
m bɛ na mita	I am coming to take (shall take)
ŋ ka mita	that I may take

12. There is no true Passive Voice, but a Neuter-Passive is formed by inflexion of the Stem.

13. Word order in the simple sentence is Subject–Object–Verb:

MALINKE **a soo buɡu**   he the horse struck

[1] *Dictionnaire Français-Malinké et Malinké-Français.*

KPELLE	ŋa ŋaloŋ kaa	I a man saw
MENDE	ŋgí mahɛ̃í lɔ́á	I the chief have seen

14. In the Genitive construction the *nomen rectum* precedes the *nomen regens*, and so does the Possessive Pronoun.

It seems to be characteristic of some MANDE languages that in the Genitive construction or with Possessives a grammatical distinction is made between

(a) parts of the body,
(b) names of relatives,
(c) other Nouns.

In MENDE, for example, there is no tonal change in names of parts of the body, and no consonantal or tonal change in names of relatives (see also the VAI and MALINKE examples below).

MALINKE	Musa ba	Musa's mother
KPELLE	kaalon (ŋɔ) kpalaŋ	the chief's farm
MENDE	màhɛ̃í wɛ̀lɛ̀í	the chief's house
MALINKE	ḿ ba	my mother
	m bulɔ	my hand
	nna bunɔ	my house
KPELLE	ŋa pɛlɛi	my house
MENDE	nyá wùí	my head
VAI	na keŋ	my house
	ŋ kuŋ	my head

15. The Adjective (including Numeral) and the Demonstrative Pronoun follow the Noun, e.g.:

KPELLE	pɛlɛ kwele	white house	bɛlɛ kwelei	the white house
	pɛlɛ kweleŋa	white houses	bɛlɛ kweleŋai	the white houses

Note that the Definite Suffix -i and the Plural Suffix -ŋa are attached to the Adjective and not to the Noun.

Section III
ISOLATED UNIT: SONGHAI

SONGHAI. Dialect Cluster.

Where spoken: In the whole valley of the middle Niger, from Djenné in the west to the borders of Nigeria in the east; from the oases of the Sahara in the north into Dahomey in the south-east—an area comprising the ancient kingdom of Songhai under the reign of the famous Askia dynasty.

SONGHAI is the language of commerce throughout most of this area, and is spoken as a second language by many speakers of other languages. There is, however, practically no vernacular literature.

The three dialects of the SONGHAI Cluster are very closely interrelated and are mutually intelligible; they are, however, recognized as separate, and the dialects and their speakers are known by different names.

Dialect: SONGHAI (SONGHAY, Fr. SONRHAÏ, SONRAÏH, &c.), own name **sŏŋai kine** (speech of the *SONGHAI*) or more often, **koira kine** (speech of the country), and, in the west, **jene kine** (speech of Djenné).

Spoken by: SONGHAI, call themselves **sŏŋai** or **sŏyai, sŏŋoi, sŏyɔi**; also known as *HABE*[1] and *KURIA*; in the north-western part of the SONGHAI language area from Djenné to Niamey.

Number: French Sudan 125,127;[2] 98,858;[3] Haute-Volta 6,330;[2] 34,131;[3] Niger 80,162;[2] 4,603;[3] 93,000.[4]

Dialect: ZARMA (DYERMA), own name **zármà**.

Spoken by: ZARMA (*DYERMA, DYABARMA, DYARMA, DJERMA, ZABARMA, ZABIRMAWA*, &c.), call themselves **zármà**; in Niger Colony, Niamey, and Dosso, extending into Sokoto Province of Nigeria.

Number: Niger 175,000;[4] Nigeria 12,390 (1931 Census).

One Gospel has been published; the New Testament is in the press (1950).

Dialect: DENDI.

Spoken by: *DENDI*, called **dandawá** (Sing. **dandá**) by the *HAUSA*; south of the *ZARMA*, on both banks of the Niger around Karimama and Gaya; also in Dahomey, in the Kouandé, Djougou, and Parakou area; a few in Nigeria, in Kontagora Division of Niger Province, where they are known as *DANDAWA*.

Number: Niger 8,976;[2] Dahomey 14,912.[2]

The *MARANSE* in *MOSSI* country, in the region of Kaya and the eastern part of Cercle Ouahigouya, speak a SONGHAI dialect.

Number: about 2,000.

---

[1] But see note on p. 61. [2] du Picq, *La langue songhai*.
[3] Le Gouvernement Général de l'Afrique Occidentale Française, 1931.
[4] *Le Niger* (Gouvernement Général de l'Afrique Occidentale Française publication).

ISOLATED UNIT: SONGHAI

Linguistic notes on SONGHAI

SONGHAI is unrelated to any other known language or Language Group. The following points may be noted:

1. The labio-velars **kp, gb** are absent.[1]
2. There are no Noun Classes.
3. Word Formatives are Affixes (mostly Suffixes), e.g.:

Noun Formatives:

ŋwa-li	food	<**ŋwa**	eat
kaŋ-iya	falling	<**kaŋ**	fall
i-bi-o	a black one	<**bi**	black (Adjectival Nominal)

Adjective Formative:

sayi-nte	rich	<**sayi**	be rich

Verbal Derivative:

ŋwa-ndi	feed	<**ŋwa**	eat (Causative)

4. The Plural is formed by Suffix (SONGHAI **-yo**, ZARMA **-ai**). Note that when an Adjective follows the Noun, the Suffix is attached to the Adjective and not to the Noun.

SONGHAI	**turí**	tree	Plur.	**turi-yo**
ZARMA	**tulí**			**túlí-ài, tulyài**
ZARMA	**bɔlo bi**	black man		**bɔlo-bi-ai**

5. Word order in the Sentence is Subject–Object–Verb:

a na hali kaŋ	he (then) water drank
a na tuli a na za	he (then) wood he (then) cut

6. In the Genitive construction the *nomen rectum* precedes the *nomen regens*:

hal fu	man's house
kɔi bali	chief's horse
fu banda	house's rear (behind the house)
sõŋai kine	Songhai speech

The Possessive Pronoun also precedes the Noun:

ili kɔi	our master
ai fu	my house

7. The Adjective follows the Noun (see § 4).

8. Vocabulary shows some resemblance to the MANDE languages (and to some other languages).

[1] Except as a dialectal variant in DENDI as spoken in Djougou (due to the influence of neighbouring languages). Cp.

SONGHAI	**kwara**	town	Djougou	**kpara**
	kwalé	be white		**kpalé**
	kɔ́i	master		**kpé**

Section IV
ISOLATED LANGUAGE GROUP: KRU

Consists of: BETE   Dialect Cluster.
           BAKWE   Dialect Cluster.

Where spoken: Liberia, mainly in the south-east; Ivory Coast, as far east as River Sassandra.

Note: The name KRU (of unknown origin) is used by Europeans to denote a number of tribes speaking related dialects, and the dialects as a whole. The people are also sometimes known as *KRUMEN* (Fr. *KROUMEN*).

Linguistic information on these dialects is scanty and consists for the most part in vocabularies only, so that no definitive classification can be made. There appear, however, to be two main Dialect Clusters. Many of the names given by different writers as those of dialects may be names of tribes, tribal sections, or localities; moreover, there is some overlapping and confusion of nomenclature.

BETE. DIALECT CLUSTER.

Where spoken: In the eastern part of the KRU language area, in the Ivory Coast between Rivers Sassandra in the east and Bandama in the west.

Dialects probably belonging to this Cluster are spoken by:

DIDA, in Cercle Lahou.
  Number: 56,000 (Labouret).
  The same dialect appears to be spoken by the *LOZWA, YOKO, GOBWA* and *JIVO* (all in approximately the same area).
  IFAN gives a long list of 'DIDA dialects', but many of these appear to b place-names, and it is possible that they are the names of localities where th dialect is spoken, perhaps with slight variations.
  The WAWI of Clarke[1] is identical with the dialect of the *DIDA*.
  Two Gospels have been translated.

KWAYA, also known as *ZEGBE*; west of the *DIDA* in the valleys of the R Fresco and Yobehiri.
  Clarke's 'Friesko', 'Friesco' and 'Eple' appear to be vocabularies of this dialec

GODYE (GODIA), call themselves *GODYE* or *GO*; west of the *KWA⅄* around Kotrou. Other names which may be those of sections of the trib or of other tribes, speaking this dialect, are: *LEGRE, NOGBO, BALEK KOTROKU* (Clarke's KOTRAHU).
  Number: 2,000 (Labouret).

NEYO (NO, NEWO, NIHIRI), call themselves *NEYO* and their dial NEWOLE; on the coast between Rivers Wawa in the east and Fanoko in west, and on both banks of the River Sassandra as far as the rapids of Zelega.

[1] *Specimens of dialects. . . .* (1848–9).

ISOLATED LANGUAGE GROUP: KRU

There are two sections of the tribe, *BOKRA* (Clarke's BUKRA) and *KEBE*, also known as 'Drewin'. The ANDONE of Clarke appears to resemble this dialect.

Number: 4,500 (Labouret).

KWADYA, call themselves *KWADYA* or *KWA*, and their dialect KWADRE-WOLE; on both banks of River Sassandra from Grigibile to Kwati.

Number: 2,000 (Labouret).

The dialect of the *GIBO* of Maburi appears to resemble closely that of the *KWADYA*.

BETE (dialect called by IFAN: BETEGBO); north of the *GODYE* and *KWADYA*, from Kwati in the south to just beyond Lat. 7, and from *KWENI* country in the east to River Sassandra in the west.

Number: 153,000 (Labouret).

The tribe appears to consist of several sections: IFAN names several BETE 'dialects': LOBLE, DAKUYA, GUIBONO, BOBONO, ZELMOGBO, YOKOGBO.

BOBWA, also known as *WAGA*, *WADYE*, *WAYA*, *WAA*, *WOBE* (Fr. *OUOBI*); in a narrow strip of territory between the *BETE* and *BAKWE* in the south and MANDE-speaking tribes in the east, north, and west.

According to Bertho[1] WOBE and GERE (see p. 40) belong to the KRU Group.

It is not known whether the *AHIZI* (*AÏZI*) on Ebrié Lagoon between Dabou and Krafi speak a KRU dialect or one of the KWA Languages (Lagoon Group) (see p. 78).

Number: 3,200 (Labouret).

BAKWE. DIALECT CLUSTER.[2]

Where spoken: In the western part of the KRU language area in Liberia, and in the Ivory Coast west of River Sassandra.

Dialects probably belonging to this Cluster are spoken by:

BAKWE (*BAKWO*), on the left bank of the River Sassandra, inland from the *HWANE*.

Number: 2,500 (Labouret).

Koelle's GBE[3] and Clarke's PORI[4] appear to be the same as this dialect.

According to IFAN, a BAKWE dialect is spoken by the *BOUDOUKWA* in Cercle Sassandra, which differs from the BAKWE of Tabou and is more nearly related to the dialect of the *NEYO* (BETE Cluster).

---

[1] 'Wobê et gêré, dialectes très voisins l'un de l'autre, appartiennent manifestement au groupe krou, marquant au sein de ce groupe la liaison entre les dialectes dida-bété d'une part et les dialectes gbakoué-kplakpo d'autre part.' 'La place du dialecte adiukru . . .' (*Bull. IFAN*, 1950, p. 1080).

[2] In the BAKWE dialects the Suffixes **-po**, **-pwe**, **-bo**, **-bwe**, denote the people, **-wi**, **-bi**, the language.

[3] Koelle, *Polygtotta Africana*.

[4] Op. cit.

ISOLATED LANGUAGE GROUP: KRU

HWANE, call themselves *HWANE* or *HWĀLE*, called *HWĪNE* or *HWĪLE* by the *ABRI*, also known as *BODO*; on the coast, west of the *NEYO* as far as River Nonwa.

The *OBWA* to the north speak a very closely related dialect.

PYA, call themselves *PYA* or *PYE* (**pyɛ**), also known as *OMELOKWE*; in the basin of River San Pedro west of the *HWANE*.

ABRI, call themselves *ABRINYA* and their dialect ABRIWI, ABRIBI (the Europeanized form of this name being the place-name Béréby), called *AULO* or *AULOPO* by the *NEYO*; on the coast south of the *PYA*. This dialect is also spoken by the *BOKWE*, *IRAPWE*, *OREPWE*, and *TUYO*.

Clarke's 'Tabu' and 'Grand Béréby' may be the same as this dialect.

GWEABO, adjacent to the *GREBO* on River Cavally.

According to Sapir[1] the *GWEABO* should be distinguished from the *GREBO*, as they speak a different 'language'. Many of the names of *GWEABO* tribes are, however, the same as those of *GREBO* tribes.

The *GWEABO* tribes are: *NYABO* (**nyãbo**) (including the *PLA* (*PLAPO*, dialect PLAPI), *NIMIAH* (**nĩwĩɛ̃**), *BOLOKWE* (**bolokwɛ̃**), *DREBO* (*TREMBLE*) (**drɛbo**), *GBWOLO* (**gbwɔlo**).

Clarke's NABWA KRU and BARBOE probably represent varieties of this dialect.

KRU-speaking tribes in eastern Liberia:

There are three groups of tribes in eastern Liberia, speaking related (but not always inter-intelligible) dialects:[2]

GREBO, call themselves *GREBO*, called *BOEZONYO* by the *KRAN*; between River Cess in the west and River Cavally in the east, and extending into the Ivory Coast (but see *GWEABO*); also extending inland for about 50 to 70 miles. They are known as 'Bush *GREBO*' (or 'Half-*GREBO*') and 'Beach *GREBO*'.

GREBO tribes include: *PALIPO* (*PALEPO*, *BADEBO*, *PADEBU*) in the north and *BAROBO* in the centre of the *GREBO* area. The *JABO*, west of Cape Palmas around Nimiah, are said to be a *GWEABO* section, although Herzog[3] states that their 'language' differs from that of the *GWEABO*.

Christaller's BWIDABO appears to be GREBO.

GREBO is used in religious education; parts of the Bible and some other religious books have been published.

KRAN (*KRAHN*), called *PAHN* (a nickname) by the *GREBO*, call themselves by their various tribal names; between Rivers Cess and Cavally, inland from the *KRU*, and extending into the Ivory Coast.

KRAN tribes include: *TCHIEN*, call themselves **tiɛ̃**, called *GIEN* (*KIEN*) by

[1] 'Some Gweabo Proverbs' (*Africa*, 1929).
[2] Much of the information on KRU-speaking tribes in Liberia was provided by the Rev. I. T. Jensen.
[3] *Jabo proverbs*.

ISOLATED LANGUAGE GROUP: KRU

the Liberians and others,[1] north and west of Tchien; *NEABO, TWABO (TE, TEPO)* dialect TEWI, called *HORO* by the *ABRI*, on River Cavally north of the *GREBO*; *SAPO (SA,* **sapã**), said to call themselves **pulu pany,**[1] in the south-eastern part of *KRAN* territory.

Total number of KRAN: 42,000 in Liberia, perhaps 100,000 in all.[2]

KRAN is used in religious education; a few Scripture portions have been published.

KRU, called *MENA YU* by the *GREBO, KLAO* by the *KRAN*; on the coast between St. John and Cess rivers, extending inland for 30 to 40 miles. They are known as 'Bush *KRU*' and 'Beach *KRU*'.

Mellish mentions a dialect **dɔ wuɖu,** spoken by one of the 'Bush *KRU*' tribes.

KRU is used in religious education; one Gospel and some other religious books have been published.

The *KRA (KRÃ)*, on the coast between Nifu and Bafu, appear to be a part of the *KRU*; they are also known as *NANNA KRU, KRAO, KRAWO*.

Dialect: BASSA, own name **basɔ**, called **ǵbɔ** by tribes of the interior, **mani** by the *KRU*.[2]

Spoken by: *BASSA*,[3] call themselves **báasà**, called **félà** by the *KPELLE*; between Monrovia and River Cess (except for most of the immediate coast), extending inland for about 100 miles.

Number: about 150,000.

Mellish distinguishes four BASSA 'dialects':
maa bã, spoken near Monrovia;
ǵi ǵban (ǵibi), in the west;
ni boɛ̀ kwiɖin and **kɔɔ,** in the River Cess area.

BASSA is used in religious education; parts of the Bible and some other religious books have been published. The *BASSA* have in recent years invented a syllabic script and this has been used, to a very slight degree, for the production of literature.

Other KRU-speaking tribes in Liberia are:

DE, call themselves **dewɛ̃mã** and their dialect **dewɛ̃ wulu;** also known as *DEWOI, DO,* and called **dɔŋɔi** by the *GOLA*; west of Monrovia.
This dialect is now being replaced by GOLA and VAI.

KWAA, called **bɛɛlɛ** by the *KPELLE*; south of the *BANDI* and *GBUNDE* (MANDE-speakers).

Linguistic notes on the KRU Dialects

1. Auer[4] distinguishes ten vowels in *GREBO*, while in other dialects only seven have been noted.

---

[1] Schwab, *Tribes of the Liberian hinterland.*   [2] Information from the Rev. G. D. Mellish.
[3] To be distinguished from the various *BASSA* of Nigeria (see pp. 86, 103) and the BANTU-speaking *BASA* of the Cameroons.
[4] *Elements of the Gedebo language.*

ISOLATED LANGUAGE GROUP: KRU

2. The labio-velar consonants **kp** and **gb** occur.
Combinations of a consonant with **l** or **r** are common, e.g.:

    GREBO **ble** cow;   **bro** earth;   **kri** farm;   **ka bokro** goat.

h can be combined with a liquid, semi-vowel or nasal (**hl, hm, hn, hny, hw**, &c.), e.g.:

    DE   **ŋhm** five;   **hmlegbo** six
    GREBO **hmu** five

3. Tone is significant, but has been studied in detail only in JABO[1] and GWEABO.[2] In GREBO the 1st and 2nd Personal Pronouns are distinguished by tone only:

	Sing.			*Plur.*	
	Subject	Object	Possessive	Subject	Object
1.	m̀, nè	mò	nà	à	àmò
2.	ḿ, né	mó	ná	á	ámó

4. Roots (which may also be complete words) are mostly monosyllabic, consisting of CV:

    GREBO   **bo** foot   **bɔ** black   **ba** to hurt
                bi to play   **bɛ** to cut   **ble** cow   **hmu** five

Some disyllabic Roots also exist (form CVCV):

    GREBO   **keni** reed   **kema** a bird   **yibo** to know

5. Suffixes are used as Noun Formatives, e.g.:

    GREBO   **-ɛ, -mɔ, -da** form Verbal Nouns:

                ku-ɛ   death<**ku** die
                nu-mɔ   doing<**nu** do
                yibo-da knowledge<**yibo** know

-de forms Nouns from Adjectives:

                kũkũ-de old age<**kũkũ** old

-ɔ forms the Noun Agent:

                wa-ɔ   saviour<**wa** save

Compound Nouns are very common, e.g.:

    GREBO   **lu-kɛ-po-dɛ**   head-back-placing-thing (pillow)
                kpo-ne-nɔ-ɔ ⎫ man of good behaviour (good man)<
                kpo-ne behaviour, ⎪ **nɔ** be good, **ɔ-** (Suffix denoting person)
                kpo-ne-nɔnɔ-ɛ ⎬ kindness
                kpo-ne-nunu-dɛ ⎭ benefaction (**nu** do, **dɛ** thing)

6. There are no Noun Classes.

---

[1] Herzog, *Jabo proverbs from Liberia*.
[2] Sapir, 'Notes on the Gweabo language of Liberia' (*Language*, 1931).

ISOLATED LANGUAGE GROUP: KRU

7. The Plural of Nouns is formed by Suffixes (sometimes with stem-elision), e.g.:

GREBO wa-ɔ   Plur. wa-o   saviour
       ki-nyɔ   ki-nyo   Portuguese
       ǵi   ǵi-a   leopard
       jɔ   jɔ-e   rat
       bli   ble   country
       bli-pe   bli-wɛ   countryman

Note also: de Plur. de-no mother
           yu   yu-ru, yi-ru child

8. There is no grammatical gender, except that persons and things are distinguished in the 3rd Pers. Pronoun, e.g.:

GREBO   *Persons*   *Non-Persons*
                Sing.   Plur.   Sing.   Plur.
       Subject   ɔ   o   ɛ   e
       Object   nɔ   no   nɛ   ne
       Poss.   ɔnɛnɛ   onɛnɛ   ɛnɛnɛ   enɛnɛ
       Demonst. nɔno   nono   nɛno   neno

9. Verbal Derivatives are formed by Particles, mostly Suffixes, e.g. GREBO

   -o Direction away from the speaker:
               hada carry   hada-o carry away

   -e Causative or Applicative:
               we   come out   we-e   cause to go out
               pe   put   pe-e   put to

   -de Applicative or Instrumental:
       kya-da laugh (Past)   ɔ kya-de-da mɔ   he laughed at me
       nu   do   ɔ nu-ne-na nɛtu[1] he did it with a stick

   -r- or -l- Reversive:
               ka close   krɛ open
               cp. ABRI ka close, kra open; NEYO ka open, kla close

   -e Intransitive-Passive:
               ɛ nu-e it was done; kɔ-e to be born

10. Tenses are formed by means of Auxiliaries or Suffixes, e.g.

GREBO ɔ mi di-mɔ   he will come (Future)
       ɔ mi-a di-mɔ   he will come (Immediate Future)
       ɔ mi wa di-mɔ   he will come (Far Future)
       ɔ di-da   he came (Past)[2]
       ɔ di-ɛ   he came (Immediate Past)
       ɔ di-dɔ   he came (Near Past)[2]

[1] Note assimilation with preceding nasal.
[2] Cp. ɔ nu-na he did; ɔ nu-nɔ (Near Past) with assimilation to preceding nasal.

ɔ di-nɔ	he habitually comes (Habitual)	
ɔ di-ma	he continually comes (Continuous)	
ɔ yi-di	he is (was) coming (Progressive) (yi = be)	
te ɔ na-di	that he may come (Optative)	

be- expresses Compulsion:

bè nu	I am to do	bé nu	you (Sing.)	bo (be-ɔ) nu	he
bà nu	we are to do	bá nu	you (Plur.)	bo nu	they

11. Negation is expressed by Negative Particles, e.g.:

ABRI n di le   I am coming   e n di be le   I am not coming
      di   come (Imper.)   a di   do not come

12. There is normally no Passive Voice, but a specialized use of the 3rd Person Plural (but see § 9).

13. Word order in the simple sentence is Subject–Verb–Object or Subject–Object–Verb, e.g.:

NEYO e li ma   I eat banana
      na ka ma li   I am banana eating
      e yi ma li   I go banana eating (Future)
      e a ma li   I have banana eaten

The Indirect Object precedes the Direct, e.g.:

GREBO e nyɛ buo tu   I give father stick

14. In the Genitive construction the *nomen rectum* precedes the *nomen regens*, with or without a Linking Particle:

GREBO buo tu or buo a tu   stick of father
   (Note also **buo ɔ tu**, ɔ being the Possessive Particle 'his').
TEWI   di a wu   child of mother (brother)

The Possessive Pronoun precedes the Noun:

TEWI   na di   my mother

15. The Demonstrative Pronoun follows the Noun:

TEWI   bla u   this rice

16. The KRU dialects are closely interrelated both in vocabulary and structure, but are not inter-intelligible. Their nearest relations are the KWA languages, but the greater part of their vocabulary is exclusively their own.

Section V

THE GUR LANGUAGES (LARGER UNIT)

THE GUR languages are spoken in French Sudan, Haute-Volta, the northern part of the Ivory Coast, the Northern Territories of the Gold Coast, northern Togoland (British and French), and Dahomey, and into Nigeria in the east. In the north they are bounded by SONGHAI, TUAREG, and FULANI, in the west by the MANDE languages (with considerable overlapping), in the south and south-east by the KWA languages, in the east and north by NUPE, BUSA, KAMBARI, HAUSA, and DYERMA.

The term GUR languages was adopted by Christaller[1] from a suggestion of G. A. Krause. It is derived from the names *GURMA*, *GURUNSI*, &c., of frequent occurrence among speakers of these languages. The name 'Voltaic' (Fr. Voltaïque) has also been applied to this larger unit.

SINGLE UNIT: SENUFO

SENUFO. DIALECT CLUSTER.

The name SENUFO (Fr. SÉNOUFO), originally a name given by the AKAN-speaking peoples, is used by Europeans, and by other African tribes, to denote both the dialects belonging to this Cluster, and the people speaking them. *SYENA*, *SYENE*, &c. (by which names some of the tribes are known), are probably variants of the same name.

Where spoken: In the western part of the GUR language area, in French Sudan, Ivory Coast, and Haute-Volta.

Total number of speakers: Estimated by Labouret at about 750,000; 850,000.[2]

Dialects belonging to this cluster are spoken by:

BAMANA (*BAMBARA*), call themselves **bamana, bambara, bãbara** (local variants of the name) or (in the south) **syeneye, sendeye**; called *BAMANA SENUFO* by MANDE-speaking people;[3] also known, in different parts of the *SENUFO* area, as *MINIANKA* (*MINIA*), *TAGBA* (*TAGWA*).

Where spoken: French Sudan, Cercle Koutiala, and the southern part of San (*MINIANKA*); Haute-Volta, Cercle Bobo Dioulasso; Ivory Coast, Sikasso (**syeneye**), the Boundiali–Korhogo area, and as far south as Seguéla.

SENADI is given by Welmers[4] as the name of the dialect (called by him 'language of the SENUFO group' spoken at Korhogo, and SUP'IDE as the name of that spoken at Sikasso.

[1] 'Sprachproben aus dem Sudan' (*Z. Afr. Spr.*, 3, 1889–90).
[2] France d'outre-mer leaflets.
[3] To distinguish them from the *BAMBARA*, who speak a MANDE dialect (see p. 34).
[4] 'Notes on two languages in the Senufo group' (*Language*, 1950).

FOLO (*FORO*) on both banks of River Bandama around Kouton and Niélé (north-west of Kong).
   Number: 23,790.[1]

KARABORO, called *KOROMA, KAROMA* by the *GOUIN* and *TURUKA*, referred to by IFAN as *KAMA*; in Haute-Volta, Cercle Bobo Dioulasso, south-east of Banfora.
   Number: 7,500;[2] 13,500.[3]

MBWIN (Fr. *MBOUIN*), around Léra, near the sources of River Comoë (but see *GOUIN, MBOUIN* under *LOBI*, p. 59).
   Number: 31,875.[1]

NAFANA, call themselves **ʃínyewolɛ̀ nafâme** ('the people'),[4] called **mfantera** by AKAN-speakers, also known as *GAMBO*, and as *PANTARA* (*BANDARA, GBANDARA, VANDRA*), from Banda, the main centre of the eastern *NAFANA*; much scattered: some between the Black Volta and Bondoukou, extending into the Gold Coast.

KOMONO (but see under LOBI, p. 59, and BAULE, p 81).

DYIMINI (*JIMINI, GIMINI, DJIMINI*), called *BAMBARA* by the *DYULA* (this being merely a general name denoting 'non-*DYULA*'); south of Kong, north of the *BAULE*. Outlying sections are to be found in the Gold Coast; according to IFAN they are also to be found around Katiola.
   Number: 25,000 (Labouret).
   IFAN mentions two 'dialects' spoken by the *GIMINI*: KAKONO and KOTOLO.

NOHOLO (Fr. *NAOULOU*), in canton Séguéla, east of Odienné.

TAGWANA (*TAGBONA*, Fr. *TAGOUANA, TAKPONIN*), called *KANGA BLE* ('Black *DYULA*') by the *BAULE*; east of River Bandama, north of the *BAULE*, west of the *DYIMINI*; also extending across the Bandama.
   Number: 35,000 (Labouret).
   The dialect spoken by the *MANDAGA* in the Konodougou area is almost identical with that of the *TAGWANA*.

TAFILE (*TAFIRE, TAFIRI*), between Kong and River Bandama.

KPALAGHA (*PALLAKA, KPALLAGA*), call themselves **kpalaya**, called **palaya, palaxa, palaka**, by MANDE-speakers and others: between the upper Bandama and upper Comoë rivers in the Korhogo–Firkessédougou area.

PADOGHO (Fr. *PADORHO, BODORO*), between Diébougou and Lorhosso (but see under LOBI, p. 59)?

TUSIA (Fr. *TOUSSIA*), south-west of Bobo Dioulasso.
   Number: 15,500 (Labouret).

---
[1] Delafosse, *Haut-Sénégal-Niger*.　　　　[2] Tauxier, *Les Gouin et les Tourouka*.
[3] *La Haute-Volta* (Gouvernement Général de l'Afrique Occidentale Française).
[4] Rapp, 'Die Náfana-Sprache ...' (*M.S.O.S.*, 1933).

THE GUR LANGUAGES 57

TIEFO (TYEFO), called *TYEFORO* by the *GOUIN* and *TURUKA*; in the Bobo Dioulasso area; according to IFAN their dialect is also spoken by the *KAMA* of Banfora (see *KARABORO* above). Delafosse's map[1] shows KIEFO, south of Bobo Dioulasso.
Number: 6,500 (Labouret).

DOGHOSIE (**doyosye**) (see under LOBI, p. 60), said by Tauxier[2] to speak a SENUFO dialect.

KULELE, called *PAMA* by the *WARA*, mentioned by Tauxier[3] as being in the same area as the *WARA* and *NATIORO* (see below). According to Ferréol[4] the '*COULAILAI*' are a section of the *SENUFO* of Banfora.
Number: 15,000.[5]

NATIORO (NATYORO), call themselves **samitemi** (Sing. **sămu, samina**), called *NATIORO* by the *DYULA*; west of Banfora.
Number: 1,000.[3]

According to Tauxier their dialect closely resembles that of the *WARA*, but perhaps shows some MANDE FU influence; according to Ferréol[4] it differs from the dialect of the *WARA*.

WARA (Fr. *OUARA, OUALA*), call themselves *SAMA* (cp. *NATIORO*); south-west of Banfora.
Number: 2,136.[3]

The short vocabulary given by Tauxier is insufficient to show the relationship of this dialect; on Delafosse's map it is shown as a MANDE dialect, while according to Ferréol[4] it may belong to the AKAN group of KWA languages.

VIGE (VIGYE, Fr. *VIGUIÉ, VIGUÉ)*, south-west of Bobo Dioulasso.
Number: 3,500 (Labouret).

TYEBALI (Fr. *TIÉBALA*), a section of the *SENUFO* in the Banfora area.
Number: 2,000.[5]

The following tribes are mentioned by Delafosse,[6] but nothing further is known of them:

KADLE (KANDERE), in canton Tengréla;
PONGALA (PONGA), in canton Kassire;
NYENE (Fr. *NIÉNÉ*), in cantons Kouto, Kolia, Tombougou, Niodougou;
KYEMBAGHA (Fr. *KIEMBARHA, KIEGBAGHA*), in cantons Nganndana (among the *FOLO*) and Korhogo; ,
ZONA, in canton Kebi;
NAFAGHA (Fr. *NAFARHA*), in cantons Komboro-dougou, Sinématiali, Karakoro, Kagbolodougo and Kadioha;

---

[1] *Carte ethnographique de l'Afrique Occidentale Française.*
[2] 'Les Dorhossié et Dorhossié-Finng du cercle de Bobo Dioulasso' (*J. Soc. Afric.*, 1931).
[3] 'Deux petites populations peu connues de l'Afrique Occidentale Française: les Ouara ou Ouala, et les Natioro' (*J. Soc. Afric.*, 1939).
[4] 'Essai d'histoire et d'ethnographie de quelques peuplades de la subdivision de Banfora' (*Bull. Com. Études hist. et scient. de l'A.O.F.*, 1924).
[5] Tauxier, 'Les Gouin et les Tourouka'.   [6] *Le peuple Siéna ou Sénoufo.*

KAFIBELE (*KAFIGE, KAFUGULO*), in cantons Sirhasso and Kannorhoba;
KAFOLO, in cantons Gujembe, Dikodougou, and Kadioha.
KASEMBELE (Fr. KASSEMBÉLÉ) in cantons Katiali, Niofouin, and Siempurgo;
GBATO, in cantons Nafon, Nganahoni, and Yérikiele;
NIAGHAFOLO (Fr. *NIARHAFOLO*), in canton Firkéssedougou.

Single Unit? KULANGO

KULANGO, own name **kóláŋò, kpélégò, koláyo**. Dialect Cluster?

Spoken by: *KULANGO* (Fr. *KOULANGO*), call themselves **kolã-mbio** (Sing. **kolayo**), or **kolambo** (Sing. **kolam, kolaŋo**); called **ŋkoramfo** by AKAN-speaking people, **ŋgorafo, kolamvo** by the *BRONG, PAXALA* by the *DYULA*. In Kong they are also known as *NABE, NAMBAI*, and *ZAZERE*, in Bondoukou as *NGWALA*.

Where spoken: Ivory Coast between Rivers Comoë and Black Volta, between Lat. 9.25 and 7.12; also west of the Comoë in Cercle Kong, and extending into the Gold Coast in the south-east.

Number of speakers: 40,000 (Labouret).

Dialects: Delafosse[1] distinguishes four dialects spoken in the following localities:
Kong;
Bouna;
Nasian;
Bondoukou.

The following may also speak dialects belonging to the same Cluster:
LOGHON (Fr. *LORHON, LORON*), perhaps the same as *NABE* (i.e. *KULANGO* of Kong); call themselves *LOMA, LOGOMA, LOGHOMA*.[2]
Tauxier gives vocabularies of three 'dialects' from different localities.
Number: 5,000 (Labouret).

TEGESYE (Fr. *TEGUESSIÉ*), called *TUNBE* by the *BIRIFO*. According to Tauxier they are related to the *LOBI*, but some, at least, of them have adopted the dialect of the *LOGHON*. According to his vocabularies, however, 'TEGUÉ' and 'LORON' are not identical.
Number: 2,000 (Labouret).

Language Group: LOBI-DOGON

Consists of: LOBI   Dialect Cluster.
            BOBO   Dialect Cluster.
            DOGON   Dialect Cluster.

Where spoken: Mainly in Haute-Volta, extending into French Sudan, Ivory Coast, and part of the Gold Coast.

LOBI. Dialect Cluster.

Dialect: LOBI.
Spoken by: *LOBI*, in Haute-Volta, Cercle Gaoua, Ivory Coast, Cercle Bondoukou, and perhaps in the adjacent parts of the Gold Coast.

---

[1] *Haut-Sénégal–Niger*.   [2] Tauxier, *Le Noir de Bondoukou*.

THE GUR LANGUAGES

Number: Haute-Volta 83,328,[1] Ivory Coast and Haute-Volta 211,000.[2]
Parts of the Bible have been translated.

Note: Vocabulary comparison[3] shows that this dialect appears to differ considerably from that spoken by the *LOBER* of the Gold Coast. It is possible that the latter may rather correspond to BIRIFO (see p. 66).

Of the dialects spoken by the following, some are known to be closely related to LOBI, so that they may be considered as dialects of one Cluster; others are perhaps also related.

DYAN (DYANU, DYANE, DIAN), call themselves **dyã**, called **dyãnu, dyãne** by neighbouring tribes; in Cercle Gaoua, subdivision Diébougou, north of the *LOBI*.
Number: 8,380.[2]

ZANGA, in four villages in the west of the NUNUMA area and the extreme north of the DAGARI area. This dialect is only known from numerals[4] but appears to be related to that of the *DYAN*.

MORU (MYORO, NYORU), in Ivory Coast, Cercle Kong.
No linguistic material is available. This dialect has been regarded by Delafosse and Tauxier as a LOBI dialect, but it is asserted by neighbours of the *MORU* that they speak an AKAN dialect (see pp. 79–81).

KOMONO (KUMWENU), on the upper Comoë River south of the *DOGHOSIE*.
Number: 3,060.[2]
No linguistic material is available. It is uncertain whether the *KOMONO* speak a dialect of this Cluster or one akin to SENUFO (see p. 56) or to BAULE (see p. 81).

GAN (GAN-LOBI), call themselves **gã**, also known as *GANE*; in Cercle Gaoua around Lorhosso.
Number: 5,350;[2] with the 'BODORO' 51,000 (Labouret).
According to Labouret the *PADOGHO (BODORO)* (see p. 56) are a section of the *GAN-LOBI* and speak the same dialect.

(Fr.) *GOUIN (MBOUIN)*, call themselves **mbwẽ (mbwɛ̃?)** or **kpẽ**, in Cercle Bobo Dioulasso, subdivision Banfora, and around Léra, near the sources of River Comoë.
Number: 55,127.[2]
Note: See also *MBWIN* under SENUFO, p. 56.

TURUKA (TURKA, Fr. *TOUROUKA)*, call themselves **gbẽ** or **kpẽ**, called *ISIEMA* by the *GOUIN*, also known as (Fr.) *PAIN, KPAIMBA*; in Cercle Bobo Dioulasso, subdivision Banfora.
Number: 25,060.[2]
The *GOUIN* and *TURUKA* speak closely related dialects.[5]

---
[1] *La Haute-Volta*.   [2] France d'outre-mer leaflet.
[3] Labouret, *Les tribus du rameau Lobi*; Rattray, *Tribes of the Ashanti hinterland*.
[4] Tauxier, *Le Noir du Soudan*.
[5] Delafosse, *Langues du Soudan et de la Guinée*; Tauxier, 'Les Gouin et les Tourouka . . .' (*J. Soc. Afric.*, 1933).

DOGHOSIE (Fr. *DORHOSSIE*), call themselves *DOKHOBE* or *DOGHOHE*; north of the *KOMONO* in Cercle Bobo Dioulasso, in two sections, the '*DOGHOSSIE* proper' and the '*DOGHOSSIE FING*' (Black *DOGHOSIE*).
Number: 7,500 (Labouret).
According to Labouret[1] they speak a LOBI dialect, but see also under SENUFO, p. 57.

BOBO. DIALECT CLUSTER.

Spoken by: *BOBO*, call themselves **bwa**.

Where spoken: French Sudan and Haute-Volta, in an area bounded by San in the north, the bend of the Black Volta in the south, Bobo Dioulasso in the south-west. MANDE languages are also spoken in a considerable part of this area.

Number of speakers: Haute-Volta 168,654;[2] French Sudan 120,000.[3]

Very little is known about the dialects spoken by the *BOBO*. The following sections of the tribe perhaps speak dialects of one Cluster:

BOBO FĬ (*BOBO FING, FINNG*) ('Black *BOBO*'), called *BULSE* by the *MOSSI*; in French Sudan, Cercles Koutiala and San; Haute-Volta, Cercles Tougan and Bobo Dioulasso.
According to Prost[4] the speech of the *BOBO FĬ* belongs to the MANDE Larger Unit (see p. 40).

SANKURA, call themselves *ZARA*, east of the *BOBO FĬ*, extending across the Black Volta, north of the *ISALA*, west of the *NUNUMA*.

BOBO GBE ('White *BOBO*') or *TYAN* (*KYAN*), called *TYANSE* by the *MOSSI*; in French Sudan, Cercles San and Bandiagara.

BOBO WULE (*ULE*, Fr. *OULÉ*) ('Red *BOBO*') or *TARA*, called *TARASE* by the *MOSSI*, also known as *PWE*; in Cercles Tougan and San, east of the *BOBO GBE*.
Parts of the New Testament have been mimeographed; the whole New Testament has been translated, but not yet published (1950).

NYENYEGE (Fr. *NIÉNÉGUÉ*), also known as (Fr.) *BOUAMOU* (cp. **bwa**); east of the *BOBO FĬ* and *BOBO WULE* in Cercles Bobo Dioulasso, Ouagadougou, and Gaoua; also, according to Labouret,[1] in Koudougou and Tougan.

DOGON. DIALECT CLUSTER.

According to Delafosse,[5] closely related dialects are spoken by the following:

DOGON (*DOGOM*), call themselves **doġŏ** or **doġom** (Sing. **doġo**), called *KIBISSI* by the *MOSSI*; in French Sudan, Cercles Bandiagara and Hombori; Haute-Volta, Cercle Ouahigouya.

---
[1] *Les tribus du rameau Lobi.*   [2] *La Haute-Volta.*   [3] Leaflet issued by France d'outre-mer.
[4] *La Langue Bisa.*   [5] *Haut-Sénégal–Niger.*

THE GUR LANGUAGES

Number: 148,898[1] (including *TOMBO*).

According to Griaule, several dialects are spoken by the *DOGON*, but these have not been studied.

TOMBO, in Cercle Hombori, also San, Mopti, and Bandiagara. According to both Delafosse and Tauxier,[2] these people call themselves *TOMBO*; Arnaud,[3] however, suggests that this is the BAMBARA name for the inhabitants of Bandiagara plateau and Hombori mountains (i.e. *DOGON*). Labouret includes *TOMBO* in *DOGON*; according to Griaule the *TOMBO* (or *TOMMO*) are *DOGON* living north and north-west of Sanga.

Note: The names *HABE* (**haβe**, Sing. **kado**) or **hombeβe** are applied by the *FULANI* to the *DOGON* (and *TOMBO*), and the name *HABE* has been used, both in the plural and in the singular form (*HABBÉ*, *CADO*), by some French writers; it does not, however, apply to DOGON speakers only, but is used by the *FULANI* to denote people other than *FULANI*, *ARABS*, or *BERBER*, and also occurs in other areas (e.g. French Cameroons and Senegal).

Single Unit: GRUSI

GRUSI. Dialect Cluster.

Note: The name *GRUSI* (*GRUSSI*, *GURUNSI*, *GURUMSI*, Fr. *GOUROUNSI*), is generally applied to all the tribes listed below, and to their dialects; individual names of tribes and dialects are, however, also used by Europeans as well as by the people themselves.

Dialect: KASENA, own name KASENE or KASEM.

Spoken by: *KASENA* (*KASSENA*, *KASSUNA*, *KASINA*, Fr. *KASSÉNA*, *KASSOUNA*), call themselves *KASENA*, *KASUNA*, *KASON* (local variants of the name), called *KASOMSE* by the *MOSSI*, *YULE* or *YULSE* by the *NANKANSE*, *WULISI* by the *TALLENSI*, also known as *GAPERSHI*, 'Kipirsi', *BINYINU* (according to various writers); in Haute-Volta, Cercle Ouagadougou, with main centre Tiébélé; also in the north of the Gold Coast.

Number: Haute-Volta 41,458;[4] Gold Coast 43,930 (1921 Census); 32,868 (1948 Census).

There are three main sections of the tribe:

KASENA BURA (*KASSON BURA*);
KASENA FRA (*KASSON FRA*);
KASENA NAGWA;[5]
those in the Gold Coast are called *AWUNA* or *ACULO* (*ADJOLO*, *KIALO*, *AKIULO*) and call themselves **acülό**.
One Gospel has been translated into 'KASSENA'.

A closely related dialect is spoken by:

NUNUMA, call themselves *NUNUMA*, *NURUMA*, *NUNA*, or *NIBULU*,

---

[1] 1938 figures, from Griaule, *Masques dogons*.   [2] *Le Noir du Yatenga*.
[3] Quoted by Dieterlen, *Les âmes dogons*.
[4] *La Haute-Volta*.   [5] Tauxier, *Le Noir du Soudan*.

called *NUNA* by neighbouring tribes; in Haute-Volta, Cercle Ouagadougou; according to IFAN also in Cercle Tougan (speaking a dialect called LELA).

The *MENKIERA* are said to be a section of the *NUNUMA*.[1]

Number: Haute-Volta 15,038;[2] total 42,500 (Labouret).

LELE, LERE occur as variants of a name of the *KASENA*; according to IFAN, LELA is the name of a dialect of NUNUMA, spoken in Cercle Tougan. With this, cp. the *LELESE* of Tauxier[3] which he also compares with *LILSE* (see *KURUMBA, FULSE*, p. 63).

According to F. J. Nicholas[4] *LYELE* (L'ÉLÉ in his orthography) is the name of the dialect spoken by the *LYELA* (*L'ÉLA*) of Cercle Koudougou in Haute-Volta (60,793 in 1931).

Dialect: TAMPRUSI, own name TAMPOLE or TAMPELE.

Spoken by: *TAMPRUSI*, call themselves *TAMPOLENSE*, also known as *TAMPOLEM, TAMPOLEMA*; in the Gold Coast, in the central part of Mamprussi District, also west of the *DAGOMBA* on the right bank of the White Volta.

The dialect spoken by the *VAGALA* (sometimes erroneously referred to as *GONJA*), a small tribe west of the *DAGOMBA*, appears to be practically identical with TAMPRUSI.

Dialect: KANJAGA, own name **buile** (BULUGU, BULEA).

Spoken by: *KANJAGA (BUILSA)*, call themselves *BUILSA* (Sing. *BULUG* or *BULO*); in the Gold Coast west of the *NANKANSE* and *TALENSI*.

Number: 58,524.[5]

Note: Koelle's GURESHA appears to be this dialect. According to Rattray[6] *KANJAGA* is really a place-name, applied by Europeans to the tribe and its dialect.

Other dialects apparently belonging to this Cluster are spoken by:

DEGHA, call themselves *DEGHA* (**deγa**?), called **buru** by the *MOSSI* and others, **mmofo** by the *BRONG, DYAMU, DYAMURU, DYOMA* by some of the MANDE-speaking peoples; in the Gold Coast, in the bend of the Black Volta north-west of Kintampo, and north-west of Assafumo; also over the border into the Ivory Coast.

Number: about 800 in the Ivory Coast.[7]

SITI, call themselves *KIRA*, called *SITIGO* by the *KULANGO, KONOSARALA* by the *LOBI, PAXALA* by the *DYULA* (but see *KULANGO*, p. 58); on the Gold Coast–Ivory Coast border in two villages on the right bank of the Black Volta south-east of Bouna.

[1] Tauxier, *Le Noir du Soudan*.
[2] *La Haute-Volta*.
[3] *Nouvelles notes sur le Mossi et le Gourounsi*.
[4] 'Les surnoms-devises des L'éla . . .' (*Anthropos*, 1950).
[5] 1948 Census.
[6] *Tribes of the Ashanti hinterland*.
[7] Tauxier, *Nouvelles notes sur le Mossi et le Gourounsi*.

THE GUR LANGUAGES

KURUMBA (Fr. *KOUROUMBA*) or *FULSE*, call themselves *KURUMBA*, *KURUMA* (Sing. *KURUMDO*) and their dialect KURUMFE, called *FULSE* by many of their neighbours, *LILSE, NIMSE, NYONYOSE* by the MOSSI; in Haute-Volta, mainly in Cercle Ouahigouya, north of Yatenga and *MOSSI* country, extending north into *DOGON* territory.

Number: 80,000.

The *DEFORO* between Djibo and Dori among the *MOSSI* appear to be a section of the *KURUMBA* and to speak their dialect.[1]

Number: 6,100.[2]

SISALA (HISSALA, ISSALA, SISAI), call themselves *LA-ISA* or *SISALA* and their dialect **sisale,** called *SISAI, PASALA, DEBE, TAMBOBOBA, GALEBAGLA, BAGBALA, KWAMA* by other tribes; in Cercle Ouagadougou, subdivision Léo, extending into the Gold Coast west of the *NANKANSE* and *KANJAGA*.

Number: Gold Coast 39,539;[3] Haute-Volta 2,957.[2]

Note: Clarke's vocabularies of CAMBA and NIBULU appear to be this dialect (but see NUNUMA, p. 61).

BUGULI (BUGURI, Fr. *POUGOULI)*, in Cercle Gaoua, subdivision Diébougou.

Number: 7,460.[2]

A vocabulary collected by Bertho[4] and headed 'PILA-PILA de Kilir et de Tanéka, dans la région de Djougou'. (Dahomey) is clearly a GRUSI dialect, and largely identical with KANJAGA (but see also *PILAPILA* under *GURMA*, p. 68). This 'Kilir' is the same as 'Kyilinga', a place-name also used to denote a GRUSI dialect spoken in Dahomey (Djougou and Atacora).

Language Group: MOSSI

Consists of:
MOSSI	Dialect Cluster.
DAGOMBA	Dialect Cluster.
NANKANSE	Language?
TALENSI	Language.
WALA	Language?
DAGARI	Dialect Cluster?
BIRIFO	Language?
NAMNAM	Language?

Where spoken: Haute-Volta and the Northern Territories of the Gold Coast, extending into Togoland (British and French).

MOSSI, own name **more, mole.** Dialect Cluster.

Spoken by: *MOSSI*, call themselves **mosi, moisi, moʃi**[5] (Sing. **moya, moaya**), called **mose** by thr *KUSASI*, *GURMAKE* by the *FULANI*, *BEMBA (BEMBRA)* by the *GURMA*.

[1] Urvoy, *Petit atlas ethno-démographique du Soudan entre Sénégal et Tchad*.
[2] *La Haute-Volta*.   [3] 1948 Census.   [4] In a personal communication.
[5] -si, -se (-sa) are Plural Suffixes occurring in many GUR languages.

Where spoken: Haute-Volta: mainly in Cercles Kaya, Ouagadougou, Tenkodogo, and parts of Cercles Tougan, Ouahigouya, Fada N'Gourma; also to the south-west in Cercle Bondoukou.

Number of speakers: about 2 millions.[1]

Dialects: According to Alexandre[2] there are four main dialects:
SAREMDE;
TAOLENDE;
YADRE (YANSI);
and the dialect spoken in Ouagadougou.

According to Bertho[3] two dialects of MOSSI are spoken in French Togoland, in the Lama-Kara area, by:

NAWDAM (Fr. *NAOUDAM, NAOUDEMBA, NAOUDEBA*), called *LOSSO*[4] by the *KABRE* (27,000);

YANGA, south and south-east of Tenkodogo (7,000).

MOSSI is also spoken by the *SILMI-MOSSI* (*SILMISSI, SILMI*), i.e. *FULANI* living among the *MOSSI* who have largely adopted the language (15,000),[5] and by the *YARSE* (over 72,000[6]), *DYULA* colonists in *MOSSI* country (cp. *YADRE, YANSI*?).

Parts of the Bible have been translated, and there is a considerable amount of vernacular literature, mainly religious.

DAGOMBA. DIALECT CLUSTER.

Dialect: DAGOMBA, own name **dagbane**.

Spoken by: *DAGOMBA*, call themselves **dagbamba** (Sing. **dagbambe**), called ŋwana by the *GONJA*; mainly in the Gold Coast, from Lat. 9° N. nearly to Lat. 11° N., between Rivers Oti and White Volta, with main centres Yendi (the capital of the old Dagomba Kingdom), Tamale, and Gambaga; also extending across the River Oti in the south-east.

Number: Gold Coast 172,739.[7]

There are dialectal variations of DAGOMBA in the three main centres.

DAGOMBA is used in elementary education, and has been standardized. The 'Africa' orthography is used. There is a small printing press in Tamale, under the Dagomba Native Authority, for the publication of vernacular literature. Parts of the New Testament have been published.

GBANYANG (GBANIAN, **ŋgbanye**) is the name given by Delafosse[8] as that of a DAGOMBA dialect, spoken in parts of Gonja[9] territory of the Gold Coast among the *GUANG*. (Note, however, that Rattray's 'GBANYA' vocabulary[10] is GUANG; see p. 81).

[1] According to J. F. Hall, Director of Protestant Missions, Ouagadougou.
[2] *Grammaire Mossi*.   [3] In a personal communication.
[4] Fröhlich, 'Notes sur les Naoudeba du Nord-Togo' (*Bull. IFAN*, 1950). (See also p. 69.)
[5] *La Haute-Volta*.   [6] Tauxier, *Le Noir du Soudan*.   [7] 1948 Census.   [8] *Carte ethnographique*....
[9] Gbanyang, Gbanya, Gonja are all forms of the same name.   [10] Rattray, op. cit.

THE GUR LANGUAGES

Dialect: KUSASI, own name **kusale, kusas piat** (speech of the *KUSASI*).

Spoken by: *KUSASI* (*KUSSASSI, KUSSASSE*), call themselves **kusasi** (Sing. **kusage**), called *FRA, FRAFRA* (their usual greeting) by neighbouring tribes (cp. also *KASENA FRA*, p. 61); in the north-eastern part of the Northern Territories of the Gold Coast, north-east of Gambaga, extending into French Togoland.

Number: Gold Coast 93,064;[1] 7,916 in Haute-Volta.[2]

Dialect: MAMPRUSI, own name **mampulugu, mamprule**.

Spoken by: *MAMPRUSI* (*MAMPRUSSI*), call themselves **mampulusi** (Sing. **mampuluga**), **mampuliga, mampele**, called *DAGBAMBA* by the *KUSASI*; south and south-west of the *KUSASI* in the Gold Coast and British Togoland.

Number: 85,000 (Labouret); Gold Coast 49,998.[1]

Parts of the Bible have been translated.

Dialect: NANUMBA, own name **nanune**.

Spoken by: *NANUMBA*, in the Gold Coast and Togoland, between Rivers Oti and Daka (Kulukpene), south of Yendi, with main centre Bimbila.

Note: It is not certain whether KUSASI, MAMPRUSI, and NANUMBA are to be considered as dialects of DAGOMBA or as separate languages.

NANKANSE, own name **naŋkane** (or **gureŋe**[3]). LANGUAGE?

Spoken by: *NANKANSE* (*NANKANA*), call themselves **naŋkanse**; according to Rattray they call themselves **gurense** (Sing. **gureŋa** or **guriŋa**) and are called **naŋkanse** by the *KASENA*; also known as *FRAFRA* (see also *KUSASI*).

Where spoken: In the Gold Coast north-west of the *MAMPRUSI*, and in the adjacent part of Haute-Volta.

Number of speakers: 105,000 (Labouret).[4]

TALENSI, own name **talene**. LANGUAGE.

Spoken by: *TALENSI* (*TALLENSI, TALLENSE, TALANSI, TALENSE*), call themselves **talis, talensi** (Sing. **taleŋa, taleŋga**).

Where spoken: Gold Coast, Zuarungu District, in most of the southern part of the District, mainly in the Tong Hills.

Number of speakers: 35,000.[5]

WALA. LANGUAGE?

Spoken by: *WALA*, call themselves *ALA* (Sing. *WALO*) or **wale**.

Where spoken: Gold Coast, Wa District, south of the *DAGARI*.

Number of speakers: 17,538 (1921 Census), 25,923.[4]

Note: According to Rattray[6] the name *WALA* is derived from the town Wa, and denotes not one tribe, but a heterogeneous people living in the Wa area.

---

[1] 1948 Census. [2] *La Haute-Volta*. [3] Rattray, op. cit.
[4] Note that the 1948 Census gives the following figures: *NANKANNI* 59,748; *FRAFRA* 174,954.
[5] Fortes, *Dynamics of clanship among the Tallensi*. [6] Op. cit.

DAGARI (DAGATI), own name **dagare**. DIALECT CLUSTER?

Spoken by: *DAGARI* (*DAGATI, DAGATSI, DAGARTI*), call themselves daġaaba (Sing. daġaao).

Where spoken: Gold Coast, in the north-western part of the Northern Territories; Haute-Volta, Cercle Gaoua, subdivision Diébougou.

Number of speakers: Gold Coast 36,500 (1921 Census); 119,216;[1] Labouret's total figure 75,000 probably refers to Haute-Volta only.

There appear to be several sections of the *DAGARI*, possibly speaking different dialects:

BIRIFO (but see below);
DAGARI;
LOBI–DAGARI;
SOGHOLE or *DAGARI-FĬ* ('Black *DAGARI*');
DAWARI (a dialectal form of the name *DAGARI*).

Delafosse[2] further distinguishes a dialect spoken by the *DAGARI WULE* or *WULEWULE* ('Red *DAGARI*') on the right bank of the Black Volta.

BIRIFO. LANGUAGE?

Spoken by: *BIRIFO* (*BIRIFOR*).

Where spoken: Haute-Volta, Cercle Gaoua, subdivision Kampti, extending into the Gold Coast.

Number of speakers: 90,000 (Labouret); Haute-Volta 48,696;[3] Gold Coast (LOBI (BIRIFOR)) 40,520.

Note: *BIRIFO* is also given as the name of a section of the *DAGARI* (see above); comparison of vocabularies shows that this language appears closely to resemble the speech of the *LOBER* in the Gold Coast,[4] which, however, differs from that of the *LOBI* (see p. 59). The location of *BIRIFO* and *LOBER* also seems to correspond.

NAMNAM (NABDAM), own name **nabt**, also known as NABDE, NABTE, NABDUG, NABRUG. LANGUAGE?

Spoken by: *NAMNAM* (*NABDAM*), call themselves *NABDAM* or *NAMNAM* (Sing. *NABT*).

Where spoken: Gold Coast, west of the Red Volta, north of the *TALENSI*, east of the *NANKANSE*.

Number of speakers: 8,063 (1921 Census).

SINGLE UNIT: GURMA[5]

GURMA. DIALECT CLUSTER.

Dialect: GURMA.

[1] 1948 Census. [2] *Vocabulaires comparatifs* ... (see Bibliography). [3] *La Haute-Volta*.
[4] Labouret, *Les tribus du rameau Lobi*; Rattray, *Tribes of the Ashanti hinterland*.
[5] Much of the information on the GURMA dialects was supplied by Père J. Bertho; see also his 'Langues voltaïques du Togo-nord et du Dahomey-nord' (*Notes afr.*, 1949).

Spoken by: *GURMA* (Fr. *GOURMA*), call themselves **binumba** (Sing. **bimba**), called *GURMA*, **gurmancɛ** (*GURMANTCHE*, Fr. *GOURMANTCHE*, &c.), by neighbouring tribes; between *MOSSI* country and the Niger, in Haute-Volta, Cercles Ouagadougou, Kaya, Dori, Fada N'Gourma, and Saẏ (mainly in Fada N'Gourma); also in French Togoland, Cercle Mango, and Dahomey, Cercles Atacora and Djougou.
Number: 127,000 (Labouret).

Dialect: KASELE, own name **cɛ** ('language').
Spoken by: *KASELE* (*KASSELE*), call themselves **akasele**, called **camba, cansi,** by neighbouring tribes (see also *TOBOTE* below); in French Togoland, Cercle Sokode, east of Sokode in Camba, Alibi, and Kusuntu.
Number: 20,000.

Dialect(s) spoken by: *TOBOTE*, call themselves **tobɔte** or **tebɔte** (Sing. **kobɔke**), also known as *CEMBA* (*CHAMBA, TSCHAMBA, TSCHAMINA, BITSHAMBA*) and as 'Bassari'; in Cercles Sokode, Bassari, and neighbourhood, and in the Gold Coast, between the *TEM* and *DAGOMBA*.
Number: 28,000; Gold Coast Census 1948: 12,489.

Dialect: KONKOMBA (KOKOMBA), own name **dikpaŋkpamdi.**
Spoken by: *KONKOMBA* (*KOKOMBA*), call themselves **kpuŋkpamba** or **kpakpamba,** called **kɔkwamba, kɔŋkomba** by neighbouring tribes, also known as **copowá** (the name of part of their country); in British Togoland north of Bassari, south of the *CAKOSI* and *MOBA*. According to Akenhead[1] the *KOMBA* are a separate tribe, related to the *KONKOMBA*, and are in the Gold Coast, Eastern Dagomba Division, north-east of Gushiago, and in Chereponi Subdivision north-east of Yendi.
Number: 16,000 (Labouret); Gold Coast Census 1948: 59,640.

Dialect: **moa.**
Spoken by: *MOBA* (*B'MOBA, BIMOBA*), call themselves **mɔba** or **mɔwa** (other versions of the name being **mɔaba, mɔab, mɔban, mɔwan**), called **bemá** by the *KUSASI* (the *MOBA PUŊPARIENE* of Groh[2]); in British Togoland, on the Gambaga Plateau. According to Akenhead[1] they are also in the Gold Coast, in Mamprussi Division and Chereponi Subdivision of Eastern Dagomba.
Number: 90,000;[3] 72,000 (Labouret).
Parts of the Bible have been translated.

Dialects apparently belonging to this Cluster are spoken by:

SOMBA (*SOMA, SOME*), call themselves **bɛtammaribɛ** (**bɛtãmmadibɛ** according to Mercier[4]) or **tamaba** and their dialect **ditamaba** (Bertho) or **tamari** (Hall), and known as *TAMBERMA*[5] in Togoland; in Dahomey, Cercles Atacora and Takamba, and in the adjoining part of French Togoland.
Number: Dahomey: 45,000 (Bertho); 72,000.[6]

[1] Department of Agriculture report (unpublished).
[2] 'Sprachproben aus zwölf Sprachen des Togohinterlandes' (*M.S.O.S.*, 1911).
[3] According to J. F. Hall, Director of Protestant Missions, Ouagadougou.
[4] 'Le consentement au mariage et son évolution chez les Betammadibe' (*Africa*, 1950).
[5] **bɛ-tammari-bɛ** and **tamber-ma** are variants of the same name, **bɛ-, -bɛ** and **-ma** being Class Affixes.   [6] *Le Dahomey* (France d'outre-mer publication, 1948).

According to Mercier[1] this is rather a separate language than a dialect, and has itself dialectal variants, including NIENDE.

Note: According to Desanti[2] *SOMBA* is a collective name used by Europeans to denote various people between the Togo border and Atacora mountains, including the *YOABU* (see below). J. F. Hall gives the figure 100,000 for *SOMBA* and '*YOUWABOU*' together.

YOABU (Fr. *YOABOU*), on the Togo–Dahomey border (Natitingou area).
Number: 8,000 (Bertho); see also under *SOMBA*.

The *YOABU* do not appear to be a separate tribe, but a caste of blacksmiths; it is not certain whether they speak a separate dialect, but the vocabulary of Mercier[1] entitled WOABA of Natitingou certainly differs from the other dialects dealt with in his article.

NATEMBA (*NATIMBA*), west of the *YOABU*.
Number: 17,000 (Bertho).

TAKEMBA (*TANKAMBA*), north of Natitingou.

(Fr.) *TAYAKOU*, north of Natitingou.

BERBA, in the region of Tanguiéta.
Number: 44,000 (Bertho).

Note: Both Bertho and Mercier[1] distinguish between the dialect spoken by the *BERBA* of Tanguiéta and BARIBA (see p. 70).

SORUBA–KUYOBE (Fr. *SOROUBA*), call themselves *BIYOBE* (*MEYOBE*), called *SOLAMBA* by the *KABRE* (from Sola, the name of the district in which they live); on the Togo–Dahomey border north-west of Djougou.
Number: 5,000 in Dahomey; the majority (number not known) in Togo.

DYE (*NGAMGAM*), in northern Togoland (shown on Mercier's map[1] west of the *NATEMBA*).

PILAPILA (*KPILAKPILA*) or *YOM*, in north-western Dahomey, around Djougou.

Marty[3] distinguishes two tribes or sections: *YOBA*, in the plains of Djougou, and *TEMBA*, in the hills of Tanéka. Apparently, however, they speak the same dialect.

According to Bertho *PILAPILA* is a nickname used by neighbouring tribes and derived from the greeting habitually used by these people.
Number: 28,000;[4] about 40,000 (Bertho).

The dialect of the *PILAPILA* appears to be related to that of the *CAMBA* of Bassari (see *KASELE* and *TOBOTE* above); but see also note on p. 63.

Single Unit? TEM

TEM, own name **tem**. Language, with associated dialects.[5]

[1] 'Vocabulaire de quelques langues du Nord-Dahomey' (*Études dahoméennes*, 1949).
[2] *Du Danhomé au Bénin-Niger*.
[3] *Études sur l'Islam au Dahomey*.   [4] *Le Dahomey* (France d'outre-mer publication 1948).
[5] Information mainly from J. Bertho, and from Fröhlich, 'Généralités sur les Kabrè du Nord-Togo' (*Bull. IFAN*, 1949).

THE GUR LANGUAGES

Spoken by: **TEM** (*TIM, TIMU*), call themselves **temba** or **tembia** (Sing. **temne**), called *KOTOKOLI* by the *HAUSA* and others (this name is frequently used by the French in the form *COTOCOLI*).

Where spoken: Mainly in central and northern French Togoland, in the Sokode, Lama-Kara, Bassari, and Sansane Mango area.

Number of speakers: According to Bertho 244,000, mainly in Lama-Kara subdivision. This figure does not include speakers of TEM dialects (see below).

Dialects: Closely related dialects are spoken by the tribes listed below. According to Bertho these dialects are only to a limited extent inter-intelligible, but a common form based on TEM is understood by all speakers of TEM dialects, as well as by other neighbouring tribes.

Number of speakers: Owing to confusion of nomenclature, it is not always possible to determine to which tribes the figures available refer. Fröhlich gives 209,500 for *LAMA*, which apparently includes *KABRE* and also *SORUBA* (see p. 68); Labouret's figure of 90,000 for *KABRE* seems to include *DOMPAGO*, also *SOMBA* and *PILAPILA* (see pp. 67–68). Other figures are given under the tribal names.

KABRE (*KABURE, KABYE*, Fr. *KABRÈ, CABRÈ, CABRAI*), call themselves *KABIEMA* or *KABREMA* (Sing. *KABIETO*), called *KATIBA, KORETIBA* by the *NAWDEM, KOWREMBA* (according to Fröhlich) by the *LAMBA, NANGBA* by the 'Bassari'; in Cercle Sokode.

LAMBA (*LAMBA ANIMA, NAMBA*), call themselves *LAMA*, called *LUNAMBA* by the *KABRE, NAMBANE* by the *CAKOSI, BULUFAI* by the *YORUBA, MAGBARA* by the *KOTOKOLI* (*TEM*); in the Lama-Kara area, extending into Dahomey. According to Fröhlich, there are three sections of the *LAMBA*, speaking dialects which he designates MANGANEPO or MANGANAPO, MANGANASISE, MANGBARA.

Number: 18,000 (Labouret).

Note: There is some confusion and overlapping of nomenclature: the name *LOSSO* is used by the *KABRE* to denote the *NAWDAM* (see p. 64); it is also, however, used by Europeans for the *LAMBA* (also known as *KABRE LAMBA*). Further confusion is caused by the use of the names *KABRE LOSSO, LOSSO LAM*(*LAMBA*), *LOSSO YAKA* (part of the *KABRE*?).

DOMPAGO, also called *LOGBA*[1] (*LEGBA*); on the Togoland–Dahomey border east of the *KABRE*, west of Djougou, around Tsheti and Dume.

Number: 14,000.[2]

DELO, call themselves **delo, lǝlo**, or **lölo**, called *NTRIBU* or *TRIBU* by neighbouring tribes; east of Kete Krachi in British Togoland.

According to Mischlich[3] a very similar dialect is spoken by the *CALA* (*TSHALA*), in the north-eastern part of Nawuri, who call themselves **cãla**.

---
[1] Not to be confused with the *LOGBA* whose language belongs to the 'Togo Remnant' Group (see p. 96).   [2] *Le Dahomey*.   [3] In an unpublished MS.

'Bago', in French Togoland between Tshaudjo and Kpetsi, with main centres Sara, Afridjo, Kusuntu, and Bago.

ANIMERE, call themselves **anímère**, around Amanta (Pampawie), Kunda in *DELO* country, Kejebi near Dutukpene, east of River Oti.

This dialect is related to TEM, but also shows affinities with the 'Togo Remnant Languages' (see pp. 96 ff.). Unlike TEM and the other GUR Languages it forms Noun Classes almost exclusively by Prefixes.

Bertho mentions a dialect spoken by the '*BODON*' in the Yendi area, as being similar to TEM, but no further information is available.

Single Unit? BARGU

BARGU (BARIBA), own name **bargú**. Language?

Spoken by: *BARGU (BARIBA, BERBA,*[1] *BARBA, BORGAWA, BOGUNG, BORGU*, &c.), call themselves **barba** (Sing. **bargú**).

Where spoken: North-eastern Togoland and northern Dahomey, with main centres Parakou, Nikki, Kandi, Djougou, and Kouandé; extending eastwards into Nigeria (Ilorin Province).

Number of speakers: French Togoland 70,000,[2] Dahomey 151,000,[3] Nigeria 18,542 (1931 Census).

A vocabulary of BATONNUN in the possession of C. K. Meek is clearly BARGU. IFAN mentions a dialect MOKOLLE, spoken in Kandi.

N. W. Thomas[4] includes the speech of the *LARU* (*LARUAWA*) near Bussa town in Nigeria, and the *LOPAWA* (of whom nothing further is known) as belonging to the 'Volta', i.e. GUR languages.

Linguistic notes on the GUR Languages

1. Most of the languages have seven vowel phonemes: **i, e, ɛ, a, o, ɔ, u**; some distinguished between **i** and **ɪ** and between **u** and **ʊ**; e is sometimes centralized (**ə**).

Diphthongs, lengthened vowels, and nasalized vowels are rare.

2. Labio-velar consonants **kp, gb, ŋm, ŋw** are of frequent occurrence in all the GUR languages.

Syllabic nasals occur in Affixes.

3. Tone is important, but not to the same degree as in, for example, the KWA languages. Tonal doublets are rare. Stress is either absent or of little importance, a high-toned syllable being sometimes stressed.

In TOBOTE, which forms Noun Classes by Prefixes and Suffixes, many Nouns

---

[1] Not to be confused with BERBA of Tanguiéta (see p. 68).
[2] Desanti, op. cit.
[3] *Le Dahomey*.
[4] In Meek, *The northern tribes of Nigeria*, vol. ii.

THE GUR LANGUAGES

have a sequence of high-low-high tone, so that the Class Affixes have high tone, while the Noun Root has low tone:

ó-nè-lé, Plur. bé-nè-bé   man   ké-jì-ké, Plur. ń-jì-ŕń   knife

In TEM, change of tone plays a part in the conjugation of the Verb (see § 10).

4. The majority of Roots (Noun and Verb) are monosyllabic and consist of CV; some Roots consist of CVC; disyllabic Roots also exist; e.g.:

DAGOMBA	dì	eat	du	climb	bí-à	child	kab-le	bundle
MOSSI	lì	eat	dʊ	climb	bí-yà	child		
TEM	dì	eat	fa	give	bo	go;	vɔke	bind

5. Noun Formatives take the form of Suffixes, e.g.:

DAGOMBA	zi-le	load	<zi	carry
	zi-zi-ra	carrier		
	bɔ-le-gu	hunting	<bɔ-le	hunt
	di-bu	eating	<di	eat

Compound Nouns are common (Noun+Noun or Noun+Verb), e.g.:
DAGOMBA pɛ-gul-a shepherd<pɛ-yo sheep   gule to watch
MOSSI   ŋwĭ-k-da rope-maker<ŋwĭ-kɛ make rope (ŋwĭ-ri rope)

6. Noun Classes are formed by Affixes (Suffix, Prefix and Suffix, or in some cases Prefix only), e.g.:

DAGOMBA (Suffix)

	bi-a	Plur. bi-he[1]	child
	wube-ga	wub-se[1]	hawk
	wɔbu-go	wɔb-re	elephant
	lay-fʊ	liy-ere	cowry
	wa-ho	yu-re	snake
	kɔb-le	kɔb-a	bone
	nɔ-le	nɔ-ya	mouth
	yu-ni	yu-ma	year
	zizi-ra	zizi-ra-ba	carrier

ko-m   water   so-m   gall   si-m   indigo   sɛ-m   sense

TEM (Suffix)

	lel-u	lèl-á	widow
	ke-le	ke-la	tooth
	ta-ka	ta-se	toad
	na-o	na-ne	child
	we-re	wɛ (we-a)	day
	fèná	fèná-sè	mouth
	be-ne	be-se	year

[1] Note that this Suffix is -he after a vowel, -se after a consonant (see also §§ 7, 9).

THE GUR LANGUAGES

	bo-wu	bo-ni	hole
	fun-ɔ	fun-te	feather
	li-m water	ni-m oil	dɔ-m salt
(Prefix and Suffix)			
	du-vo-re	a-vo-a	pigeon
KASELE (Prefix)			
	o-ta	i-ta	horse
	o-nyi	be-nyi	person
	bu-ci	i-ci	tree
	ki-nyi-mi	i-nyi-m	bird
	ko-koko	te-koko	feather
	n-yɛ	i-yɛ	fruit

In several languages—notably the SENUFO dialects and the LOBI–DOGON Group—the Class system is defective.

7. There is Concord between the Noun and other parts of speech, but the Concord is not developed to the same extent in all languages.

Concord with Adjectives:

KASELE	o-ta o-mama	Plur. i-ta i-mam	red horse
	o-nyi o-mama	be-nyi be-mama-be	red person
	bu-ci bo-mama-bo	i-ci i-mama	red tree
	ki-nyi-mi ke-mama	i-nyi-m i-mama-m	red bird
	ko-koko ko-mama	te-koko te-mama-nte	red feather
TEM	simi-ka kasa-ŋka	simi-si kasa-se	fine bird

In MOSSI and DAGOMBA only a limited number of Class Suffixes are used with Adjectives:

DAGOMBA	wɔɣel-le Plur. wɔɣel-a	tall
	yare-ga yar-se	bad

When a Noun is followed by an Adjective, the Suffix is attached to the Adjective and not to the Noun:

DAGOMBA	ti-a	ti-he[1]	tree
	ti-wɔɣel-le	ti wɔɣel-a	tall tree
	ti-yare-ga	ti yar-se[1]	bad tree
KANJAGA	ti-b	ti-ʃa	tree
	wɔŋ	wɔn-ta	tall
	ti wɔŋ	ti wɔn-ta	tall tree

There is Concord between the Noun and the Pronoun, e.g.:

TOBOTE	o-tam o-mbina	i-tak i-mbina	this horse
	ku-di ku-mbina	a-di ŋɛ-mbina	this house
TEM	du-vo-re cen-de	a-vo-a cen-a	this pigeon

[1] See note to § 6.

8. There is no grammatical gender, except that in some languages a distinction is made between persons and non-persons in the 3rd Person Pronoun, e.g.:

DAGOMBA Sing. **o** (person)   **di** (thing—all Classes)
                Plur. **bɛ**   **di**

In the GURMA dialects, however, the 3rd Person Pronoun is in agreement with the Noun.[1]

9. Verbal Derivatives are formed by means of Suffixes, e.g.:

DAGOMBA **labe** return   **lab-se**[2] cause to return (Causative or Transitive)
                du   climb   **du-he**[2] cause to climb

10. Tenses are formed mainly by Suffixes and Particles, e.g.:

DAGOMBA **di** eat; Present **di-ra**; Perfect **di-ya**;
Progressive with Object **di-re-la**, without Object **di-re-me**
Future   **n ni di**   I shall eat
           n ni di-ra I shall be eating
Habitual **o yaa kyaŋ** he habitually goes

Particles denoting time (Adverbs) can stand between the Subject Pronoun and the Tense Particle, or after the Tense Particle, e.g.:

DAGOMBA **n sa ni di**   I shall eat tomorrow
               n daa ni di I shall eat some day
               n pa ni di   I shall eat some time ahead
               n ni ti di   I shall eat at some indefinite time

In TEM different Tenses are characterized by change of initial consonant and of tone:[3]

Imperfect and Iterative	Imperative	Durative	Aorist and Infinitive	
dárà	tárà	dáré	táré	divide
ģìsì	kísì	ģìsí	kìsí	refuse
vɔ́kè	fɔ́kè	vɔ́ké	fɔ́ké	bind
vá	fá	và	fà	give

11. Negation is expressed in various ways, e.g.:

DAGOMBA **o be nya o**   he did not see him (**be** not to do)
               di ka duu ni it is not in the house (**ka** not to be)
               o ku di   he did not eat
               di di   do not eat (Prohibitive)

---
[1] Bertho, 'Langues voltaïques du Togo-Nord et du Dahomey-Nord' (*Notes afr.*, 1949).
[2] See note to § 6.
[3] Müller, 'Beitrag zur Kenntnis der Tem-Sprache' (*M.S.O.S.*, 1905).

TEM (Negative Particle **da (ta)**. Note vowel assimilation and change of tone).

má dá lá	I did not say	è dà lá	he did not say
mɛ́ dɛ́ dí	I did not eat	ɛ̀ dɛ̀ dí	he did not eat
mó dó dó	I did not sleep	è dò dó	he did not sleep

The Particle denoting prohibition is **ka**. Note also change of initial consonant.

ŋ̀ gà lá	do not say	é kà lá (Plur.)
ŋ̀ gɛ̀ dí	do not eat	é kɛ̀ dí

KANJAGA (Nasal and change of tone)

o jànjá	he came	o n jánjà	he did not come
data á kɔ́yá	the wood is dry	data à ŋ kɔ́yà	the wood is not dry

ka ŋ kyaŋ	do not go (Prohibitive)
ka n yi yilɛ	do not sing a song

12. Word order in the simple sentence is usually Subject–Verb–Object, e.g.:

DAGOMBA   doo ma bɔhe paya ma   the man asked the woman

In some languages, including all the SENUFO dialects, the order is Subject–Object–Verb, e.g.:

FORO (SENUFO)	m ma simu syo	I have oil brought
BARGU	o nyim no	he the water drank

13. In the Genitive construction the *nomen rectum* precedes the *nomen regens*, with or without a Linking Particle, e.g.:

MOSSI	ti biga	tree's child (fruit)
KASELE	onyi kudi	man's house
BARGU	sunu dondu	elephant's tooth
TEM	ŋgo bu	mother's child

The Possessive Pronoun precedes the Noun, e.g.:

DAGOMBA	m ba	my father
	bɛ naa	their chief
TEM	ma gale	my reading (**kale** to read)
	ma gbao	my buffalo (**kpao** buffalo)
	ma jokoto	my trousers (**cokoto** trousers)
	ma vɛde	my hoe (**fɛde** hoe)
	ma do	my bee (**to** bee)

14. The Adjective (including Numeral) follows the Noun, e.g.:

KASELE   o-ta o-mama   red horse (see § 7)

Adjectival ideas are, however, often expressed by Verbs, e.g.:

KASELE   **bɔ**   be black   **jo**   be good   **pe**   be white

THE GUR LANGUAGES

15. The Demonstrative Pronoun follows the Noun, e.g.:

TOBOTE **o-tam o-mbina** this horse (see § 7).

16. Postpositions are used to indicate place. They mostly consist in Nouns in the Genitive construction, e.g.:

DAGOMBA ni   inside   **du ni**   in the house
         zuyo   head   **adaka zuyo**   on the box
SISALA   ŋ harɛ behind me (my back)

Dative relationship is often expressed by the Verb 'to give'.

17. The GUR languages have a considerable common vocabulary.

Section VI
THE KWA LANGUAGES (LARGER UNIT)

THE KWA languages are spoken in the eastern part of the Ivory Coast, the southern part of the Gold Coast, Togoland, and Dahomey, and the south-western part of Nigeria.

The term KWA languages was first used by G. A. Krause in 1885, and propagated by Christaller.[1] It is derived from the word for 'people' in many of these languages, which contains the root **kwa**.

LANGUAGE GROUP ? 'LAGOON'

Consists of: ALADIAN   Language?
            AVIKAM   Language?
            GWA   Language?
            KYAMA   Language?
            METYIBO   Language?
            ABURE   Language?
            AKYE   Language or Dialect Cluster.
            ARI   Language?
            ABE   Language?
            AHIZI   Language?

Most of these languages are known from vocabularies only; it is thus not possible to make any definitive classification of them. It appears, however, that they are sufficiently closely interrelated to be provisionally grouped together.

Where spoken: In the lagoon area of the Ivory Coast, between Grand Bassam and Grand Lahou.

(Fr.) ALADIAN, own name **aladyã**. LANGUAGE?

Spoken by: (Fr.) *ALADIAN (ALADYAN, ALAGIAN, ALLADYAN)*.

Where spoken: In Cercle Abijan, on the narrow strip of land between the sea and Ebrié lagoon, from Petit Bassam to Krafi (Kraffy).

Number of speakers: 7,000 (Labouret); 8,000.[2]

One Gospel has been translated.

AVIKAM. LANGUAGE?

Spoken by: *AVIKAM*, called *BRINYA* (Fr. *BRIGNAN*) by the *ANYI* and others; also known as *GBANDA, KWAKWA, LAHU* (Lahou, place-name).

---
[1] 'Sprachproben aus dem Sudan' (*Z.A.S.*, 1889–90).
[2] Bertho, 'La place du dialecte adiukru . . .' (*Bull. IFAN*, 1950).

THE KWA LANGUAGES

Where spoken: West of the *ALADIAN* as far as Dibou, with main centre Grand Lahou. On the banks of River Bandama they are mixed with *ANYI*, *ADYUKRU*, and *ARI*.

Number of speakers: 7,000 (Labouret); 9,000.[1]

ALADIAN and AVIKAM show vocabulary relationship, but not very close. Many of the *AVIKAM* also speak ANYI.

GWA, own name **ŋgoya** or **ŋgoga**. LANGUAGE?

Spoken by: *GWA*, called *MBATO* (*MGBATO*) by the *ANYI* and others; also known as 'Potu' ('Potou').

Where spoken: East of the *ALADIAN*, on Potou Lagoon in the neighbourhood of Bingerville.

Number of speakers: 4,000 (Labouret); 6,000.[1]

KYAMA. LANGUAGE?

Spoken by: *KYAMA* (*KIAMA*), call themselves **kyama**, called 'Ebrie' by the *ABURE* and *NZIMA*.

Where spoken: North of Ebrié Lagoon between Rivers Comoë and Agnéby; also in a few places on the coast east of Petit Bassam.

Number of speakers: 11,500.[2]

KYAMA and GWA appear to be very closely related.

One Gospel has been translated into 'Ebrie'.

METYIBO. LANGUAGE?

Spoken by: *METYIBO* (*MEKIBO*), called *VETERE*, *VETRE*, *EWUTRE*, *EWUTURE*, *BYETRI*, *PAPAIRE* by neighbouring tribes; those at Sanwi are called *AGUA* by the *ANYI*.

Where spoken: On the lagoons of Assinie and Grand Bassam.

Number of speakers: 4,000 (Labouret); 3,000.[3]

ABURE, own name **abure**. LANGUAGE?

Spoken by: *ABURE* (Fr. *ABOURÉ*), call themselves **abure**, called *AKAPLESS* by Europeans (a corruption of '(Chief) Aka's place'); also known as 'Abonwa'.

Where spoken: West of Abi Lagoon, as far as Grand Bassam.

Number of speakers: 7,000 (Labouret); 8,200.[3]

---

[1] Bertho, loc. cit.
[2] B. Bouscayrol, 'Notes sur le peuple Ebrié' (*Bull. IFAN*, 1949).
[3] Bertho, loc. cit.

The *AGWA* (Fr. *AGOUA*) in the same area speak a dialect which appears to be connected with both ABURE and the ANYI dialects, the ABURE element being perhaps predominant.

AKYE, own name **atyɛ**. LANGUAGE or DIALECT CLUSTER.

Spoken by: *AKYE* (Fr. *ATTIÉ, ATCHI, ATSHE*), call themselves **atyɛ**, called *KUROBU* by the *BAULE* (IFAN mentions a tribe *KROBOU, KOBOU*).

Where spoken: In the hinterland of the lower Comoë river, north of the *KYAMA* and *GWA*.

Number of speakers: 52,500 (Labouret); 60,000.[1]

There are several sections of the tribe, with dialectal variations: *BODE* (*AKYE-KOTOKO*), *NEDI* (*MEMMI*, **ɛtɛpɛ**), *ATOBU, NGADYE, KETE*.

One Gospel has been translated.

ARI, own name **ari**. LANGUAGE?

Spoken by: *ARI*, call themselves **ari**, called *ABIJI* by the *ANYI* and *ADYUKRU* (*IFAN* mentions both *ABIDJI* and *ABIGI*; cp. place-name Abijan).

Where spoken: Between River Bandama and the *AKYE*, north of the *ADYUKRU* west of the *KYAMA*.

Number of speakers: 6,000; 11,000.[2]

ARI contains many loan-words from both ADYUKRU and ANYI. Most of the *ARI* understand *ANYI*.

ABE. LANGUAGE?

Spoken by: *ABE* (*ABBEY*), call themselves **abɛ**.

Where spoken: Between River Bandama and the *AKYE*, north of the *ARI* (according to IFAN, with main centre Agboville).

Number of speakers: 20,000 (Labouret); 25,000.[2]

According to IFAN, ABE is also spoken by the *BAULE* in that area; many of the *ABE* understand ANYI.

AHIZI. LANGUAGE?

The speech of the *AHIZI* (*AIZI*, *AÏZI*) on Ebrié Lagoon between Dabou and Krafi may belong to this Group, or may be a KRU dialect (see p. 49).

LANGUAGE GROUP: AKAN

Consists of: TWI-FANTE   Dialect Cluster.
           ANYI-BAULE   Dialect Cluster.
           GUANG   Dialect Cluster.

---

[1] Bertho, loc. cit. He distinguishes between the ATTIE and the KROBU (1,300) in two villages west of Agboville. [2] Bertho, loc. cit.

Where spoken: In the southern part of the Gold Coast, in Central Togoland, and in the Ivory Coast north of the Lagoon Group, as far west as River Bandama.

Note: The name *AKAN* was originally a collective name used to cover the inhabitants of Akwapem, Akem, Asante (Ashanti), Akwamu, and some other territories, but is now used by Europeans to denote the whole group of people speaking languages of this Group (also known as 'the AKAN-speaking peoples').

TWI, own name **twi kasa** (the TWI language). DIALECT CLUSTER. Called **simú, simúsɛ** by the *AVATIME*, **sɛkɔ́pɔ** by the *SANTROKOFI*, **sɛkɔ́bɔ́** by the *LIKPE*, **sidabé** by the *AKPAFU*.

Spoken by: TWI (*TSHI, OTWI, OTSHI*), call themselves **twi, atwi**[1] (the name **twifo**, Sing. **otwini**, denotes members of the TWI-speaking peoples). The following names are used for the *TWI*, but sometimes also for all AKAN-speakers, by other tribes: **tõ, ton** by MANDE-speakers, **tonawa** by the *HAUSA*, **blu** by the *EWE*, **bemúma** by the *AVATIME*, **bakɔ́pó** by the *SANTROKOFI*, **madabé** by the *AKPAFU*, **bakɔ́bɔnyà** by the *LIKPE*, **KAMBOSI** by the *DAGOMBA*, *KAMBON* by the *GRUSI*.

Where spoken: In the Gold Coast between Rivers Tano (Tanno) and Volta; one tribe (*AKWAMU*) on both banks of the lower Volta. The *TWI* are bounded on the west by the *ANYI* and *BAULE*, on the north by the *GUANG* and *BRONG*, on the east by *EWE* and speakers of the 'Togo Remnant Languages', on the south-east by the *GÃ*.

Number of speakers: over 1,000,000.

Dialects: There are four main dialects:[2]

AKWAPEM (AKUAPEM, AKWAPIM), spoken in the south-east of the TWI area.

AKEM (AKYEM), spoken west and north-west of AKWAPEM.

ASANTE (ASHANTI), spoken north-west of AKEM.

FANTE (FANTI), spoken on the coast between the *ADANGME* and *AHANTA*. Speakers of FANTE are not generally included in the *TWI*, but are referred to as *FANTE*.

Although linguistically FANTE may be considered as a TWI dialect, it has attained the status of a literary language. There is a considerable amount of vernacular literature, both in FANTE and in the other dialects, including the whole Bible in TWI (ASANTE) and FANTE; a weekly paper is published in FANTE.

ANYI-BAULE. DIALECT CLUSTER.

Spoken by: (1) *ANYI* (Fr. *AGNI*), a collective name for several tribes, mainly in the eastern part of the language area; (2) *BAULE* (Fr. *BAOULÉ*) a collective name for several tribes, mainly in the western part of the language area (*BAULE* is also the name of one particular tribe).

[1] With palatalized **w**.
[2] Christaller gives a number of other names of dialects, most of which, however, represent local variants of the four main dialects.

THE KWA LANGUAGES

Where spoken: In the Ivory Coast, north of the Lagoon languages, east of River Bandama, and in the adjoining part of the Gold Coast.

Number of speakers: ANYI 79,000, BAULE 373,000 (Labouret).[1]

ANYI dialects are spoken by the following:

NZIMA (NZEMA), called *AMANYA, AMANAHEA, AMRAHIA, AMREHIA* by the *FANTE* and others, *ASOKO* by the *BAULE* and by other *ANYI*-speakers, *ZIMBA* by MANDE-speakers, *AWA* by the *ASSINIE*, *GURA* by the *FANTE, APLONI, APLONIYO* by the *NEYO* (this is the origin of the name *APOLLONIA* (Fr. *APPOLONIEN*) used by Europeans); in the Gold Coast and Ivory Coast between Ankobra and Assinie, with a few small colonies along the coast west of Assinie.

AHANTA (ANTA); east of the *NZIMA*, mainly between Rivers Ankobra and Pra.
This dialect closely resembles that of the *NZIMA*.

AFEMA, also known as *SAMWI, SĀWI*; in the lagoon area of the Ivory Coast. This dialect is almost identical with that of the *NZIMA*.
The following are said to be the names of other closely related dialects: PEPISA, AOWIN (own name **aŋwoŋwĭ**), JOMORO (AJOMORA), VALWA (EVALWE).

ANUFO, call themselves **anufɔ**; north of the *NZIMA* on Tanno river and lagoon, their dialect is also known as BRUSA (BRUSSA, BRISSA, BURESSYA). See also ANUFO, below.

BETYE, on the right bank of River Comoë, and in a few villages on the left bank.

NDENYE, between River Comoë and the Gold Coast border.

SAFWI (**sɛxwi**), also called *ASSAYE*; on the Gold Coast–Ivory Coast border east of the *NDENYE*.

DYABE, at Assikasso.

The dialect ANUFO (**anufɔ**) or **tsekɔhale**, spoken by the *CAKOSI (CHOKOSI, TSCHOKOSSI, TIOKOSSI)*, in northern Togoland (British and French) and the Gold Coast, closely resembles the ANYI dialects. According to Bertho[2] it is 'presque un simple patois' of the ANYI dialect spoken in Abengourou. It is spoken in the Sansane Mangu area; also, according to IFAN, in Dahomey, around Natitingou; also in the Gold Coast, in Dagomba District among the *KONKOMBA*.

Number: Togoland 16,000 (Labouret); Gold Coast 10,753.[3]

One Gospel has been translated into ANYI.

BAULE dialects are spoken by the following:

MORONU; in the Ivory Coast, between Rivers Nzi and Comoë.

---
[1] Labouret gives the general heading *BAULE*, with subdivisions *AGNI, BAULE*, and *ABRON* (see *BRONG*, p. 82). [2] MS. vocabulary. [3] 1948 Census.

THE KWA LANGUAGES

WURE (WORYE); north of the *MORONU*.

BAULE (BOWLI, Fr. *BAOULÉ)*; between Rivers Nzi and Bandama.
One Gospel has been published; the New Testament is in preparation (1950).

NGANU (NGANO), also called *GARA, ANNO*; in Cercle Baoulé, around M'Bahiakro.

NDAME, north-west of the *BONNA* between River Comoë and the Gold Coast border.

BONNA (BONDA, BONNALI, MONNAI, BWANDA); between Assikasso and the *BRONG*, on the Gold Coast border.

'Dadyessu', in the Gold Coast, Aouwin District.

SIKASSO-NYARENE, east of Assikasso.

BINYE (BINIK); east of River Comoë, south of the *BRONG*, north of the *AFEMA*.

The dialect of the *KOMONO (KUMENU, KUMWENU)* is said to belong to this Cluster (but see under SENUFO, p. 56 and LOBI, p. 59).

Delafosse also includes under the heading *BAULE*: *NGE*; *ABE* of Mango; *BOMO*; *AGBENGAU (AGBENYAO)*; *GYASSALE (TYASALE)*.

GUANG. DIALECT CLUSTER.

The name GUANG is used by Europeans and others to cover all the dialects of this Cluster, and the tribes speaking them, and is recognized by most of them as well as their own tribal names. The present Gonja District of the Gold Coast takes its name from the old Gonja Kingdom, GONJA and GUANG being variants of the same name (other variants are gwanja, gbanya, gbanyaŋ, ŋgbanje, gbanje, &c.).

Dialect: GUANG (GONJA), own name àgbànyìtò or ŋbanyato.

Spoken by: *GUANG (GONJA)*, call themselves ŋgbànyà (Sing. kàgbànà), called gonjawa by the *HAUSA*, ntafo by the *TWI* (from nta, the TWI name for *GUANG* country, hence also used for other people in the same area), also called gwaŋ by the *TWI* and *EWE*; between the White Volta and Daka rivers, mainly in Gonja District, Gold Coast.

Note: Rattray's vocabulary entitled GBANYA[1] is GUANG (see p. 64).

Other dialects are spoken by:

NAWURI (NAWURU), between the lower Oti and Daka rivers. *Number*: 1,936.[2]

ATYOTI, call themselves àtyòtí; north of the *ADELE*, east of River Oti.

ANYANGA, call themselves ànyàŋá; between the Togo mountains and River Mono, in the Blita–Agbandi–Dofoli area.
This dialect has been influenced by both EWE and TEM.

---

[1] *Tribes of the Ashanti hinterland.*   [2] 1948 Census.

NCUMURU, own name of dialect **ncumuru** or **caŋborəŋ**; north of Krachi, on the lower Oti and Daka rivers.

Number: 6,711.[1]

'Krachi', call themselves **ka-cé sensá**; between Salaga and Buëm.

NKUNYA, on the left bank of the Volta between Buëm and *EWE* country.

A dialect known as NKAMI, **ŋkɛmi** or GABI, spoken on the right bank of the Volta, is very closely related to that of the *NKUNYA*.

'Anum' and 'Boso', north of Akwamu.

'Late' (**lɛtɛ**), called **datɛ** by the TWI; in Akwapem; the same dialect is spoken by the **kyerɛpɔŋ** (own name of dialect **ɔkere mmiri**).

'Afutu' (**òfútú, àbútú, àwútú, fétú**); on the coast, in Afutu, Sanya, Bereku, Simpa (Winnebah) and Apa.

GOMOA, on the coast, in *FANTE* country.

Dialect: BRONG.

Spoken by: BRONG (*ABRONG, ABRON*) (**broŋ, abroŋ, bono, ɛbono, burum, burom** are various versions of the name); west of the Volta, mainly south of River Pru (Pra) around Atebubu; also farther west in the Nkoranza–Kintampo–Techiman area (but TWI is widely spoken and gaining ground in this area).

Number: 21,500 (Labouret; included under BAULE, see p. 80).

The dialect spoken by the *BERI* in the Ivory Coast, in Taghadi village between Bonna and Bondoukou, belongs to the GUANG Cluster.

Single Unit: GÃ-ADANGME

GÃ-ADANGME. Dialect Cluster.

Where spoken: In the south-eastern part of the Gold Coast, from the mouth of the Volta to beyond Accra, south of the *TWI*.

Speakers of these dialects are collectively called **gɛ̃, gɛdyi** by the *EWE*, **ŋkranfó** (Sing. **okranni**, from **ŋkraŋ** = Accra) by the *TWI*.

Dialect: GÃ.

Spoken by GÃ, in Accra and neighbourhood; colonies of GÃ-speaking people live in Togoland (mainly in the Anecho area) and along the coast of Dahomey (where they are called *GẼ* (Fr. *GAIN*) or *AMINA*); some of them have, however, lost their own language in favour of EWE, and others are doing so.

Dialect: ADANGME.

Spoken by: *ADANGME* (*ADANGBE*), call themselves **daŋmeli**; in the town of Ada and the immediate hinterland of the *GÃ*.

Dialect: KROBO (or a dialectal variant of ADANGME).

Spoken by: *KROBO*, call themselves **kloli**; north of the *GÃ* and *ADANGME*.

[1] 1948 Census.

There is considerable vernacular literature in GÃ, including the whole Bible (in 'Accra').

Single Unit: EWE

EWE, own name **evegbe**, called **si-nyigbe-sɛ** by the *AVATIME*, **siyikpe** by the *SANTROKOFI*, **sinyigbe** by the *LIKPE*. Dialect Cluster.

Spoken by: *EWE* (*EVE, EHWE*, &c.). The name *EWE* is applied to all speakers of these dialects; they are called **bubutubí** by the *AWUNA*, **benigbe** by the *AVATIME*, **bayikpé** by the *SANTROKOFI*, **manyigbe** by the *AKPAFU, BOWLI* or *AYIGBE* by the *GÃ* and *ADANGME*. In the west they are called *HŬA* by the *TWI*. The central and eastern *EWE*, especially those near the coast, are called *POPO* by the *YORUBA* (this name is officially recognized in southern Nigeria), **ima** by the *KPOSO*. Other names found in older literature are *EIBE, KREPI, KREPE*.

Where spoken: Southern British and French Togoland and Dahomey and the south-eastern corner of the Gold Coast, mainly between the lower Volta and the Dahomey–Nigeria border. On the north-west the *EWE* area extends as far as about Lat. 7 (farther east, as far as Lat. 8). North of Atakpame (Togo) EWE is spoken in several towns, particularly in the region of Kpesi (Kpetsi, Pessi).

Number of speakers: over 1,000,000.

Dialect: AWUNA, own name **aŋlɔ**.
Spoken by: *AWUNA*, call themselves **aŋlɔ**, called **aŋwona** by the *TWI, AHOULAN* or *ANLO* by the French; on the coast between the Volta and Lome.
Number: about 5,000 in the coastal villages.

Other EWE dialects are spoken between the *AWUNA* and the northern limits of the EWE-speaking area, west of the Lome–Atakpame railway. These western dialects are more closely related to each other than to the rest of the Cluster.

Dialect: GẼ (Fr. GUINGBE, GAINGBE, MINA), own name **gẽ**, also known as 'Anecho'.
Spoken by: *GẼ* (Fr. *GUIN, GAIN, MINA*), call themselves **gẽ**; in French Togoland, Cercle Anecho, between Lome and Ouidah (Whydah, Peda).
Number: 62,000.[1]

The dialect known as WATYI (Fr. OUATCHI) is substantially the same as **aŋlɔ**. It is spoken in Cercle Anecho, also in Atakpame, and in Dahomey in the Athiémé-Grand Popo region.
Number: 124,000.

The dialect spoken by the *AJA* (*ADYA, ADJA*) in the Tokpli area on the left bank of River Mono in French Togoland, and across the border into Dahomey, is also closely related.
Number: Togo 3,000.[1]

---

[1] Information supplied by the Commissaire de la Republique au Togo, in reply to a questionnaire.

Dialect: GŨ ('Alada'), own name **gũgbe**.
Spoken by: GŨ (Fr. *GOUN, EGUN*), call themselves **gũ**; in the south-eastern corner of Dahomey, with main centre Porto Novo.

Dialect: Fɔ̃ (FON), own name **fɔ̃gbe**, often called 'Dahoméen' by the French.
Spoken by: Fɔ̃, call themselves **fɔ̃**; also known as (Fr.) *DJEDJI*; in the southern part of Dahomey, Cercles Savalou, Abomey, Porto Novo, Cotonou, Ouidah.
Number: 375,899 together with the *AJA*;[1] 836,000 with the AJA.[2]

IFAN also mentions a people called *KOTAFON* (**kotafɔ̃**) in Athiémé (Dahomey), who speak a dialect which differs slightly from Fɔ̃.

Dialect: MAHI.
Spoken by: MAHI (**maxé**), north of the *Fɔ̃*, with main centre Savalou.
Number: 12,066.[1]

GŨ, Fɔ̃, and MAHI are more closely related to each other than to the rest of the Cluster.

The dialect spoken by the *EWE* section of the population of Atakpame town and neighbourhood is known as HUDU. A similar dialect is spoken in Kpesi, north of Atakpame.

Three dialects of EWE—AWUNA (AƉLƆ), GẼ, and GŨ—are used for literary purposes. There is a considerable amount of vernacular literature, religious and educational, in AƉLƆ, including the whole Bible; some religious and school books have been published in GẼ; there is a Bible in GŨ, as well as some readers; one Gospel has been published in 'POPO'.

SINGLE UNIT: YORUBA

YORUBA. DIALECT CLUSTER.

Spoken by: *YORUBA*, call themselves **yorùbǎ** or **yoòbǎ** (but also use their tribal names—see below). The *YORUBA* in Dahomey are known as *NAGO (ANAGO*, Fr. *NAGOT*), originally a name given to them by the *Fɔ̃*; in Atakpame they are called *ANA*; *YORUBA* emigrants in Sierra Leone are known as *AKU*.

Where spoken: South-western Nigeria, west of the Niger Delta, and extending inland for about 200 miles to the middle Niger; also in Dahomey and French Togoland (Atakpame).

Number of speakers: Nigeria 3,116,164; Dahomey, estimated at 100,000.[3]

Dialects: Dialectal divisions correspond approximately to tribal; all the dialects are closely interrelated. The *YORUBA* tribes are:[4]

OYO ('*YORUBA* proper'), call themselves **ɔyɔ̃**; mainly in Oyo Province.

IFE, call themselves **ifɛ**; in Ife-Ilesha Division of Oyo Province.

[1] Le Gouvernement Général de l'Afrique Occidentale Française (Paris, 1931).
[2] *Le Dahomey*.   [3] Parrinder, 'Yoruba-speaking peoples in Dahomey' (*Africa*, 1947).
[4] Most of the names of *YORUBA* tribes are also those of localities and often of administrative areas (Division or District).

THE KWA LANGUAGES

IJESHA, call themselves ìjɛ̀ʃà (Ilesha (**ilɛ̀ʃà**) being a place-name); in Ife-Ilesha Division.

ILA, call themselves **ìlă**; in Ife-Ilesha Division.

IJEBU, call themselves **ìjèbŭ**; mainly in Ijebu Province and Colony.

EKITI, call themselves **èkìtì**; in Ondo Province, extending into Ilorin and Benin Provinces.

ONDO, call themselves **òndŏ**; south of the *EKITI* in Ondo Province.

EGBA, call themselves **ɛ̀gbá**; in Abeokuta Province, Egba and Ilaro Divisions, and in Dahomey and French Togoland.

OWO, call themselves **ɔ̀wɔ̀**; in Ondo Province.

Other *YORUBA* tribes in Ilorin, Benin, and Kabba Provinces (of whose dialects less is known) include: *AWORO (AKANDA)*;[1] *BUNU (EKI)*; *OWE*; *JUMU*; *IWORO*; *IGBONA*; *AKOKO* (**àkókó**); *YAGBA* (**yàgbà**); *GBEDDE*.

A YORUBA dialect, less closely related to the other members of the Cluster, is spoken by: *JEKRI (ITSEKIRI, ISHEKIRI, SHEKIRI, JEKIRI)*, called **ʃɛ̀kírì** by the *YORUBA*, *IWERRI* by the *BINI* and others; in the Niger Delta, mainly in Warri Province, but also in Benin, Colony, Calabar, Ondo, and Owerri.
Number: 9,128.

A dialect of YORUBA is also spoken by the *IGALA (IGARA)* of Igala Division, Kabba Province, and Idoma Division, Benue Province.[2]

Note: *OKPOTO* is the name of a section of the *IGALA*—but see *KWOTTO* under *IGBIRA*, p. 87; see also *IDOMA*, p. 140.

YORUBA is used as a medium of education (primary), and taught as a subject in higher standards. There is a considerable vernacular literature, mainly religious and educational, and including the whole Bible. Several vernacular periodicals are published. The literary language is mainly based on the OYO dialect, but forms from other dialects are included.

Language Group: NUPE

Consists of: NUPE Dialect Cluster.
GBARI Dialect Cluster.
IGBIRA Dialect Cluster.

Where spoken: Nigeria, north of the *YORUBA*, *BINI*, and *IGBO*.

NUPE, own name **ezi nupe**. Dialect Cluster.

Spoken by: *NUPE*, call themselves **nupeciʒi, nupenciʒi** (Sing. **nupeci, nupenci**), called **nufawa** by the *HAUSA*, **abawa** by the *GBARI* of Kuta, **ampeyi** or **nife** by the *GBARI* of Paiko and Birnin Gwari, **anupecwayi** by the *KAKANDA*, **anupe** by the *JUMU* and *IGBIRA*, **anuperi** by the *EBE*, **takpa (tapa)** by the *KAMBARI*, *YORUBA*, and *EWE*.

[1] Not to be confused with *KAKANDA* (see p. 86).
[2] According to R. G. Armstrong (personal communication), IGALA should be regarded as a separate language.

Where spoken: Ilorin and Niger Provinces, north of the *YORUBA* on both banks of the Niger from Bussa rapids to the Niger–Benue confluence, with main centre Bida.

Number of speakers: 326,017 (it is not clear, however, which speakers of NUPE dialects are included in this figure).

Dialects:[1] Dialects of this Cluster are spoken by the following:

NUPE ('*NUPE* proper'), i.e. all *NUPE* tribes except those listed below. This dialect is understood by all speakers of other NUPE dialects.

EBE (*ABEWA*), called *AGALATI* by the *KAMBARI*, *ANUPE* by the *BARGU*; in Kontagora Division, Niger Province.

DIBO or ʒitako, called *GANAGANA* by the *HAUSA*; in the south-eastern part of Niger Province.

BASSA-NGE (*IBARA*);[2] in Bassange District, Igala Division.

KUPA (*KUPANCHI*, erroneously known as *GUPA*); on the south bank of the Niger near the *KAKANDA*.

Dialect (or closely related language?) spoken by:

KAKANDA (sometimes erroneously called *AKANDA*),[3] called *SHABE* by the *IGARA*, *EHABE* by the *IGBIRA*, also known as *HYABE* and *ADYAKA-TYE*; in Kabba Province, on the south bank of the Niger.

There is some vernacular literature in NUPE, including the New Testament and parts of the Old; also one Gospel in 'BASSA'.

GBARI. DIALECT CLUSTER.

Spoken by: *GBARI* (*GWARI*, *GWALI*, *GOALI*), call themselves **g̣bari**.

Where spoken: Zaria, Benue, and Niger Provinces, north of the Niger–Benue confluence.

Number of speakers: 154,910.

Dialects: There appear to be several dialects, including the following:
GBARI GYENGUEN (MATAI, GANGAN);
GBARI YAMMA of Paiko;
GBARI YAMMA GAYEGI;
GBARI KANGYE (KWANGE).

The GBARI dialects are closely related to NUPE; according to Temple[4] they differ considerably from each other.

There is some vernacular literature in all four dialects, including several books of the New Testament in GBARI MATAI, and one each in GBARI of Paiko and GAYEGI.

---

[1] Nadel, *A Black Byzantium*.
[2] Temple, *Notes on the Tribes, Provinces, Emirates and States of the Northern Provinces of Nigeria*. For other *BASSA* see p. 103.
[3] See *AKANDA* under *AWORO* (*YORUBA*), p. 85.   [4] Op. cit.

THE KWA LANGUAGES

IGBIRA. DIALECT CLUSTER.

Spoken by: *IGBIRA* (*IGBIRRA*), called *EGBURA* by the *IGALA*, *KOTO-KORI* by the *YORUBA*, *KATAWA* by the *HAUSA*, and officially known as *KWOTTO*, a name derived from *KWOTTO-GARA* (*OKPOTO-GARA, OKPOTO-IGALA*), the *HAUSA* name for the *IGBIRA-PANDA* (on confusion of nomenclature see *IDOMA*, p. 140).

Where spoken: Mainly in Kabba Province, around the Niger–Benue confluence.

Number of speakers: 147,325.

Dialects of this Cluster are spoken by:

IGBIRA-PANDA, also known as *IGBIRA-LELE, KWOTTO*, and 'Umaisha *IGBIRA*'; on the Benue–Kabba Province border.

IGBIRA-HIMA (*IHIMA*), also known as 'Okene *IGBIRA*'; in Aworo Division, Kabba Province.

IGBIRA-IGU (*EGU, IKA*), also known as *BIRA, BIRI*, and called *IGBIRA-REHE* by the *IGBIRA-PANDA*; in the southern part of Niger Province.

'Igara', in Igara village,[1] in *KUKURUKU* country near the *SEMOLIKA*.

There is some vernacular literature in IGBIRA, including one Gospel.

LANGUAGE GROUP: BINI (EDO)

Consists of: BINI   Language.
               ISHAN   Dialect Cluster?
               KUKURUKU Dialect Cluster.
               SOBO   Dialect Cluster.

Where spoken: Nigeria, mainly in Benin, Warri, and Ondo Provinces.

BINI (EDO). LANGUAGE.

Spoken by: *BINI*, also called *EDO* (**èdó**). The name EDO (the old name of Benin) is used by some writers (e.g. Thomas)[2] to cover all the languages of this Group.

Where spoken: Benin, Warri, and Ondo Provinces, extending into Owerri and Colony.

Number of speakers: estimated by Melzian[3] at 90,000–100,000; the 1931 Census figure of 508,351 (Northern and Southern Provinces) probably includes all speakers of the BINI Language Group. According to Melzian the language is on the whole homogeneous although there are some minor local differences.

The whole New Testament and parts of the Old have been translated.

---

[1] Not to be confused with *IGALA* (see p. 85).
[2] In Meek, *The northern tribes of Nigeria*.
[3] *A concise dictionary of the Bini language*.

ISHAN. DIALECT CLUSTER?

Spoken by: ISHAN (*ESA, ISA*), call themselves ésá.

Where spoken: North of the *BINI*, in Ishan Division, Benin Province.

Number of speakers: 92,754.[1]

According to Talbot the *ISHAN* are a part of the *BINI*. There are said to be several dialects, but their names and distribution are not known. ISHAN is closely related to BINI.

KUKURUKU. DIALECT CLUSTER.

Spoken by: *KUKURUKU*.

Where spoken: Benin Province, Kukuruku, and part of Ishan Divisions; also in Igbira Division, Kabba Province.

Number of speakers: Northern Provinces 32,000 (1916);[2] Southern Provinces 93,000 (1921).[1]

Dialects: Information about the dialects and their distribution is scanty and confusing; according to Melzian the dialects include the following (some at least of the names given are those of localities):

'Auchi' (**auci**), in and around the town of Auchi;
FUGA, between Auchi and the *WANO*;
WANO, in the west of the *KUKURUKU* area on the Niger;
IBILO, in the north-west;
SEMOLIKA, in the north-west;
IBIE–OKPEPE, in the north (Thomas)[3] gives the names *IBIE* (tribe), Opepe (town);
OTWA, in the west.

Another dialect is known as ORA, spoken south and south-west of the main *KUKURUKU* area, north of the *ISHAN*. Parts of the New Testament have been translated into this dialect.

SOBO. DIALECT CLUSTER.

Spoken by: *SOBO*, a general name used by Europeans to denote all the tribes listed below.

Where spoken: Warri Province, mainly in Urhobo Division; also in Jekri-Sobo Division.

Number of speakers: estimated at about 108,000.[4]

The *SOBO* consist of two main sections, speaking different dialects:

URHOBO, in the west of Urhobo Division.
There are several local variants in the dialect of the *URHOBO*, of which

---

[1] Talbot, *The peoples of Southern Nigeria*.   [2] Temple, op. cit.
[3] In Meek, *The northern tribes of Nigeria*.
[4] Rev. J. W. Hubbard, *The Sobo of the Niger Delta*.

that spoken by the *AGBADO* 'clan' is understood by all *URHOBO* and is recognized by Europeans as being the predominant dialect. Melzian gives OKPARA-AGBADO as the name of a SOBO dialect.

ISOKO (IGABO), in the eastern part of Urhobo Division.

Note: The name *SOBO* is an anglicized form of *URHOBO*; the names *URHOBO* and *ISOKO* are, however, now gaining ground among Europeans. The *SOBO* are called *BIOTU* (a nickname) by the *IJƆ*; the *ISOKO* are (or were) called *IGABO* (a term of contempt) by the *KWALE IGBO*, and this name has in the past been used by Europeans.

SOBO dialects are also spoken by neighbouring *ABO-IGBO* and *IJƆ*, and by other inhabitants of Jekri-Sobo Division.

Parts of the Bible have been translated into URHOBO and ISOKO; the New Testament in SOBO is in the press (1950).

Other people included in the general name SOBO, who speak either SOBO dialects or separate, but related, languages, are:

EROHWA (εrohwa), east of the *SOBO*.

EVHRO, in the west, and in Jekri-Sobo Division.

OKPE, in two areas, west and east of the main *SOBO* area.

According to Hubbard[1] URHOBO, ISOKO, EROHWA, EVHRO, and OKPE are all separate languages, EROHWA and EVHRO having a slight resemblance to URHOBO and ISOKO and to each other, while OKPE is less like the rest and more like BINI.

SINGLE UNIT: IGBO

IGBO (IBO), own name iɓo. DIALECT CLUSTER.

Spoken by: *IGBO* (*IBO*, iɓo). This is a general name used by Europeans to denote people speaking dialects of one Cluster. It is now also used by the *IGBO* themselves, to denote (1) their language; (2) IGBO-speaking groups other than one's own; (3) one's own group, when speaking to Europeans.

Where spoken: Southern Nigeria: Onitsha, Owerri, Rivers (east), Ogoja (west), Benin (south-east), and Warri (north-east).

Number of speakers: 3,184,585.

Dialects: Dialectal differences correspond roughly to regional. The *IGBO* consist of a number of territorial units or local communities, which may be grouped as follows:

'Northern' or 'Onitsha', in Onitsha Province, and the northern part of Okikwi Division of Owerri Province. There are several dialects, of which those of Nri-Awka (with variant in Onitsha town) and Enugu have been distinguished; some dialects spoken in the north of this area are said to show affinity with 'Owerri IGBO'.

[1] Rev. J. W. Hubbard, *The Sobo of the Niger Delta*.

'Southern' or 'Owerri', in Owerri Province, subdivided into *ISU-AMA, ORATTA-IKWERRI, OHUHU-NGWA, ISU-ITEM*.

'Western', subdivided into Northern *IKA*, Southern *IKA* (*KWALE*) and 'Riverain'. There are several dialects, some of which show affinity with 'Onitsha IGBO'.

'Eastern' or 'Cross River', subdivided into *ADA* (*EDDA*), *ABAM-OHAFFIA, ARO*; in parts of Owerri, Ogoja, and Calabar Provinces.

'North-eastern' or *OGU UKU*.

The main recognized dialects are those of Owerri and Onitsha.

There is considerable vernacular literature in IGBO (various dialects). An attempt has been made to promote the use of 'Union IGBO', a synthesis of the dialects spoken in Bonny, Owerri, Arochuku, Ngwana, and Onitsha, and this has been used by Protestant Missions, but has not had much success, owing to its artificiality.

The whole Bible has been translated into 'Onitsha' IGBO, parts of the New Testament into 'Isuama' and 'Delta' or 'Lower' IGBO, and the whole Bible into 'Union' IGBO.

Linguistic notes on the KWA Languages

1. In most of the languages there appear to be seven vowel phonemes. TWI and FANTE have nine vowels,[1] IGBO eight.

Vowel length is of secondary importance.

Nasalized vowels are very common in several languages.

In some languages, e.g. TWI, FANTE, EWE, YORUBA, and IGBO, vowel assimilation is so regular that one can speak of a tendency to vowel harmony.

Diphthongs are frequent, triphthongs also occur.

2. The labio-velars **kp** and **gb** are common.[2] In IGBO **kp** is implosive; **gb** in YORUBA is often implosive. **kp** and **gb** are absent in TWI and FANTE, but found in western AKAN dialects. In NZIMA **kp** and **gb** occur only before back vowels, while before front vowels they are replaced by **tp** and **db**.

In EWE there are two d-sounds, one alveolar (**d**) and one post-alveolar, retroflex (ɖ), e.g.:

        dà   snake   ɖà   hair

In some languages a distinction is made between labio-dental and bilabial sounds, e.g. in EWE between **f**, **v** and **ƒ**, **ʋ**, in BINI between **v** and **ʋ**.

In TWI the sounds **tw, dw, hw, w** are palatalized before front vowels. Palatalized **ky** (dial. **ty**), **gy** (dial. **dy**), **hy** (German '*ich*-sound') and **ny** occur as well as **k, g, h, n**.

Note initial consonant combinations in EWE, in which **l** or **r** form the second part, e.g.:

        blá   to tie   trì   to be thick

---

[1] In the general spelling only seven vowels are distinguished.

[2] *gb* in IGBO is not a voiced labio-velar sound, but a conventional spelling for implosive ɓ.

3. Tone is of outstanding importance in all these languages.

EWE is the classical—and rare—example of a language in which tone is almost exclusively lexical.

In YORUBA the lexical tone is sometimes altered through elision or assimilation.

In TWI tone is grammatical as well as lexical.

In IGBO grammatical tone is present to a marked extent; lexical tone is present as well.

In YORUBA there are three tone levels (high, mid, low), with resulting combined tones (falling, rising, &c.), e.g.:

   bá meet ba hide bà perch

The existence of an independent mid-tone (mid-tone toneme) is an important characteristic of this language.

In EWE the role of the mid-tone is more restricted; it occurs in Verbal Roots.

In TWI and GÃ there are only two basic tones, but in ADADME there are three as in YORUBA.

In IGBO there are two main tone levels.

Stress is of little importance in most, if not all, languages.

4. Most Roots (Verb or Noun) are monosyllabic, consisting in CV.

In EWE a Stem consisting of more than one syllable is either a compound or a loan-word.

Reduplication as a semantic and grammatical element is common, e.g. for the formation of Adjectives from Verbs.

5. Compound Nouns are very frequent and so are compound Verbs.

6. There are no true Noun Classes. Rudimentary Noun Classes are, however, to be seen in many languages, e.g. TWI;

   ǹ-sú water ò-sú rain à-sú collection of water

There is no Concord with other parts of speech.

In the northern dialects of GUANG (e.g. GONJA) there are Noun Classes formed by Prefixes; in the southern dialects, however, there is no system of Noun Classes; Nouns have vocalic or nasal Prefixes as, e.g., in TWI (see below, § 7).

7. Nouns often have a vowel or nasal Prefix. This Prefix is used to form Nouns from Verbs, e.g.:

TWI	a-dɔw	hoeing	<dɔw	hoe
	n-na	sleeping	<da	sleep
EWE	o-gblo	breadth	<gblo	be broad
YORUBA	ɛ-da	creature	<da	create
NUPE	i-bi	wickedness	<bi	be bad

In EWE and YORUBA these Prefixes do not change, but in other languages they may change according to number (see § 8).

In TWI Nouns may be formed by Suffixes, or by Suffixes and Prefixes, e.g.:

hoa-e	whiteness<hoa		be white
tu-i	a brush	<tu	to brush
ɔ-pra-e	broom	<pra	sweep
ŋ-kasa-e	talking	<kasa	talk

8. The formation of the Plural is not uniform. In some languages the Plural may be formed by change of Prefix, e.g.:

TWI	ɔ-hene	Plur. a-hene	chief
	o-nipa	n-nipa	man
BINI	o-xwae	i-xwae	basket

In other languages the Plural is formed by addition of a Suffix, e.g.:

NUPE	(-ʒi)	doko	doko-ʒi	horse
GÃ	(-i)	gbɛ	gbɛ-i	way

The western AKAN languages also use Suffixes and Prefixes, e.g.:

NZIMA   ɔ-sɔfu   a-sɔfu-ma   priest

In EWE the 3rd Person Plural Pronoun is suffixed, e.g.:

ame   ame-wo   man

while in YORUBA it is prefixed, e.g.:

igi   awɔ̃-igi   tree

9. There is no grammatical gender.

Note, however, the distinction between persons and things in the 3rd Person Pronoun Singular, e.g. in TWI and the southern GUANG dialects:

	Persons	Things
Sing.	o	ɛ (GUANG e)
Plur.	wɔ	ɛ (GUANG e)

10. Case is expressed by position in the sentence. Genitive tone is found in IGBO and BINI. The dative is often expressed by the Verb to give.

11. Personal Pronouns. Examples of the Subject Pronoun:

		TWI	EWE	YORUBA	IGBO
Sing.	1.	me	me	mo, ni, ŋ	mu, m
	2.	wo	e, ne, wo	o	gi, ge, i, e
	3.	ɔ, ɛ	e, wo	o	o, ɔ, ya
Plur.	1.	yɛ	mie, mi, yewo	a	ahyi
	2.	mo	mie, mi	ɛ	unu
	3.	wɔ, ɛ	wo	nwɔ	ha

THE KWA LANGUAGES 93

12. There are no morphological Verb Classes. Tonal Classes arise in so far as the Verbal Roots have different tones.

13. There are no Verbal Derivatives.
There is no Passive Voice. An impersonal form of the Verb in IGBO is expressed by omission of the Subject.

14. The Verb Root is invariable. Tense is mostly expressed by particles or by reduplication, Person and Number by the Subject Pronoun. Examples from TWI and EWE.

Note that in TWI Negation is expressed by a low-tone homorganic nasal Prefix.

TWI	ɔ́kɔ́	he goes	Neg. ɔ̀ŋkɔ́
	ɔ̀kɔ́	he is gone	
	ɔ̀kɔ́è	he went	ɔ̀ŋkɔ́è
	wákɔ̀	he has gone	wàŋkɔ́
	ɔ̀rékɔ̀	he is going	ɔ̀rèŋkɔ́
	ɔ̀bɛkɔ́	he will go	ɔ̀ǹŋkɔ́
	ɔ̀rèbèkɔ́	he is going to go	
	nà wàkɔ́	he may go	nà wàŋkɔ́
	kɔ́!	go!	ŋ̀kɔ́!
	ɔ́ŋkɔ́	let him go	ɔ̀ŋŋkɔ́
	mã̀ ɔ̀ŋkɔ́	let him go	mmã̀ ɔ̀ŋŋkɔ́
ASANTE	ɔ́kɔ́	he goes	ɔ̀ŋkɔ́
EWE	mèyì	I went, I go	
	màyì	I shall go	
	máyì	I will go	
	mèlè yìyìm̀	I am (was) going	
	mènɔ̀ yìyìm̀	I was continually going	
	mánɔ̀ yìyìm̀	I shall be continually going	
	mènɔ̀à yìyìm̀	I am in the habit of continually going	
	mèlè yìyì ɡé	I am going to go, intend to go	
	mèyìnà	I am (was) in the habit of going	
	yìyì	going	

Note vowel assimilation in the Habitual Tense of the Verb in GUANG, which is formed by means of the Verb **ta** to stay, to be in a place:

n ta tsa	I am in the habit of dancing
n tɔ yɔ	going
n to tsu	taking
n te dzi	eating

15. For Negation in TWI see § 14.
In EWE Negation is expressed by **mé-** and **ò**, e.g.:

àmèà yì   the man went   àmèà méyì ò   the man did not go

In YORUBA Negation is expressed by the Particle **ko** or a variant of it.

In IGBO a Negative Suffix is added to the Root of the Verb or to other Tense-denoting elements.

16. Word order in the simple sentence is Subject–Verb–Object, e.g.:

    TWI   ɔ́ bɔ́ɔ́ àhìná   he broke a pot.

The EWE construction:

    élè àtí tsòḿ   he is tree cutting

is not an exception, as **àtí** stands in genitival relationship (he is in tree's cutting).

17. Word order in the Genitive construction is twofold. In the west (including EWE) the *nomen rectum* precedes, in the eastern languages (including YORUBA) it follows the *nomen regens*, e.g.:

    EWE   fìà xɔ̀ or fìà ʄé xɔ̀   the chief's house
    YORUBA   èdè yorùbá   the language of the Yoruba

In NUPE as a rule the *nomen regens* precedes, e.g.:

    rakũ nya lati   camel of the bush (giraffe)

But in many compound Nouns the *nomen rectum* precedes, e.g.:

    eya zũma   boat's bottom
    eyi kpaca   cornstalk

18. Adjectives (including Numerals) follow the Noun.

Section VII[1]

ISOLATED LANGUAGE GROUPS OR UNITS (CLASS LANGUAGES)

The grouping of these languages together is linguistic only in so far as languages which form Noun Classes (by Prefix or Suffix or both), and which do not belong to any of the Larger Units, are treated in one section of the Handbook for purposes of convenience.

They are dealt with on a roughly geographical basis (west to east):

(a) Togoland (British and French);
(b) Nigeria (mainly Northern Provinces, but including some languages spoken in the Southern Provinces);
(c) British and French Cameroons.

Linguistic material on the majority of these languages consists of vocabularies only, with sometimes a few sentences (as in the vocabularies of Meek), and occasional Gospel translations. Any attempt at classification into Groups (except in a few cases) would thus be premature, and the lesser-known languages are therefore provisionally regarded as Isolated Units. This does not, of course, exclude the possibility of interrelationship between any of these Units, which only further research could bring to light.

In area (c) the linguistic situation is particularly involved, largely owing to the extreme fragmentation and intermingling of the tribes, tribal sections, 'clans', and village groups. In some parts of the area every village has its own language or dialect, often incomprehensible even in neighbouring villages. The situation is further complicated by the use, among Europeans and others, of several collective names (e.g. *WIDEKUM, TIKAR, TIGONG*), each of which covers a number of small groups of people whose languages or dialects may or may not be interrelated (see also Section VIII, Non-Class Languages).

Some previous attempts at classification of languages in this area have been made.[2] The danger of classification on an insufficient basis can be seen in the intricate tables of interrelationship drawn up by Talbot, according to which it would be possible not only to link up, however tenuously, the Class languages of Southern Nigeria (the 'Semi-Bantu' languages) among themselves, but also to show their affinities with non-Class languages ('Sudanic') on the one hand, and with Bantu languages on the other. While such affinities may in fact exist, it is impossible to establish any valid conclusions on the basis of available information.

[1] In Sections VII and VIII the following sources are quoted without further footnote reference: Meek, *Tribal Studies in Northern Nigeria*; Talbot, *Southern Nigeria*; Tessmann, 'Die Völker und Sprachen Kameruns' (*Petermanns Geogr. Mitt.*, 1932).

[2] Talbot and Tessmann; see also Greenberg, 'Studies in African linguistic classification' (*Southwestern J. Anthrop.*, 1949).

ISOLATED LANGUAGE GROUPS OR UNITS
(a) CLASS LANGUAGES OF TOGOLAND

ISOLATED LANGUAGE GROUP: 'TOGO REMNANT LANGUAGES'[1]

Consists of: AVATIME   Language.
NYANGBO   Language?
TAFI   Language?
LOGBA   Language.
LIKPE   Language.
AHLƆ̃   Language.
LEFANA   Language.
BOWILI   Language.
AKPAFU   Language.
SANTROKOFI   Language.
LOLOBI   Language?
ADELE   Language.

These languages are spoken in central British and French Togoland, mainly in the district known as Buëm. They appear, from available linguistic material, to constitute a Language Group. There is some vocabulary resemblance to the KWA languages, but the Class system is reminiscent of BANTU. They are therefore provisionally regarded as an Isolated Language Group.

AVATIME, own name **siyasɛ**.[2] LANGUAGE.

Spoken by: *AVATIME*, call themselves **kedemɔnye** or **kanɛma** (Sing. **kedeanɛ**).

Where spoken: In seven villages in the central Togo hills.

NYANGBO. LANGUAGE?

Spoken by: *NYANGBO*, call themselves **batruɡbu** (Sing. **atruɡbu**), called **ba-traɡbɔ** by the *AVATIME*.

Where spoken: In a few localities in the neighbourhood of the *AVATIME*.

Number of speakers: under 2,000.

TAFI. LANGUAGE?

Spoken by: *TAFI*, called **baɡbɔ** by the *AVATIME*.

Where spoken: In four localities near the *AVATIME*.

Number of speakers: under 1,000.

NYANGBO and TAFI are very closely related to AVATIME, and may even be dialects of it.

LOGBA, own name **sɛkpana**, called **sinuɡbe** by the *AVATIME*. LANGUAGE.

Spoken by: *LOGBA*,[3] call themselves **akpana**, called **banuɡba** by the *AVATIME*.

---
[1] This is the name given to the Group by Westermann ('*Togorestsprachen*').
[2] **si-** and **-sɛ** are Class Affixes.
[3] Not to be confused with the *LOGBA* (*DOMPAGO*), see p. 68.

CLASS LANGUAGES

Where spoken: North and north-east of the *AVATIME*.

Number of speakers: under 2,000.

LIKPE, own name sɛkpɛlé or likpɛlɛ, also called MU. LANGUAGE.

Spoken by: *LIKPE*, call themselves bakpɛlé(nya) (Sing. ɔkpɛlɛ(nya)), called *MU* by the *EWE* (a general term also used for other small tribes living north of the *EWE*, the name *LIKPE* being used specifically for this tribe).

Where spoken: In six localities east of Buëm.

Number of speakers: about 3,000.

AHLɔ̃, own name ago. LANGUAGE.

Spoken by: *AHLɔ̃*, call themselves bogo (Sing. ogo or ogoebi).

Where spoken: In the central Togo hills, north-east of the *LIKPE* near the source of River Dayi.

Number of speakers: under 1,000.

LEFANA (LELEMI), own name lɛlɛmi. LANGUAGE.

Spoken by: *LEFANA*, call themselves lɛlɛmi, also known as 'Buëm' and 'Borada'.

Where spoken: In Buëm, where it is the main language of the district; also (with slight dialectal variations) in Borada town.

Number of speakers: under 3,000.

Two religious booklets have been published.

BOWILI, own name siwuri. LANGUAGE.

Spoken by: *BOWILI*, call themselves bawuri(nya) (Sing. uwurinya).

Where spoken: In a few localities in Buëm.

Number of speakers: about 600.

AKPAFU, own name siwu, called sifu by the *LIKPE*. LANGUAGE.

Spoken by: *AKPAFU (APAFU)*, call themselves mawu, ma'u (Sing. owu, o'u), called bafu by the *SANTROKOFI*, befunya by the *LIKPE*, bavũnɛ by the *BOWILI*, apafo by the *AKAN*.

Where spoken: In Buëm, on a ridge between the central Togo and Nkunya hills.

Numbers of speakers: about 1,500.

SANTROKOFI, own name sɛlɛ. LANGUAGE.

Spoken by: *SANTROKOFI*, call themselves balɛ (Sing. ɔlɛ).

Where spoken: In southern Buëm (the name of the tribe is said to be that of their former main centre, a hill in southern Buëm, from which they have moved to their present location in the neighbouring plain).

Number of speakers: under 1,000.

LOLOBI. LANGUAGE?

Spoken by: *LOLOBI*.

Where spoken: In two localities south of the *AKPAFU*, east of the *SANTROKOFI*.

ADELE, own name **sɛderɛ**. LANGUAGE.

Spoken by: *ADELE*, call themselves **bɛderɛ** or **bɛdrɛ** (Sing. **oderɛ**).

Where spoken: North of the *KPOSO*.

Linguistic notes on the Togo Remnant Languages

1. The sound-system of these languages is similar to that of the GUR languages (see p. 70).

Note the correspondence of voiced and voiceless sounds in some languages:

SANTROKOFI	li-fu	AVATIME	li-vu	fear
	kpa		gba	to lead

The voiceless sound is, at least in most cases, the original one.

2. Tone is significant, tonal doublets being somewhat more common than in the GUR languages. Dynamic stress is either absent, or of little significance.

3. Word Roots are monosyllabic and consist for the most part of CV.

4. Apart from the Class Prefixes there are few Noun Formatives, e.g.:

SANTROKOFI	ɔ-kpɛ	work	<kpɛ	do
	ku-kpí	death	<kpí	die
AVATIME	ku-tse	dying	<tse	die
	kù-bábá	coming	<bá	come
	kí-bábà	that which is coming (has come)		
	ɔ̀-bábá	he who is coming (has come)		

Compound Nouns are very common, e.g.:

AHLɔ̃	i-si o-ku	drum beating	<ku i-si	beat drum
	ɔ-fɛ o-fe	farming	<fe ɔfɛ	go to farm
	ɔ-fɛ-fe-ŋoti	farm-going-person (farmer)		

5. Noun Classes are formed mostly by Prefixes, in a few cases by Suffixes, e.g.:

AVATIME	o-ka	Plur.	ba-ka	father
	o-ne		be-ne	mother

li-nyi	e-nyi	name
li-mɛ	a-mɛ	embryo
ki-dɔ	bi-dɔ	thing
ke-dzi	ku-dzi	market
ka-se	ku-se	tail
ku-si	si-si	feather
ku-nɛ water	ku-mu	oil
ku-tse dying	ku-nya	illness

si-ya-sɛ the Avatime language **si-nyigbe-se** the Ewe language.

Note, however, that in many languages there are some Nouns, mostly denoting persons, and sometimes animals, of which the Plural is formed by Suffixes, e.g.:

ADELE nã   Plur. nã-ɛbɛ   mother
nunu   nunu-ɛbɛ   grandmother

6. There is Concord between the Noun and other parts of speech in all languages, e.g.:

Adjective (and Numeral):

ADELE	ɔ-tembi ɔ-ke	one branch
	a-bi a-nyɔ	two seeds
	e-tene ɛ-kpara	good man
	i-daŋ i-bo	high mountains
	m-bia m-pi	small chairs
	di-beŋ de-derɛ	big drum
AVATIME	ɔ-no ɔ-bidi	big man

Demonstrative Pronoun:

AVATIME   o-se ɔ-lɔtsya   this tree

7. There is no grammatical gender.

8. Case is expressed by position in the sentence.

9. Tenses are formed by Particles, e.g.:

AVATIME	màbá	I am coming
	máàbá	I shall come
	màtrábá	I am going to come
	mìzɛ́bá	I used to come
	máàzɛ̀bá	I shall (continually) come
	àtɔ́bà[1]	you shall come (Compulsive)
	àtɔ̀bá	they shall come

10. Negation is expressed by Particles, also by change of Tone.

11. There is no Passive Voice.

[1] Note change of tone.

12. Word order in the sentence is Subject–Verb–Object, e.g.:

ADELE ɛ kpàra de-ǵbara   she sweeps the court

13. In the Genitive construction the *nomen rectum* precedes the *nomen regens*, e.g.:

ADELE ɛ-kɔ ǵe-kpa   cow's hide
bu-tu a-ni   water's inside (in the water)

The Possessive Pronoun precedes the Noun, e.g.:

ADELE me n-te   my father

14. The Adjective (including the Numeral) follows the Noun (see § 6).

15. The Demonstrative Pronoun follows the Noun (see § 6).

Isolated Unit: KPOSO

KPOSO, own name **ikpɔsɔ**. Dialect Cluster.

Spoken by: KPOSO (KPOSSO), call themselves **akpɔsɔ**.

Where spoken: French Togoland, west of Atakpame.

Dialects: there are two dialects, spoken in the north and south of the KPOSO area.

Linguistic notes on KPOSO[1]

1. There are Noun Classes in the Singular, though not in the Plural. Almost all Nouns have a vowel Prefix, e.g.:

a-lúkù	tooth	ɛ-ló	hair
e-ví	breast	i-tukpá	goat
ɔ́-vɛ	sun	o-ɣlo	rat
u-tu	ear		

2. The Plural is formed by suffixing **-wani**. Nouns denoting persons form the Plural by change of Prefix (**ɔ-** or **o-**/**a-**; **u-**/**e-**) as well as suffixing **-wani**.

3. The vowel Prefixes are used as Noun Formatives, e.g.:

a-lá	dance	<lá	dance
ɛ́-lɛ̀	sleep	<lɛ̀	sleep
u-dyɛ	quarrel	<dyɛ	quarrel
i-dɔ	laziness	<dɔ	be lazy
ɔ-dyi	food	<dyi	eat
e-mú	eye	<mu	see

i- is used to form names of languages: **i-kpɔsɔ**.
u- is used to form names of countries: **u-ma** the Ewe country.

The Suffix **-ni** forms Noun Agents: **a-lá lá-ni** dancer (lit. dance-dancer).

[1] Wolf, 'Grammatik der Kposo-Sprache' (*Anthropos*, 1909). (Note that tones are marked on some words.)

CLASS LANGUAGES

4. There is a Definite form of the Noun, made by suffixing -é:

    u-vi-é   the child   **i-tʃu-é**   the tree

5. Word order in the simple sentence is Subject–Verb–Object.

6. In the Genitive construction the *nomen rectum* precedes the *nomen regens*, with Linking Particle ɔ (for persons), **ayi** (for things and inferior persons), e.g.:

    u-lɛ ɔ-na   cow's mother
    u-lɛ ay-uvi   cow's child
    veġele ay-ɔsɛ   horse's tail (or **veġele ɔsɛ**)

The Possessive Pronoun precedes the Noun, e.g.

    an ɛkule   my house (**anu**   my)

7. KPOSO has vocabulary relationship to the Togo Remnant languages. It also has some affinities with YORUBA.

Isolated Unit: KEBU

KEBU, own name **kə-ġbəri-kə**. Language.

Spoken by: *KEBU*, call themselves **e-ġbətɛ-bə** (Sing. **ġbə-tɛ**), called *KEBU* by neighbouring tribes.

Where spoken: North of the *KPOSO* in French Togoland, west of Kpessi (Kpetsi).

Linguistic notes on KEBU

Nouns are divided into four Classes; they have a Suffix, sometimes also a Prefix, in the Singular, Prefix and Suffix in the Plural. Note also change of consonant in many cases, e.g.:

		Plur.	
1.	pi-i	e-bi-bə	child
	tõ-ir	a-dɔm-bə	slave
	kpã-ir	a-ġbam-bə	hunter
	susu-ir	e-zusu-bə	fly
2.	ku-tu-kə	u-tu-ġbə	forehead
	ki-ti-kə	u-ti-ġbə	powder
3.	don-di	e-rõ-ir	tooth
	dree-di	e-tree-ir	neck
	ġɔŋ-gɔn-di	a-kɔŋ-gɔ-ir	shoulder
	vutu-ri	e-futu-ir	stomach
4.	ġbɛ-wo	a-kpɛ-ɛ	throat
	ġo-ri	e-ko-e	charcoal
	tuyo-ri	a-tuyo-e	evening

(b) CLASS LANGUAGES OF NIGERIA[1]

Isolated Unit ? RESHE

RESHE, own name TSURESHE. Language.

Spoken by: *BARESHE*, called *GUNGAWA* by the *HAUSA*.

---

[1] Most of the information on Northern Nigeria is taken from Meek, *Tribal Studies*, supplemented by personal communications from H. D. Gunn and MS. material from the International African Institute's Ethnographic Survey.

Where spoken: On the islands of the middle Niger, in Sokoto Province, Yauri Emirate, and in Agwarra District of Bussa Emirate, Ilorin Province.

The BARESHE are fishermen living on the islands.

Linguistic notes on RESHE[1]

1. Nouns are divided into Classes, formed by Prefixes.

2. There is Concord with Pronouns, Adjectives (which follow the Noun), and Verbs.

3. Nouns are formed from Verbs by means of Prefixes.

ISOLATED LANGUAGE GROUP ? KAMBARI

Consists of: KAMBARI Language?
  DUKA Language?
  and perhaps also
  KAMUKU Dialect Cluster?
  DAKAKARI Language or Dialect Cluster?

Where spoken: Northern Nigeria, mainly in Sokoto and Niger Provinces.

KAMBARI (KAMBERI, KAMBALI, KAMBERCHI), own name EVADI. LANGUAGE?

Spoken by: *KAMBARI* (*KAMBERI*, &c.), called *KAMBERAWA* by the *HAUSA*; also known as 'Yauri'.

Where spoken: Niger Province, Kontagora Emirate, Rejau (Rijau), Kumbashi and Ibelu Districts; Sokoto Province, around the town of Yauri and to the north; also in Ilorin Province, Agwarra District and Kaiama Emirate, and extending into the eastern corner of Dahomey.

Number of speakers: 66,975.[2]

Two Gospels have been translated.

DUKA (DUKANCHI). LANGUAGE?

Spoken by: *DUKA*, call themselves *HUNE*; they also recognize the name *DUKAWA*, by which they are known to the *HAUSA*.

Where spoken: Niger Province, Kontagora Emirate, north of the *KAMBARI*.

Number of speakers: 18,778.[3]

The following may also belong to the same Language Group, or may be Isolated Units:

KAMUKU. DIALECT CLUSTER?

[1] Harris, 'Notes on the Reshe language' (*Afr. Stud.*, 1946).
[2] Figures for Nigeria are taken from the 1931 Census, or from recent Government figures (the latter marked *), unless otherwise stated.
[3] MacBride, 'Notes on the Rijau District' (unpublished MS.).

Spoken by the following closely related tribes or tribal sections:

KAMUKU, called *JINDA* by the *HAUSA*, *MAJINDA* by the *KAMBARI* and *BASSA-KADUNA*, *KENJI* by the *NUPE*; in Niger Province, Kuta Division, Kamuku, Kusheriki, Kwongoma, Tegina and Allawa Districts; Zaria Province, Birnin Gwari District.
Number: 17,386.
There appear to be several dialects, spoken by two main sections of the tribe, in Makangara (the people being known as *ACHIFANCHI KAMUKU*) and Tegina, where, however, HAUSA is superseding the local dialect or dialects.

NGWOI (NKWOI, INGWO, INGWE); Niger Province, Kuta Division, in a few villages in Tegina and Kwongoma Districts.
Number: 829.[1]

URA, in Kuta Division, Kusheriki District.

So called *BAUSHI (BAUCHI, KUSHI)*, scattered in Kuta Division, mainly in Tegina District.
Number: 2,295.

PONGO (PONGU), call themselves *ARRINGEU*; in Kuta Division, mainly in Tegina District (possibly a section of the '*BAUSHI*').
Number: 2,983.

The *BASSA* in Abuja Division of Niger Province, Koton Karifi Division of Kabba Province, and Nassarawa Division of Benue Province, speak a dialect possibly belonging to this Cluster; also the *BASSA-KOMO* of Igala Division, Kabba Province.[2]
One Gospel has been published in BASSA.

DAKAKARI (DAKARCHI), own name **dɛkərici**.[3] LANGUAGE or DIALECT CLUSTER?

Spoken by: *DAKAKARI*, called *DAKARAWA* by the *HAUSA*; also known as *CHILILA*.

Where spoken: Mainly in Kontagora Division, Niger Province.

Number of speakers: 38,914 excluding the *BANGAWA* (Census figures are, however, confused and unreliable).

The main sections of the *DAKAKARI* are:

BANGI (BANGAWA), 6,926, in Donko and the surrounding part of Zuru Native Authority Area and in the southern part of Sokoro Emirate;

KELAWA (KELLINI), also known as *ADOMA*,[4] possibly the same as the HAUSA name *DOMAWA* (the *FAKARA* (people of Fakai), a mixture of *HAUSA* and *DAKAKARI*, are practically indistinguishable from the *KELAWA*);

LILAWA (LILA, LILANA).

It is not known how far these tribal divisions correspond to dialectal.

[1] 1934 Government figures.
[2] The *BASSA-KADUNA* (so-called by Europeans) in Kuta and Kontagora Divisions, now only speak HAUSA, according to MacBride.   [3] Information from I. Richardson.
[4] Not to be confused with *IDOMA* (p. 140). Cp. also *DOMA* under *JABA* (p. 105).

ISOLATED LANGUAGE GROUPS OR UNITS

A Gospel has been translated.

Krause[1] mentions SHINGINI, spoken by the *ASHINGINI* in Kontagora Division, north of the *NUPE*, but no further information is available.

It is not known what language or dialect is spoken by the *ACHIFAWA* (*ACHIPAWA*) among the *DAKAKARI* and *DUKA*. They appear not to be the same as the *ACHIPAWA* or *ACHIFANCHI KAMUKU* (see p. 103).

The vocabulary of GURMANA[2] shows some resemblance to KAMUKU. On the other hand, Kurmin Gurmana is the name of one of the units of the *GWARI* (*GBARI*) Federation, the people being called *GWARI MATAI* (see p. 86).

Isolated Language Group ? KATAB

Consists of: KATAB   Dialect Cluster.
                 JABA   Language?
                 IRIGWE   Language?
                 GANAWURI Language?

Where spoken: Zaria and Plateau Provinces.

KATAB. Dialect Cluster.

Closely related dialects are spoken by the following tribes or tribal sections:

KATAB, call themselves **tyap**,[3] called *ATYAP* by the *KAGORO*; Zaria Province, Zaria Emirate, Katab District.
     Number: 19,852.*

KACHICHERE, call themselves **atıʃɛraak**, called **titʃaat** by the *KATAB*; in Katab District.
     Number: 699.*

MORWA (*MOROA*), call themselves, and are known to their neighbours as, *ASOLIO*, called *AHOLIO* by the *KATAB*, *ASULIO* by the *KAGORO*; on the borders of Zaria and Plateau Provinces, in Moroa Independent District.
     Number: 5,726.*

ATAKA (*ATTAKA*); Moroa Independent District.
     Number: 3,963.*

KAGORO, call themselves **agwɔlɔk**, called *AGWOT* by the *KATAB*, *AGURO* by the *MOROA*; Zaria Province, Zaria Emirate, Kagoro District.
     Number: 9,261.*

The following tribes appear also to speak dialects which are related to the KATAB Cluster, and may form part of it.

---

[1] 'Beiträge zum Märchenschatz der Afrikaner' (*Globus*, **72**).
[2] Johnston, *Bantu and Semi-Bantu languages*.
[3] Note that many of the names given by Meek may be in the singular, those occurring in his vocabularies being in the sentence 'I am a. . . .'

CLASS LANGUAGES

KAJE, call themselves *BAJU*, called *AJIO* by the *KAGORO*; Katab District.
Number: 24,105.*

KAMANTAN, call themselves *ANGAN* (Sing. *ZAMANGAN*); Katab District.
Number: 3,634.*

Note: The *KAMANTAN* are possibly an offshoot of the *KADARA*, who are, however, described by Temple[1] as speaking 'a distinctive language'; Thomas[2] also mentions *KADARA* (*PEDA*).

KAGOMA; Plateau Province, Jemaa Division, adjacent to the *KAJE*.
Number: 6,126.[3]

IKULU (*IKOLU*), call themselves *ANKULU*, (*BA*)*NKULU*;[4] Katab District, west of the *KATAB*, north of the *KAJE*. Possibly the same as the *KADARA*.
Number: 5,961.*

JABA. LANGUAGE?

Spoken by: *JABA*, call themselves *HAM* (hʌm), called *ADA* by the *KATAB*; according to Struck,[5] called *DOMA* by the people of Benue.[6]

Where spoken: Zaria Province, Zaria Emirate, Jaba Independent District.

Number of speakers: 25,396.*

Parts of the New Testament have been translated.

IRIGWE. LANGUAGE?

Spoken by: *IRIGWE* (*IRREGWE*, *AREGWE*), called *IDAFAN* by the *KATAB*.

Where spoken: Plateau Province, mainly in Jos Division, Birom Tribal Area (formerly Kwal District).

Number of speakers: 12,059.[3]

Parts of the Bible have been translated.

This language is tentatively included in the KATAB Group on the strength of Meek's statement that the phonology of JABA and that of 'AREGWE of Bauchi Plateau' are closely related.

The following may also belong to the same Group:

GANAWURI. LANGUAGE?

Spoken by: *GANAWURI* (so-called by the *HAUSA* and others), call themselves *ATEN*,[3] called *ETIEN* by the *KATAB*.

Where spoken: Plateau Province, Jos Division.

---

[1] *Notes on the Tribes, Provinces, Emirates and States of the Northern Provinces of Nigeria.*
[2] In Meek, *Northern Tribes.*   [3] Ames, *Gazetteer of Plateau Province.*
[4] To be distinguished from *BAKULŬ* (*WURKUM*) (see p. 115).
[5] *Linguistic Bibliography of Northern Nigeria.*
[6] The use of the name *DOMA* has led to confusion with the *IDOMA*, whose language is, however, not related, so far as is known (see p. 140).

ISOLATED LANGUAGE GROUPS OR UNITS

Number of speakers: 4,104.[1]

This language is stated by Ames to be inter-intelligible with the neighbouring KATAB dialects.

A Gospel has been translated.

Other Class Languages of Zaria and Plateau Provinces (unclassified)

BIROM. LANGUAGE?

Spoken by: BIROM (BI ROM), call themselves **biroom**,[2] called *SHOSHO* (from the word used by them as a greeting) by the *HAUSA* and others, **akuut** by the *KATAB*, also known as *KIBO, KIBBO, KIBYEN*.

Where spoken: Plateau Province, in the central and southern part of Jos Division (Birom Tribal Area), extending into Pankshin Division.

Number of speakers: No reliable figures are available owing to confusion of nomenclature. Estimates vary between 40,000 and 100,000.

According to Meek the *BEROM* of the Bauchi Plateau speak a language cognate with that of the *CHAMBA* (but see p. 49). Thomas classes the language as 'possibly Semi-Bantu'. Numerals of 'Rop' (a *BIROM* village) given by Meek show some resemblances to CHAWAI, and a KIBYEN vocabulary[3] suggests affinities with PITI and CHAWAI.

A Gospel in 'BURUM' (= BIROM?) has been published.

The *BIROM* are often confused with the *BURUM* of Kanam Independent District, of whose language nothing is known except that they call it BOHUM.[2]
Number: 9,494.*

The *BIROM* are also sometimes confused with the *RON* (*BARON*) (see p. 138).

CHAWAI. DIALECT CLUSTER?

Dialect: CHAWAI.
Spoken by: CHAWAI (CHAWE, CHAWI), call themselves **atsam** (Sing. **tsam**), called *ATSAMA* by the *KATAB*; in Zaria Province, Katab District, north of the *KATAB*.
Number: 9,594.*

> *Note*: Although there are no Noun Classes in CHAWAI there is no doubt of its very close relationship in vocabulary with the other dialects listed below, in which there are Noun Classes.

Two Gospels have been translated.

Dialect: KURAMA.
Spoken by: *KURAMA*, call themselves **akurmi** (Sing. **bukurmi**), called *AZUMU* by the *KAHUGU*; in Lere District, north of the *CHAWAI*.
Number: 11,292.*

---

[1] Ames, *Gazetteer of Plateau Province*.
[2] Ames, op. cit., quoting the Rev. T. L. Suffill and Dr. P. W. Barnden (**bi-** being a Plural Suffix).
[3] Collected by the Rev. T. L. Suffill.

Closely related dialects are also spoken by:

JANJI, in Lere District, among the *KURAMA*.
Number: 360.*

PITI, call themselves *ABISI* (Sing. *BISI*), called *EPIT* by the *KATAB*; in Lere District south-east of the *KURAMA*.
Number: 1,589.*

JERAWA. DIALECT CLUSTER?

Information on the people known as *JERAWA* in Plateau Province, in the northern part of Jos Division, is extremely confused.

JERAWA appears to be a name applied by Europeans to (1) the people of Jere and neighbourhood (probably originally the HAUSA name for these people), (2) by extension, to a number of village groups in the area, including the *AMAP* of Amo, the *BUJAWA* of Buji, the *CHOKOBAWA* of Chokobo, the *SANGAWA* and the *RIBINAWA*. The name *RIBINAWA* (*REBINAWA*) is, however, a further source of confusion, as it is used to cover several of the people known as *JERAWA*, while *NARABUNA*, perhaps a version of the same name,[1] is also used inclusively.

There is further confusion between the *JERAWA* and *JARAWA* (see p. 115) and the *JERA* (p. 157).

Statements made by various writers about the languages or dialects spoken by these people are no less confused. It would appear that some or all of them speak dialects which may perhaps be related to CHAWAI (or to KATAB).

Class languages are also spoken by the following:

NUNKU (*MADA*), call themselves *YIDDA*, called *MADA* by the *HAUSA*; in Plateau Province, Southern Division, Nungu and Wamba Districts, also in Bauchi Province.
Number: 23,442.

EGON (*EGGON*), call themselves **megoŋ** (Sing. **abegoŋ**, **bugoŋ**), formerly known as 'Hill *MADA*'; Plateau Province, Southern Division.
There are two dialects: MATATARWA and MATENGALA, of which the latter does not appear to have Noun Classes.[2]
A Gospel has been translated.

RINDRI (*LINDIRI*), formerly known as *NUNGU*; in Wamba Division.
Their language is said to be closely related to that of the *EGON*.

NINZAM, north of the *EGON* and *RINDRI*.
A vocabulary of AYU[3] shows some resemblance to NINZAM.

RUKUBA, on the Zaria Province–Jos Division boundary.
A Gospel has been translated.

YESKWA, Keffi Emirate, Benue Province.

[1] ANO RIBINA = people of Riban; RIBINA-WA = HAUSA version of the name.
[2] MS. vocabularies.   [3] Meek, MS. vocabularies.

ISOLATED LANGUAGE GROUPS OR UNITS

GURE-KAHUGU. DIALECT CLUSTER.

Closely related dialects are spoken by:

GURE, call themselves *IGBIRI*, called *PUGBIRI* by the *KAHUGU*; in Zaria Province, Zaria Emirate, Lere District, north of the *KURAMA*.
Number: 3,787.*

KAHUGU (*KAPUGU*), call themselves *ANIRAGO* (Sing. **punɪraɡo**) (= men), called *AGARI* by the *KURAMA*, *KAGU* by the *GURE*; south of the *GURE*.
Number: 1,163.*

The following vocabularies[1] are considered by van Bulck to have some affinity with the GURE–KAHUGU dialects:

NINGAWA
BUTAWA } in the north-western part of Bauchi Province, mainly in Ningi
CHAMO } Independent District and Lame District, also in the extreme south-
KUDAWA } west of Kano Province.
SHENI; Lere District.

Linguistic notes on some Class Languages of Northern Nigeria

Although linguistic material available[2] is insufficient to establish any definite inter-relationship, there is sufficient phonetic and vocabulary resemblance between the KATAB and CHAWAI Groups and the GURE-KAHUGU Cluster, at least, for their common features to be described.

1. All these languages appear to have the following vowels: **i, ɪ, e, ɛ, a, ɔ, o, u** (Meek does not note **ᴜ**); also centralized **ə** and in some languages **ʌ**.

Nasalization occurs, and the vowel **a** is sometimes long.

Characteristic consonants and consonant combinations are:
Palatalized:

    KATAB ɛlyam[3]   KAGORO alyɛm   CHAWAI lyam tongue
    GURE uġyara   KAHUGU puġyara slave   JABA kye finger

Labialized:

    KATAB ġafwɔ finger-nail; ɔxwo slave; ʒwɔm elephant; ʃwɔi bee; ɔkwɔn tree; fufwo ear

    KAGORO dʒwak snake
    KAJE bara ʃiġɔtswa all the houses -hwa two hwɪt arrow amvwat frog
    JABA hwo name fwik nose
    KURAMA lɪvwa finger buġwɔma chief

Note also in JABA: ɬio back; ðu goat.

---

[1] Collected by various administrative officers.
[2] Meek's vocabularies (orthography slightly adapted).
[3] Written ʌ by Meek.

CLASS LANGUAGES 109

Labio-velar **kp** and **gb** occur. In EGON there is also **tp** before front vowels. Nasal Compounds occur. Other consonant combinations include:

| KAJE | katɔntsɔn | morning | JABA | bohovro | frog |
| KAHUGU | pukarma | chief | KURAMA | wuspi | five |

2. Tone has been noted in KATAB, KAGORO, and CHAWAI; in some cases the Singular and Plural of Nouns are distinguished by Tone only.

3. Most of these languages have more or less clearly discernible Noun Classes, formed mainly by Prefixes, and in a few cases by Suffixes. Formation of Plural by change of Tone has also been noted (KATAB and KAGORO).

Available material is insufficient for a full list of these Prefixes to be given.

Examples:

KATAB Group

Prefix: KATAB	ɛ-li	Plur. lɪ-	eye (also in KAGORO and MORWA)
	o-bu	ka-	tree
	ɔ-kwɔn	ka-	dog
	ɔ-xwo	ya-	slave
	ka-faŋ	ɪm-	stone
Suffix: KATAB	xie-t	-n	arrow (also in MORWA)
KAJE	ɪhwɪa-t	-n	arrow

No apparent change:

KATAB gasɔn   finger   (KAGORO gasuɔŋ, MORWA gaʃuɔŋ)
       ʃuʃwo   ear   (KAGORO cucuwo, MORWA fufwo)

KAJE appears to have a general Plural Prefix **a-**, except for persons (Sing. **a-**, Plur. **ba-**, e.g.: a-kwa, Plur. ba- slave).

JABA appears to have a general Plural Prefix **bo-**.

CHAWAI Group

KURAMA	ɔ-to	Plur. a-	ear
	li-lu	a-	knee
	bu-gwɔma	a-	chief
	bɪ-riare	a-	slave
	o-kaza	tɪ-	leg
	lɪ-vwa	tɪ-	finger
	o-ta	ti-	bow
	bu-rɔga	i-	elephant
	o-daro	in-	leopard
	o-sa	im-	hill

CHAWAI has no Noun Classes, the Plural being formed by Prefix **a-**:

tɔŋ   Plur. a-   ear

GURE-KAHUGU Dialect Cluster

These dialects appear to have a greater variety of Prefixes, e.g.:

KAHUGU	pu-ġyara	Plur. a-	slave
	pu-co	ma-	father[1]
	ka-buna	na-	leg
	kɪ-roġo	ɛ-	elephant
	ku-bi	mɪ-ġbi	leopard
	wu-ta	tu-	bow
	wo-nibo	tu-	river
	ru-bo	tu-	finger
	pɪ-sop	ɪ-	fly
	ka-niŋ	a-	bird
	ka-wə	nə-[2]	stream
	ka-nu	nu-[2]	pot (GURE kɪ-nu, Plur. nɪ-).

4. Concord between the Noun and other parts of speech is clear in GURE-KAHUGU, less so in other languages, e.g.:

KAHUGU	kona kanaŋ	my child
	nona nanaŋ	my children
	puġyara i ġya	the slave comes
	aġyara a pɪsa	the slaves go
	ato aba	two eyes
	ɪpɪs ɪba	two hands
	tubo tuba	two fingers
	rubo ruŋ	one finger
	lɪpe lɪŋ	one egg
KURAMA	atɔ aria	two ears
	tɪvwa tɪria	two fingers
	lɪŋma lɪdi	one egg

5. There is grammatical Gender in the 3rd Person Pronoun in KAHUGU:

ma ribe i	I see him	ma ribe kinne	I see her
puġyara i ġya	the slave comes	ki ġya	she comes

6. Word order in the simple sentence is Subject–Verb–Object.

7. In the Genitive construction the *nomen rectum* follows the *nomen regens*, usually without Linking Particle (but with optional Linking Particle **fu** in JABA). The Possessive Pronoun follows the Noun, e.g.:

KATAB	ɔxwo ġwam	the chief's slave	ɔxwo nu	my slave
KAJE	akwa ġwam		akwa nzuk	
JABA	ġan pop (ġana fu pop)		ġan mi	

[1] Words for father, mother, often appear to have irregular Plural forms in these languages.
[2] Note assimilation of Prefix-vowel to Root-vowel.

CHAWAI	ku rɛs (kuŋ = slave)	ku mi
KURAMA	bɪlarɪ boġwɔma (bɪlare = slave)	bɪlar ɪbam
KAHUGU	puġyare karma (puġyara = slave)	puġyar naŋ

8. Adjectives and Numerals follow the Noun.

Isolated Unit ? LALA

LALA. Dialect Cluster

The name LALA (originally given by the *FULANI*, but recognized by the speakers) denotes the language (or dialects).

Spoken by: a number of small tribes, most of whom are collectively known to Europeans and others as *YUNGUR* (they do not use this name themselves). They are called **ġbɪnna** by the *BATA-GUDU*, **abadira** by the 'Libo', **yuŋgɪrba** by the *LONGUDA*, *RABECHA* by the 'Gabin'. They call themselves by their own tribal names: *ROBA* (**rɔba**), *MBOI, HANDA, TAMBU, SUBKTU, PURA(BIRRA), BINNA* or **ġbɪnna**.

Where spoken: Adamawa Province, Yungur District, and in the adjacent parts of Song and Ganda Districts.

Number of speakers: *YUNGUR* 17,218, *LALA* 9,733, *ROBA* 1,335, other *BINNA* 2,268.

Linguistic notes on LALA

1. Implosive ɓ and ɗ have been noted.

2. The Plural of Nouns is formed by change of Suffix, or by addition of Suffix. In the 'Libo' dialect there appears also to be a Singular Prefix **i-**.

3. There are Inclusive and Exclusive forms of the 1st Person Plural Pronoun.

4. Word order is Subject–Verb–Object.

5. In the Genitive construction the *nomen rectum* follows the *nomen regens*.

Isolated Unit ? LONGUDA

LONGUDA. Dialect Cluster.

Spoken by: *LONGUDA*, call themselves *NUNGU-RABA* (**nɔ̃guraya**), called **ajitɔra** by the 'Libo'.

Where spoken: Adamawa and Bauchi Provinces, on the right bank of River Gongola, east of the Longuda Hills.

Number of speakers: 11,809.

Dialects: There are at least two dialects, spoken by the 'Hill' and 'Plains' LONGUDA respectively.

ISOLATED LANGUAGE GROUPS OR UNITS

Linguistic notes on LONGUDA

1. There do not appear to be implosive or labio-velar sounds.

2. The Plural of Nouns is formed by change of Suffix, according to Meek, but from some of his examples it would appear that some Nouns have a Singular Suffix, which is dropped in the Plural.

3. There are Inclusive and Exclusive forms of the 1st Person Plural Pronoun.

4. Word order is Subject–Verb–Object.

5. In the Genitive construction, the *nomen rectum* follows the *nomen regens*.

ISOLATED UNIT ? TULA

TULA. LANGUAGE?

Spoken by: *TULA*, call themselves *KOTULE*.

Where spoken: Bauchi Province, in the south-eastern part of Gombe Division.

Number of speakers: 19,209.

A Gospel has been translated into TULA.

According to Temple[1] the *DADIA* (about 2,300), who live in the *TULA* area, speak TULA.

Linguistic notes on TULA

1. Six Noun Classes can be distinguished, which are characterized by Suffixes.

2. There is Concord between the Noun and Qualificative.

3. In the Genitive construction the order is *nomen regens*+*nomen rectum*+Class Pronoun referring to *nomen regens*.

ISOLATED UNIT ? WAJA

WAJA. LANGUAGE?

Spoken by: *WAJA*.

Where spoken: Bauchi Province, north-east of the *TULA*.

Number of speakers: 19,718.

Two Gospels have been translated.

According to Temple[1] the *WAJA* speak a language connected with that of the *TERA* (see p. 157).

ISOLATED LANGUAGE GROUP ? TIV

Consists of: TIV Language.
and perhaps BITARE Language?

[1] *Notes on the Tribes, Provinces, Emirates, States.* . . .

CLASS LANGUAGES 113

  EKOI Dialect Cluster.
  BOKI Dialect Cluster?
  JAR Dialect Cluster?
  MBEMBE Dialect Cluster.
  'Mekaf' Language?
  and perhaps other languages or dialects.

Where spoken: Mainly in the Northern Provinces (Benue, Plateau, Adamawa); some languages which may belong to the Group are spoken in the eastern Provinces of Southern Nigeria and in the British Cameroons.

TIV. LANGUAGE.

Spoken by: *TIV* (*TIVI*, *TIWI*), call themselves **tiv**, called *MBITSE* or *MBICHI* ('strange settlers') by the *JUKUN*; also known as *MUNSHI* (*MUNCHI*) and *APPA* (cp. *JUKUN*, p. 140).

Where spoken: Benue Province, Tiv Division, also in Wukari, Lafia, and Nassarawa Divisions, and extending into the southern part of Plateau Province; in the south, extending into parts of Ogoja and Cameroons Provinces.

Number of speakers: Northern Provinces 573,605; MacBride[1] estimates the total number of TIV-speakers at 700,000–800,000.

There is some vernacular literature in TIV, including the New Testament and Psalms.

The relationship of the following languages and dialects to TIV is far from certain; they are very little known.

BITARE. LANGUAGE?

Spoken by: *YUKUTARE*, one of the tribes collectively known as *TIGONG* (see also pp. 141, 143).

Where spoken: British Cameroons (territory administered under Adamawa Province), in the southern part of Gashaka District.

The speech of the people of Abõ and Batu, in the same area as the above, may also be related to TIV; there is some vocabulary resemblance with BITARE.

Languages or dialects spoken by:

YERGUM (*YERGAM*), also known as *APPA*; in Plateau Province, Shendam Division, south-east of Pankshin.
 Number: 29,763.
 One Gospel has been translated into 'YERGUM or TAROH'.

The *EREGBA* (*REGBA*) south-west of the *YERGUM* may be related to them, or perhaps to the *JUKUN*. Nothing is known of their speech; it may be extinct.

[1] MS. notes.

B 2138

ISOLATED LANGUAGE GROUPS OR UNITS

KUTEV (*MBARIKE, ZOMPER, ZUMPER, JOMPRE*, &c.), in Benue Province east of the *TIV* on the Cameroons border, in Donga and Takum Districts of Wukari Division.

Number: 15,592* in Takum District.

They can all speak JUKUN (see p. 141).

BORITSŨ, called *DIFU* by the *JUKUN*, *AFITENG* by the *KUTEV*.

Perhaps the same as, or a section of, the *YERGUM*.

EKOI. Dialect Cluster.

Spoken by: *EKOI* (a name originally used by the *EFIK* for the *EJAGHAM*, but now used to cover several people speaking related dialects).

Where spoken: Mainly in Ogoja Province, but also in Calabar Province and the British Cameroons.

Number of speakers: 94,345.

Dialects: There appear to be many dialects, spoken by the various *EKOI* sections, which include:[1]

EKOI (ekɔi): *EJAGHAM* (*EJAKAM, EJAM, EZAM*) (ejaɢam);
(5 dialects)   *KEAKA*;[2]
   NKUM (*NKUMM*);
   OBANG (ɔbaŋg);
   EKWE;[3]
MANTA (3 dialects);
ASSUMBO;[4]
NDE.

Note that Talbot includes *BANYANGI* with sub-section *ANYANG*. The speech of the *BANYANGI* is, however, a BANTU language, while that of the *ANYANG* (Bruens's *TAKAMANDA*) appears to belong to the EKOI Cluster.

Abraham[5] points out that there is vocabulary resemblance between TIV and EKOI.

BOKI (NKI, OKII), own name ókîî.[6] Dialect Cluster?

Spoken by: *BOKI*, call themselves **vaanɛroki**.[6] *BOKI* is a name used to cover a number of small tribes, collectively known to the *TIV* as *DAMA*.

Where spoken: South of the *TIV*, mainly in Ogoja Province, but also in British Cameroons, Mamfe Division, west of Mamfe.

Number of speakers: 85,670.

---

[1] Information mainly from Talbot, *Southern Nigeria*.
[2] According to I. Richardson, **keaqa** is the name given by the *BANYANGI* to the EKOI dialects.
[3] According to I. Richardson, *EKWE* is merely another version of ekɔi.
[4] Possibly the same as Talbot's *BADZUMBO* or aʒumbo, in the northern part of Bamenda Province.
[5] *The Tiv people*.   [6] I. Richardson.

Dialects: There appear to be many dialects spoken by the *BOKI* (some of them may, however, be separate languages). The following names (of tribes or localities) are given by various authors:

BOKI (NKI), also known as *OSIKOM*;
YAKORO (DAMA KURA);
GAYI (ALEGI, UGE);
'Basua';
'Bendega' (but Thomas classes 'Bindiga' under EKOI);
BETE (MBETE). This dialect is said to differ considerably from the others.
According to Thomas there are about fifteen dialects in all.

BOKI 'has affinities with EKOI, but where it differs is still further removed from TIV'.[1]

JAR.[2] DIALECT CLUSTER?

The name *JARAWA* appears to be applied to a number of village groups in Jos Division of Plateau Province, and in parts of Pankshin and Shendam Divisions, also in Bauchi Province. Some of these people are said to speak closely related dialects, while others apparently do not. There is, however, considerable confusion of nomenclature with the *JERAWA* (see p. 107) and even the *JERA* (p. 157).

Dialects are said to be spoken by the following:

BANKALAWA;
BADAWA;
BOMBARAWA (BAMBARO, &c.); Lame District;
JAKU of Galembi, &c.;
JARAWA of Bununu ('Plains *JARAWA*');
'Hill *JARAWA*' (whose dialect appears to differ considerably).

A Gospel and Prayer Book in JARAWA have been published.

The language of the *BAKULŬ* (also known as *WURKUM*—but see p. 141) of Kulung, north of Lau, is said to be practically identical with JARAWA, and to have Noun Classes in the Singular, but not in the Plural. There is concord with other parts of speech, and some roots are strikingly reminiscent of BANTU.[3]

The speech of the following localities appears also to be related to JARAWA:

Mama and Kwarra, in the vicinity of Wamba, south of Jos;
Bari, 15 miles north of Numan, on River Gongola;
Mbula, 10–15 miles east of Numan. (Note that Thomas[4] suggests a connexion between 'the languages of the JARAWA group' and MBOA of Adamawa, also NAGUMI on the upper Benue, of which nothing further is known.)

---

[1] Abraham, op. cit.
[2] This is the name used by Abraham (op. cit.) to denote the language.
[3] MS. vocabulary compiled by Rev. E. W. Guinter.
[4] In Meek, *Northern Tribes*.

MBEMBE. Dialect Cluster.

Spoken by: MBEMBE,[1] a name originally used by the *EFIK* for the *OSHOPONG*, but now used to cover several tribes or sections speaking related dialects.

Where spoken: Ogoja Province.

Number of speakers: 43,086.

Sections of the *MBEMBE* include:

OSHOPONG (ESHUPUN);

ADUN (ARUN); Thomas[2] gives two dialects, spoken at Apiapun and Oderiga; 'Obubra'.

'Mekaf'. Language?[3]

Where spoken: In two 'towns', known as 'Big' and 'Small' Mekaf, in Bamenda Province, British Cameroons.

The people of Mekaf call themselves strangers and assert that before settling in Mekaf they had dealings with the *TIV*, whose language they understood because of its likeness to their own.

The languages or dialects spoken by the following may also be connected with this Group:[4]

ORRI; in Ogoja Province.[5]
Number: 8,607.

IYALA; in Ogoja Province.
Number: 22,525.

UKELLE (ukɛle); in Ogoja Province.
Number: 20,336.

YACHE?

Of these, *ORRI*, *IYALA*, and *UKELLE* are grouped together under the general heading *ORRI*.

Note: Abraham[6] applies the name 'BANTU' to TIV, EKOI, JAR, and possibly also BOKI and MBEMBE.

Linguistic notes on TIV

1. There appear to be eight vowel phonemes: **i, e, a, o, ɔ, u, ə** (higher central vowel), **ä** (lower central vowel).

Nasalization occurs, but only as an alternative for vowel+nasal.

When two vowels come together, the syllabic value of both is preserved, e.g. **kúûl** finger-nail.

---

[1] To be distinguished from the *MBEMBE* of the Cameroons (see p. 141).
[2] In Meek, *Northern Tribes*.   [3] From an unpublished article by Bruens.
[4] Talbot, op. cit. (figures also from Talbot).
[5] According to R. G. Armstrong (in a personal communication), ORRI and IYALA are not related.
[6] Op. cit.

2. Labio-velar **kp** and **gb** are common. **ɣ** and **v** are of frequent use and often occur finally; they can be syllabic. The affricates **ts** and **dz** occur.

Syllabic nasals occur. There are true nasal compounds as well as heterosyllabic nasal combinations (cp. the Genitive Particle and Subject of Verb in Classes 7 and 8 in the table of Affixes below).

A characteristic feature of the language is Palatalization of the consonant following **i** (thus **ky, ty, ny**, &c.). The result of the Palatalization of **ts** and **dz** is **c** and **j**; **s** becomes **ʃ** (Law of Palatalization).

Velarization also occurs, e.g.: **kw, gw, kpw**, &c.

3. There are three significant tone-levels: high, mid, and low, and all possible combinations.

Tone is both lexical and grammatical, and is of great importance. Tone Classes in the Noun are numerous.

Stress does not play an important part.

4. Nouns are composed of Affixes and Noun Stem. In a few cases the Affixes have been lost, in some other cases an intrusion of the Prefix into the core of the Stem has taken place. Nominal Stems are monosyllabic: CVC (rarely CV), or disyllabic: CVCV or CVVC.

Verb Roots may be monosyllabic:

CV	**nǎ**	give	**kpwɔ́**	die
VC	**àr**	reach	**èr**	do
CVC	**ŋbày**	roast	**yàr**	go

Composite tones in monosyllabic Roots are probably due to contraction, e.g.:

hâ pour **ʃî** remain

Disyllabic Roots consist of:

CVV	**wùà**	kill	**sɔ́ɔ̀**	sting
CVCV	**yɪrà**	call	**sómbò**	snap
CVVC	**sààn**	love	**ndòòr**	shake down fruit
CVCVC	**rùmùn**	agree	**ŋgòhòr**	receive

There are some trisyllabic Roots.

5. There is a Verbal Noun Formative, consisting of Suffix **-n** (see, however, § 13). For other formative elements see § 7.

6. There are eleven Noun Classes, characterized by Affixes (Prefix, Suffix, or both).

The Plural is expressed by transferring the Noun from a Singular to a Plural Class. Most of the Singular Classes have more than one corresponding Plural Class. But, with few exceptions, each Noun can take only one of the possible Plural forms.

There is Concord between the Noun and other parts of speech; some examples are shown in the table of Affixes below (see also § 7).

Table of Affixes[1]

Class		Class Affixes		Concords	
		Prefix	Suffix	Genitive Particle	Subject of Verb
1.	Sing.	à-, ì-		ù-	á-
2.	Sing.	ì-		ì-	ì-
3.	Sing. Plur.	í-		í-	í-
4.	Sing.			úù-	ú-
5.	Sing.		-ɣ	kù-	kú-
6.	Sing.	í-	-ɣ	kì-	kí-
7.	Sing. Plur.		-v	m̀bù-	mbú-
8.	Plur.	í-	-v (-mbiv)	m̀bì-	mbí-
9.	Plur.	á-		á-	á-
10.	Plur.	m	-m	mȧ-	má-
11.	Plur.	ù-, m̀bà-	-v	m̀bà-	vɘ́-

Nouns of Class 1 take Plurals of Class 3, 9, 11.
,, ,, 2 ,, ,, ,, 3, 9, 11.
,, ,, 3 ,, ,, ,, 9.
,, ,, 4 ,, ,, ,, 3, 9.
,, ,, 5 ,, ,, ,, 3, 8, 9, 10.
,, ,, 6 ,, ,, ,, 8, 9, 10.
,, ,, 7 ,, ,, ,, 3, 8.

7. Adjectives are in concordial agreement with the Noun, generally by Suffix where it exists, sometimes also by Prefix. The Adjective follows the Noun, the Genitive Particle in agreement with the Noun standing between them, e.g.:

(a) Class Affixes preserved:
    Cl. 11 **ùbó m̀bà[2] ùkásév** ugly women (ugly ones of female)
    Cl. 8 **ícímbív m̀bì cɘ́v[3]** old grass (grass of old)

(b) Class Suffix only preserved:
    Cl. 11 **kásév m̀bà bóv** bad women
    Cl. 6 **ícíɣ kì[2] íríɣ** black ink

(c) No Class Affix preserved:
    Cl. 1 **kwȧsɘ ù bó** bad woman
    Cl. 2 **ìkóndó ì ír** black clothing

8. There is a Locative Case, used with or without Preposition. It is characterized by change of tone and in the Singular there is mostly no Class Affix, the Class Suffix being always dropped.

---

[1] Exceptional forms are not taken into account here.
[2] Note slight change of tone.
[3] From Root **tsɘ́v** with Palatalization.

CLASS LANGUAGES

9. The Personal Pronouns (Independent or Objective) are:

	Sing.	Plur.
1.	mo, m	sə
2.	wə, u	nə
3.[1]	un	və

10. The Possessive Pronoun for the 3rd Person Singular or Plural (**na** and **və** respectively for the Personal Classes 1 and 11) immediately follow the Noun. Those for the 1st and 2nd Persons are made up of (*a*) Class Prefix (if any), (*b*) Infix **-a-**, (*c*) pronominal element.

Note: The Class Prefix is **w-** in Classes 1 and 4 and is omitted in Classes 9, 10, and 11. The pronominal element is omitted before a Class Suffix.

11. The conjugation of the Verb is homogeneous. The Stem of the Verb can have several different tone patterns, but the conjugational Prefixes do not change their tone within one single Tense, e.g. (Past Tense):

ḿ yèm   I went   ḿ và   I came   ḿ wùà   I killed

12. Verbal Derivatives have not been observed.
There is no special Passive form; an impersonal Pronoun **i-** is used.

13. The Verbal Noun has in most cases a Suffix **-n** and it has a special tone pattern, e.g.:

Stem for Past Tense   *Verbal Noun*
sɔ̀ŋgɔ́   to slit   sɔ̀ŋg-ó-n   act of slitting

If the Verbal Noun takes the tone pattern of the Past Tense, it replaces a finite Verb in the Past depending on a governing Verb, e.g.:

á kìmbìr pìnə̀n   he repeated the act of asking (in the past)—he asked again (the true Verbal Noun would be **pìnə́n**).

Verbal Noun forms replacing the Recent Past and showing its tone patterns exist.

14. The Verb Stem varies in tone according to Tense, and there are cases in which it varies also for Person. In one Tense there are also alternative tone patterns. Besides this the Verb Stem can show alterations in form. All this makes it difficult to establish a basic Stem characterized by a special tone, and the limited possibilities of tone patterns, e.g. in the Past, show that tone is linked with grammatical categories rather than of etymological significance.

15. Some Verbal Stems refer to one number of an Object only, e.g.:

ġbihi   throw away one thing   ha   throw away many things

16. The Verb is conjugated by prefixing a pronominal element to the Stem. The pronominal elements vary in tone or form according to Tense.

---

[1] Pronouns for Class 1 (Sing.) and 11 (Plur.) only are given here.

The following Tenses exist: Past, Recent Past, Subjunctive, Future (in two variations), Habitual, and Progressive.

For change of tone in the Pronoun, and of tone and form in the Stem, cp.:

	Past		*Subjunctive*		*Recent Past*	
Sing. 1.	ḿ pìnə̀	I asked	m̀ pínə́	that I may ask	ḿ pĭn	I recently asked
2.	ú pìnə̀		ù pínə́		ú pĭn	
3.	á pìnə̀		à pínə́		á pín	
Plur. 1.	sə́ pìnə̀		sə̀ pínə́		sə́ pín	
2.	nə́ pìnə̀		nə̀ pínə́		nə́ pín	
3.	və́ pìnə̀		və̀ pínə́		və́ pín	

17. Verbal and Copula Negation are expressed by the negative Postpositions **da**, **dzə**, **ga**, e.g.:

  á kàhà súrə́ gá he hoed the farm not
  ká wán nà gá it is his son not
  ká mò dzə́ it is I not

18. Word order in the sentence is Subject–Verb–Object.

19. There are Copula forms for each Noun Class, resembling in form the Demonstrative Pronouns, e.g.:

  ḿ ŋgù kwá ŏr I am a young man

20. For word order in the Genitive Construction see § 7.

For Adjectives see § 7.

Note on 'Mekaf'[1]

An examination of the Class system of 'Mekaf' shows:

(*a*) Ten Affixes have been noted: 7 Prefixes and 3 Suffixes.
(*b*) In two Plural Classes ('animal' and 'fluid' Classes) the Affixes are used as both Prefix and Suffix.
(*c*) There is a Plural Class formed by change of tone only.
(*d*) There is Concord between the Noun and other parts of speech.

Note on BOKI[2]

1. There are Noun Classes. Plurals are formed by change of Prefix; some Nouns have no distinct Plural form.

2. There appears to be Concord.

3. The Personal Pronouns are:

	Subject	*Object*
Sing. 1.	me	mɛ
2.	wɔ'ɔ	yɔ
3.	nyi	a

[1] From an unpublished article by Bruens. [2] From I. Richardson.

	Subject	Object
Plur. 1.	bɛvɛ	bɛ
2.	bẽva	bẽ
3.	mbɛ	ambɛ

4. The Copula appears to resemble the Demonstrative.

Isolated Unit: IJƆ

IJƆ (IJAW). Dialect Cluster?

Spoken by: IJƆ (IJAW, IJOH), call themselves **ijɔ**.

Where spoken: South-western Nigeria, mainly in Owerri Province, Degema Division, Warri Province, Western Ijaw Division, and Ondo Province, Okitipupa Division.

Number of speakers: 156,436.

Dialects: IJƆ is very little known, and no detailed information is available on the dialects and their distribution. According to Talbot the *IJƆ* consist of three main (geographical) divisions, each comprising several tribes or tribal sections speaking different dialects:

'Kalabari' and *OKRIKAN*, in the east;

'Lower *IJAW*', comprising 'Brass *NEMBE*', 'Brass *IJAW*', and 'Ogbinya', in the centre;

'Western *IJAW*', comprising *ATISSA*, *MIMI* and 'Warri', adjacent to the *SOBO*; these sections of the *IJƆ* also speak *SOBO* dialects.

Parts of the Bible have been translated into 'Patani (Kolokuma)' and 'Nimbi (Brass)'.

Linguistic notes on IJƆ

1. There appear to be Noun Classes, formed by Prefixes and Suffixes.

2. Tone seems to play a part in the formation of the Plural of Nouns.

3. The Personal Pronouns appear to have high tone in the 1st Person, low tone in the 2nd Person (Sing. and Plur.).

4. In the Genitive construction the *nomen rectum* precedes the *nomen regens*, e.g.:

    alabɔ chief **omonibɔ** slave
    alabɔ monibɔ the chief's slave

The Possessive Pronoun precedes the Noun, e.g.:

    ɔro monibɔ his slave

5. Word order in the simple sentence is Subject–Object–Verb, e.g.:

    amɛn omonibɔ macim we the slave call

6. Adjective, Numeral, and Demonstrative Pronoun precede the Noun, e.g.:

tɔro	eye	ma tɔro	two eyes
obiri	dog	dob obiri	large dog

Isolated Unit ? LUKÖ

LUKÖ, own name **lukö (lukə)**. Language.

Spoken by: *YAKÖ (YAKURR)*, call themselves **yakö (yakə)**.[1]

Where spoken: In the extreme south of Ogoja Province, Obubra Division, with main centre Umor (Ugep).

Number of speakers: about 20,000.[2]

LUKÖ has Noun Classes formed by Prefixes. There is Concord between the Noun and other parts of speech.[3]

(c) CLASS LANGUAGES OF THE BRITISH AND FRENCH CAMEROONS[4]

Information on most of these languages and dialects is very slight; it is possible that there is a closer interrelationship between at least some of them than would appear from the provisional classification given below, but much further research is needed.

Isolated Unit? BALI (ŋ́gàa kà)[5]

BALI, own name **ŋ́gàa kà**. Language?

Spoken by: *BALI*, call themselves **banyɔŋa** (Sing. **munyɔŋa**).[6]

Where spoken: British Cameroons, Bamenda Province, Bali **(ba'ni)** town and surroundings.

This is the language fostered before the First World War by German missionaries and administrators under the name of BALI. It is now, however, less widely used, Pidgin and DUALA having largely taken its place.

There is some vernacular literature, including the New Testament.

Linguistic notes on BALI ngàa kà[7]

1. The Noun Class system is not clear and would seem to be on the point of disappearing[8]; there is no distinct Plural form for most Nouns. (Note, however, that

---

[1] See footnote 1 to Forde, 'Ward organization among the Yakö' (*Africa*, 1950).
[2] Forde, *Marriage and the family among the Yakö*.   [3] Information from M. Guthrie.
[4] Information on this section mainly from I. Richardson; also from: Bruens, 'The structure of Nkom and its relation to Bantu and Sudanic' (*Anthropos*, 1942/5), and unpublished material; E. Meyer, 'Stand und Aufnahmen der Sprachforschung in Kamerun' (*Z. Eingeb. Spr.*, 1942), and unpublished material; Kaberry, MS. notes; Talbot, *Southern Nigeria*.
[5] To be distinguished from BALI **(ndaGam)**, see p. 150.
[6] Cp. NYONGNEPA under CHAMBA, p. 150.
[7] From I. Richardson, and E. Meyer, loc. cit.
[8] 'Das Präfixklassensystem des Bali entstammt offenbar den Bantusprachen, doch ist die Zahl der Klassen stark reduziert, und ihre Präfixe sind abgeschliffen. . . . Das Klassensystem ist nicht charakteristisch und ausschlaggebend für diese Sprache.' E. Meyer, loc. cit.

CLASS LANGUAGES

some Nouns have Plural forms reminiscent both of BANTU and of the BAMILEKE languages (Richardson).)

2. There is an Inclusive and an Exclusive form of the 1st Person Plural (Meyer).

3. There are many Tenses of the Verb, both in the Simple and Progressive forms (i.e. two Aspects of the Verb?) (Meyer).

4. Vocabulary shows considerable resemblance to BANTU.

Isolated Language Group? NSAW-KOM

The languages and dialects provisionally grouped together under this heading are those called BAFUMBUM-BANSAW by Talbot, NKOM by Bruens, WE by Meyer. Note that most of the peoples speaking them are also known as *TIKAR*;[1] they are indicated below by [*TIKAR*].

Where spoken: British Cameroons, Bamenda Province.

Languages and/or dialects which may be interrelated are spoken by:

NSAW (BANSAW, BANSO, NSO) [*TIKAR*], own name of language **làmsɔ'**; in Bansaw Tribal Area, with main centre Kumbo.
  Number: 9,339;* according to Richardson's informant ('from the latest census') total *c.* 40,000.
  According to Kaberry there are many dialects.
  Before the war the language was used in mission schools; a catechism has been published.

KOM (NKOM, BIKOM, BAMEKON) [*TIKAR*], own name of language **ètáŋ ekóm,** with dialectal variants **tsaŋ** and **kidʒɛm,** according to Bruens; west of the *NSAW* (a variant of **kidʒɛm** being spoken at Babanki-Tungo).
  Number: 13,454;[2] according to Bruens, *c.* 15,000.

mmɛ (a place-name in the south of Fungom Tribal Area), a 'language' closely resembling KOM (Bruens).

BUM, north of the *KOM*, and speaking a related language or dialect.

NSUNGLI (NSUNGNI, NSUGNI, NDZUNGLE, ZUNGLE) [*TIKAR*]; north of the *NSAW*.

According to Kaberry *NSUNGLI* is a collective name covering several people speaking closely related dialects:
  WIYA (NDU); *WAR (WA, MBWAT)*; *TANG.*
According to Meyer the dialect of Tamanken is a NSUNGLI dialect. Talbot considers the *NSUNGLI* to be part of the *NSAW*.

FUNGOM [*TIKAR*] (their speech being known as 'We', according to Meyer); in Fungom Tribal Area.

---

[1] For TIKAR see p. 125.   [2] 1927 Government figures.

Dialect: òsò, spoken by áwíésò (Sing. wúsò), at Esu (Richardson).
The language is closely related to KOM, according to Bruens. The *FUNGOM* are possibly the same as Talbot's *BAFUMBUM*.
Number: 5,260 TP.*[1]

'Wum', in Aghem Tribal Area. The language is said to be understood by the adjacent *FUNGOM* (Richardson).
Number: 1,769.*

Note: In the north of the area a different language is spoken which is incomprehensible in the south; JUKUN is used as a lingua franca in the north (Richardson).

Bruens also refers to ɥe and ɥum as related languages (cp. 'We' and 'Wum'?).

Linguistic notes on the NSAW-KOM Group

NSAW[2]

1. Particular consonants noted include:

   final syllabic nasals;
   trilled **r**, especially final;
   retroflex **z**;

2. There are Noun Classes; the Plural is formed:
   (*a*) by change of Prefix (**ki-/vi-** being the commonest);
   (*b*) by addition of Suffix (**-si** being the commonest);
   (*c*) some Nouns do not differentiate between Singular and Plural.

3. There is Concord between the Noun and other parts of speech.

Note: The old people are said to speak 'a different language', with more **ki-/vi-** Nouns, also **li-/ma-** Prefixes, and with less Suffixes.

KOM[3]

1. Particular sounds noted include:
   unrounded back vowels;
   nasalized vowels;
   semi-vowel ɥ.

2. The Root is monosyllabic: CV or CVC (final consonant **n**, **s**, or **f**).

3. There are Noun Classes; the Plural is formed:
   (*a*) by Prefix;
   (*b*) by omission of Prefix;
   (*c*) (in one case only) by addition of Suffix.

---

[1] TP = taxpayers. The total figure may be reckoned at approximately 4½ times the taxpayer figure.
[2] From I. Richardson.
[3] Bruens, loc. cit.

'We'[1]

1. Particular sounds noted include:
   frequent use of diphthongs;
   glottal stop.

2. There are Noun Classes, including four Plural Classes. The Plural is formed by Prefix.

3. Concord is strictly observed. But note that, e.g. in the Genitive construction, the Class Prefix is used as a Suffix:

   ífau   leaf   fɔ́kâ'   tree   fáu-i fɔ́kà'   leaf of tree

When the Noun is the Subject of a sentence, or is followed by a Demonstrative, the Class Prefix is dropped from the Noun, and the Pronoun shows the Class.

4. Verbal Derivatives are formed by Suffixes; there is no Passive.

Isolated Unit? TIKAR

TIKAR, own name **lĕd tùmu** (Meyer). Dialect Cluster?

Spoken by: TIKAR (*TIKARI, TIKALI*), call themselves **laŋ tumu** (Meyer).

Where spoken: French Cameroons, on both sides of River Mbam, between the *MAMBILA* in the north-west and the *VUTE* in the south-east.

Number of speakers: 8,863+1,660 among the *BAMUM*.[2]

Dialects: There are two main dialects, spoken north and south of River Mbam respectively (Richardson).

Linguistic notes on TIKAR (Southern or NGEMBI dialect)[3]

1. Particular sounds noted include:
   nasalized vowels;
   semi-vowel ɥ;
   syllabic nasals.

2. There are Noun Classes; the Plural is formed by:

   (a) addition of Prefix, e.g.:

wúŋ	Plur. mɛ̀wúŋ	fire
tɔ́	bùtɔ́	fish-hook
kwɛ́	bùkwɛ́	skin
kɥê	bùkɥê	mat
ŋ́gà	bɛ́ŋgà	crocodile

[1] Meyer, loc. cit.
[2] I. Dugast, 'Inventaire ethnique du sud-Cameroun' (*Mém. IFAN*, 1949). Note that the Nigerian Census of 1931 gives the figure 107,966 in the Northern Provinces, but the name *TIKAR* is loosely used to cover a number of tribes (see under NSAW-KOM, pp. 123–4) and this figure cannot be considered even approximately correct.   [3] From I. Richardson.

(b) some Nouns make no distinction, e.g.:

    ńyá   animal/s
    ǹdʒwí dog/s

3. No clear Concord system is discernible.

4. The Personal Pronouns are:

	Subject	Object	Possessive
Sing. 1.	mɔ̀	mɔ́	yɛ̌
2.	?	wʊ́	
3.	à	nʊ́	
Plur. 1.	bu	bu (tone uncertain)	
2.	?	bí	
3.	bɛ̀	bɔ́	

5. Examples of Tenses and word order:

    bu ʄwɛ̌ gbɛ̀rì   we bought bananas (Subj.–Verb–Obj.)
    bu tɔ́ gbɛ̀rì ʄwɛ̌ we buy bananas (now) (Subj.–Particle–Obj.–Verb)
    bu yɛ́ gbɛ̀rì ʄwɛ̌ we shall buy bananas

6. In the Genitive construction the *nomen regens* precedes the *nomen rectum* without Linking Particle, e.g.:

    àkwɔ́ mlɛ́   hoe (of) woman
    bùkwɔ́ bɛ́yí hoes (of) women (note **mlɛ́**, Plur. **bɛ́yí** woman)
    kwɔ́ yɛ̌   my hoe

Isolated Language Group? WIDEKUM

The name WIDEKUM, as well as being the name of a place and of its inhabitants, is used to cover a number of peoples (indicated by [WIDEKUM] below). Some of them are known, and some alleged, to speak related languages and/or dialects. It is not impossible that some of these languages may prove to be related to the BAMILEKE languages (see p. 128).

Where spoken: British Cameroons, Bamenda Province.

Speakers of these languages or dialects include:

WIDEKUM (MBUDIKEM, BURRIKEM, TIWIRKUM), own name of language **íyìríkùm**; at and around Widekum between Bamenda and Mamfe (Richardson).

MOGAMO (MOGAMAW, MEGAMAW, MOGHAMO) [WIDEKUM], call themselves **mɔ́γámò**, called **mɔgamu** by the WIDEKUM.
    Number: 4,326 TP.*

ŋgámámbó, called **mitaa** by neighbouring peoples; at Bafawchu in Ngemba Tribal Area; originally from Widekum (Richardson).

MENEMO (*BAMETA, META, MUTA*—but cp. **mitaa** above) [*WIDEKUM*]; north-north-west of Bali.

Number: 2,892 TP* (Talbot gives the figure 20,291, but includes several other small groups of people).

NGONU (*ANGONO, NGUNU, NGWO*), name of language NGWA (Bruens) [*WIDEKUM*]; in the western part of Bamenda Province.

Number: 2,211 TP.*

Their language is said to differ considerably from WIDEKUM, but may perhaps be related to it (Richardson).

NGEMBA (*MOGIMBA, MEGIMBA, NGOMBA*) [*WIDEKUM*]; in two separate areas with slight dialectal variations, north and south of the *MENEMO* and Bali respectively (Richardson).

Number: 5,158 TP* (Talbot gives 29,379, but this figure includes some other groups).

NGI (*MINGI, NGIE, AGIE, UGIE*) [*WIDEKUM*] (included in the *MENEMO* by Talbot); in the south-western part of Bamenda Province.

Note: Nothing further is known of the *MELAMBA*, said by Talbot to be located between the *MOGIMBA* and *BANSAW*. He gives the figure 17,963.

According to Talbot the *BAFUT* (*FUT, BUFU, FU*) speak a MOGIMBA dialect. They are, however, not known as *WIDEKUM*, but as *TIKAR* (see pp. 123, 125). They live north-east of Bali, adjacent to the *MOGIMBA*.

Number: 6,300 TP.*

The speech of the *AGE* or *ESIMBI* [*WIDEKUM*] in the western part of Bamenda Province is said not to be understood by the *WIDEKUM* (Richardson).

Number: 1,040 TP.*

Linguistic notes on the WIDEKUM Group

WIDEKUM[1]

1. Particular sounds noted include:

   many centralized vowels;
   unrounded **ɯ**;
   syllabic nasals;
   unexploded plosives.

(cp. BAMUN, p. 131).

2. There are Noun Classes; the Plural is formed by change of Prefix.

3. There is Concord between the Noun and other parts of speech.

4. The Personal Pronouns are:

	Subject	Object
Sing. 1.	mɔ́	ɛ́mʊ́
2.	ɔ̀wɔ̀	ɛ́wɛ̀
3.	mɛ́n	ámɛ́n

[1] Information from I. Richardson.

	Subject	Object
Plur. 1.	bà	ɛ́wá
2.	mbú or vú?	áwú
3.	òmɛn	ɔ̀mɛ́n

5. The vocabulary shows some correspondence with BANTU, but the Noun Classes do not seem to correspond.

BAFUT[1]

1. There are Noun Classes; the Plural is formed by change of Prefix.

2. There is Concord between the Noun and other parts of speech, e.g.:

azo	Plur. njo	thing
ati	üti	tree
muŋwį ku̱la	buŋwį bu̱la	this knife
nüli̱hi̱ nu̱la	mi̱hi̱ mu̱la	this eye
nu̱ ģu̱la	bö bu̱la	this man

3. The vocabulary shows little resemblance to BANTU.

Isolated Language Group? BAMILEKE[2]

The name BAMILEKE is used by Europeans to designate a number of languages and/or dialects spoken in the French Cameroons, and the people speaking them. These people have no common name, but use the name *BAMILEKE*. The languages are sometimes also referred to by Europeans as 'Grassfield', and this name, recognized by the *BAMILEKE* themselves, has become **grafi** or **grafil** in Pidgin.

The BAMILEKE languages are to some extent interrelated, though the degree of relationship cannot be established with any accuracy, as the speech of every village differs in varying degrees from that of other villages. Some relationship with the WIDEKUM languages is not impossible (see pp. 126–7).

Pidgin is widely used among the *BAMILEKE*.

Where spoken: In the whole of Bamileke region, except for the *DIBUM* in the south-east, whose language is BANTU, and the *MBO* west of Dshang (BANTU language?); also spoken by the many *BAMILEKE* who have emigrated to other areas.

Number of speakers: total population of Bamileke region 425,900, plus emigrants (perhaps 40,000–50,000).

The total number of languages and/or dialects is not known. The following are some of those known to Europeans (note that in most cases the name given as that of the language is that of the locality where it is spoken):

DSHANG (DSCHANG, CHANG), own name ásùŋl(i)átʃàŋ or -atsaŋ; in subdivision Dschang.

---

[1] M. Guthrie, *The classification of the Bantu languages*, p. 19. Note that k̲, g̲ are used for x, ɣ.
[2] Information from I. Richardson, unless otherwise stated.

CLASS LANGUAGES

Number: not known; the population of the subdivision is 158,000, but this includes speakers of other languages.

The speech of the *BANGWA* (own name ŋwɛ) in the British Cameroons, in the extreme east of Mamfe Division, is very closely related to DSHANG.

BABADJOU, own name (ɛ)tsaso (from the native name of Babadjou village); in Babadjou chefferie and neighbourhood. The language is said to differ from other BAMILEKE languages.

BAGAM, own name **tsoɣap¹**; in Bagam chefferie and neighbourhood (near Bati).[1]

BAMOUGOUM, own name **nɛɣa pamuŋgup¹**; Bamougoum chefferie in Bafoussam subdivision.
Number (population of chefferie): 14,000.
The language resembles BAMEKA (pop. 6,000) and BAMENDJOU (own name **nɛɣa mundʒu**) (pop. 11,000), also BANSOA and BALESSING in Dshang subdivision.

BAFOUSSAM, own name **fusap¹ (fusam̩, fulsap¹)**; in Bafoussam subdivision.

BANDJOUN (BANDJOUM), own name **ŋgomandʒũ**; in Bandjoun chefferie and surroundings.
Number (population of chefferie): 27,000.
The speech of Baham chefferie (own name **ŋgomahũm**) (pop. 13,000) is closely related to BANDJOUN.

BABOUANTOU, own name **ɣö pa papwantu**; in the north-eastern part of Bafang subdivision. It is said to be closely related to BAFANG.

BAFANG,[2] own name **ɣəəfa', yəlafa'**. DIALECT CLUSTER?
The name **fefe (fɛ'ɛfɛ')** is used to denote the language of the whole Bafang area, as opposed to **ɣəəfa'** spoken in Bafang itself, by people calling themselves **puaafa'**.
There are many dialects, spoken in the villages surrounding Bafang (e.g. **ŋka'** spoken in Banka, **ɣəlabuunʃa**, &c.)
Number (population of subdivision): 67,500.[3]
BAFANG is used in missions. A catechism has been published.

BAKOU, own name **ɣəəkuu,** spoken west of Bafang, is said to be almost identical with BAFANG.

Dialects of the Bangou–Batchingou–Bamana area. At least one dialect is closely related to BANGANGTE (see below).

Dialects of the Bangwa–Batouffam area. At least one dialect is closely related to BANGANGTE. (Not to be confused with Bangwa in the British Cameroons—see above.)

BANGANGTE, own name **ndʒubʊɣa**, spoken by the **baɣa** in the chefferie of Bangangte, but understood throughout the whole subdivision, although other

[1] Not to be confused with Balibagam (see p. 150).
[2] To be distinguished from Beba Befang (see p. 152).
[3] *Mémento Cameroun* (Service de Presse et d'Information du Cameroun, 1949).

local dialects are also spoken; also spoken by emigrants from Bangangte to other areas.

Number (population of chefferie): 66,700.

BANGANGTE is used by French Protestant missions (Roman Catholics use Pidgin). There is some vernacular literature.

Dialect or language of Batongtou.

Possibly also belonging to this Language Group:

BANKWET and BANA.[1]

BAMUN (BAMUM), own name ʃúpàmʌ́m. LANGUAGE.

Spoken by: *BAMUN* (*BAMUM*, (Fr.) *BAMOUM*).

Where spoken: French Cameroons, throughout the administrative area of Fumban.

Number of speakers: 74,848.[2]

BAMUN has a script of its own, invented by Sultan Njoya during the last century. There is some vernacular literature, including a considerable part of the New Testament. BAMUN is used as a lingua franca in the southern part of Ndop Tribal Area, British Cameroons.

Linguistic notes on the BAMILEKE Group

BAMILEKE languages.[3]

1. Particular sounds noted include:

   many central vowels, which are largely indeterminate and indistinguishable;
   double vowels;
   two varieties of **a** (front and back);
   semi-vowel **ɥ**;
   unexploded plosives;
   glottal stop;
   fricative **x** and **ɦ**;
   aspirated **k**^{h};
   syllabic nasals;
   explosive and implosive **b, ɓ** (no labio-velar **gb**);
   many curious consonant combinations.

   Examples from BAFANG (fɛ'ɛfɛ'):

zák	Plur. ǹzák	thigh	zɔ̀k	Plur. ńzɔ̀k	knee
ŋ́gàp	ŋ́gàp	chicken	lɔ̀x	ńdɔ̀x	stone
lɔ́x (no Plur.)		sleep	ɦʊ́	ńɦʊ̀	leaf

2. There are Noun Classes, but very indeterminate. The Plural is formed by addition or change of Prefix (**mə-** being a common Plural Prefix); some Nouns make no distinction.

[1] See Ad. Léger, 'Contribution à l'étude de la langue Bamiléké' (*J. Soc. Afric.*, 1932).
[2] Dugast, 'Inventaire ethnique du sud-Cameroun'.
[3] I. Richardson.

3. There appears to be Concord of a sort, e.g. with Possessives (see § 4).

4. An Inclusive/Exclusive distinction in the 1st Person Plural Possessive Pronoun has been noted in DSHANG, e.g.:

Inclusive: Sing. **wúpe** Plur. **púpe** our (person)
ʒúpe **tʃúpe** our (thing)
Exclusive: Sing. **wɔ́yɔ** Plur. **pɔ́yɔ** our (person) (i.e. belonging to you and me only)
zɔ́yɔ **tsɔ́yɔ** our (thing)

5. The vocabulary shows considerable resemblance to BANTU.
The material of Léger[1] is insufficient to deduce the Noun Classes, but shows evidence of Concord.
His examples include (orthography that of the author):

mo	Plur.	*po*	child
membo mumban		*pombo punban*	uncle
fono		*m'fono*	body
tung		*n'tung*	ear

BAMUN[2]

1. Particular sounds noted include:

nasalized vowels;
double vowels;
unrounded **ɯ**;
syllabic nasals;
ejective **k'**;
unexploded plosives, e.g. **k'wút⁀** leg, Plur. **ŋk'wút⁀**; **lwɔ́p⁀** fish-hook.

2. There are Noun Classes; the Plural is formed by:

(*a*) change of Prefix: **mɔ́n** Plur. **pɔ́n** child
mə́sì **pə́sì** bird
(*b*) change of Tone: **ǹʃééʃə̀** **ǹʃèèʃə̀** mat
fɯ̂ɯfwét⁀ **fɯ́ɯfwɛ̀t⁀** wind
(*c*) reduplication **ǹdáp⁀** **ǹdáp⁀ǹdáp⁀** house
(*d*) some Nouns do not distinguish between Singular and Plural:
kɔŋ chest/s

3. There does not appear to be Concord. The Demonstrative distinguishes Number but not Class, e.g.:

ǹdá yì this house Plur. **ǹdá ʃì** (note dropping of final **p⁀**)
mə́nyí íyɯ̀ə̀ that knife **pə́nyí ʃù ə̀**

4. Word order in the simple sentence is Subject–Verb–Object.

[1] Loc. cit. [2] I. Richardson.

5. Examples of Tenses:

pǔ yùùn	we bought (recent)
pǔ pí yǔǔn	we bought (yesterday)
pǔ kà pí yùùn	we bought (long ago)
pǔ tí nǎǎ ndʒúún	we are buying
pǔ náá ntúɔ yùùn	we shall buy (Auxiliary Verb tuɔ = come)
pǔ nǎǎ ndɔ́' yùùn	we shall buy (Far Future)

6. Negation is expressed by means of the Particle **máà**.

7. In the Genitive construction the *nomen regens* precedes the *nomen rectum* without Linking Particle.

Miscellaneous notes

Talbot's BEBA BEFANG, Tessmann's BAFINGE, perhaps refer to an area in the British Cameroons, Bamenda Province: Biba Befang. The inhabitants are said to be related to the *WIDEKUM*, but now to speak a different language, unrelated to others in the neighbourhood (Richardson).

Ndop is the name of a Tribal Area in the British Cameroons. The name has no linguistic significance: BAMUN is used as a lingua franca in the southern part of the area (Richardson).

Section VIII
ISOLATED LANGUAGE GROUPS OR UNITS (NON-CLASS LANGUAGES) OF NIGERIA AND THE CAMEROONS

In this section are dealt with those languages and/or dialects which have no Noun Classes. Apart from this negative characteristic, there is not sufficient evidence to justify any attempt at classification, except in a few cases into Groups. Further research is needed, as most of these languages are very little known.

Isolated Unit:[1] IBIBIO-EFIK

IBIBIO-EFIK. Dialect Cluster.

Spoken by: *IBIBIO*.
   Note: This is the name of the largest of several groups of tribes, and is used by Europeans collectively to cover all the groups.

Where spoken: Nigeria, south and south-east of the *IGBO*, mainly in Calabar Province, but also in parts of Owerri Province and the British Cameroons.

Number of speakers: total estimated at over 1,000,000.[2]

Dialects: Dialectal divisions correspond approximately to tribal. The main *IBIBIO* subdivisions (groups of tribes) are:

(Eastern): *IBIBIO*; in Calabar Province, and Aba Division of Owerri Province.
   Number: 79,946 TP.

(Western): *ANANG*; in Calabar Province, and Aba Division of Owerri Province.
   Number: about 7,300 TP.

(Northern): *ENYONG*; in Calabar Province, and Bende Division of Owerri Province.
   Number: about 6,600 TP.

(Southern): *EKET*; in Eket Division, Calabar Province.
   Number: 22,180 TP.

(Delta): *ANDONE-IBENO*; in Calabar Province.
   Number: 7,292 TP.

(Riverain): *EFIK*; in Calabar Province, and Kumba (and Victoria) Divisions of the British Cameroons.
   Number: 8,755 TP.

---

[1] See, however, M. M. Green, 'The classification of West African tone-languages: Igbo and Efik' (*Africa*, 1949).
[2] 1944–5 figures for *IBIBIO* tribes supplied by G. I. Jones.

IBIBIO dialects strongly influenced by IGBO are spoken by the following:

ITO (**ito**), a small section near Arochuku;

ITUMBUZO (**itu mba uzo**), an outlying section near Bende.

EFIK is the best-known dialect, and the one which has become the literary language. Other sections of the *IBIBIO* accept it as such, though speaking their own dialects. The use of EFIK is spreading, and there is a considerable literature, mainly religious and educational, including the whole Bible (at present being revised).

The speech of the following shows some resemblance to the IBIBIO-EFIK Cluster, but relationship is uncertain:

OGONI, call themselves *KANA*, called *OGONI* by the *IGBO*; in Calabar Province, Opobo Division, and Owerri Province, Ahoada Division.
Number: 76,313 (Talbot).
According to Talbot there are several dialects, which differ considerably from each other.
Parts of the New Testament have been published in OGONI, also a few other religious books.

ANDONI, in Calabar Province, south of the *OGONI*.

Linguistic notes on IBIBIO-EFIK

1. EFIK has seven vowel phonemes: **i** (with two members, one of which is centralized and used in closed syllables), **e** (slightly retracted), **ɛ**,[1] **a, ɔ, o** (with two members, the close one used in closed syllables), **u**. IBIBIO appears to have only six vowel phonemes.

The falling diphthongs **ei, ai, ɔi, ui** occur. Rapid pronunciation of vowel combinations such as **ie, ia,** produce the rising diphthongs **ye, ya,** &c.

Vowel length is not significant in EFIK, and if it appears is due to contraction. In IBIBIO, on the other hand, it is of considerable grammatical importance, often differentiating Singular and Plural Verbs.

Nasalization is rare and not significant.

Regular vowel assimilation plays a role in the conjugation of the Verb (see § 14).

2. Labio-velar **kp** occurs, but not **gb**.
There are no true nasal compounds.
Syllabic nasals are common.
Consonantal combinations (e.g. **br, tr, kpr**) occur, but are rare. Some consonants can be doubled.

3. There are two basic tone levels, high and low. Falling and rising tones also occur. A mid, or lowered high, tone is found, as a lexical tone, after another high tone in some Nouns, and also occurs in certain grammatical constructions.

Stress is of secondary importance. Stressing of the Root syllable has been observed.[2]

---

[1] Not differentiated from **e** in the official orthography.
[2] I. C. Ward, *The phonetic and tonal structure of Efik*, p. 29.

4. Most Nouns have a vowel (more rarely a nasal) Prefix. In many cases this Prefix is used to form Nouns from Verbs. The Noun Root is mostly monosyllabic (CV or CVC) or disyllabic (CVCV or CVCVC; sometimes CVV or CVVC), e.g.:

-tó	tree	-bɔ̀ŋ	chief	bíà[1]	yam
-bùòt	head	-dùdù	strength	-búbɔ̀k	post

A few Roots consist of CCV: **-frê**[2] brains; **-ŋwâ** cat.

Verbal Roots are mostly monosyllabic (CV or CVC) or disyllabic (CVCV; there is some reason to believe that these are derived from Roots of the type CVC).

The tonal structure of the syllable is restricted to the pattern high, low, or rising (low-high in disyllables), e.g.:

dép	buy	kéré	think
dù	live	dòrì	put
kǎ	go	fèhé	run

5. There are no Noun Classes. Adjectives and Verbs agree with their Nouns in Number.

6. A Verbal Noun is formed by the Prefix **edi-**. Two kinds of Noun Agent are formed by Prefixes.

7. The Plural is formed either by change of the initial vowel, or, more usually, by addition of a Prefix, e.g.:

      ófǹ Plur. **ifǹ** slave

8. There are special tone-patterns for the Genitive construction, which are the same as those used with Adjectives, e.g.:

ùbóm	canoe	ódúdú úbòm	hole of the canoe
íkɔ́t	bush	àŋwâ ìkɔ̀t	cat of the bush (bush cat)
ówó		ìtîm òwò	doorpost of the man

9. There is no grammatical gender.

10. The forms of the Subject Pronouns (Pronominal Prefixes) differ in Positive and Negative (see §§ 14, 15). The Independent Personal Pronouns, Objective Pronouns, and Possessives in EFIK are:

	Independent	*Object*	*Possessive*	*Plur.*
1.	àmì	mî	mì	ǹnyìn
2.	àfò	fî	fò	m̀bùfò
3.	ènyé	ènyé	ésìé	m̀mɔ́

There are also Referring Pronouns: Sing. **ímɔ́**, Plur. **m̀mìmɔ́**.

11. The conjugation of the Verb is homogeneous; there are no morphological Verb Classes or Tone Classes.

---

[1] One of the rare examples of a Noun without Prefix.
[2] Also pronounced as a disyllable **fərê**.

12. EFIK does not seem to possess a great number of Verbal Derivatives. Some Verbs have a Reflexive–Passive formed by a vowel Suffix. A few Verbs form an Inversive by the Suffix **-re**. In IBIBIO, however, Verbal Derivatives (Reflexive–Passive, Inversive, Reciprocal) are much more common.

13. The Verb Root is not invariable. It changes its inherent tone in some Tenses, either throughout the Tense (e.g. Conversational Present and Habitual) or in some Persons of certain Roots (Interrogative).

From the Verb Root may be distinguished the Tense Stem, i.e. the Root enlarged by a Tense Prefix, e.g. **nám** do; **kánám** (Stem of Perfect Tense). This Prefix has in the majority of cases a constant tone, but can vary in tone according to Tense (thus distinguishing Conditional from Final) or Person (in the Present Perfect). In form this Prefix is liable to vowel assimilation.

In some Verbs a Plural Stem is formed from the Verb Root either by a Suffix or by other means. This system is much more developed in IBIBIO than in EFIK.

14. The Verb is conjugated by adding Pronominal Prefixes to the Root (or Plural Stem) or to the Tense Stem. The Pronominal Prefixes are:

	Sing.	*Plur.*
1.	nasal	i
2.	harmonizing vowel	e
3.	harmonizing vowel	e

The tones of the Prefixes vary in different tenses. In most Tenses the 2nd and 3rd Persons are distinguished by tone (see below).

There are five Simple Tenses[1] (Pronominal Prefix+Root): Narrative, Conversational Present, Interrogative, Conditional, and Subjunctive (Hortative), and a number of Compound Tenses (Pronominal Prefix+Tense Stem): two Futures, Present Perfect, Perfect, another Conditional, Final, and Habitual.

Change of tone in the Root and Pronominal Prefix are shown in the following examples (Verb **dù** to live):

		Narrative	*Subjunctive*	*Perfect*
Sing.	1.	ń-dù	ń-dû	ŋ́-kó-dù[2]
	2.	ó-dù	ò-dû	ò-kó-dù
	3.	ó-dù	ó-dû	ó-kó-dù
Plur.	1.	í-dù	ì-dû	ì-kó-dù
	2.	é-dù	è-dû	è-kó-dù
	3.	é-dù	é-dû	é-kó-dù

15. There are six Negative Tenses: Simple Form, Perfect, Future, Conditional, Habitual, and Subjunctive. For the first five of these Tenses there is a special set of Pronominal Prefixes. These five Tenses have a Suffix (**-ke** with varying tone) and special tone patterns.

[1] The terminology is that used by I. C. Ward, op. cit. [2] From **-ká** by assimilation.

The Negative Personal Prefixes are:

	Sing.	Plur.
1.	nasal	í
2.	ú	í
3.	í	í

e.g.: ń-dép-ké I do not buy; í-sí-dèp-kè he does not habitually buy.

The Negative Subjunctive is formed by attaching the Positive Pronominal Prefixes (see § 14) to a Negative Stem consisting of the Prefix di- or ku-+Verb Root. The tone of the Pronominal Prefix is low for all Persons, but there is a characteristic tone pattern for the Tense, e.g.:

kút	to see	ǹ-dí-kùt	that I may not see
wòt	to kill	è-dí-wòt	that you may not kill
		ò-kû-wòt	that he may not kill

16. Word order in the simple sentence is Subject–Verb–Object.

17. In the Genitive construction the *nomen rectum* follows the *nomen regens*. For Genitive tone pattern see § 8.

18. Adjectives (including ordinal Numerals) precede the Noun, which has the same tone pattern as in the Genitive construction.
Cardinal Numerals follow the Noun.

19. The Copula is expressed by a Verb, e.g.:

enye edi akamba owo   he is a great man (**di** = to be)

Note on OGONI and ANDONI[1]

1. In OGONI monosyllabic Roots (CV) are very common.

2. Most Nouns have no Prefix in OGONI, but ANDONI has Noun Prefixes, e.g.

OGONI **tɔn**   ANDONI **ɔtɔn** ear

3. In both languages the *nomen rectum* precedes the *nomen regens*; the Possessive Pronoun precedes the Noun in OGONI, follows it in ANDONI, e.g.:

| OGONI | **na be** | my name | ANDONI | **ŋguŋ a** | my child |
| | **olo be** | your name | | | |

4. Adjectives, Numerals, and Demonstratives precede the Noun in OGONI; the Numeral follows in ANDONI, e.g.:

OGONI	**to**	house		
	ba to	two houses		
	ba tɔŋ	two ears	ANDONI	**otɔn ɛba**

[1] From the slight material given by N. W. Thomas, *Specimens of languages from Southern Nigeria*.

ISOLATED LANGUAGE GROUPS OR UNITS

Isolated Language Group or Unit? ANGAS

Where spoken: Nigeria: Plateau Province.

ANGAS. Language or Dialect Cluster?

Spoken by: *ANGAS* (*ANGASS*), call themselves *KERANG* (*KARANG*) or *KARANG-MA* (**-ma** being a Plural Suffix).

Where spoken: Pankshin Division of Plateau Province.

Number of speakers: 55,242.[1]

The *ANGAS* are in two sections, known to Europeans as 'Hill' and 'Plains' *ANGAS*; the latter are also said to call themselves **gurna**.

Parts of the New Testament have been translated, and there are a few readers and elementary religious books.

The following either speak dialects of the ANGAS Cluster, or languages belonging to the same Group:

ANKWE, call themselves *KEMAI* (*GOEMAI*); south of the *ANGAS* in Shendam Division.
   Number: 13,507.[1]
   A Gospel has been published.

SURA, in Pankshin Division, North and South Sura Districts.
   Number: 20,107.[1]
   Parts of the Bible have been published in 'SURA (MAGHAVUL)', and there are a few primers.

Linguistic and dialectal subdivisions are not known. A number of small tribes or tribal sections are connected with the *ANGAS–ANKWE–SURA*, but are regarded as separate for Census purposes. Opinions differ as to whether they all speak dialects of this Cluster; some of them may speak languages or dialects related to TIV.

The speech of the following may also be related to ANGAS:

RON (*BARON*)[2] (called *CHALA* in the Census); in the south-eastern part of Pankshin Division.
   Number: 11,613.
   Probably include the people referred to by Thomas[3] as *NAFUNFIA*.

PYEM (*PAIEMA, PAYEMA, PEMAWA*, &c.), also known as 'Gindiri'; in Pankshin Division and on the Bauchi–Plateau Province border.
   Number: 7,732.

Note: Foulkes[4] draws attention to affinities of ANGAS with HAUSA; relationship cannot, however, be shown to be sufficiently close to justify the classification of ANGAS in the CHADO-HAMITIC Languages. ANGAS has no grammatical gender.

---
[1] Ames, *Gazetteer of Plateau Province*.
[2] Not to be confused with *BIROM* or *BURUM* (see p. 106).
[3] In Meek, *Tribal Studies*.
[4] *Angas manual*.

Isolated Unit? JEN

JEN. Language or Dialect Cluster?

Spoken by: JEN, call themselves **dza**.

Where spoken: Nigeria: Adamawa Province, on the north bank of the Benue about Lat. 9° N., Long. 11° E.

According to Meek the phonology of JEN differs from other languages in the neighbourhood; linguistic material is not sufficient for any classification to be made.

There may be several dialects: Meek gives vocabularies of JEN and of the dialect of the *MUNGA*, possibly an offshoot of the *JEN*.

Note: The *JEN* are included in the *BACHAMA* in the Census, but there appears to be no justification for this, at least on linguistic grounds.

Isolated Language Group? MUMUYE

Consists of: MUMUYE   Dialect Cluster?
'Yendang'   Dialect Cluster?

Where spoken: Nigeria: Adamawa Province, mainly in Muri Division, in the hill country between Jalingo in the west and Mayo Belwa in the east.

The name *MUMUYE* is a general term applied to various people speaking dialects of both Clusters; many of them acknowledge the name, but they mostly call themselves by their own local names.

The division of dialects spoken by the so-called *MUMUYE* is based on Meek.

MUMUYE. Dialect Cluster?

Number of speakers: 79,272 (it is not clear, however, which peoples are included in this figure—see below).

Dialects which appear to be closely interrelated are spoken by:
PUGU ('Hill *MUMUYE*'); 'Zinna'; 'Ding-ding'; *YAKOKO* (**yakɔkɔ**); *GOLA*; 'Bajama'.

A Gospel and primer have been published in MUMUYE.

'Yendang'. Dialect Cluster?

Dialects which appear to be closely interrelated, but to differ from the MUMUYE dialects, are spoken by:

'Yendang' (1,984) and 'Waka', east of Zinna in Bajama District;

'Kumba', 'Yofo', 'Sate', 'Kuseki'; in Mayo Belwa District;

BALI and *PASSAM* (locality not stated);

'Gengle' (call themselves *WEGELE*), 'Kugama' (call themselves *WEGAM*) and 'Teme'; in Mayo Belwa District.

ISOLATED LANGUAGE GROUPS OR UNITS

Isolated Unit? IDOMA[1]

Note: There is very great confusion of nomenclature as between the *IDOMA*, *IGBIRA* (see p. 87), and *IGALA* (see p. 85); moreover, the *JABA* are also said to be known as *DOMA* (see p. 105); the name *OKPOTO (KWOTTO)*, originally used by the *HAUSA* and *FULANI*, is applied by Europeans to (*a*) the *IDOMA* and their language, the *IDOMA* even being sometimes called *OKPOTO IGALA*, (*b*) part of the *IGALA*, (*c*) a section of the *IGBIRA*, (*d*) a section of the *ORRI* (see p. 116).

IDOMA. Dialect Cluster.

Spoken by: *IDOMA*.

Where spoken: Nigeria: Benue Province, mainly in Idoma Division, west of the *TIV*.

Number of speakers: 117, 773 (this figure is, however, unreliable).

Dialects: Abraham[2] distinguishes the following dialects (the same names are used for the people speaking them, and are mostly those of localities):

OTUKPO
IGUMALE
OKWOGA
OTUKPA
AGATU

The OTUKPO dialect is understood by all *IDOMA*.

Parts of the New Testament have been translated, and some tentative translations of religious books have been made into the IGUMALE dialect.

The *ARAGO* of Lafia Emirate are also said to be a section of the *IDOMA* and to speak an IDOMA dialect.

Number: 13,293.

A Gospel and primer have been published.

The *IDOMA* are said to be of *JUKUN* origin, and their language to be to some extent connected with JUKUN,[3] but available evidence is not sufficient to show whether IDOMA and JUKUN should be considered to belong to one Group.

Isolated Unit? JUKUN

JUKUN. Dialect Cluster.

Spoken by: *JUKUN (JUKUM, JUKŪ, JUKON)*, also known as *KUROROFA (KURARAPA, KWARARAFA), URAPANG, GBAGBANG, BAIBAI, APPA (APA, AKPA), KE (WIKE), NDAMA*, called **kwana** by the *BACHAMA*, **jukun** by many of their neighbours, **kwanaba** by the *LONGUDA*, **wapā** or **can** by the *TIGONG*, **ocan** or **can** by the 'Batu', **kpā** by the 'Nyidu'.

---

[1] R. G. Armstrong (in a personal communication) states that IDOMA is related to IGALA (see p. 85).   [2] *The principles of Idoma.*

[3] Temple, *Notes on the Tribes, Provinces* . . .; Abraham, *The Tiv people.*

NON-CLASS LANGUAGES

Where spoken: Nigeria: mainly in Benue and Adamawa Provinces, with centres Wukari and Donga.

Number of speakers: 31,975 (but this figure includes the *RINDRI* (see p. 107) of Wamba District, and does not include the peoples speaking JUKUN as second language).

Dialects: According to Meek there are six dialects, of which five are spoken in the following areas:

Donga;
Wukari; the people call themselves **wapã**;
Kona; the people call themselves **jibə**;
Gwana and Pindiga;
Wase Tofa in Plateau Province;
the sixth dialect is that spoken by the *JIBU* (*JIBAWA*; Tessmann's *DSCHUBU*?) in Adamawa Province between Gashaka and Bakundi.

JUKUN is also spoken by the WURBO ('people of the water'), a fishing people scattered along the Benue between Lau and Abinsi; it is used as a lingua franca over a considerable area. It is also spoken by the *KENTU* as well as their own language or dialect.

According to Meek there is considerable difference between the dialects, that of Wukari being markedly different from the rest.

One Gospel has been published in each of the dialects of Kona, Wukari, and Donga; there are also some elementary readers.

Some of the so-called *TIGONG* (*TUGUN*, *TUKUN*)[1] of Adamawa Province (mandated territory) are said by Meek to speak dialects which are closely related to JUKUN in vocabulary and grammar, though not in phonology. From his vocabularies it would appear that in these dialects the Plural is formed by various Suffixes, while in JUKUN the Singular and Plural seem to be identical.

Note: The name *WURKUM* (*WURKUN*), used by some writers as a tribal name, is really only the JUKUN name for several small tribes or sections,[2] some of whom possibly speak JUKUN dialects.

A Gospel has been published in 'WURKUM'.

Isolated Unit? MBEMBE[3]

MBEMBE (IZARE, NSARE), own name **ñɔ̀àlé**. Dialect Cluster?

Note: The name AKONTO has also been applied to this language.

Spoken by: *MBEMBE*[4] (a collective name for several tribes or sections, also known as *TIGONG*).[1]

---

[1] For other '*TIGONG*' see pp. 113, 143. [2] See also p. 115.
[3] Information from I. Richardson, unless otherwise stated.
[4] Not to be confused with the *MBEMBE* of Ogoja Province (see p. 116), nor with the *MBEM* of Bamenda Province. The latter are said to speak a language related to that of the *NFUMTE* (*MFUMTE*), but nothing further is known of their speech. Both *MBEM* and *NFUMTE*, together with the *MBAW* (*MBO*), were formerly known as *KAKA* or *KAKA-NTEM*.

Where spoken: British Cameroons, Bamenda Province, Mbembe District; also in Wukari Division, Benue Province.

Number of speakers: 2,893 TP.*

According to E. Meyer there is considerable difference between the dialects (or languages) spoken by the *MBEMBE*; Richardson, however, reports that the language is stated to be uniform.

Linguistic notes on MBEMBE

1. Particular sounds noted include:

    implosive **kɓ, gɓ**;
    consonant combinations with **r**, e.g.: **θr, ðr, fr, vr**, &c.;
    syllabic **w**.

2. There are no ascertainable Noun Classes. Note, however, that according to Meyer the dialect of **akwɛŋko** (place-name) has a Class system of sorts, Singular and Plural of Nouns being formed by Suffixes, but there is no Concord.

3. The Plural is formed:

    (a) by change of final vowel, e.g.:

θrì	Plur.	**θrǎ**	thigh
m̀frú		**m̀fræ̀**	spear

    (b) by change of tone, e.g.:

vè	**vé**	animal

    and by various other means (never, however, by Prefix).

4. Tone is significant, e.g.

vè	see	**vè**	animal	**vé**	animals
θɛ̀	cry			**θɛ́**	work

5. Roots are monosyllabic (CV).

6. There is vocabulary resemblance with JUKUN.

Isolated Unit? NDORO

NDORO. Language?

Spoken by: *NDORO* (**ndɔro**).

Where spoken: Cameroons: Gashaka District, and Benue Province, Wukari Division.

Number of speakers: 1,169.

Meek 'provisionally' includes NDORO in the 'NKI' Group (see BOKI, pp. 114–15), but adds, 'it can hardly be classed as a Semi-Bantu language'.

NON-CLASS LANGUAGES

Isolated Unit? KENTU

KENTU. Dialect Cluster?

Spoken by: *KENTU*, call themselves **etkyẽ**.

Where spoken: Benue Province, Wukari Division, Donga District, and across the border into the Cameroons (Gashaka District).

Number of speakers: 6,330* in Donga District.

Meek, who gives two vocabularies, of KENTU and 'Nyidu', 'provisionally' includes KENTU in the 'NKI' Group, but the vocabularies show no evidence of Noun Classes.

All the *KENTU* also speak JUKUN.

Isolated Language Group? MAMBILA

Consists of: MAMBILA Dialect Cluster.
BUNGNU Dialect Cluster?

MAMBILA. Dialect Cluster.

Spoken by: *MAMBILA* (*MABILA, MAMBILLA, MAMBERE*), call themselves **nor** ('men'), called **ba-mɛmbila** by the 'Abö', **omavırre** by the 'Batu', **kətɔba** by the *KILA* (blacksmiths among the *MAMBILA*), **luɛn** by the *BUNGNU*. Some of the *MAMBILA* are also known as *TORBI* (probably a FULANI name); the southern *MAMBILA* are also known as *TAGBO, TONGBO*, or *LAGUBI*.

Where spoken: Nigeria: Adamawa Province (mandated territory), Gashaka and Mambila Districts, on the Mambila plateau; there are said to be some *MAMBILA* in Bamenda Division, British Cameroons, and in the French Cameroons.

Number of speakers: 15,835.[1]

Dialects: According to Meek there are two main dialectal divisions:
Northern, including the villages of Kuma, Titon, Kabri;
Southern, including the villages of Warwar, Mbamgam, Wa.

The language or dialects spoken by the following are closely related to MAMBILA, but not sufficiently to be considered MAMBILA dialects, according to Meek:

BUNGNU, also known as *KAMKAM, KAKABA*, call themselves *BUNGNU*; adjacent to the *MAMBILA*.
Number: 800.

'Magu' (also sometimes known as *TIGONG*—see also pp. 113, 141), and 'Ndunda'. Meek heads his vocabulary of this dialect MVANIP, without further explanation of the name.

Linguistic notes on MAMBILA[2]

1. Eight cardinal vowels and five centralized vowels have been noted; the latter include two with lip-rounding (**ü** and **ö**).

[1] Government figures.   [2] E. Meyer, 'Mambila-Studie' (*Z. Eingeb. Spr.*, 1939/40).

2. Consonants include the labio-dental affricate **bv** and the dental fricative **θ**. **t**, **d**, and **n** are dental.
Labio-velar **kp** and **gb** do not occur; there are no implosives.
Nasal compounds occur.

3. Tone is of lexical and perhaps also of grammatical importance. There is strong stress.

4. Roots normally begin with a consonant. The forms CV, CVC and CVV, CVVC are of frequent occurrence.

5. There are no Noun Classes; there is no grammatical gender.

6. The Plural of Nouns is not normally differentiated from the Singular; in some cases a Plural Suffix **-bo (-bə)** is used. The Plural of Nouns denoting persons may also be formed by the addition of **ba** (= people).

7. Case is shown by position in the sentence.

8. There are Prepositions and a few Postpositions.

9. The Verb Root is invariable in shape. Reduplication of the Root occurs, but without morphological significance, i.e. only in cases where the Verb stands without a following Object.

10. The only trace of Verbal Derivatives known is an Inversive, formed by various Suffixes. There is no Passive.

11. The following Tenses have been noted:
Simple form: Subject (Pronoun or Noun)+Verb Root;
Perfect, with Suffix **-í (-é)** and a verbal Postposition denoting completion;
Habitual, formed with a Particle following the Root;
Future, formed with a Particle preceding the Root.

12. Negation is expressed by a negative Particle immediately following the Verb Root, e.g. **me kɛl wal** I know not.
There is a Negative Copula which stands at the end of the sentence; it appears to be identical with the word for 'No'.

13. Word order in the simple sentence is Subject–Verb–Object. If the Verb is negatived the order is Subject–Object–Verb.

14. In the Genitive construction the *nomen rectum* follows the *nomen regens* and has the Suffix **-i** or **-e**, e.g.:

jü baturəm-i language of the European

15. Subject and Predicate may be, but are not always, joined by a Copula.

NON-CLASS LANGUAGES

16. The vocabulary, apart from some loan-words from Bantu and other Class languages and from VUTE, appears to be entirely unrelated to any other language.

ISOLATED UNIT: VUTE

VUTE. LANGUAGE OR DIALECT CLUSTER.

Spoken by: *VUTE* (*WUTE*, *BUTE*, also known as *BABUTE*, *BABUTI*), call themselves *VUTERE* (Sing. *VUTE*).

Where spoken: Scattered over a wide area in the French Cameroons north of River Sanaga, east of the *TIKAR*, extending north to Tibati, east to *BAYA* territory.

Number of speakers: 16,121.[1]

Little is known about VUTE, and the dialectal differences have not been studied.

According to Tessmann the following speak dialects related to VUTE:

'Galim', among the *MBUM*;

SUGA (*SSUGA, JEMJEM, NJEMNJEM*), on River Gendero.

ISOLATED LANGUAGE GROUP? MBUM[2]

Consists of:
MUNDANG	Dialect Cluster.
MANGBAI	Language?
TUPURI	Dialect Cluster.
KERA	Language?
MONO	Language?
MBUM	Dialect Cluster.
KARI	Dialect Cluster.

Where spoken: Over a wide area in the French Cameroons, extending into Chad.

MUNDANG. DIALECT CLUSTER.

Spoken by: *MUNDANG* (Fr. *MOUNDAN*), called *BANA*, *MBANA* by the *FULANI*.

Where spoken: In two areas: north-west of Binder in the southern part of Maroua subdivision, and in Lere subdivision.

Dialect spoken in Lere.
Number: 45,148.

Dialect spoken in Gelama (Gelami) (this dialect differs somewhat from the others).
Number: not known; few.

Dialect spoken by *JASING* (*JASSING, YASSING*).
Number: 25,000.

---

[1] Dugast, 'Inventaire ethnique du sud-Cameroun'.
[2] Much of the information on this group, including population figures, was supplied by Fr. van Bulck.

The IMBANA of Barth[1] is a MUNDANG dialect.

Parts of the New Testament have been published in MUNDANG.

MANGBAI. LANGUAGE?

Spoken by: *MANGBAI* (*MANGBEI*), call themselves **mambai**.

Where spoken: In Guidar and Garoua subdivisions, and in one village in Chad.

Number: French Cameroons 3,051, Chad 860.

TUPURI. DIALECT CLUSTER.

Spoken by: *TUPURI*, call themselves **tupuri** in the west, **tuburi** in the east; also known as *NDORE*, which name they themselves acknowledge.

Dialect spoken at Kaele.
Number: 24,310.

Dialect spoken at Yagoua (French Cameroons) and Fianga and Pala (Chad).
Number: 62,200.

The dialect given by Mouchet[2] is identical with the MATA of Lukas.[3]

There are also about 15,000 *TUPURI* mixed with *FULANI*, who probably speak FULANI.

KERA. LANGUAGE?

Spoken by: *KERA*, call themselves **kɛɾa**.

Where spoken: North and south of Lake Tikem.

Number of speakers: 15,000.

It is not certain whether KERA is to be considered as a separate language, but it differs considerably from TUPURI, according to van Bulck.

MONO. LANGUAGE?

Spoken by: *MONO*, call themselves **mɔ̃nɔ̃**.

Where spoken: North-east of Rei Buba (Rey Bouba).

It is not certain whether MONO is to be considered as a separate language.

MBUM. DIALECT CLUSTER.

Spoken by: *MBUM*.

Where spoken: widely scattered, mainly between Tibati in the south-west and the area north-east of Ngaoundere.

Number of speakers: *c.* 20,000, according to E. Meyer.

---

[1] In Benton, *Notes on some languages of the western Sudan*.
[2] 'Vocabulaires comparatifs de 15 parlers du Nord-Cameroun' (part 1) (*J. Soc. Afric.*, 1938).
[3] *Zentralsudanische Studien*.

NON-CLASS LANGUAGES

Dialects: According to information given to van Bulck, *MBUM* dialects are spoken by:
- mbum njal;
- mbum babal;
- mbum ŋger (*MBERE*), east of the main *MBUM* area, mainly between Rivers Wina and Wora;[1]
- mbum tiba.

The *PERE* (*KEPERE, KPER, RIPERE*, &c.), south of the main *MBUM* area, south-east of Yoko, are also said to be a part of the *MBUM* and to speak a MBUM dialect, which they call kəpɛrɛ.[2]

The *PANI* are also said to be a part of the *MBUM*; on the other hand, they may be the same as the *PANA* (see below under KARI).

Many *MBUM* are Islamized and now speak ARABIC; they are known as *MBUM BELAKA*.

Parts of the New Testament have been translated into MBUM.

KARI. DIALECT CLUSTER.

Dialect spoken by *KARI* (*KALI, KARE*), in the French Cameroons, Kare mountains, east of Rei Buba; in Chad, between Lia and Pawa.

Dialect spoken by *TALI*,[3] in Chad.

Dialect spoken by *PANA*, in Chad.

Dialect spoken by *GUNJE*, in Chad.

Speakers of the last three dialects together number about 40,000.

Linguistic notes on the MBUM Group

1. Labio-velars are characteristic of the Group;
   TUPURI has **b, ɓ**, and **p**;
   KERA has flapped **ɽ**;
   TUPURI and MUNDANG have **v** and **f** as well as bilabial **ʋ** and **ƒ**.

2. Tone is both lexical and grammatical; there are probably three levels (noted in TUPURI by Mouchet[4] and in MBUM by Tessmann[5] and Flottum).[6]

3. The Plural is formed by a Suffix of the shape **-ri**.

4. Mouchet notes a 3rd Person Feminine Pronoun in MONO and MUNDANG. Otherwise there does not appear to be grammatical Gender.

---

[1] Sometimes known as *LAKA MBERE*, but appear to be quite distinct from the *LAKA* whose language belongs to the BONGO-BAGIRMI Group. [2] According to I. Richardson.
[3] '*TALLA*' is erroneously included among the BAYA-speaking tribes by Bruel (*La France Équatoriale Africaine*) and Poutrin (*Esquisse des principales populations* . . .). [4] Loc. cit.
[5] 'Die Sprache der Mbakka-Limba, Mbum und Lakka' (*M.S.O.S.*, 1930).
[6] 'Le lapin et la famine' (*Ét. Camerounaises*, 1950).

5. Verbal Derivatives are frequent and are formed in many different ways, e.g. by tone, by change of Root vowel, &c.

6. The Verb system appears to vary greatly as between languages. Tenses are formed mostly by change of tone, sometimes by Suffix.

In MBUM the Verb is conjugated by placing pronominal forms before the Verb Stem, e.g.:

Pronoun+Verb Stem+**ra**	Narrative
Pronoun+Verb Stem+**wa**	Perfect
Pronoun+Verbal Noun+**mo**	Future
Pronoun+**ka**+Verbal Noun	Progressive

7. Word order in the simple sentence is Subject–Verb–Object.

8. In the Genitive construction the *nomen rectum* follows the *nomen regens*, with Linking Particle, probably in non-Intimate Genitive.

9. The Qualificative follows the Noun.

10. Vocabulary relationship between the languages is shown especially in Numerals,[1] Pronominal Stems (Personal and Demonstrative), and in words such as 'ear', 'nose', 'tooth', 'water', &c.

Isolated Language Group? CHAMBA

Consists of:
DURU	Dialect Cluster?
CHAMBA	Dialect Cluster.
CHAMBA DAKA	Dialect Cluster?
VERE	Dialect Cluster?

Where spoken: British and French Cameroons.

DURU. Dialect Cluster?[2]

Dialects possibly belonging to one Cluster are spoken by the following:

DURU (DURRU), in French Cameroons between Rivers Benue and Faro, also east of the Benue among the *MBUM*.
   Number: 2,000.[3]

   Note: *DUI* is the name of a section of the *DURU* at the foot of the Sari massif, some of whom appear also to be known as *PANI*.
   Strümpell's vocabularies of Northern (DUI) and Southern DURU show slight divergencies only.[4]

'Sari' ('Ssari'), on Sari massif north of the *DURU*.

---

[1] Note that Numerals of this Group show some resemblance to those of SOMRAI.

[2] Figures for the DURU Cluster from Griaule, 'Vocabulaires Papé, Woko, Kutinn, Namtchi et Séwé du Cameroun septentrional' (*J. Soc. Afric.*, 1941), unless otherwise stated.

[3] 'Inventaire ethnique et linguistique du Cameroun sous mandat Français' (*J. Soc. Afric.*, 1934).

[4] 'Vergleichendes Wörterverzeichnis der Heidensprachen Adamauas' (*Z. für Ethnol.*, 1910) (hereafter referred to as 'Adamaua').

NON-CLASS LANGUAGES

PAPE, call themselves *PANON* (**panõ**?), called *PAPE* by the *FULANI*; on Sari massif, south and west of the *NAMCI*.
Number: 3,664.
This dialect appears to be almost identical with that of the 'Sari'.

NAMCI (*NAMTCHI, NAMJI*, &c.); in the neighbourhood of Poli.
Number: 11,156.
There appear to be several dialects, of which that spoken in the south shows considerable resemblance to the dialects of the 'Sari' and *PAPE*, while those spoken at Poli and Sewe (north-west of Poli) closely resemble each other and the dialect of the *WOKO*. Baudelaire[1] differentiates between the *DUPA*, adjacent to the *PAPE*, whose dialect is related to DURU, and the *DOAYO* of Poli who speak a different dialect. Both are known as *NAMCI*.

WOKO (*VOKO, BOKO*), south-east of the *NAMCI* on the spurs of the Sari massif.
Number: 946.

KOTOPO (*KOTOFO, KOTTOFO, KOTPOJO*), in the Kontcha area, east and west of River Mao Deo.
Struck[2] differentiates between KOTPOJO and KOTOPO, stating that the latter is a dialect of the former.

KOMA, west of River Mao Deo.
Number: 2,907.
Tessmann[3] considers the dialect of the *KOMA* to be related to the DURU dialects, on the basis of unpublished material collected by Dühring.

KUTINN (*KUTIN*), west of River Nyal (tributary of River Faro).
Number: 426.
Griaule considers their dialect to be related to DURU.

CHAMBA. DIALECT CLUSTER.

The name *CHAMBA* covers a number of small groups of people in Nigeria (Benue and Adamawa Provinces), British and French Cameroons. According to Meek they call themselves *SAMA, SAMABU* (-**bu** being a Plural Suffix), and are called **diŋyim, diŋi, dima** by neighbouring tribes.

The following *CHAMBA* groups speak dialects which are closely interrelated, and which show some vocabulary resemblance to the DURU Cluster:

CHAMBA of Donga, call themselves **diŋa**;

CHAMBA LEKON (*LEKO, LAEGO*) and *CHAMBA* of Kugana, on the French Cameroons border;

'Wom', call themselves *PEREBA*, called *ZAGAI* by the *VERE*; in Adamawa Province, Vere District;

---

[1] 'La numération de 1 à 10 dans les dialectes Habé de Garoua, Guider, Poli et Rey Bouba' (*Bull. Soc. Et. Camerounaises*, 1944). Note the use of the name *HABE* to cover several tribes, and cp. note under DOGON, p. 61.   [2] Introduction to Strümpell, 'Adamaua'.
[3] 'Die Völker und Sprachen Kameruns.'

MUMBAKE (MUBAKO), call themselves *NYONGNEPA*;[1] in Adamawa Province;

KOLBILA (KOLBILLA, KOLBILARI), adjacent to the *DURU* at Bantadje, in French Cameroons.

The *BALI* of Bamenda Province, British Cameroons, are a *CHAMBA* offshoot, and a dialect which appears to be almost identical with that of the *CHAMBA* of Donga[2] is spoken by some of them (for the speech of the other *BALI* see p. 122). This dialect is **ndaɢam**, spoken by the **nɛkɔvibla** of Balikumbat, also at Baligasho and Baligansi, and at Balibagam[3] on the French Cameroons border.

> *Note*: Another name used as that of a language is **mubakʊ** (Richardson), **məbakɔ** (Vielhauer[4]), or **mubako** (Meyer); this language is said to be a different language from BALI (**ŋɡaa ka**), and to be a non-Class language, 'the original BALI language'.[5] According to Meyer it is still spoken in a few homesteads. It is not clear whether this is another name for **ndaɢam** or not.

CHAMBA DAKA. DIALECT CLUSTER?

The dialects of the following *CHAMBA* peoples in Adamawa Province are closely interrelated, according to Meek, but differ considerably in vocabulary from both the CHAMBA and DURU Clusters:

CHAMBA DAKA, call themselves **sama**; in Muri Emirate and British Cameroons;

CHAMBA (TSUGU), in Adamawa Province;

CHAMBA of Nassarao, Adamawa Province;

LAMJA of Maio Faran.

One Gospel has been translated into CHAMBA DAKA.

VERE. DIALECT CLUSTER?

Spoken by: VERE (*VERRE, WERE, YERE*—Griaule's spelling *VÉRÈ*[6] suggests that the name may be **verɛ**; said to call themselves **jiri**.

Where spoken: South of Yola in Vere District on the Nigeria–French Cameroons border.

Number of speakers: Nigeria 10,866.

The *VERE* consist of a number of local groups, of which Meek gives a list; there are probably dialectal variations.

---

[1] For MUMBAKE see also note on **mubakʊ** below; for NYONGNEPA see also **nyoŋa** under BALI **ŋɡaa ka** (p. 122).

[2] From comparison of the **ndaɢam** vocabulary collected by Richardson with Meek's CHAMBA of Donga.

[3] Not to be confused with Bagam on the French side of the border, where a BAMILEKE language is spoken (see p. 129). [4] *Grundzüge einer Grammatik der Balisprache*.

[5] According to I. Richardson's informant, the official interpreter.

[6] 'Vocabulaires Papé, Woko....'

NON-CLASS LANGUAGES

The vocabulary shows resemblance to the DURU and CHAMBA dialects, but no further linguistic material is available. Note, however, that changes in the form of the attribute suggest a concord between Noun and attribute, and thus perhaps a kind of class division of the Noun. It is therefore far from certain that VERE belongs to this Group.

Linguistic notes on BALI ndaGam[1]

1. Particular sounds noted include:

   long vowels;
   several central vowels;
   unrounded ɯ;
   unexploded plosives;
   dental t;
   implosive kɓ, gɓ, ɓ, ɗ;
   q and G.

2. There are no Noun Classes. Singular Nouns end in -a, Plurals in -bla (-bəla, -bila).

3. There appear to be two level tones, high and low, also rising and falling tones.

Isolated Unit? FALI

FALI. Dialect Cluster.

Spoken by: FALI.

FALI is a collective name given by the *FULANI* to a number of tribes or tribal sections. Some of them speak interrelated dialects, and acknowledge the name *FALI*, but call themselves **mɔŋɔ** or **mɔŋgɔ**. The speech of other so-called *FALI* appears to be related to the BURA and BATA Groups of the CHADIC languages (see pp. 154, 156).

Where spoken: Mainly in French Cameroons, northward from Garoua to about Lat. 10° N.

Dialects:[2] FALI dialects are spoken by the following:

FALI of Bouzoum, north of Peske, east of Gider.
   Number: 11,600.

FALI of Peske, Bori, and Zabkar, call themselves **ni-gɔbri-ai** (Sing. **ni gɔbri**).
   Number: 8,201.

FALI of Durbayi.
   Number: 5,953.

FALI of Kangu plateau, call themselves **ni-kaŋ**.
   Number: (see p. 152).

---

[1] From I. Richardson.
[2] Information from Lebeuf, 'Les rites funéraires chez les Fali'(*J. Soc. Afric.*, 1938) and 'Vocabulaire comparé de 16 villages Fali' (*J. Soc. Afric.*, 1941), and from van Bulck.

ISOLATED LANGUAGE GROUPS OR UNITS

FALI of Tingelin plateau, call themselves **ni-gɔbri**; also the people of Banayo village and neighbourhood.

Number: 18,000 together with the FALI of Kangu.

Strümpell[1] includes under *FALI* the *DABA* (but see pp. 158–9), 'Mubi' (but see CHEKE, p. 156), and others.

According to Lebeuf[2] a FALI dialect is spoken at Bela in Nigeria, but van Bulck queries this statement.

---

[1] 'Wörterverzeichnis der Heidensprachen des Mandara-Gebirges' (*Z. Eingeb. Spr.*, 1922/3) (hereafter referred to as 'Mandara').

[2] 'Vocabulaire comparé. . . .'

Section IX
THE CHADIC LANGUAGES
LARGER UNIT?

THE CHADIC and CHADO-HAMITIC languages are spoken in an area centred on the neighbourhood of Lake Chad. The term CHADIC is here used to denote languages spoken mainly south-west of Lake Chad. They have certain elements in common (see p. 160) with other languages spoken south of Chad, which, however, also show distinct HAMITIC features (see pp. 169–70) and are therefore termed CHADO-HAMITIC.[1]

The CHADIC languages are mostly very little known, and the classification given here must therefore be regarded as tentative.

LANGUAGE GROUP ? BURA

Consists of: BURA   Language?
MARGI   Dialect Cluster.
and perhaps other units.

Where spoken: Nigeria: Adamawa and Bornu Provinces, extending into the French Cameroons.

BURA. LANGUAGE?

Spoken by: BURA (*BURRA*, Fr. *BOURRAH*), call themselves **bura,** called **huve** by the *BATA-GUDU*, *HUVIYA* by the *HONA*, **tɔxrica** by the 'Gabin'.

Where spoken: Bornu Province, Bornu Emirate, Biu Division, and Mokolo sub-division in the French Cameroons.

Number of speakers: Nigeria 72,213; French Cameroons 16,500.[2]

A section called *BURA KOKRA* (23,144) is reported north-west of Biu, but nothing is known of their speech.[3]

BURA is used for education in mission schools. The New Testament has been translated, and is being revised (1950); there are a few readers.

BURA is also spoken by the *BABUR* (*BABIR*, *PABIR*), called **pabɪr** by the *MARGI*, **babɪr** by the *SUKUR*; in Bornu Province, north-west of Biu.

Note: MAGHA appears to be the name of a language spoken west of the *BABUR*, of which, however, nothing is known.[3]

---
[1] A similar situation may be observed in the case of the NILOTIC and NILO-HAMITIC languages.
[2] 'Inventaire ethnique et linguistique. . . .'
[3] Information from M. Pindar, Visiting Teacher, Biu.

MARGI. DIALECT CLUSTER.

Spoken by: *MARGI* (*MARGHI*), call themselves **margi**, called **mırki** by the *FALI* of Kiria, **buxɪdɪm** by the *SUKUR*.

Where spoken: In the south-eastern part of Bornu Province, and in Adamawa Province, east of the *BURA*.

Number of speakers: 151,223 (including the *CHIBBAK*).

Dialects: Vocabularies of MARGI dialects spoken in the following localities have been collected:

Lasa, Minthla, Molgoy, 'the plains'.

Parts of the New Testament have been translated.

Note: *DUHU* appears to be the name either of a part of the *MARGI* or of a related tribe.[1]

Vocabularies of the dialects spoken by the following closely resemble those of MARGI dialects; they may thus belong to the same Cluster:

KILBA, call themselves **xibba** or *NDIRMA*, called **wudiŋ** by the *CHEKE*, **pɛlla** by the *CHIBBAK*; in Adamawa Province, Kilba District, south-east of the *BURA*.
Number: 22,799.

CHIBBAK (*CHIBBUK*, *CHIBBOK*, *KIBAKU*), call themselves **kəbʌk**; west of the *MARGI*.
Number: (included in the *MARGI* figures).
This dialect is inter-intelligible with some of the MARGI dialects.

The languages or dialects of the following may also be related to the BURA Group:

MAYA, in the French Cameroons south of Mora.[2] No linguistic material is available.

FALI of Kiria in Uba (Wuba) District of Adamawa Province. The vocabulary appears to be akin to the BURA Group (for other FALI see pp. 151–2, 156, 158).

LANGUAGE GROUP: BATA

Consists of:
- BATA — Dialect Cluster?
- NJAI — Dialect Cluster?
- CHEKE — Language?
- HIGI — Dialect Cluster.
- 'Woga' — Dialect Cluster?

Where spoken: Nigeria: Adamawa Province; British and French Cameroons.

[1] Tessmann, op. cit. [2] Mouchet, 'Vocabulaires comparatifs . . . (part 1)'.

THE CHADIC LANGUAGES 155

BATA. DIALECT CLUSTER OR CLUSTERS?

Spoken by: *BATA* (*BATTA*), a collective name used by the *FULANI* for a number of tribes, tribal sections, or local groups (who call themselves by their own local names), called ɓoati by the *NJAI*, ɓete by *GUDU*, bɪrsa by the people of Libo, dunu by those of Gengle and Kugama.

Where spoken: Adamawa Province, on both banks of the Benue, and on the Benue and Faro rivers in French Cameroons, also in the British Cameroons south of Mubi.

Number of speakers: Nigeria 23,003; French Cameroons, see below.

Dialects: There appears to be considerable divergence between those dialects of which something is known, so that it is far from certain whether they constitute one or more Clusters. They are spoken by:

ZUMU (*JIMO, ZOMO*), in Nigeria, in and around Zumu; the same dialect is spoken by the people of Malabu (about 45 miles east of Yola), Kofa, Bulai, and by the *MULENG*. All these people are also known collectively as *JIRAI*. Strümpell's WADI of Wapango[1] appears to resemble this dialect.

GUDU, in Nigeria, about 10 miles west of Song; the same dialect is spoken by the people of Kumbi.

NJAI (*NZANGI, ZANI, ZANY, NJEL, NJENY*), call themselves nzaŋyɪn (Sing. nzaŋɛ); in British and French Cameroons. The same dialect is spoken by the *HOLMA* (*KURNDEL*), and the same, or a closely related dialect, by the *GUDI* (*GUDE*) in French Cameroons.
  Number: French Cameroons: NJAI 9,518,* GUDI 4,312.*
  The JEN given by Mouchet[2] is apparently this dialect, as are also Strümpell's NJEI and KOBOTSCHI.
  Note: Meek includes the dialect of the *NJAI* among the BATA dialects. According to van Bulck it differs considerably from the dialect of the *BATA* of Garoua, although the *NJAI* claim to understand the speech of the Nigerian *BATA*.

BATA of Garoua, French Cameroons (fishermen on the Benue).
  Number: estimated at 2,000 by van Bulck.

Dialect: BACHAMA.[3]

Spoken by: *BACHAMA*, call themselves bacama or ɓoare, called abacama by the people of Libo, besema by the *YUNGUR*, bwareba by the *LONGUDA*; in Nigeria, on the banks of the Benue near Numan.
  Number: 11,850 (but this figure includes some non-BACHAMA speakers, e.g. the JEN (see p. 139)).
  A Gospel has been translated into this dialect.

Note: Some of these dialects show CHADO-HAMITIC influence in that they have grammatical gender (see p. 160).

[1] 'Mandara.'   [2] 'Vocabulaires comparatifs ... (part 2).'
[3] 'The Bachama and Bata speak the same language' (Meek, *Tribal Studies*).

CHEKE. LANGUAGE?

Spoken by: *CHEKE*, called **mapodi** by the *NJAI*.

Where spoken: British Cameroons, Mubi District, and across the border into French Cameroons.

Strümpell's MUBI[1] appears to be identical with CHEKE.

Van Bulck suggests that the *CHEKE* may be the people in Guidar subdivision of French Cameroons who are known by the nickname of *SHEDE* and who call themselves **ġuġuġuju**.

HIGI. DIALECT CLUSTER.

Spoken by: *HIGI* (*HIJI*), call themselves **kamun** (= people) in British Cameroons, **kapsiki** in French Cameroons, called **hiji** by the *FULANI* and others, and sometimes known as 'Hill *MARGI*'.

Where spoken: In the Mandara mountains between Uba and Madagali.

Number of speakers: British Cameroons 6,284, French Cameroons 8,937.[2]

There appear to be several dialects; those known from vocabularies are:

Dialect spoken at Moda;

Dialect spoken at Humsi;

Dialect spoken by *HIGI WULA*;

Dialect spoken by *HIGI SINNA*;

Dialect spoken by *KAPSIKI*.

'Woga'. DIALECT CLUSTER?

Vocabularies from the following localities in Madagali District appear to be those of dialects which may perhaps constitute a Cluster:

Woga (the people call themselves *WUDIR*);

Vemgo;

Vizik;

Tur, on the French Cameroons border.

Note, however, that Vuzik and Turu are given by Lavergne[3] as place-names in *MATAKAM* country.

The speech of the so-called *FALI* of Mubi District (Ulvin and surroundings) and of Yilbu (Jilbu) appears from vocabularies to be akin to the BATA Group (for *FALI* see also pp. 151–2, 154, 158).

The language or dialect spoken by the *SUKUR* (*SUGUR*; *SSUGUR*) south of Madagali also appears to belong to this Group; it is not, however, understood by neighbouring *HIGI* or *MARGI*.[4]

Number: 1,300.

[1] 'Mandara.'
[2] 'Inventaire ethnique et linguistique. . . .'
[3] 'Le pays et la population Matakam' (*Bull. Soc. Et. Camerounaises*, 1944).
[4] MacBride, MS. notes on the *SUKUR*.

THE CHADIC LANGUAGES 157

According to Meek, the *SUKUR* are an offshoot of the *GUDUR* (*MPSAKALI*, *SHAKIRI*) in the French Cameroons, of whom, however, nothing further is known, though Gudur is mentioned by Strümpell[1] as the name of a village in the Mandara mountains, and by Lavergne[2] as a place-name in *MATAKAM* country.

SINGLE UNIT? TERA

TERA. DIALECT CLUSTER?

From vocabularies, it appears that closely related dialects are spoken by the following:

'Ganda' (Gaanda, Kanda), 'Gabin' (Kabin), and 'Boga' (Poka); in Adamawa Province, in the hill country north of Song.
Number: 5,400.[3]

HONA (so called by the *KILBA*; they recognize this name but also call themselves *FITERIYA*),[4] called *HUENE* by the *GUDU*, *BUA* by the people of Mboi, *KUTURINCHA* by the 'Gabin', **kutɛrɪŋga** by the *ROBA*; north-west of Song in Hona District, and in Ganda and Gola Districts.
Number: 6,604.

HINA (*HINNA*, *HUNNA*), call themselves **pɪlɪmdi**, in Tera District, and around Gumburku in Bornu Province.
Number: 4,350.[5]

Note: Apparently not the same as the *HINA* (*DABA HINA*) in the French Cameroons (see p. 159).

TERA, call themselves **nyimaʃi**, called *TERAWA* by the *HAUSA*; in Bornu and Bauchi Provinces on River Gongola.
Number: 18,499 (but this figure probably includes the *HINA*).
A Gospel has been translated.

There is some uncertainty about the speech of the *TERA*. According to Temple[6] their original language was BOLENCHI (see BOLEWA, p. 163), but they have adopted the *TANGALE* language, NIMALTO (see p. 164). Meek's vocabulary of TERA, however, shows undeniable resemblance to those of HONA, HINA, &c.

JERA (*JERRA*),[7] call themselves **jɛrra**; in the south-western corner of Bornu Province and the adjacent part of Bauchi Province, south of the *TERA* on both sides of River Gongola.
Number: '*JERA* of Yola' 1,856;[5] there are said to be 897 *JERA* in Biu Division, Shani District.[8]

Nothing is known of the speech of the *PUTHLUNDI* in Biu Division; it may perhaps be related either to TERA or to KANAKURU.
Number: 13,154.[8]

---

[1] 'Mandara.'
[2] 'Le pays et la population Matakam' (*Bull. Soc. Ét. Camerounaises*, 1944).   [3] Meek.
[4] Meek, *Tribal Studies*, p. 396. But in his vocabulary (p. 414) the sentence 'You are a Hona' is translated *tsi i təfətera nana*.   [5] Meek, *Tribal Studies*.   [6] *Notes on the Tribes, Provinces*. . . .
[7] Note that there is great confusion of nomenclature with the *JERAWA* (see p. 107) and *JARAWA* (see p. 115).   [8] Information from M. Pindar, visiting teacher of Biu.

THE CHADIC LANGUAGES

LANGUAGE GROUP: MATAKAM - MANDARA[1]

Consists of: MATAKAM Dialect Cluster?
'Mora' Dialect Cluster.
DABA Dialect Cluster.
MANDARA Dialect Cluster.
PADUKO Language?

Where spoken: French Cameroons.

MATAKAM. DIALECT CLUSTER?

Vocabularies of dialects spoken by the following show sufficient resemblance for them to be tentatively considered as belonging to one Cluster:

MATAKAM; mainly in subdivision Mokolo.

Number: 33,000;[2] 55,973 in subdivision Mokolo.[3]
Strümpell[4] gives vocabularies of two dialects, which show considerable differences.

MOFU (MUFFO, MUFU, MUFFU, Fr. *MOFOU)*; east of the *MATAKAM*, also farther south, east of River Lue, mainly in subdivision Maroua.
Number: 33,000.[5]
The name *BULAHAI* is also used to denote the *MATAKAM* and *MOFU* together.[3]

The speech of the *GWOZA* (ġwázà) at Gwoza west of Mora is only known from short vocabularies collected by Lukas (unpublished). The vocabulary shows some affinities with Strümpell's MATAKAM, but also with CHADO-HAMITIC languages.

'Mora.' DIALECT CLUSTER.

Van Bulck reports the existence of eleven closely related dialects spoken on Mora massif.[6]

DABA. DIALECT CLUSTER.

Dialect: GISIGA.
Spoken by: *GISIGA* (Fr. *GUISSIGA*), also known as 'Muturua' (a place-name) and as *RUM*;[7] in subdivision Kaele.
Number: 18,390.*

Dialect: MUSGOI (MUSGOY).
Spoken by: *MUSGOI (MUSGOY, MUSUGEU)*, north of the *GISIGA*.
Number: 4,313.[2]
Note: The *MUSGOI* are also known as *FALI* (but see pp. 151-2, 154, 156).

---

[1] Classification according to van Bulck. [2] 'Inventaire ethnique et linguistique. . . .'
[3] Lavergne, op. cit. [4] 'Mandara.'
[5] Marchesseau, 'Quelques éléments d'ethnographie sur les Mofu du Massif de Durum' (*Bull. Soc. Et. Camerounaises*, 1945). [6] Information obtained from Mouchet.
[7] Van Bulck, however, failed to find any trace of this name, or of the name *BALDA*, which also occurs in some works dealing with this area.

Dialect: DABA HINA.
Spoken by: *DABA HINA (INA)*,[1] in subdivision Mokolo, in and around Hina west of River Lue, opposite the *GISIGA*.
Number: 2,500.[2]

Dialect: GAWAR.
Spoken by: *GAWAR* (Fr. *GAOUAR*), in subdivision Mokolo. They are also known as *FALI*.

Numbers: van Bulck gives the total figure for *MUSGOI*, *HINA*, and *GAWAR* as 13,084.

MANDARA. DIALECT CLUSTER.[3]

Where spoken: In the Mandara mountains area, mainly in French Cameroons, but also in Nigeria: Bornu Province.

Number of speakers: 30,000–40,000.

Dialect: MANDARA.
Spoken by: *MANDARA (WANDALA)*, call themselves **wándàlà**; in the Mandara mountains, with main centre Mora.
Number: Nigeria 4,936; French Cameroons 11,860.[2]

Dialect spoken by: *GAMERGU*, called **gàmàrgú** by the *MANDARA*; in Bornu Province, on both banks of River Yedzeram, from Lat. 11° 40′ N. southwards.
Number: 9,070.
Vocabulary evidence bears out the assertion of *MANDARA* informants that this is a MANDARA dialect.

Information about the following dialects was obtained from *MANDARA* informants in Bornu; no linguistic material is available. According to these informants, the tribes speaking MANDARA dialects are:

KAMBURWAMA (**kàmbùrwáamà**), probably in the Mandara mountains (precise area not known);

MASFEIMA (**másfĕimà**), south of the *MANDARA*;

JAMPALAM (**jàmphàlàm**), east of the *MANDARA*;

ZLOGBA (**ɮògbá**), west of the *MANDARA*;

MAZAGWA (**màzàgwá**), south-west of the *MANDARA*;

GWANJE (**gwánjè**), precise area not known; their dialect is said to be closely related to that of the *GAMERGU*.

Nothing is known of the speech of the *NGASLAWE*, called **ŋàɬàwé** by the *MANDARA*, west of the *MANDARA*, except that it is said not to be a MANDARA dialect.

---

[1] Not to be confused with the *HINA* (see p. 157).
[2] 'Inventaire ethnique et linguistique. . . .'
[3] Information from Lukas.

PADUKO. Language?

Spoken by: PADUKO (*PADOGO, PADOKO, PADOKWA*).

Where spoken: French Cameroons, south of Mora.

GIDAR, spoken at and around Gidar (Gider, Guider), west of River Lue, may perhaps be a CHADIC language, strongly influenced by CHADO-HAMITIC, according to van Bulck.

Number of speakers: French Cameroons, subdivision Guider 29,887;* Chad, subdivision Lere 7,500.*

Linguistic notes on the CHADIC Languages

The CHADIC languages have certain features in common with the central CHADO-HAMITIC languages. These include:

(a) the presence of lateral sounds (note also the absence of labio-velar sounds);
(b) the distinction between Inclusive and Exclusive in the 1st Person Plural Pronoun;
(c) a common vocabulary which is small, but includes basic words such as 'four', 'ear', &c., and some common morphological elements;
(d) formation of the Plural by Suffixes;
(e) the existence of Possessive Suffixes or Possessive Pronouns which follow the Noun;
(f) Objective Suffixes in the Verb.

Points *d–f* are not confined to these two Larger Units, but occur in other neighbouring languages as well.

Word order is the same in both Larger Units (and in other neighbouring languages).

1. Lateral sounds[1] have been noted in some languages, e.g. the MANDARA dialects and the BATA dialect of the *GUDU* (but apparently not in all the BATA dialects).

Labio-velar **gb** occurs in the BACHAMA dialect.

2. Tone plays an important part in the MANDARA dialects, and probably in other languages as well.

3. There are no Noun Classes.

Grammatical Gender occurs, mostly only in the Pronoun, in the BATA dialects of the *ZUMU, GUDU, JEŊ* (according to Mouchet[2]) and of Garoua, and in GIDAR. BATA of Garoua has Gender in the Noun, Pronoun, and Adjective, GIDAR in the Noun, Pronoun (including Object of Verb), and Adjective.

4. The Plural is formed by:

Suffix in the BURA Group and in MANDARA;
Suffix and change of Root vowel in HIGI and the BATA dialect of the *ZUMU*;

---

[1] In most Gospel translations *tl, dl, ll* are used to represent these sounds.
[2] 'Vocabulaires comparatifs . . . (part 2).'

change of Suffix and Root vowel in BACHAMA;
addition or change of Suffix in the dialects of Gabin and of the *HONA*;
dropping of Suffix in PADUKO.[1]

5. The distinction between Inclusive and Exclusive in the 1st Person Plural Pronoun appears to be universal.

6. A number of Verbal Derivatives, formed by Suffixes, have been noted in BURA dialects. They include a Reflexive-Passive, a Causative, Directionals (expressing 'out of', 'away', &c.). These Suffixes can be combined together.

7. Little is known of the verbal structure of the CHADIC languages. From the scanty material available it appears that there are remarkable differences between languages.

The BURA Verb is the best known. In conjugation the Pronoun is placed before the Verb Root (or Derived Stem) in the Simple Form of the Verb. At least four further Tenses (Perfect, Habitual, Progressive, Subjunctive) are formed, the first three by a Particle standing between the Pronoun and Verb, the last by a Particle preceding the Pronoun.

Conjugation of the Verb in MANDARA has some special features which have not so far been observed in other languages of these regions. Two Tenses can be distinguished, a Future and a Preterite, the first being conjugated by Prefixes, whereas the second has Infixes, the Verb Stem appearing before and after, e.g.:

miʃ-ʃukwa (Inclusive)   ŋaʃ-ʃukwa (Exclusive)   we shall buy
ʃəkwa-myip-ʃukwa   ʃəkwa-ŋrap-ʃukwa   we bought

Reduplication of the Verb Root has also been observed by Mouchet[1] in PADUKO.

8. Word order in the simple sentence appears to be Subject–Verb–Object in all languages; in many languages the Pronominal Object follows the Verb; in PADUKO the Pronoun Subject follows the Verb, but the Noun Subject precedes it.[1]

9. In the Genitive construction the *nomen rectum* follows the *nomen regens*, directly in the languages and dialects of the *MARGI* of Minthla, *KILBA, BATA ZUMU, HONA*, and *MANDARA*,[2] with Linking Particle in BURA, MARGI of Lasa, HIGI, BACHAMA, and perhaps HINA. In the BATA dialect of the *GUDU* the Particle appears to follow the *nomen rectum*. In MATAKAM Compound Nouns show that the *nomen rectum* follows the *nomen regens* as in the other languages.

10. Possession is expressed by Possessive Suffixes or Possessive Pronouns which follow the Noun.

11. Adjectives (including Numerals) follow the Noun in most languages; in BURA and the dialect of the *KILBA* a Particle stands between them. The 'Woga' dialects deviate in that the Numeral precedes the Noun.

---

[1] 'Vocabulaires comparatifs . . . (part 2).'
[2] Mouchet (loc. cit.) notes an optional Linking Particle in MANDARA.

Section X
THE CHADO-HAMITIC LANGUAGES (LARGER UNIT)

The CHADO-HAMITIC languages are spoken over a wide area extending roughly from the western border of northern Nigeria to Wadai in French Equatorial Africa, mainly between Lat. 14° N. in the north and Lat. 10° N. in the south (Lat. 9° N. in the area south of Lake Chad).

Single Unit: HAUSA
HAUSA. Dialect Cluster.

Spoken by: *HAUSA*, call themselves **háusáawaá** (Sing. **bàháuʃè**), called **àfùnó** by the *KANURI*, also called by many other names by other tribes in Nigeria and elsewhere.

    Note: The name HAUSA is used by Europeans and others to denote the people as well as the language.

Where spoken: Nigeria: throughout a considerable part of the Northern Provinces (for main centres, see below); also to the west and south, in the Southern Provinces of Nigeria, and in numerous *HAUSA* colonies in the whole of West Africa, especially in Dahomey, Togoland, and the Northern Territories of the Gold Coast; to the east and north, in French West Africa (Cameroons) and French Equatorial Africa (Chad); also in many of the greater centres in North Africa.

Number of speakers: The total number of HAUSA-speakers cannot be estimated, in view of the enormous distribution of the *HAUSA* and the great number of those who speak HAUSA as a second language. Census figures for the *HAUSA* in the Northern Provinces of Nigeria are 3,604,016.

Dialects: No detailed survey of the dialects of HAUSA and their distribution has yet been made. Two main dialectal divisions may be distinguished in Nigeria:

    Eastern: spoken in Kano, Katagum, Hadejiya, and elsewhere;
    Western: spoken in Sokoto, Katsina, Gobir, and elsewhere.

Other main centres where HAUSA is spoken are: Zaria, Zamfara, Kontagora, Gumel, Mara'di.

HAUSA is the most important lingua franca in Nigeria, where it is the official language in the Northern Provinces. It is also widely spoken, and still more widely understood, in other West African countries.

Before the advent of Europeans, HAUSA was already a literary language, written by the malams in Arabic (Ajami) script. It is used in education, and now possesses a considerable vernacular literature. Numerous books and pamphlets have been published, and there is an important bi-weekly newspaper, *Gaskiya*, published in Kano.

The literary language is based on the dialect spoken in Kano, and enriched by numerous expressions and phrases taken from various other dialects.

THE CHADO-HAMITIC LANGUAGES 163

Language Group: BADE

Consists of: BADE Language.
BOLEWA Dialect Cluster?
KAREKARE Language.
NGIZIM Language.

Where spoken: Nigeria: mainly in Bornu Province, but also in Kano and Bauchi Provinces.

BADE. Language.

Spoken by: BADE (BEDE, BEDDE), call themselves **bade**, called **bádè** by the *KANURI*.

Where spoken: Bornu Province, south of a line from Nguru to Geidam, north-west of the *KANURI*, north and north-east of the *NGIZIM*.

Number of speakers: 31,933.

BOLEWA. Dialect Cluster?

Dialect: BOLEWA (BOLENCHI).
Spoken by: BOLEWA (BOLEA, BORLAWA), call themselves **bolewa**, called **bòlèwà** by the *KANURI*, **bolawa** by the *HAUSA* (the *BOLEWA* of Fika call themselves **fika** and are called **fikankayɛn** by the *KAREKARE*, and are also known as *ANPIKA*); in Bornu Province, in Potiskum and Fika and the surrounding area; Bauchi Province, south of the bend in the Gongola river (these two areas being separated by *FULANI*).
Number: 31,939.
Benton[1] distinguishes two 'dialects', which he calls 'Fika' and 'Bara'.

Dialect: NGAMO.
Spoken by: NGAMO (NGAMAYA), call themselves **ŋgamo** or **ŋgamaya**, called **gamawa** by the *HAUSA* and *KANURI*; in the south-western part of Bornu Province and the north-eastern part of Bauchi Province.
Number: 17,800.
NGAMO is closely related in vocabulary to BOLEWA, so that it may be regarded as belonging to the same Cluster.

KAREKARE. Language.

Spoken by: KAREKARE (KEREKERE, KERIKERI), call themselves **kɛrɛkɛrɛ**, called **kárékáré** by the *KANURI*.

Where spoken: In the western part of Bornu Province and the east of Kano Province, south of Potiskum; also in Bauchi Province.

Number of speakers: 39,124.

[1] *Notes on some languages of the Western Sudan.*

THE CHADO-HAMITIC LANGUAGES

NGIZIM. LANGUAGE.

Spoken by: NGIZIM (*NGIZZEM*), call themselves **ŋgizim**, called **ngɔ́zɔ́m** by the *KANURI*, also known (according to Meek[1]) as *KIRDIWAT* (ARABIC), called *WALU* by the *BADE*, *GWAZUM* by the *KAREKARE*.

Where spoken: South of the *BADE* in the west of Bornu Province and the east of Kano Province.

Number of speakers: 39,233.

LANGUAGE GROUP ? TANGALE[2]

Consists of: TANGALE   Language.
      KANAKURU Language.

Where spoken: Bauchi, Adamawa, and Bornu Provinces.

TANGALE. LANGUAGE.

Spoken by: TANGALE, call themselves **taŋgale**, called *JAGJAGE* by the *MANDARA*, also known as *KUMBA*.

Where spoken: Bauchi Province, north of the Benue, north-west of the *BACHAMA*.

Number of speakers: 36,020.

The New Testament and parts of the Old Testament have been translated.

According to Temple[3] the *TERA* (see p. 157) have adopted the language of the *TANGALE*, which is called NIMALTO. The *AFUDU* (*YAFFUDAWA*) also perhaps speak 'a dialect of TANGALE'.

KANAKURU. LANGUAGE.

Spoken by: *KANAKURU*, call themselves **dera**, called **bilauun** by the 'Libo', **embelıŋga** by the *ROBA*, **lıŋga** by the *YUNGUR*, *SHELLENGCHA* by the 'Gabin', **tsaba** by the *LONGUDA*.

Where spoken: Adamawa Province, Numan Division, Shellen District, and Shani and Gasi Districts in Bornu Province.

Number of speakers: 11,316.

KANAKURU is used in religious education. A Gospel has been translated into 'KANAKURA'.

LANGUAGE GROUP: KOTOKO[4]

Consists of: KOTOKO Dialect Cluster.
      BUDUMA Dialect Cluster.

Where spoken: In the Lake Chad area and to the south.

---

[1] *Tribal Studies.*   [2] See p. 175.   [3] *Notes on the Tribes, Provinces.* ....
[4] Information on this and the two following Groups from Lukas indicated by [L.]; information from van Bulck indicated by [vB.].

THE CHADO-HAMITIC LANGUAGES

KOTOKO. DIALECT CLUSTER.

Spoken by: *KOTOKO*. This is the name given by the Arabs to all speakers of these dialects, and recognized by at least some of them as well as their own tribal or local names. They are called *MAKARI* (**magəri**) by the *KANURI* (this being the name of one of their tribes), **mantage** by the *KUSERI*, **madaganye** by the people of Gulfei, Afade, and Makari, *SAO*, *SO*[1] by the KUKA [L.] The southern *KOTOKO* call themselves *MIDA*, and are called *LABANG* by their northern neighbours.[2]

Where spoken: South of Lake Chad, west of River Shari, on both sides of River Logone as far south as the *MUSGU* area.

Number of speakers: 27,500 in 1936 [vB.]. Duisburg gives the estimate 40,000–50,000, but it is not clear how many speakers of KOTOKO dialects are included.

The following dialects are those of which something is known; there may be others as yet unknown:

KOTOKO DAA (**kɔtɔkɔ daa**), spoken (with many local variants) between Lake Chad and Logone Gana; around Logone Gana the dialect is called **lagwane gaana** [vB.].

LOGONE, own name **lagwane** [L.], **lagwane birni** [vB.]; in and around the town of Logone Birni.

KUSERI, own name **msirr** [vB.]; the people are called **'ūsuri** by those of Logono, **miir** by those of Gulfei [L.]; at Kuseri on the left bank of the Logone south-west of Fort Lamy.

'Gulfei'; the people call themselves **málɓê** [L.] or **malgwe**, **ŋgwalkwe** [vB.], called **gwalakwe** by the people of Logone [L.]; at Gulfei (Goulfei) on the left bank of the Logone north-west of Fort Lamy.

AFADE; the people are called **avadˀə** by those of Logone [L.]; at Afade west of River Shari.

'Shawi', at and around Shawi or Shoe, on River Shari, on both sides of the French Cameroons–Chad border.

MAKARI; the people are called **mpháadə** by those of Gulfei, **mùyəbàatə** by those of Logone [L.]; at Makari (Mafate).

Note: The people of Klesem on the right bank of River Shari, and of Ngala (Nghala) on the left bank, no longer speak KOTOKO, but have adopted KANURI [vB.].

---

[1] *SAU* (*SAO*, *SO*, *SSO*) is the name of a people now extinct, but known to have been the great antagonists of the invading *KANURI* west of Lake Chad during past centuries. Von Duisburg in 1914 found an inhabitant of Ngala village south of Lake Chad who claimed to speak SAU. From his notes it can be concluded that the *SAU* spoke a KOTOKO dialect (von Duisburg, 'Überreste der So-Sprache', *M.S.O.S.*, 1914).

[2] von Duisburg, 'Mittelsudan und Zentralsahara', in *Afrika*, ed. Bernatzik.

BUDUMA. Dialect Cluster.

Dialect: BUDUMA (BUDDUMA, Fr. BOUDDOUMA).

Spoken by: *BUDUMA*, call themselves *YIDENA* or *YEDINA*, called *BUDUMA* by the *KANURI* and *KANEMBU*; on the islands in the north-eastern part of Lake Chad, and on some parts of the shore.

Number: estimated by Nachtigal[1] at 12,000–15,000, by Tilho[2] at 45,000 (probably including the *KURI*). No recent figures are available.

Dialect: KURI.

Spoken by: *KURI*, call themselves **kakáa** [vB.]; on the islands in the south-eastern part of Lake Chad.

Language Group: MASA

Consists of: MUSGU Dialect Cluster.
SIGILA Language?
MASA Dialect Cluster.
MUSEI Dialect Cluster.
MARBA Language.
DARI Dialect Cluster.

Where spoken: French Cameroons and Chad, south and south-east of the KOTOKO area.

MUSGU. Dialect Cluster.

Spoken by: *MUSGU* (*MUZGU, MUSGUM*, Fr. *MOUSGOU*, &c.), call themselves **mulwi** (they also recognize the name **mamzɔkoi**, but do not like it) [vB.]; called **mùzùgù** by the *KANURI*, **múzùgù** by the people of Logone, **musgu** by the *MANDARA, MASA* by the *KOTOKO* and others [L.].

Where spoken: South of the *KOTOKO* on both banks of the Logone, west and east of the town of Musgum (Mousgoum), extending as far as River Shari, and in the south as far as the *TUPURI* and *BANA*.

Number of speakers: French Cameroons 17,000, Chad 8,400 [vB.].

Dialects: The following dialects are known [vB.]:

pus (Cameroons);
gwai
aɓi
bɛɛgɛ }(Chad).
vulum

SIGILA. Language?

Spoken by: *SIGILA*.

Where spoken: French Cameroons, east of Mora.

SIGILA is included in this Group on the evidence of Tessmann.[3]

---

[1] *Sahara und Sudan*.   [2] *Documents de la mission Tilho* (1911).
[3] 'Die Völker und Sprachen Kameruns.'

THE CHADO-HAMITIC LANGUAGES

MASA. DIALECT CLUSTER.

Spoken by: *MASA*, call themselves **masa** (**-na** Masc., **-ta** Fem. Sing.); the name **masana** is locally used to denote their speech [vB.]; called *WALIA* by the *MUSGU* and *FULANI* [L.].

Dialects of MASA are spoken in the following areas [vB.]:
  French Cameroons: Yagoua;
  Chad: an area including Gumei, Walia, and Hara (42,000). This dialect is also known as BANA(NA).
  On River Ba Ili (1,300).

Parts of the Bible have been translated.

MUSEI. DIALECT CLUSTER.

Spoken by: *MUSEI (MUSEY, MUSSOI)*. This name, originally meaning 'slaves', is now recognized by the people themselves [vB.].

Where spoken: Chad and French Cameroons, south of the *MASA*.

Dialects [vB.]:
  masa gbaya;
  (h)ɔllɔm;
  ŋgame (GME);
  dialect of River Kabiya. The people are known as *HOHO*, and also accept the name *BANANA* (cp. under MASA above);
  dialect of the Cameroons (4 villages).

Number of speakers: Chad 41,000 (including the *MARBA*—see below); French Cameroons 7,000 [vB.].

MARBA. LANGUAGE.

Spoken by: *MARBA*.

Where spoken: On River Logone, west of Lai, south-west of Kim.

Number of speakers: 4,740.[1]

DARI. DIALECT CLUSTER.

Where spoken: Chad, south-west of the *MARBA*, south of the *TUPURI* and *MUNDANG*.

Dialects: The name DARI (a place-name) is used to cover the following dialects [vB.]:

  KADO, spoken in Pala district;
  PEVE, spoken around Lame;
  'Tshimiang' (**cimiaŋ**).

[1] 'Inventaire ethnique et linguistique. . . .'

THE CHADO-HAMITIC LANGUAGES

LANGUAGE GROUP: SOKORO - MUBI [vB.]

Consists of: JONGOR   Dialect Cluster.
           'BIDYO   Dialect Cluster.
           DANGALEAT   Language?
           MOGUM   Dialect Cluster.
           MUBI   Dialect Cluster.
           SOKORO   Dialect Cluster?

Where spoken: Chad: south of River Batha, separated from the other CHADO-HAMITIC languages by the *BAGIRMI* and other tribes.

JONGOR (DJONGOR). DIALECT CLUSTER.

Spoken by: *JONGOR* (so called by the Arabs).

Where spoken: Mainly in the Abu Telfan area, also on Jebel Geira.

Dialects: There are two dialects, which differ considerably [vB.], spoken at:

  Abu Telfan (8,000–10,000);
  Jebel Geira (Mokolo) (6,000).

Note: Two languages are spoken on Jebel Geira, the other being a KENGA dialect, belonging to the BONGO-BAGIRMI Language Group.

'BIDYO. DIALECT CLUSTER.

Where spoken: West of Abu Telfan.

Dialects [vB.]:

  'BIDYO (10,000–11,000);
  WAANA (3,000).

DANGALEAT. LANGUAGE? [vB.].

Where spoken: North of Jebel Geira, north-west of Bitkine.

Number of speakers: 16,000.

MOGUM. DIALECT CLUSTER [vB.].

Where spoken: In the Melfi-Abu Deia area.

Dialects are spoken by:

  mɔgum of Melfi (1,764);
  mɔgum of Abu Deia (3,500);
  kɔffa of Abu Deia (1,000).

MUBI. DIALECT CLUSTER.

Dialect: MUBI.
Spoken by: *MUBI*, call themselves **mónjúl** (Sing. **mínjílò**) [L.]; north-east of Abu Telfan.
Number: 22,531 [vB.].

Dialect: MASMAJE.
Spoken by: *MASMAJE*, called **másmájé** by the *MUBI* [L.]; north of the *MUBI* on the south bank of River Batha.
Number: 3,966 [vB.].

Dialect: KAJAKSE.
Spoken by: *KAJAKSE (KAJAGISE, KADJAGSE*, &c.), called **kàjágísé** by the *MUBI*, **kàjáakísɛ̀ɛ** by the *MABA* [L.]; east of the *MUBI*, west of Goz Beïda.
Number: 3,917 [vB.].

Dialect: BERGIT, own name **bɛrgit** [vB.].
Spoken by: *BERGIT (BIRGIT)*; south-west of the *MUBI* [vB.].
Number: 1,900 [vB.].

Dialect: TORAM, own name **tɔram** [vB.].
Spoken by: *TORAM*, south of Abu Deia.
Number: 3,650 [vB.].

SOKORO. DIALECT CLUSTER? [vB.].

Dialect: SOKORO, own name **sokɔrɔ**.
Spoken by: *SOKORO*, on the north-east of Melfi massif, in the Bédanga, Ngogmi, and Erla area; also to the south of Djebren.
Number: 4,077.[1]

Dialect: BAREIN, own name **barein**.
Spoken by: *BAREIN (BARAÏN, BARAIN)*, at the foot of the mountains between Fandiala and Telgo, south of the *SOKORO*.
Number: 1,896.[1]

Dialect: SABA, own name **saba**.
Spoken by: *SABA*, east of the *SOKORO*, north-east of Melfi.
Number: 1,725.

Note: The *TUNJUR* of Melfi (about 50 people living on the Kutuku–Djebren road) speak a related dialect. All other *TUNJUR* now speak ARABIC [vB.].

Linguistic notes on the CHADO-HAMITIC Languages

Features common to the central CHADO-HAMITIC languages (KOTOKO, MASA, and BADE Groups) and the CHADIC languages have been summarized on p. 160.

Features peculiar to the CHADO-HAMITIC languages are:

1. There is a two-class or two-gender system in the Noun with a Concord in some Qualificatives (not in Numerals), and in the Verb if the Pronoun is expressed. Apart from HAUSA, special forms of the Noun, from which its Gender can be concluded, do not seem to exist. But the difference in form always exists in some Person of the

---

[1] According to Hersé ('Observations sur les margayes de Melfi', *Bull. Inst. Et. Centrafr.*, 1947), both the *SOKORO* and the *BAREIN* are decreasing in numbers.

Pronoun, so that we can distinguish Masculine and Feminine Pronominals. This two-gender system resembles that of the HAMITIC languages, and in the Pronominals there is often even etymological relationship.

2. There are some Plural forms which otherwise are only to be found in the HAMITIC languages.

3. The CHADO-HAMITIC languages have a very small HAMITIC vocabulary, containing Pronominal Roots, Nouns, and Verbs.

HAUSA

1. There are five vowel phonemes. Vowel length is of great importance.

HAUSA has three implosive sounds: ɓ, ɗ, and 'y (rare). It has the ejectives k' (in the recognized orthography ƙ), s' (the most usual pronunciation of the sound written ts), and in some instances c'. There is a flapped retroflex ɽ (not distinguished in orthography from rolled r).

Consonantal length is important.

There are no true nasal compounds.

2. HAUSA has a characteristic syllabic structure. Every syllable begins with a consonant.[1] A syllable is either open or closed by one consonant only. A closed syllable always has a short vowel.

Certain laws control the final consonant of a syllable, especially in the dialect of Kano. The final consonant is either assimilated to the following consonant or there is the following change:

> final labials or velar plosives (b, f, k, g, and sometimes m) are changed to u (i.e. unsyllabic w);
> alveolar plosives and fricatives (t, d, s, z) to r;
> final nasals become ŋ.

3. There are two basic tone levels, high and low. Falling tones also occur. Rising tones are very rare.

Tone is of restricted significance etymologically, but has morphological value in so far as it builds up tone patterns which are morphologically characteristic.

Stress is prevalent to a considerable extent. Its influence on tone has not yet been studied.

4. Verbal Roots are mostly monosyllabic, the form CVC being commoner than the form CV, but disyllabic Roots of the form CVCC are also frequent. The vowel of the Root may be either short or long.

Noun Roots show similar forms to the Verb Roots, but disyllabic and polysyllabic Roots are frequent.

5. Compound Nouns and Verbs are rare.

[1] It must be remembered that in HAUSA the glottal stop (') is a consonant, and therefore that words which in the official orthography begin with a vowel, begin in reality with a glottal stop.

6. There are many Noun and Verb formatives, e.g. for the Noun Agent **má-** is prefixed and **-íi** suffixed, and a Noun expressing place is formed in the same way, but with different tone patterns on the Root, e.g.:

másàllàacíi person who prays   **másálláacíi** mosque (place of prayers).

Other Nouns are formed by the Prefix **ba-** and often a Suffix **-e**, indicating a person, e.g.:

bà-háuʃ-è a Hausa

Abstract Nouns are normally formed by Suffixes, e.g.:

k'árán-cíi smallness

For Verb formatives see § 12.

7. The Plural formation is extremely complicated. Two main principles are used:

(1) reduplication of either the whole of the Noun or the last consonant with different vowels, e.g.:

gídáa compound   Plur. **gídàa-jée** (<*gídàa-dée)

(2) Suffixes (of which there are many), e.g.:

rìigáa gown   Plur. **ríig-únà**

As many Plurals of the first type have undergone sound-changes in which the original reduplication has been lost, one can distinguish a third group of Plurals characterized by some inner vowel-change, e.g.:

gúlbíi river   Plur. **gúlàabée** (<*gúlbàa-bée)

8. There is grammatical Gender in the Noun as well as in the Pronoun, including the Subject Pronoun of the Verb. The Noun is thus divided into two Singular Classes, Masculine and Feminine. Plurals must be considered as a third Class (Plural Class); there is no gender distinction in the Plural.

Gender in the Noun cannot always be recognized from the form, but can be seen from any kind of Concord (Genitive, Qualificative, Subject Pronoun, &c.), e.g.:

gídá-ŋ Áudù	compound of Audu
góoná-r Áudù	farm of Audu
máatá-n Áudù	wives of Audu
záakì yáa gúdù	the lion ran away
gíiwáa táa gúdù	the elephant ran away
máatáa sún gúdù	the women ran away

Note that there is a Definite form of the Noun with the Suffix **-n** (Masc. and Plur.) or **-r** (Fem.) with falling tone on the last syllable if possible.

9. Case is shown by position in the sentence and by Prepositions. There are a few

Locative Case forms, formed either by loss of Suffix or by change of vowel quantity, e.g.:

ká	locative of káì head
wútá	locative of wútáa fire
wá yáarò	to the boy (yáarò boy)

10. The Personal Pronouns are as follows:

		Independent	Object (tone varies)
Sing.	1.	níi	ni
	2. Masc.	kái	ka
	Fem.	kée	ki
	3. Masc.	ʃíi	ʃi
	Fem.	ítá	ta
Plur.	1.	múu	mu
	2.	kúu	ku
	3.	súu	su

Note the absence of the distinction between Inclusive and Exclusive forms which is characteristic in many CHADO-HAMITIC languages (see p. 161).

The Subject Pronouns vary according to Tense (see § 15).

There is an Indefinite Pronoun used as Subject of the Verb only:

   án káʃè ʃí one killed him

11. There are no morphological Verb Classes on the whole, but there are a few remnants of a second morphological Class which appears to have died out in HAUSA. These remnants consist of the Future of the Verb 'to go' and two Imperatives, which all have the Pronominals after the Stem, e.g.:

  záà ní I shall go **jè ká!** go! **yáa kà!** come!

There are no Tone Classes.

12. Verbal Derivatives are formed by Suffixes, e.g.:

hàrb-áa	shoot at (cp. the Basic form hárb-à shoot off)
hárb-è	shoot down
bùg-ú	be thoroughly beaten
sáy-óo	buy and bring
sáy-ás	sell
bùb-búg-à	(<*bùg-búg-à) beat many times, many things successively, &c.

There is a further Verbal Derivative used before the Preposition **ma** to. It is similar in form to the Causative (**-ás**), but its use is restricted.

In the first Verbal Derivative given above there is a change of final vowel when followed by an Object, e.g.:

náa hàrb-í mùtûm	I shot at a man
náa hàrb-ée ʃì	I shot at him

The term 'mutable' or 'changing' Verb has been applied to this form by grammarians. The change being characteristic of a Verbal Derivative only, this term is misleading.

13. In some Verbs the Verbal Derivative in -**u** is an Intransitive–Passive. It could therefore be said that a Passive form exists, but its use as a simple Passive is not general. Active forms with the Indefinite Pronoun are used instead.

14. Generally speaking, the Verbal Root does not undergo any change in form. There are some cases in which the Root undergoes a vowel change in a Verbal Derivative or in an Imperative, e.g.:

    ɗìib- to take out   **ɗèeb-í!** take out!   **ɗèeb-** remove

but this is rare.

The tonal structure of the Root is, comparatively speaking, constant in the Basic as well as in any one Derived Form throughout all the Tenses, but it changes according to the Verbal Derivative (being always high in the -**óo** form and in the Causative) and often in the Imperative.

In conjugation the Subject Pronoun precedes the Verb Stem. Number, Gender, and Simple Tenses[1] are all shown in the Subject Pronoun.

15. The following Tenses exist:

Simple Tenses:

Subjunctive	ǹ káamà	that I may catch
Historical Past	ná káamà	I caught
Past	náa káamà	I have caught
Intentional (Future)	zân káamà	I intend to catch
Future	náà káamà	I shall probably catch
Habitual	ná kàn káamà	I habitually catch

Compound Tenses:

Progressive	ń nàa káamàawáa	I am catching
Relative Progressive	ní kèe káamàawáa	I am catching

16. Verbal Negation is expressed in different ways. While the majority of the Tenses are negated by **bà** before and **bá** after the Verb, the Progressive has one negative Particle only, and the Subjunctive is negated by **kádà**, e.g.:

bà náà káamà bá	I shall probably not catch
báa nàa káamàawáa	I am not catching
kádà ǹ káamà	that I may not catch

Copula Negation is expressed by **bàa** before and **bá** after the word to be negated, e.g.:

    bàa ʃíi bá it is not he

[1] The term Simple Tense is here used to distinguish the combination of Subject Pronoun and Verb Stem from the so-called Progressive, which is composed of the Verb 'to be' and a Verbal Noun, and can therefore be called a Compound Tense.

17. Word order in the simple sentence is Subject–Verb–Object. The Indirect Object precedes the Direct Object, e.g.:

    náa káamà dóokì   I have caught the horse
    náa káamà wà yáarò dóokì   I have caught the horse for the boy

18. In the Genitive construction the *nomen rectum* follows the *nomen regens* with a Linking Particle **n** (Masc. and Plur.), **r** (Fem.), e.g.:

    ǵídá-n sárkíi   the compound of the chief
    ǵóoná-r sárkíi   the farm of the chief
    máatá-n sárkíi   the wives of the chief

The fuller forms of the Genitive Particle **na** (Masc. and Plur.), **ta** (Fem.), are also used under certain circumstances.

19. The Adjective is either in the Genitive construction, preceding the Noun, or (less often) directly follows the Noun, e.g.:

    k'àrámí-n dóokì   a small stallion
    k'àrámá-r ǵóoɗìyáa   a small mare, but
    ǵàrí bàbbá   a big town

Numerals generally follow the Noun.

20. The Copula is **nee** (Masc. and Plur.), **cee** (Fem.); the tones vary. This Copula follows the Predicate, e.g.:

    Áudù sárkíi ńee   Audu is a chief
    Kàndé màatársà cée   Kande is his wife
    súu sàráakúnà née   they are chiefs

The omission of the Copula is confined to elliptical sentences and mostly restricted to poetical speech.

Other CHADO-HAMITIC Languages
(on the BADE, KOTOKO, and MASA Groups see also p. 160)

BADE Group

1. The Plural is formed:

(*a*) mainly by Suffixes, of which the prevalent elements are:

    BADE   **-eet, -t, -n**
    KAREKARE   **-n, -ai, -o, -cino**

(*b*) by reduplication of the penultimate consonant of the Noun in BADE (etymologically the last consonant, BADE Nouns being enlarged by a Suffix **-n**), with different vowels, e.g.:

    BADE **udən** knife   Plur. **udaden**

Reduplication of the final consonant of the Noun has also been noted in NGIZIM, e.g.:

        duku horse   Plur. **dukakin**

(c) in BADE, by vowel change, e.g.:

        mdən man   Plur. **mdan**

2. In the Genitive construction the *nomen rectum* follows the *nomen regens*, directly in most languages, with Linking Particle **k** in NGIZIM.

TANGALE Group

1. In TANGALE the Plural is formed in some cases by prefixing **ana-**; in KANAKURU by Suffix or Suffix-change.

2. The *nomen rectum* follows the *nomen regens* without Linking Particle in TANGALE, the *nomen regens* being often shortened by losing its final vowel (a kind of *status constructus* of the SEMITIC languages).
In KANAKURU there is a Linking Particle.

Note: The formation of the Plural by Prefix in TANGALE and the structure of the Verb in both TANGALE and KANAKURU show that these two languages can only tentatively be classed as CHADO-HAMITIC.

KOTOKO Group

1. The Plural is formed:
(a) by lengthening the final consonant (infrequently);
(b) by the Suffixes **-e, -en (-nye<ni+e** in 'Gulfei'); **-ai, -ei, -e** in BUDUMA (the Plural Suffix **(-w)a** has been introduced from KANEMBU);
(c) by internal vowel change;
(d) by a combination of (b) and (c).

2. Verbs are conjugated by prefixing the Personal Pronouns to the Verb Stem.

3. Tenses and Verbal Derivatives are formed as follows:
(a) Past Tense, by the use of an Infix between the Pronoun and the Verb Stem, e.g.:

        ġ-a-l you went

(b) Future Tense, by a Prefix, e.g.:

        sa-ġə-l you will go ('Gulfei' **na-ġ-yim** you will eat)

(c) Perfect Tense and some Verbal Derivatives such as the Passive, and others expressing local modifications (e.g. motion towards), by Adverbs which generally stand at the end of the sentence, e.g.:

        a-stə buluunaanii ya he has gone (**stə**) to his hole (**buluunaa**)

4. The *nomen rectum* follows the *nomen regens*, generally with a Linking Particle.

5. In BUDUMA, KANURI influence is to be seen in the introduction of a number of Postpositions and many KANURI words.

MASA Group

1. The phonetic structure of MUSGU as well as that of MASA is characterized by a tendency towards vowel harmony.

2. The Plural is formed by Suffixes, e.g. **-ai, -akai, -aad** in MUSGU.

3. Gender is shown in the Noun in MASA by the Suffixes **-na** (Masc.), **-ta** (Fem.) in the Singular; no distinction of Gender is made in the Plural. There are separate Masc. and Fem. forms of the Pronoun, including the Object Infix [vB.].

4. Mouchet notes an Inclusive/Exclusive distinction in the 1st Person Plural Pronoun in MASA.[1]

5. The Verb in MASA is conjugated by putting special forms of the Personal Pronouns before the Verb Stem, but the Pronoun is omitted if the Subject is a Noun. The Verb Stem undergoes several modifications by Suffixes or Particles, the latter generally standing at the end of the sentence.

Tenses and Verbal Derivatives made in this manner are: Perfect, Perfective, Durative, Passive-Intransitive, Reciprocal, Directional, and probably others [L.].

6. In MASA, Auxiliary Verbs can stand between the Pronoun and the Verb Stem (perhaps here a Verbal Noun), to express (*a*) a Future, (*b*) a form of possibility [L.].

7. The *nomen rectum* follows the *nomen regens*, with Linking Particle.

MUBI-SOKORO Group

1. There are no lateral sounds.

2. Plurals in MUBI are formed by inner vowel change, by Suffixes, or by a combination of both. In many cases the Plural form arises from a reduplication of the last (sometimes the last but one) consonant of the Singular, e.g.:

    ģip knee Plur. **ģaabab**
    lisi tongue   **lesas** [L.]

Some Plurals are formed by change of tone [vB.].

In JONGOR the Plural Suffix is **-ģi** or **-aģi** (cp. KENGA, SARA, and other languages of the BONGO-BAGIRMI Group).[2]

3. There are three Genitive Particles in MUBI, Masculine, Feminine, and Plural, which stand between *nomen regens* and *rectum*.

In DANGALEAT the Linking Particle is **k**, in JONGOR **k(i)**.[2]

---

[1] 'Vocabulaires comparatifs... (part 2).'
[2] From MS. vocabularies collected by A. J. Arkell, headed KARBO [= DANGALEAT] and MOKALO [= JONGOR].

THE CHADO-HAMITIC LANGUAGES

4. The Inclusive/Exclusive distinction in the 1st Person Plural Pronoun has been observed by van Bulck in all languages investigated.

5. Conjugation of the Verb in MUBI is in many points similar to that of KOTOKO. While a Present and Preterite Tense are conjugated by Prefixes, a second Preterite has Suffixes only [L.].

BIBLIOGRAPHY

GENERAL

CLARKE, JOHN. 1848. Specimens of dialects: short vocabularies of languages, and notes of countries and customs in Africa. Berwick-upon-Tweed and London. Pp. v+104.

DELAFOSSE, M. 1904. Vocabulaires comparatifs de plus de 60 langues et dialectes parlés à la Côte d'Ivoire et dans les régions limitrophes. Paris: Leroux. Pp. 284.
> Many of the languages and dialects dealt with are still virtually unknown, and subsequent attempts at classification are largely based on the material in this book.

—— 1912. Haut-Sénégal–Niger. Paris.
> Vol. 1 contains a section on languages.

—— 1924. Les langues du Soudan et de la Guinée. In: Meillet, A., and Cohen, M., Les langues du monde. Paris: Champion.

DREXEL, A. Gliederung der afrikanischen Sprachen. Anthropos, **16–20**, 1921–5.

GREENBERG, J. H. Studies in African linguistic classification. 1. The Niger-Congo family; 3. The position of Bantu. Southwestern J. Anthrop. **5**, 1949, 2, 79–100; 4, 309–17.

JOHNSTON, SIR H. H. 1919 and 1922. A comparative study of the Bantu and Semi-Bantu languages. 2 vols. Oxford: Clarendon Press [hereafter referred to as 'Bantu and Semi-Bantu'.]
> Vocabularies and notes on a great number of languages; some of the material is taken from Koelle (*see below*).

KOELLE, S. W. 1854. Polyglotta Africana. London: Church Missionary Society. Pp. 188, folio.
> Consists of vocabularies of a great number of languages and dialects of West Africa. Some of these are even now very little known. Many of the statements of subsequent writers are based on the material in this book.

LAROCHETTE, J. La racine du type CV dans les langues soudanaises. Zaïre, **4**, 6, 1950, 583–612.

WESTERMANN, D. 1927. Die westlichen Sudansprachen und ihre Beziehungen zum Bantu. M.S.O.S. Beiheft (Jahrg. 30). Berlin: de Gruyter. Pp. 313.

—— Nominalklassen in westafrikanischen Klassensprachen und in Bantusprachen. M.S.O.S. **38**, 1935, 1–53.

—— Charakter und Einteilung der Sudansprachen. Africa, **8**, 1935, 129–48.

—— Pluralbildung und Nominalklassen in einigen afrikanischen Sprachen. Abh. d. dtsch. Akad. d. Wiss. z. Berlin 1945/6, Phil.-hist. Klasse **1**. Pp. 27.

WIESCHHOF, H. A. Sur un exemplaire annoté d'un ouvrage de Maurice Delafosse. C.R. 1ᵉ Conf. Int. des africanistes de l'ouest, IFAN, Dakar, 1951, pp. 224–6.
> An account of notes made by Clozel in his copy of Delafosse's Vocabulaires comparatifs..., now in the library of the University of Pennsylvania.

SECTION I
THE WEST ATLANTIC LANGUAGES

GENERAL

MIGEOD, F. W. H. 1911 and 1933. The languages of West Africa. 2 vols. London: Kegan Paul.
> Contains specimens of a number of languages and dialects, with grammatical notes.

THOMAS, N. W. 1916. Specimens of languages from Sierra Leone. London: Harrison & Sons. Pp. 62.

WESTERMANN, D. Die westatlantische Gruppe der Sudansprachen (Westafrikanische Studien 5). M.S.O.S. **31**, 1928, 63–86.

1. ADYUKRU

BERTHO, J. La place du dialecte adiukru par rapport aux autres dialectes de la Côte d'Ivoire. Bull. IFAN, **12**, 4, 1950, 1075–94.
> Contains a vocabulary of 120 words and comparisons with other languages.

DELAFOSSE, M. 1901. Essai de manuel de la langue agni. Paris.
> Contains a vocabulary of ADYUKRU, and a bibliography.

2. GOLA

ROHDE, H. Texte in der Golasprache. In: Westermann, D., Die Kpelle (*see* II. 2).
WESTERMANN, D. 1921. Die Gola-Sprache in Liberien. Hamburg. Pp. 178.
  Grammar, texts, and vocabulary.

3. KISSI-LANDOMA GROUP

CLARKE, M. L. 1929. Limba–English dictionary. Freetown: Government Printer (multigraphed). Pp. 150.
FODAY, J. E. B. Names of the twelve months of the year in Temne, with notes and translation. School Notes, Sierra Leone, **6**, 1941, 13–17.
HOUIS, M. Les minorités ethniques de la Guinée côtière. Situation linguistique. Ét. Guinéennes, **4**, 1950, 25–48.
—— Contes baga (Dialecte du Koba). Ét. Guinéennes, **6**, 1950, 2–15.
  Folk-tales with interlinear and free translation, and glossary.
INTERNATIONAL INSTITUTE OF AFRICAN LANGUAGES AND CULTURES. 1929. Alphabets for the Mende, Temne, Soso, Kono and Limba languages. London.
KRAUSE, G. A. Die Stellung des Temne innerhalb der Bantusprachen. Z. afr. u. ocean. Spr. **1**, 1895, 250–67.
SAMARIN, W. A provisional phonemic analysis of Kisi.
  Kroeber Anthrop. Papers, **2**, 1950, 89–102 (Univ. of California, Berkeley).
SAYERS, E. F. A few Temne songs. Sierra Leone Stud. **10**, 1927.
—— A comparative agricultural vocabulary in various Sierra Leone languages. Sierra Leone Stud. **11**, 1928.
  Includes TEMNE and LIMBA.
—— and KAMARA, M. A Timne tale with translation. Sierra Leone Stud. **16**, 1930, 21–26.
C SCHLENKER, C. F. 1861. A collection of Temne traditions, texts with translation, to which is appended a Temne–English vocabulary. London: Church Missionary Society. Pp. 298.
—— 1864. Grammar of the Temne language. London: Church Missionary Society. Pp. 414.
—— 1880. An English–Temne dictionary. London: Church Missionary Society. Pp. 403.
SUMNER, A. T. 1921. A handbook of the Sherbro language. London: Crown Agents. Pp. 132.
—— 1922. A handbook of the Temne language. Freetown: Government Printing Office. Pp. 157.
THOMAS, N. W. 1916. Anthropological report on Sierra Leone. London: Harrison & Sons.
  Part II. Timne–English dictionary. Pp. 139.
    III. Timne grammar and stories. Pp. 86.
WESTERMANN, D. Form und Funktion der Reduplikation in einigen westafrikanischen Sprachen. Afrika (Berlin), **3**, 2 [1944], 83–104.
  Examples from EWE, FUL, TWI, GA, GUANG, YORUBA, TEMNE.

4. OTHER LANGUAGES

BELLA, L. DE SOUZA. Apontamentos sobre a lingua dos Balantas de Jabadá. Bol. Cult. Guiné Portug. **1**, 4, 1946, 729–63.
CARREIRA, A., and MARQUES, J. BASSO. 1947. Subsídios para o estudo da lingua Manjaca. Centro de Estudos da Guiné Portuguesa, **3**. Pp. 175.
HOUIS, M. Les minorités ethniques . . . (*see* I. 3).
  Vocabularies of BAGA FORE and NALU, with notes.
KLINGENHEBEN, A. Die Permutationen des Biafada und des Ful. Z. Eingeb. Spr. **15**, 1924/5, 3, 180–213; **4**, 266–72.
KRAUSE, G. A. Die Fada-Sprache am Geba-Fluss im portugiesischen Westafrika. Z. afr. u. ocean. Spr. **1**, 1895, 363–72.
  Deals with BIAFADA.
MARQUES, J. BASSO. Familiaridade idiomática entre Cobiana e Cassangas. Bol. Cult. Guiné Portug. **2**, 8, 1947, 875–913.

NOGUEIRA, A. Monografia sôbre a tribo banhun. Bol. Cult. Guiné Portug. **2**, 8, 1947, 973–1008. Contains a short vocabulary.
QUINTINO, F. R. Algumas notas sôbre a Gramática Balanta. Bol. Cult. Guiné Port. **6**, 21, 1951, 1–52.
TASTEVIN, C. Vocabulaires inédits de 7 dialectes sénégalais dont 6 de Casamance. J. Soc. Afric. **6**, 1, 1936, 1–33.
BANYUN, BAYOT, BALANT, MANKANYA, MANDYAK, DYOLA, SERER-NON.
WEISS, P. H. Grammaire et lexique Diola du Fogny (Casamance). Bull. IFAN, **1**, 2/3, 1939, 412–578.
Deals with the 'Filham' dialect.
WINTZ, E. 1909. Dictionnaire Français-Dyola et Dyola-Français, précédé d'un essai de grammaire. Elinkine (Casamance): Mission Catholique. Pp. 79+185.

5. SERER

FAIDHERBE, L. L. C. Essai sur la langue Poul et comparaison de cette langue avec le Wolof, les idiomes sérères et les autres langues du Soudan occidental. Rev. Ling. **7**, 1875, 195–242, 291–321.
GREFFIER, H. 1901. Dictionnaire Français-Sérère, précédé d'un abrégé de la grammaire sérère. St. Joseph de Ngazobil. Pp. 350.
—— 1901. Grammaire Sérère. St. Joseph de Ngazobil.
HESTERMANN, F. Die Repetition in der Serersprache von Senegambia. Z. dtsch. morgenl. Ges. **69**, 1915, 107–12.
—— Der dreistufige Anlaut und die Suffixbildung in Serer. Wiener Z. Kde. Morgenl. **30**, 1918, 223–63.
HOMBURGER, L. Le sérère-peul. J. Soc. Afric. **9**, 1, 1939, 85–102.
SENGHOR, S. L. L'harmonie vocalique en Sérère (dialecte du Dyéguémé). J. Soc. Afric. **14**, 1944, 17–23.
TASTEVIN, C. Vocabulaires inédits . . . (see I. 4).

6. WOLOF

(ANON.) 1902. Dictionnaire volof-français avec abrégé de grammaire volof. St. Joseph de Ngazobil.
ANTA, DIOP CHEIKH. Études de linguistique ouolove. Présence africaine, **4**, 1948, 672–84 (in continuation).
AUGRAND, ——. 1943. Manuel ouolof. Dakar: Ed. Viale.
DELAFOSSE, M. Les classes nominales en wolof. Festschrift Meinhof, 1927, pp. 29–44.
FAIDHERBE, L. L. C. Essai sur la langue Poul . . . (see I. 5).
GRANET, ——. 1905. Manuel de conversation wolof-français. Paris.
GUY GRAND, V. J., and ABIVEN, ——. 1923. Dictionnaire Français-Volof. Dakar. Pp. 627.
HOMBURGER, L. Le wolof et les parlers bantous. Mém. Soc. Ling. Paris, **17**, 1912, pp. 26.
MOURADIAN, J. Note sur quelques emprunts de la langue wolof à l'arabe. Bull. IFAN, **2**, 3/4, 1940, 269–84.
NDIAYE, AISSETOU. Complément à une note sur quelques emprunts de la langue wolof à l'arabe. Notes afr. **41**, 1949, 26–29.
ROMARCH, ——. 1922. Recueil de morceaux religieux et profanes en langue wolof. Abbeville: Paillart.
SENGHOR, S. L. Les classes nominales en wolof et les substantifs à initiale nasale. J. Soc. Afric. **13**, 1943, 109–22.
—— L'article conjonctif en wolof. J. Soc. Afric. **17**, 1947, 19–22.
WARD, I. C. A short phonetic study of Wolof (Jolof) as spoken in the Gambia and in Senegal. Africa, **12**, 3, 1939, 320–34.

7. FULANI

ARENSDORFF, L. 1913. Manuel pratique de la langue peulh. Paris: P. Geuthner.

BRUN, J. Recueil de fables et de chants en dialecte Hal Poular. Anthrop. **14/15,** 1919/20, 180–214.
CREMER, J. 1923. Dictionnaire Français-Peul (Dialectes de la Haute-Volta). Matériaux d'ethnographie et de linguistique Soudanaises, Tome I. Paris: Geuthner. Pp. xxix+109. With introduction by M. Delafosse.
DREXEL, A. Kann das Ful als hamitische Sprache gelten? Festschrift P. W. Schmidt, Wien, 1928, pp. 45–60.
G EAST, R. M. 1934. Stories of old Adamawa. A collection of historical texts in the Adamawa dialect of Fulani. With a translation and notes. Lagos and London: West Africa Publicity, Ltd.
FAIDHERBE, L. L. C. Essai sur la langue Poul . . . (see 1. 5).
—— 1882. Grammaire et vocabulaire de la langue Poul. Paris: Maisonneuve et Cie.
FLIEGELMANN, FRIEDA. Moral vocabulary of an unwritten language (Fulani). Anthrop. **27,** 1932, 213–48.
GADEN, H. Note sur le dialecte Foul parlé par les Foulbé du Baguirmi. J. Asiatique, jan./fév. 1908. Pp. 70.
—— 1913, 1914. Le Poular. Dialecte Peul du Fouta Sénégalais. Paris: Leroux (Collection de la Revue du monde musulman).
 Vol. I. Étude morphologique, textes. Pp. 336.
G II. Lexique Poular-Français. Pp. xii+263.
—— 1931. Proverbes et maximes Peuls et Toucouleurs, traduits, expliqués et annotés. Paris: Trav. et Mém. Inst. d'Ethnol. **16.** Pp. xxxiv+368.
—— 1935. La vie d'El Hadj Omar, Qacida en Poular. Paris: Trav. et Mém. Inst. d'Ethnol. **21.** Pp. xxv+289.
GREENBERG, J. H. Studies in African linguistic classification. 2. The classification of Fulani. Southwestern J. Anthrop. **5,** 3, 1949, 190–8.
GUIRAUDON, TH. G. DE. 1887. Notes de linguistique africaine. Les Puls. Paris: Leroux.
—— 1894. Bolle Fulbe. Manuel de la langue Foule. Grammaire, textes, vocabulaire. Paris and Leipzig: H. Weltern. Pp. viii+144.
HOMBURGER, L. Morphèmes africains en peul et dans les parlers bantous. Mém. Soc. Ling. Paris, **18,** 1913.
—— 1929. Les préfixes nominaux dans les parlers peul, haoussa et bantou. Trav. et Mém. Inst. d'Ethnol. **6.** Pp. xi+166.
—— Le peul et les langues nilotiques. Bull. Soc. Ling. Paris, **37,** 1936, 58–72.
—— Le sérère-peul (see 1. 5).
—— Eléments dravidiens en peul. J. Soc. Afric. **18,** 2, 1948, 135–43.
JEFFREYS, M. D. W. Speculative origins of the Fulani language. Africa, **17,** 1947, 47–54.
JOHNSTON, SIR H. H. The Fulas and their language. J. Afr. Soc. **20,** 1920/1, 212–16.
KLINGENHEBEN, A. Die Präfixklassen des Ful. Z. Eingeb. Spr. **14,** 1923/4, 189–222, 290–315.
—— 1927. Die Laute des Ful. Z. Eingeb. Spr. Beiheft **9.**
—— Die nominalen Klassensysteme des Ful. Donum Natalicium Schrijnen (Utrecht), 1929, pp. 175–81.
—— Die Permutationen des Biafada und des Ful (see 1. 4).
—— 1941. Die Suffixklassen des Ful. Z. Eingeb. Spr. Beiheft **23.**
—— Die Klassenelemente der Zahlwörter des Ful. Z. dtsch. morgenl. Ges. **99,** 1, 1945/9, 67–92.
LABOURET, H. 1952. La langue des Peuls ou Foulbé. Mém. IFAN, **16,** pp. xi+286.
LEITH-ROSS, S. 1921. Fulani grammar. Lagos. Pp. 210.
MEINHOF, C. Das Ful in seiner Bedeutung für die Sprachen der Hamiten, Semiten und Bantu. Z. dtsch. morgenl. Ges. **65,** 1911, 177–220.
—— 1912. Die Sprachen der Hamiten. Hamburg.
 Chap. 2. FUL.
MOREIRA, J. M. 1948. Fulas do Gabú. Bissau. Pp. 328.
 Contains information on language.
PALMER, H. R. The 'Fulas' and their language. J. Afr. Soc. **22,** 1922/3, 121–31.
PFEFFER, G. Prose and poetry of the Ful'be. Africa, **12,** 1939, 285–306.

SCHULTZE, —. Fulbe-Notizen. M.S.O.S. **12**, 1909, 123–6.
STEANE, K. Kleine Fullah-Grammatik (bearb. Emil Sembritzki). Archiv f. d. Studium dtsch. Kolonialspr. **7**, 1909.
STEPHANI, FRANZ V. Materialien für das Studium der Fulbe-Sprache. M.S.O.S. **12**, 1909, 114–22.
—— 1911. Taschenbuch der Sprache der Fulbe in Adamaua. Berlin: G. Reimer.
STORBECK, F. Metoula-Sprachführer der Ful-Sprache. Berlin-Schöneberg: Langenscheidt.
—— Fulsprichwörter aus Adamaua. Z. Eingeb. Spr. **10**, 1919/20, 106–22.
—— Fultexte aus Adamaua. Z. Eingeb. Spr. **11**, 1920/1, 24–34.
TAUTAIN, L. Contribution à l'étude de la langue foule (Poular). Rev. Ling. **22**, 347–66; **23**, 28–50, 118–47, 212–21.
TAYLOR, F. W. 1921. A first Fulani reading book. London: Crown Agents.
—— 1921. A second Fulani reading book. London: Crown Agents.
—— 1930. A third Fulani reading book. London: Crown Agents.
—— 1921. A first grammar of the Adamawa dialect of the Fulani language (Taylor's Fulani–Hausa series 1). Oxford: Clarendon Press. Pp. 135.
—— 1926. A Fulani–Hausa phrase-book (Taylor's Fulani–Hausa series 3). Oxford: Clarendon Press. Pp. 158.
—— 1927. A Fulani–Hausa vocabulary (Taylor's Fulani–Hausa series 4). Oxford: Clarendon Press. Pp. 136.
—— 1929. Fulani–Hausa readings in the native scripts (Taylor's Fulani–Hausa series 5). Oxford: Clarendon Press.
—— 1932. A Fulani–Hausa dictionary (Taylor's Fulani–Hausa series 6). Oxford: Clarendon Press. Pp. 242.
—— Some English words in Fulani and Hausa. J. Afr. Soc. **20**, 1920/1, 25–32.
VIEILLARD, G. Récits Peuls du Macina et du Kounari. Bull. Com. Ét. hist. et scient. de l'A.O.F. **14**, 1931, 137–56.
—— Douroël Bâli Boûlo et Fâdia. Conte Peul du Kounari. Bull. Com. Ét. hist. et scient. de l'A.O.F. **16**, 1933, 149–54.
—— Poèmes peuls du Fouta Djallon. Bull. Com. Ét. hist. et scient. de l'A.O.F. **20**, 1937, 225–311.
WESTERMANN, D. 1909. Handbuch der Ful-Sprache. Wörterbuch, Grammatik, Übungen und Texte. Berlin: D. Reimer. Pp. 274.
—— 1910. Fullah-Übungen. Berlin.
—— 1913. Erzählungen in Fulfulde, niedergeschrieben von Abdallah Adam, transkribiert, übersetzt und mit einem Nachtrag: Erzählungen im Dialekt von Sokoto. Berlin: G. Reimer (Lehrbücher des S.O.S. **30**).
—— Form und Funktion der Reduplikation ... (see I. 3).
G WHITTING, C. E. J. 1940. Hausa and Fulani proverbs. Lagos: Government Printer. Pp. 192.

SECTION II

THE MANDE LANGUAGES

GENERAL

CLARKE, J. Specimens ... (see GENERAL).
DELAFOSSE, M. 1901. Essai de manuel pratique de la langue Mandé ou Mandingue. Paris: Leroux. Pp. 304.
    Deals mainly with DYULA, but also contains vocabularies of other languages and dialects.
HINTZE, F. Zum konsonantischen Anlautwechsel in einigen westafrikanischen Sprachen. Z. Phon. u. Spr. Wiss. **2**, 1948, 3/4, 164–82; 5/6, 522–35.
    BANDI, MENDE, KPELLE, MANYA, and KEBU.
KOELLE, S. W. Polyglotta Africana (see GENERAL).
MIGEOD, F. W. H. The languages of West Africa (see I. GENERAL).

STEINTHAL, H. 1867. Die Mande-Neger-Sprachen. Psychologisch und phonetisch betrachtet. A comparative study of MALINKE, BAMBARA, and VAI.
THOMAS, N. W. Specimens . . . from Sierra Leone (see I. GENERAL).
WESTERMANN, D. Die westlichen Sudansprachen (see GENERAL).
Pp. 144–96, the MANDE languages.

1. MANDE TAN GROUP

(ANON.) 1896. Essai de dictionnaire français-malinké. Soudan Français: Mission à Kéita. Pp. 428.
ABIVEN, —. 1896. Essai de grammaire Malinkée. Imp. de St. Michel en Priziac. Pp. 428.
—— 1900. Méthode de lecture Malinkée. Paris: André et Cie. Pp. 22.
—— 1900. Grammaire Malinkée. Paris.
—— 1900. Dictionnaire Malinké-Français. St. Michel en Priziac. Pp. 118.
—— 1900. Dictionnaire Français-Malinké. St. Michel en Priziac.
—— 1906. Dictionnaire Français-Malinké et Malinké-Français précédé d'un abrégé de grammaire Malinké. Abbeville: Paillart. Pp. xliv+176.
BARTH, H. Der verlorene Sohn in der Sprache von Shetun ku Sefe oder der Azarareye-Sprache. Z. dtsch. morgenl. Ges. **9**, 1885.
  Translation of the story of the Prodigal Son into AZER, with notes.
BASTARD, G. Essai de lexique pour les idiomes du Soudan. Rev. col. 17 Mai 1900.
  SONINKE and KHASSONKE.
G BAZIN, H. 1906. Dictionnaire Bambara-Français, précédé d'un abrégé de grammaire Bambara. Paris. Pp. 694.
BRUN, P. Proverbes et devinettes Khassonkés. Annuaire du Com. Ét. hist. et scient. de l'A.O.F., 1917, pp. 223 ff.
CHATAIGNIER, ABEL. L'impérissable beauté. Afr. Stud. **5**, 3, 1946, 195–206.
  MALINKE text with translation and notes.
—— La conception malinké de la personnalité humaine révélée par l'usage des possessifs. C.R. 1ᵉ Conf. Int. des africanistes de l'ouest. IFAN, Dakar, 1951, pp. 193–6.
COLY, DEMBA. Chant mandingue de Casamance. Notes afr. IFAN, 38, 1948, 22–24.
DAMMANN, E. Vai-Erzählungen. Z. Eingeb. Spr. **23**, 1932/3, 254–78.
—— Vai-Sprichwörter. Z. Eingeb. Spr. **24**, 1933/4, 76–79.
DELAFORGE, M. 2nd ed. 1935, 4th ed. 1947. Grammaire et méthode Bambara. Paris: Ch. Lavauzelle. Pp. 203.
DELAFOSSE, M. Les Vai, leur langue et leur système d'écriture. L'Anthrop. **10**, 1899.
—— 1929. La langue Mandingue et ses dialectes (Malinke, Bambara, Dioula). 1. Introduction, grammaire, lexique Français-Mandingue. Paris: Geuthner (Bibl. des langues orientales vivantes). Pp. 674.
ESSEN, O. v. Stimmhafte Implosive im Vai. Z. Eingeb. Spr. **26**, 1935/6, 150–8.
FAIDHERBE, L. L. C. Notes grammaticales sur la langue sarakolé ou soninké. Annuaire du Sénégal 1864.
GAMBLE, D. P. 1949. Notes on Mandinka. Bathurst: Government Printer. Pp. 16.
—— 1949. Mandinka grammar. London: Col. Office Research Dept. (duplic.). Pp. 66.
HAMLYN, W. T. 1935. A short study of the western Mandinka language. London: Crown Agents. Pp. 110.
HAMPARÉ BA, AMADOU. Les trois pêcheurs bredouilles (conte bambara). Notes afr. IFAN, **21**, 1944, 21–22.
HEYDORN, R. Das Manya. Ein in Liberia gesprochener Mandingodialekt. Z. Eingeb. Spr. **34**, 1, 1944, 25–53; **35**, 1, 1949, 47–66.
HOMBURGER, L. Le bantou et le mandé. Mém. Soc. Ling. Paris, **19**, 4, 1915, 224–42.
—— Les dialectes coptes et mandés. Bull. Soc. Ling. Paris, **30**, 1, 1930, 1–57.
HOPKINSON, E. 1911. A vocabulary of the Mandingo language as spoken in the Gambia. London: West, Newman & Co. Pp. 72.
  Another edition, with addenda 1924, pp. 72+14.

KLINGENHEBEN, A. Vai-Texte. Z. Eingeb. Spr. **16**, 1915/16, 58–133.
  With an introduction on sounds, syllables, words, tone, and stress, and on the linguistic form of the texts.
—— Zur psychologischen Struktur der Vai-Sprache. C. R. Congr. Int. Afr. Inst. Paris, 1932, pp. 89–99.
—— The Vai script. Africa, **6**, 1933, 158–71 (reprinted in Sierra Leone Stud. **19**, 1933).
—— 1933. Der Bau der Sprache der Vai in Westafrika. Nachrichten d. Ges. d. Wiss. z. Göttingen. Phil-hist. Klasse. Pp. 31.
—— Die Mande-Völker und ihre Sprache. Z. Eingeb. Spr. **34**, 1944, 1–26.
  Deals with BAMBARA and KHASONKE.
KOELLE, S. W. 1849. Narrative of an expedition into the Vy country and the discovery of a system of writing recently invented by the natives. Pp. 34.
G —— 1854. Outline of a grammar of the Vai language. London.
LABOURET, H. Les Manding et leur langue. Bull. Com. Ét. hist. et. scient. de l'A.O.F. **17**, 1, 1934, 1–270 (whole number).
—— and WARD, I. C. Quelques observations sur la langue Mandingue. Africa, **6**, 1, 1933, 38–50.
  Deals mainly with the function of tone.
MASSAQUOI, MOMOLU. The Vai people and their syllabic writing. J. Afr. Soc. **10**, 1911, 59–66.
MIGEOD, F. W. H. The syllabic writing of the Vai people. J. Afr. Soc. **9**, 1909, 46–58.
MONTEIL, CH. 1915. Les Khassonké. Paris: Leroux. Pp. 528.
  Part 3 (pp. 405–524) deals with the language.
—— La langue des Bozo. Bull. Com. Ét. hist. et scient. de l'A.O.F. **15**, 2/3, 1932, 261–399 (also as a separate reprint).
—— La langue Azer. Contributions à l'étude du Sahara occidental (ed. Th. Monod), 3. Paris: Publications du Com. Ét. hist. et scient. de l'A.O.F., Série B, No. 5, fasc. 2, 1938, pp. 213–41.
NUNN, G. N. N. 1934. Short phrase book and classified vocabularies from English into Mandinka. Bathurst: Government Printer. Pp. 29.
PÉROZ, E. 1891. Dictionnaire français-mandingue. Paris.
  Eastern and southern MALINKE.
SAUVANT, M. 1913. Manuel Bambara (grammaire et lexique). Alger.
—— 1925. Petit manuel Bambara. Alger.
—— 1926. Dictionnaire Français-Bambara et Bambara-Français. Alger.
SAYERS, E. F. A comparative agricultural vocabulary . . . (see I. 3).
—— The song of 'Mfaji—the adored of women. Sierra Leone Stud. **13**, 1938, p. 34.
  In MALINKE.
SILVA, V. L. R. DA. Pequeno vocabulario Portuguez-Mandinga. Bol. Soc. Geogr. Lisboa, 1929, 99–108, 142–51.
TAUTAIN, L. Notes sur les trois langues soninké, bamana et mallinké ou mandingké. Rev. Ling. et Philol. comp., 1887.
TAUXIER, L. 1921. Le Noir de Bondoukou. Paris: Leroux. Pp. 770.
  Appendices contain vocabularies of a number of languages and dialects.
TOULET, ——. Proverbes bambara. Bull. Com. Et. hist. et scient. de l'A.O.F. **3**, 1920, 346–7.
TRAVÉLÉ, M. 1913, 2nd ed. 1923. Petit dictionnaire Français-Bambara et Bambara-Français. Paris: Geuthner. Pp. 281.
—— 1923. Proverbes et contes Bambara. Paris.
  Texts with translation.
—— 1927, new ed. 1947. Petit manuel Français-Bambara. Paris: Geuthner. Pp. 69, new ed. 90.
WELMERS, W. E. Tonemes and tone-writing in Maninka. Studies in Linguistics, **7**, 1, 1949, 1–17.

2. MANDE FU

ADAM, J. Noms toma d'arbres et arbustes (Guinée Française). C.R. 1ᵉ Conf. Int. des africanistes de l'ouest, IFAN, Dakar, 1951, pp. 150–2.
  TOMA and Latin names.

AGINSKY, ETHEL G. A grammar of the Mende language. Language dissertation, Philadelphia, 20, 1935. Pp. 111.
AVERY, E. Mende proverbs. School Notes, Sierra Leone, **6**, 1941, 35–39.
CLARKE, W. R. E. 1941, repr. 1943. Mende phrase book. Bunubu, Sierra Leone. Pp. 34.
CROSBY, K. H., and WARD, I. C. 1944. An introduction to the study of Mende. Cambridge: Heffer, for Int. Inst. Afr. Lang. & Cult. Pp. vi+66.
  A full treatment of tone and a clear exposition of grammar, with numerous examples.
DONNER, E. Überlieferungen aus Nordostliberia. Z. f. Ethnol. **71**, 4/6, 1939, 174–200.
DUPONT, I. H. 1892. Outline grammar of the Susu language. London.
EBERL-ELBER, R. Der konsonantische Anlautwechsel in der Sprachengruppe Gbande–Loma–Mende. Mitt. d. Auslandhochschule, **60**, 3, 1937, 128–43.
—— Eine Tierfabel in der Mende-Sprache. Ethnos (Stockholm), **3**, 2/3, 1938, 47–52.
—— Two Mende tales. B.S.O.S. **10**, 1, 1939, 223–34.
FUNKE, E. Die Sprache von Busa am Niger. M.S.O.S. **16**, 1913, 52–84.
GUINEÉ FRANÇAISE, PRÉFECTURE APOSTOLIQUE. 1915. Essai de grammaire Soussou. Paris: Imp. des orphelins apprentis d'Auteuil. Pp. 125.
HEINITZ, W. Analyse eines Mende-Liedes. Vox, 1928, 9/10, 40–44.
HEYDORN, R. Die Sprache der Bandi im nordwestlichen Liberia. Z. Eingeb. Spr. **31**, 2/3, 1940/1, 81–114, 167–88.
INT. INST. AFR. LANG. AND CULT. Alphabets . . . (*see* I. 3).
JOFFRE, J. Sur un nouvel alphabet ouest-africain: Le Toma (frontière franco-libérienne). Bull. IFAN, **7**, 1945, 1–4, 160–73.
—— AND MONOD, TH. A new West African alphabet used by the Toma, French Guinea and Liberia. Man, **43**, 85, 1943, 108–12.
LAKNA, PH. Grammaire et dictionnaire Français-Susu et Susu-Français. Conakry.
LASSORT, A. L'écriture guerzée. C.R. 1ᵉ Conf. Int. des africanistes de l'ouest, IFAN, Dakar, 1951, pp. 209–15.
  A recently invented form of writing.
MICHELL, H. Notes on the Mende language and customs. Sierra Leone Stud. **3**, 13 ff.
MIGEOD, F. W. H. 1908. The Mende language. Grammar, short vocabulary, and folk-tales with English translation. London: Kegan Paul. Pp. 271.
—— 1913. Mende natural history vocabulary. London: Kegan Paul. Pp. 64.
NOLTZE, K. Märchen der Kpelle in Liberia. M.S.O.S. **37**, 1934, 162–84.
PASTOR. —. La langue Soso. La voix de Notre Dame, 4 déc. 1931, 406–9.
PROST, A. Contribution à l'étude des langues mandé-sud. Notes afr. **40**, 1948, 2–4.
G —— 1950. La Langue Bisa. Grammaire et dictionnaire. Centre IFAN, Ouagadougou, Haute-Volta. Pp. 198.
RAMBAULT (I. B. ?). 1888. Dictionnaire Français-Soso et Soso-Français. Paris: Imp. de l'Œuvre de St. Paul. Pp. 164.
SAYERS, E. F. A comparative agricultural vocabulary . . . (*see* I. 3).
—— Three Susu songs. Sierra Leone Stud. **15**, 1929, 48–50.
—— Some Susu proverbs. Sierra Leone Stud. **15**, 1929, 51–56.
SENIOR, M. M. Some Mende proverbs. Africa, **17**, 3, 1947, 202–5.
SORY, ALMAMY, and others. Trois contes soussou. Ét. Guinéennes, **1**, 1947, 23–25.
  With interlinear and free translation.
SUMNER, A. T. Grammar for beginners (Mende). Freetown: Government Printer.
—— 1917. A handbook of the Mende language. Freetown: Government Printer. Pp. 191.
—— Mendi writing. Sierra Leone Stud. **17**, 1932.
—— and HONTER, R. F. Names of diseases in Mende. Sierra Leone Stud. **6**, 1922, 41 ff.
TAUXIER, L. 1917. Le Noir du Yatenga. Paris.
  Appendices contain numerous vocabularies.
—— 1924. Nouvelles notes sur le Mossi et le Gourounsi. Paris: Larose. Pp. 206.
  Pp. 178–80, vocabularies of BOKO (from Koelle) and 'BOUSSA'.
WELMERS, W. E. 1948. Spoken Kpelle. Monrovia: Lutheran Mission (duplic.). 1950, pp. 105–18.
—— New light on consonant change in Kpelle. Z. Phonetik u. Wiss. **4**, 1/2.

WESTERMANN, D. Sprachstudien aus dem Gebiet der Sudansprachen 2. Die Kpesesprache in Liberia. M.S.O.S. **13**, 1910, 58–72.
—— 1921. Die Kpelle, ein Negerstamm in Liberia. Göttingen und Leipzig.
 Pp. 139–73, a study of the grammatical structure of KPELLE.
—— Drei Erzählungen in der Kpelle-Sprache (Liberia). Wörterverzeichnis Deutsch–Kpelle. M.S.O.S. **26/7**, 1924, 37–83.
—— Die Kpelle-Sprache in Liberia. Grammatische Einführung, Texte und Wörterbuch. Z. Eingeb. Spr. Beiheft **6**. Pp. viii+278.
—— and MELZIAN, H. 1930. The Kpelle language in Liberia. Grammatical outline, colloquial sentences and vocabulary. Berlin: Reimer. Pp. vii+85.

SECTION III
SONGHAI

C BARTH, H. 1862. Sammlung und Bearbeitung Centralafrikanischer Vokabularien. Gotha: Perthes. 2 vols.
 One of the languages dealt with is SONGHAI.
BEN HAMOUDA. Devinettes Songhay. Bull. Com. Ét. hist. et scient. de l'A.O.F. **1**, 1916, 62–67.
—— Proverbes Songhay. Bull. Com. Ét. hist. et scient. de l'A.O.F. **3**, 1918, 278–80.
CLARKE, J. Specimens . . . (see GENERAL).
 'Timbuctoo, Kissour, Tombuktu, Sansanding' are all SONGHAI.
DUPUIS, A. 1911. Les Gows ou chasseurs du Niger. Paris.
 Contains SONGHAI texts with translation.
—— 1917. Essai de méthode pratique pour l'étude de la langue Songoi ou Songaï. Paris.
 With texts and vocabulary.
FUNKE, E. Die Sprachverhältnisse in Sugu, Dahomey, Franz. Westafrika. Z. Kol. Spr. **5**, 1914/15, 257–69.
HACQUARD, —, AND DUPUIS, —. 1897. Manuel de la langue Songay, parlée de Tombouctou à Say. Paris.
KOELLE, S. W. Polyglotta Africana (see GENERAL).
MARIE, E. 1914. Vocabulaire Français-Djerma, Djerma-Français. Paris.
MIGEOD, F. W. H. Languages of West Africa (see I. GENERAL).
PICQ, ARDANT DU. Une population africaine: les Dyerma. II. La langue Songhay. Bull. Com. d'Et. hist. et scient. de l'A.O.F., 1931.
WESTERMANN, D. Die westlichen Sudansprachen (see GENERAL).
 SONGHAI included in the section on GUR languages, pp. 121–43.
—— Ein Beitrag zur Kenntnis des Zarma-Songai am Niger. Z. Eingeb. Spr. **11**, 3, 1920/1, 188–220.

SECTION IV
THE KRU DIALECTS

AUER, J. G. 1870. Elements of the Gedebo language. Stuttgart.
CHRISTALLER, J. G. Näheres über die Kru-Sprache. Z. Afr. Spr. **3**, 1889, 1–39.
 Deals with several dialects.
CLARKE, J. Specimens . . . (see GENERAL).
C HERZOG, G. 1926. Jabo proverbs from Liberia. Oxford Univ. Press. for Int. Inst. Afr. Lang. and Cult. Pp. 272.
 With a tonal analysis.
KOELLE, S. W. Polyglotta Africana (see GENERAL).
MÜLLER, F. 1877. Die Sprachen Basa, Grebo und Kru. Wien.
 Short grammatical survey; GREBO text.
PAULIAN, R. Éléments d'un vocabulaire zoologique des dialectes de basse Côte d'Ivoire. J. Soc. Afric. **16**, 1946, 23–28.
 Mainly BETE dialects.

PAYNE, J. 1864. Grebo grammar. New York.
—— 1867. A dictionary of the Grebo language. Philadelphia.
SAPIR, E. Notes on the Gweabo language of Liberia. Language, **7**, 1931, 30–41.
  A careful tonal analysis.
THOIRE, G. Le dialecte Plawi, Côte d'Ivoire. J. Soc. Afric. **3**, 3, 1933, 319–33.
  An elementary introduction.
THOMANN, G. 1905. Essai de manuel de la langue Néouolé. Paris.
THOMAS, N. W. Specimens of languages from Sierra Leone (see I. GENERAL).
WESTERMANN, D. Die westlichen Sudansprachen (see GENERAL).
  KRU dialects, pp. 52–65.

SECTION V

THE GUR LANGUAGES

GENERAL

CHRISTALLER, J. G. Sprachproben aus dem Sudan von 40 bis 60 Sprachen und Mundarten hinter der Gold- und Sklavenküste. Z. Afr. Spr. **3**, 1889/90, 133–54.
GROH, B. Sprachproben aus zwölf Sprachen des Togohinterlandes. M.S.O.S. **14**, 1911, 227–39.
KOELLE, S. W. Polyglotta Africana (see GENERAL).
MIGEOD, F. W. H. The languages of West Africa (see GENERAL).
RATTRAY, R. S. 1932. The tribes of the Ashanti hinterland. Oxford: Clarendon Press.
  Contains a section by Westermann on the GUR languages.
TAUXIER, L. Le Noir de Bondoukou (see II. 1).
—— Le Noir du Yatenga (see II. 2).
WESTERMANN, D. Die westlichen Sudansprachen (see GENERAL).
  GUR, pp. 121–43.

1. SENUFO

CHÉRON, G. 1925. Le dialecte senoufo du Minianka. Paris: Geuthner. Pp. 167.
  Grammar, texts, and vocabulary.
CREMER, J. Essai sur la langue Minianka. Bull. Com. Et. hist. et scient. de l'A.O.F. **4**, 1919, 560–616.
RAPP, E. Die Náfana-sprache auf der Elfenbeinküste und auf der Goldküste. M.S.O.S. **36**, 3, 1933, 66–69.
WELMERS, W. E. Notes on two languages in the Senufo group. 1. Senadi. 2. Sup'ide. Language, **26**, 1, 4, 1950, 126–46, 494–531.

2. KULANGO

RAPP, E. Die Sprache der Kólaŋò auf der Elfenbeinküste und der Goldküste. M.S.O.S. **36**, 3, 1933, 54–66.

3. LOBI-DOGON GROUP

GRIAULE, M. 1938. Jeux Dogons. Paris: Inst. d'Ethnol.
  Contains a considerable number of short texts, songs, &c., with translation; they are not, however, sufficient for an analysis of the language.
LEIRIS, M. 1948. La langue secrète des Dogons de Sanga. Trav. et Mém. de l'Inst. d'Ethnol. Paris, No. 50. Pp. 530.
  Deals with the secret language, but not with that of everyday life.
TAUXIER, L. Vocabulaire Dorhossié et Dorhossié Fing. J. Soc. Afric. **1**, 1931, 87–110.
—— Les Gouin et les Tourouka, résidence de Banfora, cercle de Bobo Dioulasso. J. Soc. Afric. **3**, 1, 1933, 110+128.

4. GRUSI.

CARDINALL, A. W. 1920. The natives of the Northern Territories of the Gold Coast. London.
  Pp. 113–58, grammatical sketch and vocabulary of KASSENA.

CREMER, J. 1924. Grammaire de la langue Kasséna ou Kassené. (Matériaux d'ethnographie et de linguistique soudanaises 2.) Paris. Pp. viii+64.
DIETERLEN, G. Notes sur les Kourouma du Yatenga et de l'Empire de Wagadugu. J. Soc. Afric. **10**, 1940, 181–9.
    Contains grammatical notes on KURUMA (FULSE).
FUNKE, E. Die Isala-Sprache im Westsudan. M.S.O.S. **23/25**, 1919/22, 69–87.
—— Sprachverhältnisse . . . (see III).
    Includes a vocabulary of 'KYILIŃA oder TŠYLIŃA'.
HAILLOT, J. Étude sur la langue dian. Bull. Com. Ét. hist. et scient. A.O.F. **3**, 1918, 348–80.
TAUXIER, L. Nouvelles notes sur le Mossi et le Gourounsi (see II. 2).
    Appendices consist of vocabularies of a number of languages.
WESTERMANN, D. Die Grussisprachen im westlichen Sudan. Z. Kol. Spr. **4**, 1913/14, 161–80, 312–32; **5**, 1914/15, 45–76.
    A comparative study based on ATJÜLO, KANJAGA, and ISSALA, including vocabularies from several earlier writers.
WOLF, L. Beitrag zur Kilir-Sprache. Z. Afr. Spr. **3**, 1889, 290–4.

5. MOSSI GROUP

ALEXANDRE, P. 1935. Grammaire Moré. Paris. Pp. 253.
—— 1934/5. Dictionnaire Moré-Français et Français-Moré.
BLAIR, H. A. (ed.). 1940. Dagomba (Dagbane) dictionary. Accra: Government Printer. Pp. 111.
BLUZET, R. 1901. Vocabulaire de la langue Mossi, précédé de notes grammaticales. Publication du Comité de l'Afrique Française.
DUBOIS, F. Vocabulaire Mossi. Bull. Com. de l'Afr. Française, 1898.
FISCH, R. 1912. Grammatik der Dagomba-Sprache. Archiv f. d. Studium dtsch. Kol. Spr. **14**. Berlin. Pp. x+78.
—— 1913. Dagbane-Sprachproben. Jahrb. d. Hamb. Wiss. Anst. Beiheft 8. Pp. 190.
—— Wörtersammlung Dagbáne-Deutsch. M.S.O.S. **16**, 3, 1913, 113–214.
FROGER, F. 1910. Étude sur la langue des Mossi (Boucle du Niger). Paris: Leroux. Pp. 259.
—— 1923. Manuel pratique de langue Môrè. Paris: Fournier. Pp. 326.
FUNKE, E. Vokabular der Kussassi-Sprache im Westsudan. M.S.O.S. **25**, 1922, 88–98.
LÄSSIG, R. 1928. Die Kussassi-Sprache im Westsudan. Glückstadt: Berlin Philos. Dissert. Pp. 59.
    Based on a manuscript by Funke.
MATTHEWS, J. H. English–Mole vocabulary. Gold Coast Rev., Jan.–June 1930, 41–92.
OKRAKU, S. 1917. Dagomba grammar. Oxford.
RATTRAY, R. S. 1918. An elementary Mole grammar, with a vocabulary. Oxford: Clarendon Press. Pp. 85.
SHIRER, W. L. 1939. Dagbane grammar. Tamale: Assemblies of God Mission (multigraphed). Pp. 89.
TAUXIER, L. Nouvelles notes sur le Mossi et le Gourounsi (see II. 2).
WESTERMANN, D. Die Mossi-Sprachengruppe im westlichen Sudan. Anthropos, **8**, 1913, 467–504, 810–30.

6. GURMA

DUBOIS, F. Vocabulaire Gourma. Bull. Com. de l'Afr. Française, July 1898.
MERCIER, P. Vocabulaire de quelques langues du Nord-Dahomey. Ét. Dahoméennes **2**, 1949, 73–83.
    GURMA, NATIMBA, WOABA, BERBA, SOMBA, NIENDE, YOM [PILA-PILA], WINDJI-WINDJI, BULBA.
—— Note sur les 'Pila-Pila' et les 'Taneka'. Ét. Dahoméennes, **3**, 1950, 39–71.
    Contains a short vocabulary of YOM.
MÜLLER, F. Ein Beitrag zur Kenntnis der Akasele (Tšambá)-Sprache. Anthropos, **1**, 1906, 787–803.
    A comprehensive grammatical sketch.

NICOLAS, F. J. Les surnoms-devises des L'éla de la Haute-Volta (A.O.F.). Anthropos, **45**, 1/3, 1950, 81–118.
   Contains a number of sayings with translation and glossary, and short vocabularies of several dialects.
—— Sept contes des L'éla de la Haute-Volta (A.O.F.) Anthropos, **47**, 1–2, 1952, 80–94.
WESTERMANN, D. 1922. Die Sprache der Guang in Togo und auf der Goldküste und fünf andere Togosprachen. Berlin: Reimer. Pp. 268.
   TOBOTE, AKASELE, and GURMA.
ZECH, V. Vermischte Notizen über Togo und das Togohinterland. Mitt. aus d. dtsch. Schutzgeb. **2**, 1898.
   Contains BASSARI and TSCHAMBA vocabularies.

7. TEM
LELIÈVRE, R. P. Grammaire et vocabulaire Tem.
MÜLLER, F. Beitrag zur Kenntnis der Tem-Sprache (Nord-Togo). M.S.O.S. **8**, 1905, 251–86.
WESTERMANN, D. Drei Dialekte des Tem in Togo: Căla, Delo und Bagó. Nach Aufnahmen von Mischlich. M.S.O.S. **36**, 1933, 7–33.

8. BARGU
WESTERMANN, D. Die Bargu-Sprache im westlichen Sudan. In: Die Sprache der Guang, pp. 124–42 (see v. 6).
WOLF, L. Beitrag zur Kilir-Sprache (see v. 4).
   Contains BARGU numerals.

SECTION VI
THE KWA LANGUAGES
GENERAL
CHRISTALLER, J. G. Sprachproben ... (see V. GENERAL).
CLARKE, J. Specimens ... (see GENERAL).
DELAFOSSE, M. Vocabulaires comparatifs ... (see GENERAL).
KOELLE, S. W. Polyglotta Africana (see GENERAL).
MIGEOD, F. W. H. The languages of West Africa (see I. GENERAL).
THOMAS, N. W., in MEEK, C. K. The Northern Tribes of Nigeria.
   Vol. 2, pp. 132–47, a chapter on languages.
WESTERMANN, D. Form und Funktion der Reduplikation ... (see I. 3).

1. THE 'LAGOON' GROUP
BAILLEUL, P. 1902. Petit dictionnaire de la langue abouré. Dabou.
DELAFOSSE, M. Manuel de la langue agni (see I. 1).
   Contains short vocabularies of ALAGUIAN, ARI, ABE.
DREYFUSS, C. 1900. Six mois dans l'Attié. Paris.
   Contains a vocabulary.
LATHAM, R. G. On a vocabulary of Avekoom, Ivory Coast. Proc. Philol. Soc. **4**, 1848–50, 183–4.
MERAND, P. 1902. Essai sur la langue Attié. Dabou.
PAULIAN, R. Éléments d'un vocabulaire zoologique ... (see IV).
WESTERMANN, D. Das Tschi und Guang. Ihre Stellung innerhalb der Ewe-Tschi Gruppe (Westsudanische Studien 1). M.S.O.S. **28**, 1925, 1–85.
   Deals also with languages of the 'Lagoon' Group.

2. AKAN GROUP
AKROFI, C. A. 1931. Twi kasa mmara. London.
   A grammar of TWI in TWI.
ANAMAN, B. B. 1926. Standard Nzima. Accra.

ANAMAN, B. B. 1927. English and Nzima key book. Accra.
BALMER, W., and GRANT, F. C. F. 1929. A grammar of the Fante-Akan language. London: Atlantic Press. Pp. 224.
BELLON, J. Märchen des Tschi-Volkes auf der Goldküste. Gesammelt von J. Adyaye. M.S.O.S. **17**, 1940, 1–38.
    Folk-tales with translation.
BLAIR, H. A. 1934. Gonja vocabulary and notes. Accra: Government Printer.
BONHOMME, P. J. M. 1901. Petites exercices préparatoires pour l'étude de l'Agni (Afema). Lyon.
BREW, L. H. 1917. Practical Fanti course. Cape Coast.
CHAMBERLAIN, G. D. 1930. A brief account of the Brissa language. Accra. Pp. 57.
G CHRISTALLER, J. G. 1875. A grammar of the Asante and Fante language. Basel. Pp. xxiv+203.
—— 1879. A collection of 3600 Tshi proverbs. Basel.
—— 1881, rev. ed. 1933. Dictionary of the Asante and Fante language called Tshi (Twi). Basel. Pp. xxxii+607.
—— Die Volta Sprachengruppe. Z. Afr. Spr. **1**, 1887/8, 161–88.
    TSCHI, GA, EWE, GUANG, AVATIME.
—— Sprichwörter der Tschwi-Neger. Z. afr. u. ocean. Spr. **1**, 1895, 184–7; **2**, 1896, 51–53, 241–3.
DELAFOSSE, M. Essai de manuel de la langue agni (see I. 1).
GROH, B. Sprachproben . . . (see V. GENERAL).
HINTZE, U. Untersuchungen zur sprachlichen Stellung des Nzema innerhalb der Akansprachen. Phil. Diss. Berlin 1949, IV. Pp. 137 (typescr.).
MIGEOD, F. W. H. The languages of West Africa (see I. GENERAL).
MÜLLER, F. Die Religionen Togos in Einzeldarstellungen. Anthropos, **1**, 1906, 509–21; **2**, 1907, 201–10; **3**, 1908, 272–9.
    With texts in ATAKPAME (YORUBA), KPOSO, ANYADA.
RAPP, E. L. Sprichwörter der Akan. Mit voller Tonbeziehung herausgegeben und übersetzt. M.S.O.S. **36**, 1933, 69–98.
—— 1936. An introduction to Twi. Basel: Evang. Missionsges. Pp. 119.
—— Guang-Studien 1. Sprichwörter der Kyerepɔŋ von Apirede. M.S.O.S. **42**, 1939, 127–58.
—— Die Bedeutung der grammatischen Töne im Zeitwort der südlichen Guang-Sprachen in Westafrika. Archiv f. vergl. Phon. **7**, 1943/4, 36–46.
SEIDEL, A. Beiträge zur Kenntnis der Sprachen in Togo. Z. afr. u. ocean. Spr. **4**, 1898, 201 ff.
    Material (from R. Plehn) on a number of languages.
TAUXIER, L. Le Noir de Bondoukou (see II. 1).
    Contains vocabularies of DOMA, two ANYI dialects, BRONG and BERI, the latter being identical with the GUANG dialect spoken in Salaga.
VÖHRINGER, E. F. Das Sippensystem der Twi auf der Goldküste. Ein Twi-Text übersetzt und erläutert. M.S.O.S. **37**, 1934, 143–211.
WARD, I. C. 1939. The pronunciation of Twi. Cambridge. Pp. 23.
WELMAN, C. W. [c. 1925] A preliminary study of the Nzima language. London: Crown Agents. Pp. 113.
WELMERS, W. E. A descriptive grammar of Fanti. Language, **22**, 3, 1946, Supplement. Pp. 78.
WESTERMANN, D. Die velarlabialen Laute in der Ewe-Tschi Gruppe der Sudansprachen. Z. Eingeb. Spr. **10**, 4, 1919/20, 243–61.
—— Guang-Texte in der Mundart der Landschaft Nkunya. M.S.O.S. **35**, 1932, 1–85.
—— Das Tschi und Guang (see VI. 1).
—— Die Sprache der Guang (see V. 6).
    Grammatical outline, vocabulary, and texts.
—— Form und Funktion der Reduplikation (see I. 3).
ZECH, V. Vermischte Notizen über Togo und das Togohinterland (see V. 6).
    Pp. 89 ff. and 101, GUANG vocabulary from Brong (Yeggi); pp. 138 ff., 'Reste der Gonya-Sprache in Semere'.

3. GÃ-ADANGME GROUP

CHRISTALLER, J. G. Die Volta-Sprachengruppe . . . (*see* VI. 2).
—— and BOHNER, H. 1890. Übungen in der Gã-Sprache. Basel.
FLEISCHER, C. F. 2nd ed. 1924. A new English–Ga method. Oxford. Pp. vii+183.
—— and WILKIE, M. B. Specimens of the folk-lore of the Ga-people on the Gold Coast. Africa, **3**, 1930, 360–8.
    Tales (in phonetic orthography) with translation.
RAPP, E. L. Sprichwörter der Ga. M.S.O.S. **39**, 1936, 1–24.
—— Märchen des Ga-Volkes. M.S.O.S. **39**, 1936, 24–46.
—— Adangme-Texte. Afrika (Berlin), **1**, 1942, 55–100.
—— Die Adangme-Ga Mundart von Agotime in Togo. Afrika (Berlin), **2**, 1943, 4–58.
SCHOPF, J., and RICHTER, L. 2nd ed. 1912. An English–Accra or Gã dictionary. Basel. Pp. xi+256.
WILKIE, M. B. 1930. Ga grammar notes and exercises. Oxford Univ. Press. Pp. 239.
ZIMMERMANN, J. 1858. A grammatical sketch of the Akra or Ga language and a vocabulary. . . . Stuttgart. Pp. xvi+464.

4. EWE

BERTHO, J. Parenté de la langue Yorouba de la Nigéria du sud et de la langue Adja de la région côtière du Dahomey et du Togo. Notes afr. **35**, 1947, 10–11.
BÜRGI, F. Sammlung von Ewe-Sprichwörtern. Archiv f. Anthrop. Neue Folge **13**, 1914, 415–50.
CHRISTALLER, J. G. Die Volta Sprachengruppe . . . (*see* VI. 2).
DELAFOSSE, M. 1894. Manuel Dahoméen. Paris.
HÄRTTER, G. Aus der Volkslitteratur der Evheer in Togo. Z. afr. u. ocean. Spr. **6**, 1902, 105 ff.
LABOURET, H., and RIVET, P. 1929. Le royaume d'Arda et son évangélisation au XVIIᵉ siècle. Paris. Pp. 62.
    Contains a seventeenth-century translation into Gɛ̃ of the *Doctrina Christiana*.
MERTENS, F. 1906. Deutsch–Ewe Wörterbuch. Lome.
PAKU, E. 1930. Fransegbe srɔgbale na Eveawo. Manuel de la langue française. Bremen. Pp. 120.
    Grammar of French in EWE.
PRIETZE, R. Beiträge zur Erforschung von Sprache und Volksgeist der Togo-Kolonie (Anecho). Z. afr. u. ocean. Spr., **3**, 1897, 10 ff.
    Folk-tales in the Gɛ̃ dialect.
RIEBSTEIN, P. E. 1923. Éléments de grammaire Ewe. Steyl, Holland. Pp. 60.
SCHOBER, R. Die semantische Gestalt des Ewe. Anthropos, **28**, 5/6, 1933, 621–32.
SCHÖNHÄRL, J. 1909. Volkskundliches aus Togo. Dresden and Leipzig.
    Texts and translation.
SCHROEDER, J. 1936. Formenlehre des Gɛ̃-Dialektes der Ewesprache. Dissertation Berlin, 1936. Durlach. Pp. 82.
SEIDEL, A. 1904. Togo-Sprachen. Kurze Grammatiken, Vokabulare und Phrasensammlungen der drei Hauptsprachen in Togo: Anglo-Ewe, Anecho-Ewe und Hausa. Dresden and Leipzig: Koch.
—— 1906. Lehrbuch der Ehwe-Sprache in Togo. Heidelberg.
    AWUNA dialect.
SPIESS, C. Fabeln über die Spinne bei den Ewe. M.S.O.S. **21**, 1918, 101–34, **22**, 1919 (whole number).
—— Ordalien der Ewe, Westafrika. M.S.O.S. **36**, 1933, 34–54.
    Texts with translation.
SPIETH, J. 1906. Die Ewe-Stämme. Berlin: D. Reimer. Pp. 80+962, map.
    A very rich collection of texts with translation.
TOSO, V. Ewe-Texte. Z. Kol. Spr. **7**, 1916/17, 1–24.

TROTTER, D. 1921. A grammatical guide, and numerous idioms and phrases for beginners in the Ewe dialect. [Translated from D. Westermann.] London: Harrison & Sons. Pp. 87.
WESTERMANN, D. Avatime-Fabeln mit Ewe und Deutscher Übersetzung. Z. afr. u. ocean. Spr. **7**, 1, 1903.
—— 1905/6. Wörterbuch der Ewe-Sprache. I. Ewe–Deutsch; II. Deutsch–Ewe. Berlin. Pp. 35+601; 17+235.
—— 1907. Grammatik der Ewe-Sprache. Berlin: D. Reimer. Pp. 16+158.
—— 1910, 1922, 1930. Gbesela yeye or English–Ewe dictionary. Berlin: Reimer. Pp. 347.
—— 1917. Phonetisches aus dem Ewe. Barcelona. Pp. 66.
—— Die velarlabialen Laute ... (see VI. 2).
—— 1928. Evefiala, or Ewe–English dictionary. Berlin: Reimer. Pp. 347.
—— Kindheitserinnerungen des Togonegers Bonifatius Foli. M.S.O.S. **34**, 1931, 1–69. Texts in the Gẽ dialect with translation.
—— 1931. Die Ewe-Sprache in Togo. Eine praktische Einführung. Berlin: de Gruyter. Pp. viii+95.
—— Der Wortbau des Ewe. Abh. Preuss. Akad. Wiss. phil.-hist. Klasse, **9**, 1943, pp. 23.
—— transl. BICKFORD-SMITH, A. L. 1930. A study of the Ewe language. Oxford Univ. Press. Pp. xiv+258.
WITTE, F. Lieder und Gesänge der Ewhe-Neger (Gẽ-Dialekt). Anthropos, **1**, 1906, 65–81, 194–209.
—— Sprichwörter der Ewhe-Neger, Gẽ-Dialekt (Togo, Westafrika). Anthropos, **12/13**, 1917/18, 58–83.

5. YORUBA

ADEYEMI, M. C., and LATUNDE, S. V. Yoruba conversation. Lagos.
—— —— 1932. Yoruba language simplified. Ondo.
—— —— A companion to Yoruba language simplified. Ondo.
AKINTAN, E. A. 1932. Lecture on Yoruba language with special reference to its grammar. Lagos: Ijaiye Press. Pp. 16.
—— 1941. First steps in Yoruba composition. Lagos.
—— 1942. Yoruba language as a syllabic and euphonic language. Lagos: Alebiosu Press. Pp. 10.
—— 1945. Modern grammar of Yoruba language. Lagos.
—— 1947. Lecture on the fundamental principles of Yoruba language, and common errors in the writing of Yoruba words and sentences. Lagos: B'aoku Printing Press. Pp. 18.
BAUDIN, N. 1884. Essai de grammaire Yorouba. Lyon.
—— 1885. Dictionnaire Yoruba-Français et Français-Yoruba. Lyon.
BERTHO, J. Parenté de la langue Yoruba ... (see VI. 4).
BOUCHE, P. 1880. Étude sur la langue Nago. Bar-le-Duc.
—— 1883. Les Noirs peints par eux-mêmes.
C. B. and L. B. 1908. Guide pratique de conversation en Français, Anglais et Yoruba ou Nago. Strasbourg.
DENNETT, R. E. West African categories and the Yoruba language. J. Afr. Soc. **15**, 1914, 75–80; **16**, 1917, 242–50; **17**, 1917, 66–71.
GAYE, J. A. DE, and BEECROFT, W. S. 2nd ed. 1923. Yoruba grammar. London: Kegan Paul.
—— 1923. Yoruba composition. London: Kegan Paul.
INTERNATIONAL INSTITUTE OF AFRICAN LANGUAGES AND CULTURES. 1929. Alphabets for the Efik, Ibo and Yoruba languages, recommended by the Education Board, Lagos. London.
JAMES, A. LLOYD. The tones of Yoruba. B.S.O.S., **3**, 1923, 119–28.
LASEBIKAN, E. L., and LEWIS, L. J. 1949. A Yoruba revision course. Oxford University Press.
MANN, A. Eine geschichtliche Sage aus der Zeit der ersten Niederlassungen der Egba. Z. Afr. Spr. **2**, 209 ff.
MELZIAN, H. Beobachtungen über die Verwendung der Töne in der Yoruba-Sprache. M.S.O.S. **37**, 1934, 197–233.
Contains a word-list with full tone-marks.

BIBLIOGRAPHY 193

MÜLLER, F. Ein Beitrag zur Kenntnis des Atakpame. Z. afr. u. ocean. Spr. 6, 1902, 138–66, 194–205.
—— Die Religionen Togos in Einzeldarstellungen (*see* VI. 2).
PHILPOT, W. T. A. Notes on the Igala language. B.S.O.S. 7, 4, 1933/5, 897–912.
PRICE, H. L. WARD. 1925. Yoruba phrase book with phonetic spelling. Lagos: C.M.S. Bookshop.
SEIDEL, A. Beiträge zur Kenntnis der Sprachen in Togo (*see* VI. 2).
    Contains material on NAGO.
THOMAS, N. W. 1914. Specimens of languages from Southern Nigeria. London: Harrison & Sons. Pp. 143.
TIDJANI, A. S. Formes déférentes en Yorouba. Notes afr. 17, 1943, 4–5.
WESTERMANN, D. (ed.) 1931. Yoruba-Texte. Berlin: Lautabteilung. Pp. 15.
—— Die westlichen Sudansprachen (*see* GENERAL).
    YORUBA, pp. 66–82.

6. NUPE GROUP

BANFIELD, A. W. 1914, 1916. Dictionary of the Nupe language. 1. Nupe–English. 2. English–Nupe. Shonga, Nigeria.
    With full tone-markings.
—— and MACINTYRE, I. L. 1915. A grammar of the Nupe language together with a vocabulary. London: S.P.C.K. Pp. 186.
EDGAR, F. 1909. A grammar of the Gbari language, with Gbari–English and English–Gbari dictionaries. Belfast: W. & G. Baird. Pp. 373.
    Deals with the MATAI dialect.
LOW, W. P. 1908. Gbari grammar, notes and vocabulary. Zungeru: Government Printer. Pp. 17.
WESTERMANN, D. Das Nupe in Nigeria, seine Stellung innerhalb der Kwa-Sprachen (Westsudanische Studien 4). M.S.O.S. 30, 1927, 173–207.

7. BINI GROUP

BUTCHER, H. L. M. 1936. Elementary dictionary of the Benin language. Church Missionary Society.
—— and GBINIGIE, E. O. Four Edo fables. Africa, 10, 3, 1937, 342–52.
DENNETT, R. E. Notes on the languages of the Efa (people) or the Bini commonly called Uze Ado. J. Afr. Soc. 3, 1904, 142–53.
HIDE, R. H. The Bini as a botanist. Some notes on Benin vernacular names of plants. Nigerian Field, 11, 1943, 69–79.
HUBBARD, J. W. n.d. [1951 or 1952]. Thə Soho of the Niger Delta. Zaria: Gaskiya Corporation. Pp. xxvi+369.
MELZIAN, H. 1937. A concise dictionary of the Bini language of Southern Nigeria. London: Kegan Paul. Pp. xviii+233.
    With full tone-markings.
—— 1942. Vergleichende Charakteristik des Verbums im Bini (Nigerien). Arbeiten aus d. Inst. f. Lautforschung an d. Univ. Berlin 12. Pp. 131.
—— Zum Konsonantismus in den Dialekten der Beningruppe. Archiv. f. vergl. Phon. 6, 2, 1942/3, 49–58.
STRUB, E. Essai d'une grammaire de la langue Kukuruku (Nigéria, Afrique Occidentale). Anthropos, 10/11, 1915/16, 450–65, 888–907.
THOMAS, N. W. 1910. Anthropological report on the Edo-speaking peoples of Nigeria. Part 2. Linguistics. London: Harrison & Sons. Pp. 251.
    Contains texts in EDO, ISHAN, KUKURUKU, and SOBO, a grammatical summary of EDO or WANO, a comparative dictionary of 22 dialects of the EDO language area, and an EDO–English dictionary.
WELCH, J. W. The linguistic situation in the western parts of the Niger Delta. Africa, 6, 1933, 220–2.
WESTERMANN, D. Das Edo in Nigerien (Westsudanische Studien 3). M.S.O.S. 29, 1926, 32–60.

8. IGBO

(ANON.) 1928. English–Ibo phrase book. Niger Bookshop.
ADAMS, R. F. G. 1932. A modern Ibo grammar. Oxford Univ. Press. Pp. 200.
—— Ibo texts. Africa, **7**, 4, 1934, 452–63.
    The OWERRI dialect, in the new orthography.
—— and WARD, I. C. The Arochuku dialect of Ibo. Africa, **2**, 1, 1929, 57–70.
CARNOCHAN, J. A study in the phonology of an Igbo speaker. B.S.O.A.S. **12**, 2, 1948, 417–26.
GREEN, M. M. The unwritten literature of the Igbo-speaking people of south-eastern Nigeria. B.S.O.A.S. **12**, 3/4, 1948, 838–46.
—— The classification of West African tone-languages: Igbo and Efik. Africa, **19**, 3, 1949, 213–19.
—— 1949. Igbo spelling: an explanatory statement. Cambridge Univ. Press. Pp. 7.
INT. INST. OF AFR. LANG. AND CULT. Alphabets ... (*see* VI. 5).
THOMAS, N. W. 1913/14. Anthropological report on the Ibo-speaking peoples of Nigeria. London: Harrison & Sons.
    Vol. II, 1913. English–Ibo and Ibo–English dictionary. Pp. 391.
    III, 1913. Proverbs, narratives, vocabularies, and grammar. Pp. 199.
    V, 1914. Addenda to Ibo–English dictionary. Pp. v+184.
    VI, 1914. Proverbs, stories, tones in Ibo. Pp. 14.
—— Specimens of languages ... (*see* VI. 5).
WARD, I. C. 1936. An introduction to the Ibo language. Cambridge: Heffer. Pp. xiii+215.
—— 1941. Ibo dialects and the development of a common language.
WESTERMANN, D. Das Ibo in Süd-Nigerien (Westsudanische Studien 2). M.S.O.S. **29**, 1926, 1–31.

SECTION VII

(a) TOGOLAND

1. THE TOGO REMNANT GROUP

CHRISTALLER, J. G. Die Volta Sprachengruppe (*see* VI. 2).
—— Die Adelesprache im Togogebiet. Z. afr. u. ocean. Spr. **1**, 1895, 16–33.
FUNKE, E. Die Familie im Spiegel der afrikanischen Volksmärchen. Z. Kol. Spr. **2**, 1911/12, 37–62.
    Texts in AVATIME, NYANGBO, and SANTROKOFI, with translation.
—— Versuch einer Grammatik der Avatimesprache. M.S.O.S. **12**, 1909, 287–334.
—— Deutsch-Avatime Wörterverzeichnis. M.S.O.S. **13**, 1910, 1–38.
—— Die Nyaṅgbo-Táfi Sprache. Ein Beitrag zur Kenntnis der Sprachen Togos. M.S.O.S. **13**, 1910, 166–202.
—— Einiges über Geschichte, religiöse Gebräuche und Anschauungen des Avatimevolkes in Togo. Z. Kol. Spr. **1**, 1910/11, 81–105.
    Texts with translation.
—— Die Santrokofisprache. Beitrag zur Kenntnis der Sprachen Togos. M.S.O.S. **14**, 1911, 182–226.
—— Originaltexte aus den Klassensprachen in Mitteltogo. Z. Eingeb. Spr. **10**, 4, 1919/20, 261–313.
    Texts in AVATIME, LIKPE, LOGBA, LEFANA, AKPOSO, AKPAFU, with translation.
JOHNSTON, SIR H. H. Bantu and Semi-Bantu (*see* GENERAL).
SEIDEL, A. Beiträge zur Kenntnis der Sprachen ... (*see* VI. 2).
    AVATIME, LOGBA, NYAMBO and TAFI, BORADA, BOVIRI, A(K)PAFU, SANTROKOFI, LIKPE, AXOLO.
WESTERMANN, D. Die Sprache der Guang (*see* V. 6).
—— Avatime-Fabeln mit Ewe- und deutscher Übersetzung (*see* VI. 4).
—— Die Logba-Sprache in Togo. Z. afr. u. ocean. Spr. **7**, 1903.

WESTERMANN, D. Vier Sprachen aus Mitteltogo. Likpe, Bowili, Akpafu und Adele, nebst einigen Resten der Borosprache. M.S.O.S. 25, 1922, 1–59.
—— Die Animeresprache in Togo. Nach Aufnahmen von A. Mischlich. M.S.O.S. 36, 1933, 1–7.
 Grammatical notes and vocabulary, with tone-markings.

2. KPOSO

FUNKE, E. Originaltexte ... (see VIIa. 1).
MÜLLER, F. Die Religionen Togos ... (see VI. 2).
SEIDEL, A. Beiträge zur Kenntnis der Sprachen ... (see VI. 2).
WOLF, F. Grammatik der Kposo-Sprache (Nord-Togo, West-Afrika). Anthropos, 4, 1909, 142–67, 630–59.

3. KEBU

HINTZE, F. Zum konsonantischen Anlautwecheel ... (see II. GENERAL).
MÜLLER, F. Die Religionen Togos ... (see VI. 2).
SEIDEL, A. Beiträge zur Kenntnis der Sprachen ... (see VI. 2).
WOLF, F. Grammatik des Kögböriko. Anthropos, 2, 1907, 422–37, 795–820.
 A fairly complete introduction to the language.

(b) NIGERIA

1. CLASS LANGUAGES OF NORTHERN NIGERIA

HARRIS, P. G. Notes on the Reshe language. Afr. Stud. 5, 4, 1946, 221–42.
 Grammatical notes, text with interlinear translation, and vocabulary.
JOHNSTON, SIR H. H. Bantu and Semi-Bantu (see GENERAL).
KOELLE, S. W. Polyglotta Africana (see GENERAL).
KRAUSE, G. A. Beiträge zum Märchenschatz der Afrikaner. Globus, 72, 229–33, 254–8.
 Texts in TŠI-ŠINGINI.
MEEK, C. K. 1931. Tribal Studies in Northern Nigeria. 2 vols. London: Kegan Paul.
 Contains a number of vocabularies, mostly of considerable length, together with sentences, in many languages and dialects of Northern Nigeria, the majority of which are still otherwise unknown.
THOMAS, N. W., in MEEK, C. K., Northern Tribes (see VI. GENERAL).
—— Specimens of languages ... (see VI. GENERAL).

2. THE TIV GROUP

ABRAHAM, R. C. 1933. The grammar of Tiv. Kaduna. Pp. 213.
—— 2nd ed. 1940. The Tiv people. Crown Agents.
 Pp. 6–7, short vocabularies of TIV, EKOI, and JAR.
G —— 1940. The principles of Tiv. Crown Agents. Pp. 102.
G —— 1940. Dictionary of the Tiv language. Crown Agents. Pp. ix+331.
G —— 1940. Tiv reader for European students. Crown Agents. Pp. vii+82.
DANGEL, R. Grammatische Skizze der Yergum-Sprache. Bibl. Afr. 3, 2/3, 1929, 135–46.
FITZPATRICK, J. F. J. Some notes on the Kwolla District and its tribes. J. Afr. Soc. 10, 1910–11, 16–52, 213–21, 490 ff.
JEFFREYS, M. D. W. A note on the Ekoi language. Z. Eingeb. Spr. 35, 3/4, 1950, 260–3.
JOHNSTON, SIR H. H. Bantu and Semi-Bantu (see GENERAL).
JUDD, A. S. Notes on the Munshi tribe and language. J. Afr. Soc. 16, 1916, 52–61; 1917, 143–8.
KOELLE, S. W. Polyglotta Africana (see GENERAL).
LUKAS, J. Das Nomen im Tiv. Anthropos, 47, 1–2, 1952, 147–76,
MALHERBE, W. A. 1932. Tiv–English dictionary with grammar notes and index. Lagos: Government Printer. Pp. xxxix+207.

MANSFELD, A. 1908. Urwald-Dokumente. Berlin: D. Reimer; Pp. xvi+310.
    Pp. 269–310, grammatical notes on EKOI and vocabularies with phrases of BOKI, EKOI, KEAKA, OBANG, ANYANG and BANYANG, and a text in EKOI.
MEEK, C. K. Tribal Studies (see VIIb.1).
    Vol. 2 contains vocabularies of languages and dialects which may belong to this Group.
TALBOT, P. A. 1912. In the shadow of the bush. London.
    Pp. 415–45, grammatical notes and vocabulary of EKOI.
THOMAS, N. W., in MEEK, C. K., Northern Tribes (see VI. GENERAL).
—— Specimens of languages . . . (see VI. GENERAL).

(c) CAMEROONS

ANKERMANN, B. Koelle's Mbe-Sprache. M.S.O.S. 30, 1927, 1–4.
    A language spoken in the Bali area.
BRUENS, A. The structure of Nkom and its relations to Bantu and Sudanic. Anthropos, 37/40, 1942/5, 827–66.
CRAWFORD, O. G. S. The writing of Njoya (Sultan Njoya's ideographic script for the Bamoun language). Antiquity, 9, 1936, 435–42.
DEBARGE, J. Note sur l'écriture inventée par Njoya, sultan de Bamoun. Arch. suisses d'anthrop. générale, 5, 1928/9, 243–7.
JOHNSTON, SIR H. H. Bantu and Semi-Bantu (see GENERAL).
KOELLE, S. W. Polyglotta Africana (see GENERAL).
LABOURET, H. L'écriture bamoun. Togo-Cameroun, avr.–juin 1935, pp. 127–33.
LÉGER, AD. Contribution à l'étude de la langue bamiléké. J. Soc. Afr. 2, 2, 1932, 209–27.
MEINHOF, C. Die Sprachverhältnisse im Kamerun. Z. afr. u. ocean. Spr. 1, 1895, 138–63.
    Contains a BALI [ŋgaa ka] vocabulary.
MEYER, E. Märchen in der Bali-Sprache aus dem Grasland von Kamerun. Z. Eingeb. Spr. 32, 1941, 135–60; 1942, 224–36.
—— Stand und Aufgaben der Sprachforschung in Kamerun. Z. Eingeb. Spr. 32, 4, 1942, 241–85.
TESSMANN, G. Die Völker und Sprachen Kameruns. Petermanns Geogr. Mitt., 1932, pp. 113–20, 184–91.
TISCHHAUSER, G. Bali-Wörterbuch (Kamerun). Bali-Deutsch-Englisch und Deutsch-Bali bezw. Englisch-Bali. Z. Eingeb. Spr. Beiheft.
THOMAS, N. W., in MEEK, C. K., Northern Tribes (see VI. GENERAL).
VIELHAUER, E. 1915. Grundzüge einer Grammatik der Balisprache. Basler Missionsdruckerei.
WARD, I. C. The phonetic structure of Bamum. B.S.O.S. 9, 2, 1938, 423–38.
ZINTGRAFF, E. Einiges aus der Balisprache. Z. afr. u. ocean. Spr. 1, 1895, 318–23.
    With additional note by Meinhof.

SECTION VIII

1. IBIBIO-EFIK

ADAMS, R. F. G. 1939, rev. 1943. English–Efik–Efik–English vocabulary. London: Philip, Son & Nephew. 1943 ed. pp. 258.
—— Some Efik plant names. Nigerian Field, 3, 1934, 166–7.
—— Efik vocabulary of living things. Nigerian Field, 11, 1943, 156–68; 12, 1947, 23–24; 13, 1948, 61–67.
CLARKE, J. Specimens (see GENERAL).
GASKIN, E. A. L. Twelve proverbs and one folk-story from the Efik country. Africa, 5, 1932, 68–70.
GOLDIE, H. 1868. Principles of Efik grammar with specimen of the language. Edinburgh: Muir & Paterson. Pp. 105.
—— 1874. Efik grammar in English. United Presbyt. College.
—— 1874. Efik grammar in Efik. United Presbyt. College.
—— 1874. Efik dictionary. United Presbyt. College.

BIBLIOGRAPHY

GREEN, M. M. The classification of West African tone-languages (see VI. 8).
INTERNATIONAL INSTITUTE OF AFRICAN LANGUAGES AND CULTURES. Alphabets . . . (see VI. 5.)
JEFFREYS, M. D. W. 1935. Old Calabar and notes on the Ibibio language. Calabar.
OYOYOH, O. I. 1943. A summary of study in Effik–Ibibio language with particular reference to orthography. Calabar: Henshaw Press. Pp. 20.
THOMAS, N. W. Specimens of languages . . . (see VI. GENERAL).
WARD, I. C. The phonetic and tonal structure of Efik. Cambridge: Heffer. Pp. xiii+186.

2. OTHER LANGUAGES

ABRAHAM, R. C. 1935. The principles of Idoma. Crown Agents. Pp. 429.
—— 1951. The Idoma language. Idoma word-lists. Idoma chrestomathy. Idoma proverbs. Published by the author for the Idoma Native Administration, Government of Nigeria. [Pp. not numbered.]
BENTON, P. A. Notes on some languages of the Western Sudan (see V. 6).
  Unpublished vocabularies of Barth include FALI, KOAMA a JUKUN dialect?, IMBANA (MUNDANG).
DUISBURG, A. VON. Untersuchungen über die Mbum-Sprache in Adamaua. M.S.O.S. 28, 1925, 132–75.
DÜHRING, F. K. Zusammenstellung meiner Sprachaufnahmen des Pani-Dui im Tscholere-Gebirge und des Lakka im Logone-Gebiet mit den Sprachaufnahmen des Lakka im Mayo Nakana von Strümpell. Mitt. aus d. dtsch. Schutzgeb. 33, 1925, 75–77.
FITZPATRICK, J. F. J. Some notes on the Kwolla District . . . (see VIIb. 2).
  Notes on the GURKAWA, MONTOL, and ANKWE languages.
FLOTTUM, SVERE. Le Lapin et la famine. Conte en langue Mbum. Ét. Camerounaises, 3, 29/30, 1950, 83–93.
  In the 'Africa' orthography with tone-markings. Interlinear and free translation and notes.
FOULKES, H. D. 1915. Angass manual. London: Kegan Paul. Pp. xviii+313.
FRAZER, W. K. 1908. Vocabulary of the Jukon language. Zungeru: Government Printer.
GRIAULE, M. Vocabulaires Papé, Woko, Kutinn, Namtchi et Séwé du Cameroun septentrional. J. Soc. Afr. 11, 1941, 169–85.
HOFMEISTER, J. Wörterverzeichnis der Wute-Sprache. Jahrb. Hamb. Wiss. Anst. 36, Beiheft 2, 1918, 1–14.
—— Kurzgefasste Wute-Grammatik. Z. Kol. Spr. 9, 1918/19, 1–19.
LEBEUF, J. P. Vocabulaires comparés des parlers de 16 villages Fali du Cameroun septentrional. J. Soc. Afr. 11, 1941, 33–60.
LUKAS, J. 1937. Zentralsudanische Studien. Wörterverzeichnisse der Deutschen Zentral-Afrika-Expedition 1910–11, nachgelassene Aufnahmen von Gustav Nachtigal und eigene Sammlungen. Abh. aus d. Gebiet d. Auslandkde. 45, Reihe B, Band 24. Hamburg: de Gruyter. Pp. 191.
MACLEOD, ——. 1929. Report on the Idoma language. Government Printer, Pp. 24.
MEEK, C. K. Tribal Studies (see VIIb. 1).
MEYER, E. Mambila-Studie. Z. Eingeb. Spr. 30, 1939/40, 1, 1–52; 2, 117–48; 3, 210–32.
MIGEOD, F. W. H. The languages of West Africa (see I. GENERAL).
  Includes ANGAS.
MOUCHET, J. Vocabulaires comparatifs de 15 parlers du Nord-Cameroun (part 1). J. Soc. Afric. 8, 1938, 123–43.
  Vocabularies of KALI, MÕNÕ, MUNDĂN (2 dialects), TUPURI, with some linguistic notes.
ORMSBY, G. Notes on the Angass language. J. Afr. Soc. 12, 48, 1913, 421–4; 13, 49, 1913, 54–61; 50, 1914, 204–10; 51, 1914, 313–15.
SIEBER, J. Märchen und Fabeln der Wute. Z. Eingeb. Spr. 12, 1921/2, 53–72, 162–339.
STRÜMPELL, F. Vergleichendes Wörterverzeichnis der Heidensprachen Adamauas. Z. f. Ethn. 1910, 3/4, 444–88.
  With introductory notes by B. Struck. Vocabularies of a number of little-known languages and dialects.

STRÜMPELL, F. Wörterverzeichnis der Heidensprachen des Mandaragebirges (Adamaua). Z. Eingeb. Spr. **13**, 1922/3, 47–75, 109–49.
TESSMANN, G. Die Sprache der Mbakka-Limba, Mbum und Lakka. M.S.O.S. **33**, 1930, 55–82.
—— Die Völker und Sprachen . . . (*see* VIIc).
THOMAS, N. W., in MEEK, C. K., Northern Tribes (*see* VI. GENERAL).
—— Specimens . . . (*see* VI. 5).

SECTION IX
THE CHADIC LANGUAGES

BARTH, H. Sammlung und Bearbeitung . . . (*see* III).
    Includes WANDALA.
BENTON, P. A. Notes . . . (*see* VIII 2).
CLARKE, J. Specimens of dialects . . . (*see* GENERAL).
KOELLE, S. W. Polyglotta Africana (*see* GENERAL).
KLINGENHEBEN, A. 1929. Mandara (aufgezeichnet von Carl Meinhof). Lautbibliothek, Phonetische Platten u. Umschriften, hrg. v. d. Lautabteilung d. Preuss. Staatsbibl. No. 48. Berlin.
    Gramophone records with transcription.
LAVERGNE, G. Le pays et la population Matakam. Bull. Soc. Ét. Camerounaises, **7**, 1944, 9–73.
    Pp. 64–66 text with interlinear translation.
—— 1949. Folklore africain. Les Matakam. Paris: Imp. Servant-Crouzet.
    Part 3, pp. 93–171, deals with language.
LUKAS, J. The linguistic situation in the Lake Chad area in Central Africa. Africa, **9**, 1936, 322–49.
—— Zentralsudanische Studien (*see* VIII. 2).
    PADUKO, BAZA [BATA Group], WANDALA.
—— Linguistic research between Nile and Lake Chad. Africa, **12**, 1939, 335–49.
MEEK, C. K. Tribal studies (*see* VIIb. 1).
MOUCHET, J. Vocabulaires comparatifs de 15 parlers du Nord-Cameroun (part 2). Ét. Camerounaises, **3**, 1950, 5–74.
    Vocabularies of WANDALA, PADOKO, KOTOKO, MUZUK (2), MASA, GIDAR, MUSGOY, BATA, JÉD, with some linguistic notes.
    (For part 1 *see* VIII. 2).
STRÜMPELL, F. Vergleichendes Wörterverzeichnis . . . (*see* VIII. 2).
—— Wörterverzeichnis der Heidensprachen (*see* VIII. 2).
TESSMANN, G. Völker und Sprachen . . . (*see* VIIc).

SECTION X
THE CHADO-HAMITIC LANGUAGES

GENERAL

LUKAS, J. The linguistic situation in the Lake Chad area (*see* IX).
—— Neue Aussichten zur sprachlichen Gliederung des Sudan. Int. Linguisten-Kongress, Kopenhagen, 1936, pp. 286–91.
—— Hamitisches Sprachgut im Sudan. Z. dtsch. morgenl. Ges. **90**, 3/4, 1937, 579–88.
—— Der hamitische Gehalt der Tschado-Hamitischen Sprachen. Z. Eingeb. Spr. **28**, 4, 1938, 286–99.
—— Linguistic research between Nile and Lake Chad (*see* IX).

1. HAUSA

ABRAHAM, R. C. 1934. The principles of Hausa. Kaduna: Government Printer.
—— 1940. An introduction to spoken Hausa, and Hausa reader for European students. London: Crown Agents. Pp. 213.

ABRAHAM, R. C. [c. 1940. Phonetics and tones of Hausa. Kaduna (duplic.).]
—— 1941. Modern grammar of spoken Hausa. London: Crown Agents. Pp. 172.
—— and KANO, M. 1949. Dictionary of the Hausa language. London: Crown Agents. Pp. 992.
BARGERY, G. P. 1934. A Hausa–English dictionary and English–Hausa vocabulary. With some notes on the Hausa people and their language by D. Westermann. Oxford Univ. Press. Pp. 1226.
CARNOCHAN, J. A study of quantity in Hausa. Bull. S.O.A.S. 13, 4, 1951, 1032–44.
DALZIEL, J. M. 1916. A Hausa botanical vocabulary. London: T. Fisher Unwin.
DELAFOSSE, M. 1901. Manuel de la langue haoussa ou chrestomathie haoussa précédé d'un abrégé de grammaire et suivi d'un vocabulaire. Paris: Maisonneuve. Pp. xiv+134.
EAST, R. 1938. Language examinations in the Northern Provinces of Nigeria. Jos: S.I.M. Bookshop. Pp. 136.
FLETCHER, R. S. 1912. Hausa sayings and folklore with vocabulary of new words. Oxford Univ. Press. Pp. 173.
FUNKE, E. Die Stellung der Hausasprache unter den Sprachen Togos. M.S.O.S. 19, 1916, 116–28.
—— Einige Tanz- und Liebeslieder der Hausa. Z. Eingeb. Spr. 11, 1920/1, 259–78.
GILL, J. W. Hausa speech, its wit and wisdom. Bull.S.O.S. 1, 1918, 30–46.
GREENBERG, J. H. Hausa verse prosody. J. Amer. Orient. Soc. 69, 3, 1949, 125–35.
HARRIS, H. G. 1908. Hausa stories and riddles with notes on the language, etc., and a concise Hausa dictionary. Weston-super-Mare: Mendip Press. Pp. 111–33.
—— 1908. A pocket dictionary of the Hausa language: Hausa–English. Weston-super-Mare: Mendip Press. Pp. 33.
HAYWOOD, A. H. W. 2nd ed. 1914. English–Hausa vocabulary of words in everyday use. London: Kegan Paul. Pp. 31.
HODGE, CARLETON M. Morpheme alternants and the noun phrase in Hausa. Language, 21, 2, 1945, 87–91.
HOMBURGER, L. Les préfixes nominaux . . . (see I. 7).
JAMES, A. LLOYD, and BARGERY, G. P. A note on the pronunciation of Hausa. Bull.S.O.S. 3, 4, 1925, 721–9.
KING, PHILIP V. Some Hausa idioms. J.A.S. 8, 1909, 193–201.
KLINGENHEBEN, A. Die Silbenauslautgesetze des Hausa. Z. Eingeb. Spr. 18, 4, 1927/8, 272–97.
—— Zwei geschichtliche Hausatexte. Z. Eing. Spr. 31, 1941, 114–29.
KRAUSE, G. A., ed. HEEPE, M. Gottlob Adolf Krauses Haussa-Handschriften in der Preussischen Staatsbibliothek, Hamburg. M.S.O.S. 31, 1928, 105–7, xxviii+lxxx.
LANDEROIN, M. 1910. Grammaire et contes haoussas. Paris: Larose. Pp. 292.
—— and TILHO, J. 1910. Dictionnaire Haoussa comprenant Haoussa-Français et Français-Haoussa. Paris: Larose. Pp. 163.
MIGEOD, F. W. H. 1914. A grammar of the Hausa language. London: Kegan Paul.
MILLER, W. R. 2nd ed. 1902. Hausa notes. Exeter: Jas. Townsend & Sons. Pp. 67.
MILLER, E. P. 1939. Wata biyu–Hausa grammar. Jos. Pp. 77.
MISCHLICH, A. 1902, 2nd ed. 1911. Lehrbuch der Hausa-Sprache. Lehrb. d. S.O.S. 27. Pp. 200.
—— 1906. Wörterbuch der Hausa-Sprache. I. Hausa-Deutsch. Berlin: D. Reimer. Pp. 692.
—— Hausa-Märchen. Jber. d. Frankfurter Vereins f. orient. Spr. 1913/15.
—— 1929. Neue Märchen aus Afrika gesammelt und aus der Hausasprache übersetzt. Veröffentlichungen des Staat.-Sächs. Forschungsinstituts f. Völkerkde in Leipzig, 1 Reihe, Bd. 9. Pp. 312.
—— 1942. Über die Kulturen im Mittel-Sudan. Landwirtschaft, Gewerbe und Handel, unter Beifügung der Hausa-Texte. Berlin: Reimer. Pp. 199.
—— n.d. Hausa. Metoula-Sprachführer. Berlin-Schöneberg: Langenscheidt.
OGILVIE, H. L. 3rd ed. 1947. Helps to the study of Hausa. Jos: S.I.M. Bookshop. Pp. 81.
PARSONS, ALLAN C. 1915. A Hausa phrase book with medical and scientific vocabulary. Oxford Univ. Press. 2nd ed. revised by G. P. Bargery, 1924. Pp. 118.

POWER, G. 1921. Hausa–English grammar. Nigeria (Northern Provinces) Education Dept. Pp. 108.
PRIETZE, R. Zwei Haussa-Texte. Z.A.O.S. **3**, 1897, 140–56.
—— 1904. Haussa-Sprichwörter und Haussa-Lieder. Kirchhain.
—— Die spezifischen Verstärkungsadverbien im Haussa und Kanuri. M.S.O.S. **11**, 1908, 307–17.
—— Lieder fahrender Haussa-Schüler. M.S.O.S. **19**, 1916, 1–115.
—— 1916. Haussa-Sänger. Inaugural-Dissert. z. Erlangung d. Doktorwürde d. Philos. Fakultät Göttingen.
—— Gesungene Predigten eines fahrenden Haussalehrers. M.S.O.S. **20**, 1917, 1–60.
—— Haussa-Preislieder auf Parias. M.S.O.S. **21**, 1918, 1–53.
—— Wüstenreise des Haussa-Händlers Mohammed Agigi (in Gesprächen geschildert von Ḥāžž Aḥmed aus Kano). M.S.O.S. **26/7**, 1924/5, 1–37; **28**, 1925, 175–247.
—— Die Geschichte von Gizo und Koki. M.S.O.S. **29**, 1926, 61–89.
—— Haussa des täglichen Lebens. M.S.O.S. **29**, 1926, 90–98.
—— Die Mädchen von Gaia. M.S.O.S. **29**, 1929, 135–90.
—— Lieder des Haussavolks. M.S.O.S. **30**, 1927, 5–172, i–cxi.
—— Dichtung der Haussa. Africa, **4**, 1931, 86–95.
RATTRAY, R. S. 1913. Hausa folk-lore, customs, proverbs, &c. Oxford: Clarendon Press. 2 vols., pp. 327, 315.
Arabic script, transliteration, translation, and notes.
ROBINSON, C. H. 4th ed. 1914. Hausa grammar with exercises. London: Kegan Paul. Pp. 218.
—— 4th ed. 1925. Dictionary of the Hausa Language. Cambridge Univ. Press. 2 vols., pp. xviii+476, viii+290.
STEWART, A. 1943. A Hausa–English guide. Nigeria: S.I.M. Bookshop. Pp. 32.
TAYLOR, F. W. Some English words in Fulani and Hausa (see I. 7).
—— 1933. A practical Hausa grammar. (Taylor's Fulani–Hausa series 2.) Oxford: Clarendon Press. Pp. 142.
—— A Fulani–Hausa phrase book (see I. 7).
—— A Hausa–Fulani vocabulary (see I. 7).
—— Fulani–Hausa readings (see I. 7).
TREMEARNE, A. J. N. Fifty Hausa folk-tales. Folklore, **21**, 1910.
—— 1914. Hausa folk-tales. The Hausa text of the stories in Hausa Superstitions and Customs, in Folk-lore, and in other publications. London: J. Bale, Sons & Danielsson (West African Nights Entertainment 2). Pp. xii+240.
VISCHER, H. Rules for Hausa spelling. J.A.S. **11**, 1911/12, 339–47 (also separately printed: Zungeru: Government Printing Office, pp. 11).
VYCICHL, WERNER. Hausa und Ägyptisch. Ein Beitrag zur historischen Hamitistik. M.S.O.S. **37**, 1934, 36–116.
With bibliography.
WESTERMANN, D. 1911. Die Sprache der Hausa in Zentralafrika. (Deutsche Kol. Spr. **3**.) Berlin: D. Reimer. Pp. viii+88.
WEYDLING, C. 1942. Einführung ins Hausa. Leipzig: Harrassowitz. Pp. xx+131.
G WHITTING, C. E. J. Hausa and Fulani proverbs (see I. 7).

2. OTHER LANGUAGES

BARTH, H. Sammlung und Bearbeitung . . . (see III).
LOGONE.
—— Vocabulary of Budduma, spoken by the inhabitants of the islands in Lake Chad. J. Roy. Geog. Soc. **21**, 1851, 214.
BENTON, P. A. Notes . . . (see VIII. 2).
Pp. 1–37, Notes on Bolanchi; 38–55 Notes on Budduma; and vocabularies from Barth.
DUISBURG, A. VON. Überreste der So-Sprache. M.S.O.S. **17**, 1914, 39–45.
GAUDEFROY-DEMOMBYNES, M. 1907. Documents sur les langues de l'Oubangui-Chari. Actes XIVe Congr. Int. des Orientalistes, 2. Paris. Pp. 116.
Includes KOTOKO (several dialects), BUDUMA, KURI, MASA.

GAUDICHE, —. La langue boudouma. J. Soc. Afric. **8**, 1, 1938, 11–32.
HAGEN, G. VON. Die Bana. Baessler Archiv, **2**, 1912.
    Contains a short vocabulary.
LEBEUF, J. P. Vocabulaires Kotoko: Makari, Goulfei, Kousséri, Afadé. Bull. IFAN, **4**, 1942, 160–74.
LUKAS, J. 1936. Die Logone-Sprache im zentralen Sudan. Mit Beiträgen aus dem Nachlass von Gustav Nachtigal. Abh. Kde. Morgenl. **21**, 6.
—— Zentralsudanische Studien (*see* VIII. 2).
—— 1941. Deutsche Quellen zur Sprache der Musgu in Kamerun. Z. Eingeb. Spr. Beiheft **24**. Pp. 121.
MEEK, C. K. Tribal studies (*see* VIIb. 1).
MOUCHET, J. Vocabulaires comparatifs . . . parts 1 and 2 (*see* VIII. 2, and IX).
MÜLLER, F. 1886. Die Musuk-Sprache in Central-Afrika. Nach den Aufzeichnungen von G. A. Krause hrg. Sitzungsber. d. Phil.-hist. Klasse d. Kais. Akad. Wiss. Wien, **112**, 1, pp. 353 ff. (also as a separate reprint).
STRÜMPELL, F. Vergleichendes Wörterverzeichnis . . . (*see* VIII. 2).
    Vocabularies of DARI and GIDER.
TESSMANN, G. Völker und Sprachen (*see* VIIc).

NOTES

An asterisk indicates a work or an article published before the first edition of *The Languages of West Africa* but not included in the bibliography in that edition.

Some additional abbreviations used in this supplementary bibliography:

A.L.S.	African Language Studies (London)
A.L.R.	African Language Review (London)
J.A.L.	Journal of African Languages (London—earlier volumes, East Lansing—later volumes)
J.W.A.L.	Journal of West African Languages (London, C.U.P.)
J.A.O.S.	Journal of the American Oriental Society
S.L.L.R.	Sierra Leone Language Review (Freetown)
O.U.P.	Oxford University Press
C.U.P.	Cambridge University Press
C.N.R.S.	Centre Nationale de la Recherche Scientifique, Paris.
BSELAF	Bulletin de la Societé pour l'Étude des Langues Africaines, 20 rue de la Baume, Paris, VIIIe
CLAD	Centre de Linguistique Appliquée de Dakar
GLECS	Groupe Linguistique d'Études Chamito-Semitiques, École Pratique des Hautes Études, Paris.

SUPPLEMENTARY BIBLIOGRAPHY

COMPILED BY PROFESSOR D. W. ARNOTT

This Supplementary Bibliography attempts to list all the significant books, monographs and articles concerned with West African languages that have appeared since the publication of *The Languages of West Africa*, as well as a considerable number of pre-1952 works which were not included in the original bibliography—these older works being marked with an asterisk.

A certain amount of selection has been necessary, and subjective judgments have sometimes been unavoidable. It is also possible that some important contributions have been inadvertently overlooked, but it is hoped that such omissions are few. Vernacular texts have not been included except where accompanied by a translation or commentary of some kind, or for some other special reason; nor have biblical translations, which are mostly covered by the *Bibliography of Scriptures in African Languages* listed in the General section under 'Coldham, Geraldine E'. Anthropological and sociological works have also been excluded unless they contain a significant amount of linguistic information.

Works which have recently been republished, by photographic process, by Frank Cass and by Gregg International Publishers are indicated by C and G respectively, both in the original bibliography on pp. 178–201 and in this supplementary bibliography.

Since the publication of the 1952 edition, there has been much discussion of the classification of West African languages, particularly since the appearance of Greenberg's important works, and any new publication would have to take account of this. But as the present volume is, in the main, a simple reprint of Part II of the *Handbook of African Languages*, it would be pointless and confusing to introduce in the bibliography any major changes in the classification, and languages here appear in the same sections and sub-sections as in the 1952 edition. However, in the case of Section VII (Class Languages) it has seemed appropriate to introduce some additional sub-sections, treating Tiv, Ekoi and Ijɔ separately in view of the considerable amount of recent material on these languages; and in some cases, where there seems to be general agreement that a different classification is appropriate, a note has been added indicating the alternative grouping (viz. in Section VII the 'Togorestsprachen' and Ijɔ, and in Section VIII the Ron-Angas languages).

New sections XI and XII have been added, covering respectively Kanuri, and Creoles and Pidgins; although Kanuri was not included in the West African volume of the Handbook, it is for practical purposes so much a language of West Africa that it seemed advisable to include it here.

In order to help users of the bibliography to pick out entries referring to particular languages, language names—or the names of the peoples speaking them—are printed in bold type. It has seemed best to retain the name used by the author (usually the language name, but sometimes the name of the people who speak it, or even the name given them by some neighbouring group) although this leads to some inconsistency; the author's own spelling has also been retained, except that where the language names do not appear in the title, the spelling of the main entry in the Handbook has sometimes been used.

I would like to express my gratitude to many scholars who have helped to make this bibliography as complete as possible: particularly to Professors M. Houis and G. Manessy for help with Sections II and V respectively, Professor J. Lukas, Dr. H. Jungraithmayr and Dr. P. Zima for their help with Sections IX, X and XI, Dr. Elizabeth Dunstan for her very considerable help in the final preparation of Sections VI–VIII, and Mr. Ian F. Hancock for supplying the bibliographical material for Section XII.

D. W. ARNOTT
School of Oriental and African Studies
University of London
March 1970

SUPPLEMENTARY BIBLIOGRAPHY

GENERAL

ALEXANDRE, P. Linguistique africaine. Latitudes, no. spécial, 1963 (1964), 17-26.
—— 1967. Langues et langage en Afrique noire. Pp. 171, bibl. cartes. Paris: Payot.
ARMSTRONG, R. G. 1964. The Study of West African languages. Pp. 74. Ibadan: Univ. Press.
BENDOR-SAMUEL, P. M. Phonemic problems in some West African languages. S.L.L.R., 4, 1965, 85-90.
BERTHO, J. Aperçu d'ensemble sur les dialectes de l'ouest de la Nigéria. Bull. IFAN, 14, 1, 1952, 259-71.
BLAKNEY, CHARLES. 1963. On 'banana' and 'iron': linguistic footprints in African history. Pp. 124. Hartford, Conn.: Hartford Seminar Foundation (Hartford Stud. in Linguistics.)
BRITISH AND FOREIGN BIBLE SOCIETY. See COLDHAM, GERALDINE E.
BROSNAHAN, L. F. Some aspects of the linguistic situation in tropical Africa. Lingua, 12, 1, 1963, 54-65.
COLDHAM, GERALDINE E. 1966. A bibliography of Scriptures in African languages (a revision of the African sections of the Darlow and Moule 'Historical catalogue of the Holy Scriptures', with additions to 1964). Pp. xi + 848 (in 2 vols). London: British & Foreign Bible Society.
*CZERMAK, W. 1928. Zum konsonantischen Anlautwechsel in den Sprachen des Sudan. Festschrift P. W. Schmidt, Wien, 1928, 26-44.
DALBY, D. (ed.) Studies devoted to S. W. Koelle's *Polyglotta Africana* on the occasion of its republication. S.L.L.R., 3, 1964, 58-90, bibl. (in contin.).
—— Problems of language-mapping in West Africa. Z.f. Mundartforschung (Marburg), 31, 4, 1964, 356-61.
—— Levels of relationship in the comparative study of African languages. A.L.S., 7, 1966, 171-9.
—— Reflections on the classification of African languages, with special reference to the work of Zigismund Wilhelm Koelle and Malcolm Guthrie. A.L.S., 11, 1970, 147-71.
*DELAFOSSE, M. Mots soudanais du moyen âge. Mém. Soc. Ling. Paris, 18, 1913.
DELAFOSSE, M. et CAQUOT, A. Les langues du Soudan et de la Guineé. In: Les langues du monde. Paris: C.N.R.S., 1952, 735-845.
DE LAVERGNE DE TRESSAN, M. 1953. Inventaire linguistique de l'Afrique occidentale française et du Togo. Pp. 241, cartes. Dakar: IFAN (Mém. 30).
*DESTAING, E. Notes de phonétique [Afrique occidentale]. Mém. Soc. Ling. Paris, 16, 1910, 289-99.
*EAST, R. M. 1941. A vernacular bibliography for the languages of Nigeria. Pp. iv+84.
FODOR, I. Az afrikai nyelvek osztályozásának problémái [Problems of classification of African languages]. Nyelvtudományi Közlemények [Budapest], 67, 1, 1965, bibl., map.
—— 1966. The problems in the classification of the African languages: methodological and theoretical conclusions concerning the classification system of Joseph H. Greenberg. Pp. 153, bibl. Budapest: Hungarian Acad. of Sciences Center for Afro-Asian research (Studies on developing countries, 5).
FRANCE. 1968. Centre National de la Recherche Scientifique. Colloque International sur la *classification nominale* dans les langues négro-africaines. (Aix-en-Provence, 3-7 juillet, 1967). Pp. 400. Paris: Éd. du C.N.R.S.
*GREENBERG, J. H. The classification of African languages. Amer. Anthrop., 50, 1, Part 1, 1948, 24-30.
—— Studies in African linguistic classification. I. The Niger-Congo family. II. The classification of Fulani. III. The position of Bantu. IV. Hamito-Semitic. VII. Smaller families: index of languages. VIII. Further remarks on method: revisions and corrections. S.-W. J. Anthrop., 5, 2, 5, 3, 5, 4 (1949); 6, 1, 6, 4 (1950); 10, 4 (1954).
—— 1955. Studies in African linguistic classification (Reprinted from S.-W.J. Anthrop.). Pp. 104 (maps). New Haven: Compass Publishing Company.
—— The labial consonants of Proto-Afro-Asiatic. Word, 14, 2-3, 1958, 295-302.

GREENBERG, J. H. 1963. The languages of Africa. Pp. v+171, maps. Bloomington: Indiana University Res. Center in Anthrop., Folklore & Ling. (Publ. 25): also Int. J. Amer. Ling., 29, 1 (part 2), 1963. (Expanded version of Studies in African linguistic classification, 1955.) [Reviewed in J.A.L., 2, 2, 1963, 170–1; Lingua, 13, 1964, 85–7; Word, 19, 1963, 407–17.]
—— Vowel harmony in African languages. Actes du Second Colloque International de Linguistique Négro-Africaine, Université de Dakar, 1963, 33–7.
—— Interdisciplinary perspectives in African linguistic research. Afr. Stud. Bull. [Stanford], 9, 1, 1966, 8–23.
GUTHRIE, M. 1967. Comparative Bantu. Part I, Vol. 1. The comparative linguistics of the Bantu languages. Pp. 143, topograms. Farnborough, England: Gregg. [Vol. 2 and Part II, Vols. 3 and 4 in press].
HAIR, P. E. H. An introduction to John Clarke's 'Specimens of dialects . . . .', 1848–9. S.L.L.R., 5, 1966, 72–82.
—— Collections of vocabularies of western Africa before the Polyglotta: a key. J.A.L., 5, 3, 1966, 208–17.
—— Niger languages and Sierra Leonean missionary linguists, 1840–1930. Bull. Soc. Afr. Church Hist. [Birmingham], 2, 2, 1966, 127–8.
—— A nineteenth century link between Chinese and African language studies. Bull. S.O.A.S., 29, 1, 1966, 143–5.
—— 1967. The early study of Nigerian languages: essays and bibliographies. London: C.U.P. Pp. xiv+110, ill., map. (W. Afr. language monograph Ser. 7.)
*HAUSE, H. E. Terms for musical instruments in the Sudanic languages: a lexicographical inquiry. J.A.O.S., Suppl. 7, 1948, 1–71.
*HINTZE, F. Zum konsonantischen Anlautwechsel in einigen westafrikanischen Sprachen. Z. Phon., 2, 1948, 164–82, 322–35.
*HODGSON, W. B. 1844. Languages of Soudan or Negroland. New York.
*HOMBURGER, LILIAS. De l'origine des classes nominales dans les langues négro-africaines. Lingua, 1, 2, 1948, 235–46.
HOUIS, M. Remarques sur la transcription toponymique en Afrique Occidentale Française. Bull. IFAN, 14, 1, 1952, 351–6.
—— Trois essais de classification des langues de l'Afrique noire occidentale. Notes afr. IFAN, 60, 1953, 118–19.
—— Schèmes et fonctions tonologiques. Bull. IFAN, 18 (B), 3/4, 1956, 335–68.
—— État des connaissances linguistiques dans l'Ouest africain et perspectives de recherches. Orbis [Louvain], 5, 1, 1956, 169–84.
—— Comment écrire les langues africaines. Présence afr., 17, 1957, 76–92.
—— Problèmes linguistiques de l'Ouest africain. In: Guide Bleu AOF-Togo. Paris: Hachette, 1958, ccv–ccx.
—— Quelques données de toponymie ouest-africaine. Bull. IFAN, 20 (B), 1956, 562–75.
—— Toponymie et sociologie. Bull. IFAN, 22 (B) 1/2, 1960, 443–5.
—— Mouvements historiques et communautés linguistiques dans l'Ouest africain. L'Homme, 1, 3, 1961, 72–90.
—— 1967. Aperçu sur les structures grammaticales des langues négro-africaines. Pp. iv+311 +xlviii. Lyon: Faculté de Théologie S.J.
—— Pour une typologie des séquences de propositions. J.W.A.L., 5, 1, 1968, 13–24.
—— Greenberg: The languages of Africa. Bull. IFAN, 26 (B), 1/2, 1964, 286–95.
JACQUOT, A. and RICHARDSON, I. 1956. Linguistic survey of the northern Bantu borderland, vol. 1 (ed. M. Guthrie and A. N. Tucker). Pt. 1. Report of the western team: Atlantic coast to Oubangui. Pp. 9–62, map. London: O.U.P. for Int. Afr. Inst.
KÄHLER-MEYER, EMMI. Klassensysteme in afrikanischen Sprachen. Tribus, 1952–3, 418–27.
*KLINGENHEBEN, A. Über einige Fremdwörter in sudanischen Klassensprachen. Z. Eingeb. Spr., 13, 1922–3, 302–4.
*—— Tempora Westafrikas und die semitischen Tempora. Z. Eingeb. Spr., 19, 4, 1929, 241–68.

KLINGENHEBEN, A. Zum Problem der Silbe in afrikanischen Sprachen. Afrika und Übersee, 37, 1952-3, 7-20.
—— Zur Entstehung des Klassensprachentyps in Afrika. Mitt. Inst. Orientforsch. [Berlin], 6, 1, 1958, 112-20.
—— Influence of analogy in African languages. J.A.L., 1, 1, 1962, 30-42.
KOELLE, S. W. 1964. (1st ed. 1854). Polyglotta Africana; or a comparative vocabulary of nearly 300 words and phrases, in more than one hundred distinct African languages (reprinted with an historical introduction by P. E. H. Hair). Pp. 188, map. Graz: Akademische Druck- und Verlagsanstalt and Fourah Bay College.
*LABOURET, H. La situation linguistique en Afrique Occidentale Française. Africa, 4, 1, 1931, 56-62.
LADEFOGED, P. The phonetic basis of West African Languages. Actes du Second Colloque International de Linguistique Négro-Africaine, Université de Dakar, 1963, 3-21.
—— 1968. A phonetic study of West African languages: an auditory-instrumental survey, 2nd ed. (1st ed. 1964). London: C.U.P. Pp. xvi, 74, bibl., ill., map. [Reviewed in Afr. u. Übersee 48, 1964, 152-5; J.A.L., 4, 2, 1965, 135-7, and Bull S.O.A.S., 29, 2, 1966, 430-2.]
LUBEL', L. YE. Ekspeditsiya Sovietskikh lingvistov v Republiku Mali. [An expedition of Soviet linguists to the Mali Republic]. Vestnik Akad. Nauk SSR, 9, 1964, 96-100.
LUKAS, J. (ed.) 1955. Afrikanistische studien. Pp. 416. Berlin: Ak. Verlag.
—— Der gegenwärtige Stand der Gliederung der Westsudanischen Sprachen. Tribus, 4-5, 1954-5, 87-93.
MANESSY, G. Observations sur la classification nominale dans les langues négro-africaines du Soudan et de la Guinée. Bull. Soc. Ling. Paris, 57, 1962, 126-59.
*MAUNY, R. Enquête sur les noms de métaux dans les langues africaines. Notes afr. IFAN, 50, 1951, 61.
—— 1952. Glossaire des expressions et termes locaux employés dans l'Ouest africain. Pp. 69. Dakar: IFAN (Catalogues 9).
MEEUSSEN, A. E. Tone typologies for West African languages. A.L.S., 11, 1970, 266-71.
*MIGEOD, F. W. H. 1911, 1913. The languages of West Africa. 2 vols. pp. 373, ix+436, map. London: Kegan Paul.
MONTEIL, V. La classification des langues de l'Afrique. Bull. IFAN, 27 (B), 1/2, 1965, 155-68.
—— La transcription des langues africaines (conférence à Bamako). Bull. IFAN, 28 (B), 3/4, 1966, 723-30.
MUKAROVSKY, H. G. West African and Hamito-Semitic languages. Wiener völkerkdl. Mitt., 13, 8, 1966, 9-36, bibl.
*NORRIS, E. 1841. Outline of a vocabulary of a few of the principal languages of western and central Africa. Compiled for the use of the Niger Expedition. Pp. vii+213. London.
PIKE, K. L. 1966. Tagmemic and matrix linguistics applied to selected African languages. Ann Arbor, Michigan: University of Michigan Center for Research on Language and Language Behavior. [Kasem, Vagala, Sisala, Dagaari, Bariba, Bimoba, Basari; Twi, Degema, Engenni, Igede, Yachi, Izi; Abua, Agbo, Bette, Mbembe, Etung.]
RICHARDSON, I. 1957. Linguistic survey of the northern Bantu borderland. Vol. 2. Pp. 97, map. London: O.U.P. for Int. Afr. Inst.
RODRIGUES, A. DALL'IGNA. Portugiesische Literatur über afrikanische Sprachen. Afr. u. Übersee, 42, 3, 1958, 119-34.
SEBEOK, T. A. (ed.) 1970. Current trends in linguistics. Vol. 7: Linguistics in Sub-Saharan Africa. Bloomington: Indiana University.
SIERTSEMA, BERTHA. Intonation phenomena in tone languages. Actes du Second Colloque International de Linguistique Négro-Africaine, Université de Dakar, 1963, 55-56.
SPENCER, J. (ed.) 1963. Language in Africa. Papers of the Leverhulme conference on Universities and the language problems of tropical Africa. Pp. 167. C.U.P.
—— S. W. Koelle and the problem of notation for African languages, 1847-1855. S.L.L.R., 5, 1966, 83-105.
*STRUCK, B. Einige Sudan-Wortstämme. Z.f. Kolonialsprachen, 2, 1911-1912, 231-53, 309-23.

*THOMAS, N. W. The Sudanic languages. Bull. S.O.A.S., 1, 1917–20, 107–24, map.
TUCKER, A. N. Neue Wege zur Gliederung der afrikanischen Nichtbantusprachen. Phonetica, 1, 1957, 39–52.
—— Systems of tone-marking African languages. Bull. S.O.A.S., 27, 3, 1964, 594–611.
UNESCO. Rapport final sur la réunion d'un groupe d'experts pour l'unification des alphabets des langues nationales, Bamako, 28 fév.—5 mars, 1966. Pp. 40. UNESCO/CLT/BALING/13, 15/9/66. French original and English translation. [Mandingue, Peul, Tamasheq, Songhay-Zarma, Hausa, Kanuri.]
VOEGELIN, C. F. and F. M. 1964. Languages of the world: African fascicle one. (=Anthropological Linguistics, 6, 5, May 1964.)
*WARD, IDA C. Verbal tone patterns in West African languages. Bull. S.O.A.S., 12, 3/4, 1948, 831–7.
—— Tonal analysis of West African languages. Z.f. Phonetik u. allg. Sprachwiss., 3, 1/2, 1949, 54–67.
WELMERS, W. E. Associative *a* and *ka* in Niger-Congo. Language, 39, 3, 1, 1963, 432–47.
WEST AFRICAN LANGUAGES CONGRESS. 1963. Actes du second colloque international de linguistique négro-africaine, Dakar, 12–16 avril 1962. Pp. xx+302, cartes. Dakar: Université.
*WESTERMANN, D. 1911. Die Sudansprachen: eine sprachvergleichende Studie. Pp. viii+222, map. Hamburg: L. Friederichsen. (Abh.d. Hamburgischen Kolonialinst., 3).
*—— Laut, Ton und Sinn in westafrikanischen Sudansprachen. In Festschrift Meinhof. Hamburg 1927, 315–28.
*—— Laut und Sinn in einigen westafrikanischen Sprachen. Arch. f. die gesamte Phonetik, 1, 1, 3–4, 1937, 154–72 and 193–212.
*—— Afrikanische Tabusitten in ihrer Einwirkung auf die Sprachstellung. Abhandl. d. Pr. Ak. d. W. Phil. hist. Kl., 12, 1939, 1–22.
*—— Form und Funktion der Reduplikation in einigen westafrikanischen Sprachen. Afrika [Berlin], 3, 2, 1944, 83–104.
*—— Sprachbezeichnungen und Sprachverwandtschaft in Afrika. Sitzungsber. d. deutsch Ak. d. Wiss. Phil.-hist. Kl., 1, 1948, 270.
*—— African linguistic classification. Africa, 22, 1952, 150–6.
*—— and WARD, IDA C. 1949 (2nd impression). Practical phonetics for students of African languages. Pp. 169, ill. London: O.U.P. for Int. Afr. Inst.
WILLIAMSON, KAY. Deep and surface structure in tone languages. J.W.A.L., 5, 2, 1968, 77–81.
WINSTON, F. D. D. Greenberg's classification of African languages. A.L.S., 7, 1966, 160–70, bibl.
WOLFF, H. 1954. Nigerian orthography. Pp. 61. Zaria: Northern Regional Adult Education Office for Unesco.
—— Subsystem typologies and area linguistics. Anthrop. Linguistics, 1, 7, 1959, 1–88.
ZIMA, P. Some remarks on the function of tones in African languages. Travaux linguistiques de Prague, II, 1966, 151–6.

For other articles dealing with the classification of West African languages, see under 'General' in the various sections below.

SECTION I

THE WEST ATLANTIC LANGUAGES

GENERAL

BRADSHAW, A. T. von S. Vestiges of Portuguese in the languages of Sierra Leone. S.L.L.R., 4, 1965, 5–37 [incl. **Fula, Limba, Temne, Bullom, Gola, Kissi**].
CALVET, M. J. 1967. La transcription des langues du Sénégal; problèmes théoriques pour le choix d'un alphabet official. Avec, en annexe, le Rapport UNESCO sur la réunion d'experts tenue a Bamako en 1966 pour la transcription des langues africaines. Pp. 71. Dakar: CLAD 29 bis [incl. **Wolof, Toucouleur (Fula), Diola, Serer**].

CANU, G. 1965. Les systèmes phonologiques des principales langues du Sénégal. Étude comparative. Pp. 44. Dakar: CLAD No. 13 [incl. **Bagnun, Dyola-Fogny, Peul (Fula), Serer, Wolof**].
CARREIRA, A. O fundamento dos etnónimos na Guiné portuguesa. Garcia de Orta, 10, 2, 1962, 305–23, map.
CORREA, A. A. M. Elementos para a classificação de raças e linguas na Guiné portuguesa. Lisboa: Soc. de Geog., Congr.... V. Centenario.... Guiné, vol. 2, 1946, 373–87.
DALBY, D. Language distribution in Sierra Leone, 1961–62. S.L.L.R., 1, 1962, 62–7, map.
—— The Mel languages: a reclassification of southern 'West Atlantic'. A.L.S., 6, 1965, 1–17, bibl., map. [**Temne, Baga, Bullom, Bom, Krim, Kissi, Gola**.]
—— Mel languages in the Polyglotta Africana. S.L.L.R., 4, 1965, 129–35; 5, 1966, 139–51. [**Baga, Landuma** and **Temne; Bullom, Kissi, Gola**.]
—— Languages of Sierra Leone. In: Sierra Leone in maps, ed. J. I. Clarke. University of London Press, 1966, 38–9, maps.
DO ESPIRITO SANTO, J. Nomes vernáculos de algumas plantas da Guiné portuguesa. Bol. cult. Guiné port., 3, 12, 1948, 983–1036.
GUINÉ PORTUGUESA: Brigada de estudos florestais. Nomes vernaculos de algumas plantas da Guiné portuguesa. Bol. cult. Guiné port., 11, 42, 1956, 73–81.
HAIR, P. E. H. Ethnolinguistic continuity on the Guinea Coast. J. Afr. Hist., 8, 2, 1967, 247–68.
—— An ethnolinguistic inventory of the Upper Guinea coast before 1700. A.L.R., 6, 1967, 32–70, [**Bidyogo, Biafada, Nalu** and **Landuma; 'Sapi', Baga, Temne, Bullom, Susu, Loko** and **Limba; Wolof, Serer, Tukulor-Fula; Mandingo-Flup-Dyola, Banyum** and **Brame-Pepel-Mandyak**].
—— An ethnolinguistic inventory of the Lower Guinea Coast before 1700. A.L.R., 7, 1968, 47–73, [incl. **Gola, Bullom, Krim**].
HOUIS, M. Les minorités ethniques de la Guinée côtière: situation linguistique. Et. guinéennes, 4, 1950, 25–48.
LOPES, F. C. O dinheiro nas línguas de Guiné. Mundo port. No. 139, 1945.
—— O conhecimento das línguas da Guiné portuguesa e a possibilidade de uma grafia una. Bol. cult. Guiné port., 1, 3, 1946, 453–6.
SAPIR, D. West Atlantic; an inventory of the languages, their noun class systems, and consonant alternation. In: Current trends in linguistics. Vol. 7, Linguistics in Sub-Saharan Africa, ed. Thomas A. Sebeok. Bloomington: Indiana University, 1970.
SAUVAGEOT, S. and others. Les classes nominales et leurs fonctions dans le groupe sénégalo-guinéen ou ouest-atlantique. Actes du Second Colloque International de Linguistique Négro-Africaine, Université de Dakar, 1963, 267–91 [incl. **Dyola, Serer, Wolof, Fula**].
VIEIRA, R. A. Subsidio para o estudio da flora medicinal da Guiné portuguesa. Bol. geral Ultramar, 32, 1956, 368–78; 33, 1957, 379–81.
WEIL, P. M. Language distribution in the Gambia. A.L.R., 7, 1968, 101–6, [incl. **Wolof, Serer, Diola, Fula, Manjak, Banyun, Temne, Mansuanka**].
WILSON, W. A. A. Temne and the West Atlantic group. S.L.L.R., 2, 1963, 26–9.
—— Uma volta linguistica na Guiné. Bol. cult. Guiné port., 14, 56, 1959, 569–601.
—— Numeration in the languages of Guiné. Africa, 31, 4, 1961, 372–7, [incl. **Wolof, Diola, Fula,** and many smaller languages].
—— Talking drums in Portuguese Guinea. Est. Etnol. ultramar portug., 3, 1963, 199–220, bibl., ill.

1. ADYUKRU

2. GOLA

BRADSHAW, A. T. von S. Vestiges of Portuguese... (see I. General) [incl. **Gola**].
DALBY, D. The Mel languages.... (see I. General) [incl. **Gola**].
HAIR, P. E. H. An ethnolinguistic inventory of the Lower Guinea coast... (see I. General) [incl. **Gola**].

3. KISSI-LANDOMA GROUP

BERRY, J. Nominal classes in **Hu-Limba**. Sierra Leone Stud., 11, 1958, 169–173.
—— A short phonetic study of **Sherbro (Bolom)** as spoken in Sierra Leone. Sierra Leone Stud., 12, 1959, 284–94.
—— The structure of the noun in **Kisi**. Sierra Leone Stud., 12, 1959, 308–15.
—— A note on voice and aspect in **Hu-Limba**. Sierra Leone Stud., 13, 1960, 36–40.
BRADSHAW, A. T. von S. Vestiges of Portuguese ... (see I. General) [incl. **Limba, Temne, Bullom, Kissi**].
DALBY, D. **Banta** and **Mabanta**. S.L.L.R., 2, 1963, 23–5.
—— The Mel languages .... (see I. General) [incl. **Temne, Baga, Bullom, Bom, Krim, Kissi**].
—— Mel languages in the Polyglotta ... (see I. General) [incl. **Baga, Landuma** and **Temne, Bulom, Kissi**].
—— Lexical analysis in **Temne**, with illustrative word list, J.W.A.L., 3, 2, 1966, 5–26.
—— and KAMARA, A. Vocabulary of the **Temne** Ragbenle society. S.L.L.R., 3, 1964, 35–41.
DAWSON, J. L. **Temne** witchcraft vocabulary. S.L.L.R., 2, 1963, 16–22.
FINNEGAN, R. **Limba** religious vocabulary. S.L.L.R., 2, 1963, 11–15.
HAIR, P. E. H. Notes on the early study of some West African languages [Susu, **Bullom/Sherbro, Temne**, Mende, Vai and Yoruba]. Bull. IFAN, 23 (B), 3/4, 1961, 683–95, bibl.
—— **Temne** and African language classification before 1864. J.A.L., 4, 1, 1965, 46–56.
—— An ethnolinguistic inventory of the Upper Guinea coast ... (see I. General) [incl. **Landuma, 'Sapi', Baga, Temne, Bullom, Limba**].
—— An ethnolinguistic inventory of the Lower Guinea Coast .... (see I. General) [incl. **Bullom, Krim**].
HOUIS, M. Contes **Baga** (Dialecte du Koba). Et. guinéennes, 6, 1950, 3–15.
—— Remarques sur la voix passive en **baga**. Notes afr. IFAN, 55, 1952, 91–2.
—— Le système pronominal et les classes dans les dialectes **baga**. Bull. IFAN, 15, 1, 1953, 381–404 (carte).
—— Le genre animé en **baga**. Notes afr. IFAN, 58, 1953, 25–7.
—— Le rapport d'annexion en **baga**. Bull. IFAN, 15, 2, 1953, 848–54.
MITCHELL, P. K. A note on the distribution in Sierra Leone of literacy in Arabic, Mende and **Temne**. A.L.R., 7, 1968, 90–100.
*MUKAROVSKY, H. G. 1948. Die Sprache der **Kissi** in Liberia. Abriss einer Grammatik mit Texten und Vokabular, verarbeitet nach Aufzeichnungen von Dora Earthy. Wien.
—— Abriss einer Lautlehre des **Limba**. Arch. f. Völkerkde., 17/18, 1962–63, 161–78.
—— **Sherbro, Mmani** und die westguineische Sprachgruppe. Arch. f. Völkerkde., 20, 1966, 75–88, bibl.
—— **Kisi** and Bantu. Arch. f. Völkerkde., 13, 1959, 132–75.
PAULME, DENISE. 1964. Documents sur la langue **kissi**. Lexique et textes. Pp. 167. Dakar. Documents linguistiques, 8.
PICHL, W. Comparative notes on **Sherbro** and **Krim**. S.L.L.R., 3, 1964, 42–6.
—— Einiges aus der Geschichte der **Bullom** (eine ethnolinguistische Betrachtung). Mitt. anthrop. Ges. Wien, 95, 1965, 22–6.
—— 1966. The **Cangin** group: a language group in northern Senegal. Pp. 12, bibl., map. Pittsburgh: Duquesne Univ. Inst. Afr. Affairs (Afr. reprint ser., 20).
—— 1967. **Sherbro**-English dictionary (Freetown, Fourah Bay College, 1964). Pp. xi+153, bibl., ill. Pittsburgh: Duquesne Univ. Press.
*SAMARIN, W. J. A provisional phonemic analysis of **Kisi**. Kroeber Anthrop. Soc. Pap. [Berkeley, California], 2, 1950, 89–100.
—— A tentative analysis of the pluralisation of **Kisi** nouns. Kroeber Anthrop. Soc. Pap. 5, 1951, 58–85.
SCOTT, J. P. L. 1956. An introduction to **Temne** grammar. Pp. 40. Sierre Leone: Govt. Printing Dept.
TURAY, A. K. A vocabulary of **Temne** musical instruments. S.L.L.R., 5, 1966, 27–33.

WEIL, P. M. Language distribution in the Gambia. A.L.R., 7, 1968, 101–6, [incl. **Temne**].
WILSON, W. A. A. 1961. An outline of the **Temne** language. Pp. 63. London: S.O.A.S.
—— **Temne, Landuma** and the **Baga** languages. S.L.L.R., 1, 1962, 27–38.
—— **Temne** and the West Atlantic group. S.L.L.R., 2, 1963, 26–9.
—— An interpretation of the **Temne** tone system. J.W.A.L., 5, 1968, 5–11.

4. OTHER LANGUAGES

BALANDIER, G. Toponymie des îles de **Kabak** et **Kakossa**. Ét. guinéennes, 8, 1952, 49–54.
CANU, G. 1965. Les systèmes phonologiques . . . . (see I. General) [incl. **Bagnun, Dyola-Fogny**].
*CARDOSA, H. L. Pequeno vocabulário do dialecto '**pepel**'. Bol. Soc. geog. Lisboa, sér. 20, 10, 1902, 121–8.
CARREIRA, A. Alguns aspectos da influência da língua mandinga na **Pajadinca**. Bol. cult. Guiné port., 18, 71, 1963, 345–83, map.
DALBY, D., and HAIR, P. E. H. A West African word [*myonga*] of 1456. J.W.A.L., 4, 1, 1967, 13–14. [**Manyanka-Pepel-Mandyak**.]
DE SÁ NOGUEIRA, R. Temas de linguística **Banta**: As línguas Banta e o Português. Lisboa: Instituto de Línguas Africanas e Orientais, anexo a Escola Superior Colonial.
DONEUX, J. Les systèmes phonologiques des langues de Casamance. [**Dyola, Baynuk, Banyun Mandyak, Pepel, Mankanya, Balanta**, Creole.] CLAD No. 28. Pp. 82.
—— Le **manjaku**, classes nominales et questions sur l'alternance consonantique. In: La classification nominale dans les langues négro-africaines. Paris: C.N.R.S., 1967, 261–76.
FERRY, MARIE-PAULE. Deux langues **tenda** du Senegal oriental, **basari** et **bedik**. BSELAF, 7, 1968.
—— L'alternance consonantique en **bedik**. J.W.A.L., 5, 2, 1968, 91–6.
GREENBERG, J. H. Polyglotta evidence for consonant mutation in the **Mandyak** languages. S.L.L.R., 5, 1966, 106–10.
HAIR, P. E. H. An ethnolinguistic inventory of the Upper Guinea Coast . . . (see I. General) [incl. **Bidyogo, Biafada, Nalu, Flup-Dyola, Banyun, Brame-Pepel-Mandyak**].
KENNEDY, A. M. Dialect in **Diola**. J.A.L., 3, 1, 1964, 96–101.
*LOPES, E. C. **Manjacos**: Lingua. Mundo port, 10, 113, 114, 1943.
*MARQUES, J. B. Aspectos do problema da semelhança da lingua dos **Papéis, Manjacos** e **Brames**. Bol. cult. Guiné port, 2, 5, 1947, 77–109.
MUKAROVSKY, H. G. Vers une linguistique comparative ouest-africaine: le **diola**, langue bantoue-guinéenne. Bull. IFAN, 26 (B), 1/2, 1964, 127–65.
*NGASOBIL: MISSION ST. JOSEPH. 1880. Guide de la conversation en quatre langues: Français, Volof, **Diola**, Sérère. Pp. 329 [1907 ed., pp. 295].
QUINTINO, F. R. Conhecimento da língua **balanta**, através da sua estrutura vocabular. Bol. cult. Guiné port., 16, 64, 1961, 737–68.
SAPIR, J. D. 1965. A grammar of **Diola-Fogny**. Pp. xiii+129. London: C.U.P. (W. Afr. language Monogr. series 2). [Reviewed in Africa, 36, 4, 1966, 465–66.]
—— and THOMAS, L. V. Le **Diola** et le temps. Recherches anthropologiques sur la notion de durée en Basse-Casamance (Thomas). Notes linguistiques (Sapir). Bull. IFAN, 29 (B), 1/2, 1967, 331–424.
SAUVAGEOT, S. Note sur la classification nominale en **bainouk**. In: La classification nominale dans les langues négro-africaines. Paris: C.N.R.S., 1967, 225–36.
—— *et al.* Les classes nominales . . . (see I. General) [incl. **Dyola**].
TRIFKOVIC, M. 1967. Le **Mancagne**; étude phonologique et morphologique. Pp. 314. Dakar: IFAN.
WEIL, P. M. Language distribution in the Gambia. A.L.R., 7, 1968, 101–6, [incl. **Diola, Mansuanka, Manyak, Banyun**].
*WEISS, H. 1940. Grammaire et lexique **diola** du Fogny. Pp. 168. Paris: Larose.
WILSON, W. A. A. Outline of the **Balanta** language. A.L.S., 2, 1961, 139–68.

WILSON, W. A. A. Numeration in the languages of Guiné. Africa, 31, 4, 1961, 372–7, [incl. **Diola** and many smaller languages].
—— A reconstruction of the **Pajade** mutation system. J.W.A.L., 2, 1, 1965, 15–20.

5. SERER

CANU, G. Les systèmes phonologiques . . . (see I. General) [incl. **Serer**].
*EZANNO, F. J. Quelques proverbes **sérèrs** recueillis à Fadiout (Sénégal) (avec traduction française). Anthropos, 48, 3/4, 1953, 593–6.
—— 1960. Dictionnaire **sérère**-français, précédé d'un abrégé de grammaire sérère par le P. Greffier S.Sp. Joal: Mission Catholique.
*FAIDHERBE, L. L. C. Étude sur la langue **kéguem** ou **sérère-sine**. Annuaire du Sénégal et dépendances pour l'année 1865. Saint-Louis, 1865, 173–242.
*—— 1887. Langues sénégalaises: wolof, arabe-hassania, soninke, **sérère**. Notions grammaticales, vocabulaires et phrases. Pp. 266. Paris: Leroux.
HAIR, P. E. H. An ethnolinguistic inventory of the Upper Guinea Coast . . . (see I. General), [incl. **Serer**].
*HESTERMANN, F. Der Anlautwechsel in der **Serersprache** in Senegambien, Westafrika. Wiener Z. f.d. Kunde des Morgenländes, 26, 1912, 350–62.
*LAMOISE, R. P. 1873. Dictionnaire de la langue **sérère**. Ngasobil: Mission St. Joseph.
*—— 1873. Grammaire de la langue **sérère** avec des examples et des exercises. Pp. 359. Ngasobil: Mission St. Joseph.
MANESSY, G. et SAUVAGEOT, S. (eds.). 1963. Wolof et **Sérèr**; études de phonétique et de grammaire descriptive (extraits de revues françaises, anglaises, allemandes, autrichiennes et suisses). Pp. 307, bibl. Dakar: Université (Publ. Section Langues et Litt., 12).
*MOLLIEN, G. T. 1820. Voyage dans l'intérieur de l'Afrique. Vol. 2 Vocabulaire des langues iolof, poule et **serrère**. Paris: Courcier.
*NGASOBIL: MISSION ST. JOSEPH. 1880. Guide de la conversation en quatre langues: Français, Volof, Diola, **Sérère**. Pp. 329 [1907 éd., pp. 295].
PICHL, W. Permutation et accord en **serer**. Actes du second Colloque International de Linguistique Négro-Africaine, Université de Dakar, 1963, 78–85.
SAUVAGEOT, S. and others. Les classes nominales . . . (see I. General) [incl. **Serer**].
WEIL, P. M. Language distribution . . . (see I. General) [incl. **Serer**].

6. WOLOF

AMAR, S. Influence de l'Islam sur la littérature **'wolof'**. Bull. IFAN, 30 (B), 2, 1968, 628–41.
BOILAT, Abbé. 1858. Grammaire de langue **wolofe**. Pp. vi+430. Paris: Impr. Impériale.
CALVET, M. Interférences du phonétisme **wolof** dans le français parlé au Sénégal dans la région du Cap Vert. Bull. IFAN, 26 (B), 3/4, 1964, 518–31.
—— Étude phonétique des voyelles du **wolof**. Pp. 30. Dakar: CLAD, No. 14.
—— et DUMONT, P. Le français au Sénégal. Interférences au **wolof** dans le français des élèves sénégalais. Bull. IFAN, 31 (B), 1, 1969, 239–63.
CANU, G. Les systèmes phonologiques . . . (see I. General) [incl. Wolof].
CISSÉ, B. (tr.). Poème de Moussa Ka (1883–1967) [en wolof et français] (revu et annoté par Amar Samb). Bull. IFAN 30 (B), 3, 7, 1968, 847–60.
COPANS, J. et al., 1968. Contes **wolof** du Baol (Sénégal). Pp. 184, cartes. Dakar-Hann: Centre ORSTOM.
DALBY, D. Further indigenous scripts of West Africa: Manding, **Wolof** and Fula alphabets and Yoruba 'holy' writings. A.L.S., 10, 1969, 161–81.
*DARD, J. 1826. Grammaire **wolof**. 2 vols. Pp. xxxi+213. Paris: Impr. Royale.
*—— 1855 (1re éd. 1825). Dictionnaire français-**wolof** et français-bambara, suivi du dictionnaire **wolof**-français. Pp. 242. Paris: Impr. Royale.
*DESCEMET, L. 1964. Recueil d'environ 1,200 phrases usuelles françaises avec leur traduction en regard en **ouolof** de Saint-Louis. Pp. 48. Saint-Louis: Impr. du Gouvt.
DIOP, Mme A. Test d'audiométrie vocale en **wolof**. Pp. 65. Dakar: CLAD. No. 20.

*Faidherbe, L. C. 1864. (1re éd. 1860). Vocabulaire d'environ 1,500 mots français avec leurs correspondants en **ouolof** de Saint-Louis, en poular (toucouleur) du Fouta, en soninké (sarakhollé) de Bakel. Pp. 70. Saint-Louis: Impr. du Gouvt.

*—— 1887. Langues sénégalaises: **wolof**, arabe-hassania, soninké, sérère. Notions grammaticales, vocabulaires et phrases. Pp. 266. Paris: Leroux.

*Fieldhouse, J. 1878. Grammar of the **Jolof** language. Pp. 37. London: Wesleyan Missionary Soc.

Gamble, D. P. 1958. Elementary **Wolof** grammar. Pp. 21. London: Colonial Office (Research Dept.).

—— 1958. **Wolof**-English dictionary. Pp. 29. London: Colonial Office (Research Dept.).

Grelier, S. 1965–6. Essai de comparaison morpho-syntaxique de l'anglais, du **wolof** et du français (le nominal). Pp. 142. Dakar: CLAD. No. 19.

—— 1966. Recherche des principales interférences dans les systèmes verbaux de l'anglais, du **wolof** et du français (analyse théorique et application pratique). Pp. 179. Dakar: CLAD. No. 31.

Hair, P. E. H. An ethnolinguistic inventory of the Upper Guinea Coast ... (see I. General) [incl. **Wolof**].

*Kobes, A. 1858. Principes de la langue **volofe**. Paris.

*—— 1869. Grammaire de la langue **volofe**. Pp. vi+360. Ngasobil: Mission St. Joseph.

*—— 1923 (1re éd. 1873). Dictionnaire **volof**-français. Nouvelle édition revue et augmentée par O. Abiven. Pp. viii+383. Dakar: Impr. de la Mission.

*—— 1924. Dictionnaire français-**volof**, revue et augmenté par O. Abiven. Dakar.

*Labouret, H. Remarques sur la langue des **Wolof**. In: Les pêcheurs de Guet N'dar, N. Leca. Paris: Larose, 1935, 16–27.

*Lambert, M. Grammaire **ouolove**, précédée d'une introduction intitulée: Les Ouolofs, par M. A. Renzi. Pp. 27. [Extrait de l'Investigateur (Paris), 1842.]

Manessy, G. et Sauvageot, S. (eds.). 1963. **Wolof** et Sérèr: études de phonétique et de grammaire descriptive (extraits de revues françaises, anglaises, allemandes, autrichiennes et suisses). Pp. 307, bibl. Dakar: Université (Publ. Section Langues et Litt., 12). [Reviewed in Archiv Orientalni (Prague), 33, 1965, 118.]

*Mollien, G. T. 1820. Voyage dans l'intérieur de l'Afrique. Vol. 2. Vocabulaire des langues **iolof**, poule et serrère. Paris: Courcier.

*Mouradian, J. Note sur quelques emprunts de la langue **wolof** à l'arabe. Bull. IFAN, 2, 3/4, 1940, 269–84.

*Ngasobil: Mission St. Joseph. 1880. Guide de la conversation en quatre langues: Français, **Volof**, Diola, Sérère. Pp. 329 [1907 éd., pp. 295].

Pichl, W. **Wolof**-Erzählungen. Afr. u. Übersee, 44, 4, 1961, 253–82.

—— Ein **Wolof**-Gedicht und -Lieder. Afr. u. Übersee, 45, 4, 1962, 271–85.

—— **Wolof**-Sprichwörter und -Rätsel. Afr. u. Übersee, 46, 1/2, 1962, 93–109.

—— Verschiedene **Wolof**-Texte. Afr. u. Übersee, 46, 3, 1963, 204–18.

*Rambaud, J. B. La détermination en **Wolof**. Bull. Soc. Ling. Paris, 1898, 122–36.

*—— 1903. La langue **wolof**. Pp. 106. Paris: Leroux (Bibl. École Langues orient. vivantes, 2).

*Roger, J.-F. 1829. Fables sénégalaises recueillies dans l'**Ouolof**. Paris: F. Didot.

*—— 1829. Recherches philosophiques sur la langue **ouolove**, suivies d'un vocabulaire abregé français-ouolof. Pp. 175. Paris: Doudey-Dupré.

Sauvageot, S. 1965. Le parler du **dyolof**: description synchronique d'un dialecte **wolof**. Pp. 274, carte. Dakar: IFAN (Mém. 73). [Reviewed in Africa, 36, 4, 1966, 465–6; J.A.L., 5, 1, 1966, 68–70.]

—— et al. Les classes nominales ... (see I. General) [incl. **Wolof**.]

*Speisser, F.-L. 1888. Grammaire élémentaire de la langue **volofe**. Pp. 351. Ngasobil: Mission St. Joseph.

Stewart, W. A. et al. 1966. Introductory course in Dakar **Wolof**. Pp. 230. Washington, D.C.: Centre of Applied Linguistics.

Weil, P. M. Language distribution in the Gambia. A.L.R., 7, 1968, 101–6 [incl. **Wolof**].

WILSON, W. A. A. Numeration in the languages of Guinea. Africa, 31, 4, 1961, 372–7 [incl. **Wolof**].
WIOLAND, F. Le genre en Français parlé et en **wolof**. Pp. 31. Dakar: CLAD. No. 18.
WIOLAND, F. et CALVET, M. L'expansion du **wolof** au Sénégal. Bull. IFAN, 29 (B), 3/4, 1967, 604–18.

7. FULANI (FULA)

ARNOTT, D. W. The middle voice in **Fula**. Bull. S.O.A.S., 28, 1956, 130–44.
—— Proverbial lore and word-play of the **Fulani**. Africa, 27, 4, 1957, 379–96.
—— Some features of the nominal class system of **Fula** in Nigeria, Dahomey and Niger. Afr. u. Übersee, 43, 4, 1960, 241–78.
—— The tense system in Gombe **Fula**. Afr. u. Übersee, 49, 1, 1966, 1–31; 2, 105–35; 3, 173–95; 4, 270–99.
—— The subjunctive in **Fula**: a study of the relation between meaning and syntax. A.L.S., 2, 1961, 126–36.
—— Morphological features in the verbal system of **Fula**. J.W.A.L., 2, 1, 1965, 5–14.
—— Sentence intonation in the Gombe dialect of **Fula**: a tentative analysis. A.L.S., 6, 1965, 73–100.
—— **Fula** dialects in the *Polyglotta Africana*. S.L.L.R., 4, 1965, 109–21.
—— Nominal groups in **Fula** In: Neue Afrikanistische Studien, ed. J. Lukas. Hamburg, 1966, 40–60.
—— Some reflections on the content of individual classes in **Fula** and Tiv. In: La classification nominale dans les langues négro-africaines. Paris: C.N.R.S., 1967, 45–74.
—— 1969. **Fula**. In: Twelve Nigerian languages. A handbook on their sound systems for teachers of English, ed. Elizabeth Dunstan. London: Longmans, 1969, 57–71.
—— Trilingual dictionary, **Fulfulde**-French-English. See UNESCO. 1969.
—— 1970. The nominal and verbal systems of **Fula**. Pp. 432. Oxford: Clarendon Press.
—— 1st and 2nd person pronominal forms in **Fula**. A.L.S., 11, 1970, 35–47.
BA, OUMAR. Dix-huit poèmes **peul** modernes, presentés par Pierre F. Lacroix. Cah. Ét. afr., 2, 8, 1962, 536–50.
—— 1965. Poèmes **peul** modernes. Deuxième édition. (Études mauritaniennes.) Pp. 45. Nouakchott: Imprimerie Mauritanienne.
—— Trois poèmes **poular**. Cah. Étud. afr., 8, 2 (30), 1968, 318–22.
—— Vocabulaire de base: introduction à l'étude du **poular** du Fouta sénégalais. Bull. IFAN, 30 (B), 3, 1968, 1271–82.
—— Le franc-parler **toucouleur**. Bull. IFAN, 30 (B), 2, 1968, 1581–629
—— [n.d.] Petit vocabulaire de la langue **peul** parlée au Fouta Toro. Pp. 56. Dakar: CLAD. No. 35.
*BAIKIE, W. B. 1861. Observations on the Hausa and **Fulfulde** languages. Pp. 29, London.
*BONIFACI, A. 1949. Dictionnaire de langue peule. 1. Français-peul. Yaounde: Impr. du Gouvt.
*BRACKENBURY, E. A. Notes on the **Fulfulde**. J. Afr. Soc., 15, 1915, 70–82.
*—— 1907. Short vocabulary of the **Fulani** language. Pp. 39. N. Nigeria: Govt. Printer.
BRADSHAW, A. T. von S. Vestiges of Portuguese . . . (see I. General) [incl. **Fula**].
CALVET, M. J. 1967. La transcription des langues du Senegal . . . (see I. General) [incl. Toucouleur (**Fula**)].
CANU, G. 1965. Les systèmes phonologiques . . . (see I. General) [incl. Peul (**Fula**)].
DALBY, D. Further indigenous scripts of West Africa: Manding, Wolof and **Fula** alphabets and Yoruba 'holy' writings. A.L.S., 10, 1969, 161–81.
DAUZATS, A. Quelques notes de toponymie du Nord-Cameroun. Bull. Soc. Ét. camerounaises, 4, 1943, 47–60, [incl. **Peul**].
—— 1952 (2e éd.) Éléments de langue **peule** du Nord-Cameroun. Pp. 128. Albi: Impr. Albigeoise.
—— 1952. Lexique français-**peul** et peul-français. Pp. 444. Albi: Impr. Albigeoise.

*DE LAVERGNE DE TRESSAN, Marquis. Pour une transcription phonétique **peule**, unifiée. Bull. IFAN, 13, 3, 1951, 916–23.
—— Du langage descriptif en **peul**. Bull. IFAN, 14, 2, 1952, 636–59.
—— Au sujet des **Peuls**. Bull. IFAN, 14, 4, 1952, 1512–59 (carte).
DE LESTRANGE, MONIQUE et DE LAVERGNE DE TRESSAN, Marquis. Proverbes **peuls** du Badyar et du Foûta-Djallon. Bull. IFAN, 17 (B), 3/4, 1955, 433–76.
DIALLO, OUSMANE, Le pluriel de politesse au Fouta-Diallon. Notes afr. IFAN, 32, 1946, 12–13.
DUCOS, GISÈLE E. Parallèle badiaranké-**peul**, limité à deux points de structure. J.A.L., 3, 1, 1964, 75–9.
DUPIRE, MARGUERITE et DE TRESSAN, Marquis. Devinettes **peules** et bororo. Africa, 25, 4, 1955, 375–92.
*FAIDHERBE, L. C. 1864. (1re éd. 1860). Vocabulaire d'environ 1,500 mots français avec leurs correspondants en ouolof de Saint Louis, en **poular** (toucouleur) du Fouta, en soninké (sarakhollé) de Bakel. Pp. 70. Saint-Louis: Impr. du Gouvt.
*—— et QUINTON, L. Dictionnaire de la langue **poul**. Bull. Soc. Géog. Paris, sér. 7, 2, 1881, 334–54.
*GADEN, H. Du nom chez les Toucouleurs et **Peuls** islamisés du Fouta sénégalais. Rev. Ethnog. et Sociol., 3, 1/2, 1912, 50–6.
*—— Un chant de guerre **toucouleur**. Annu. et Mém. Com. Ét. hist. et sci. A.O.F., 1916, 349–51; 1917, p. 497.
*—— Les alternances de consonnes initiales du Fouldé, dialecte **peul**, du Fouta Djallon. Outremer, 1, 3, 1929, 286–306.
*—— Quelques proverbes et maximes **peuls** et toucouleurs. Revue officiers réserve Sénégal-Mauretanie, 3, 1937, 78–81.
GAMBLE, D. 1958. Firdu **Fula** grammar. Pp. 48. London: Colonial Office (Research Dept.).
—— 1958. Gambian **Fula** verb list. Pp. 43. London: Colonial Office (Research Dept.).
—— 1958. **Fula**-English vocabulary, Gambian dialects. Pp. 33. London: Colonial Office (Research Dept.).
*GAUSSON, L. Un texte **Foulah**. Rev. Ling et Phil. Comp. (Paris), 39, 1906, 221–35.
*GIBERT, E. Étude de la langue des **Poule**. Rev. Ling. et Phil. Comp., 32, 1899, 285–304; 33, 1900, 49–66, 137–86; 34, 1901, 50–78.
GÜNTHER, W. A **Fula** word-list of the early 19th century. Africana Marburgensia [Marburg], 1, 1, 1968, 14–22.
HAIR, P. E. H. An ethnolinguistic inventory of the Upper Guinea Coast . . . (see I. General) [incl. Tukulor-**Fula**].
HAUDRICOURT, A. G. et THOMAS, JACQUELINE, M.-C. 1967. La notation des langues: phonétique et phonologie. Paris, Institut Géographique National et Institut d'Ethnologie, Pp. v+166, bibl. +2 discs. (Disc 1 includes **Fula**.) [Reviewed in Africa, 39, 1, 1969, 97.]
*HOMBURGER, LILIAS. Les représentants de quelques hiéroglyphes égyptiens en **peul**. Bull. Soc. Ling. Paris, 23, 5, 1930, 277–312.
HOUIS, M. Du rapport entre les classes et le conditionnement de l'initiale radicale en **peul**. Bull. IFAN, 21 (B), 1–2, 1959, 167–78.
JOHNSON J., and ROBINSON, D. Deux fonds d'histoire orale sur le Fouta Toro. Bull. IFAN, 31, 1, 1969, 120–37. (Catalogue of tape-recordings made at Matam and Podor, 90 in **poular**, and typed French translations.)
KASSÜHLKE, R. **Ful**texte, von Matakamleuten gesprochen. In: Neue afrikanistische Studien, ed. J. Lukas. [Hamburg], 1966, 137–43.
—— Bibelübersetzung in **Ful**. Africana Marburgensia [Marburg], 2, 1, 1969, 9–13.
KIRK-GREENE, A. H. M. The linguistic statistics of Northern Nigeria: a tentative presentation. A.L.R., 6, 1967, 75–101 [incl. **Fulani**].
KLINGENHEBEN, A. Die Pronomina o und i des **Ful**. Ethno-Glossica [Hamburg] Bd. III, 1927.
—— Zum Problem der Silbe in afrikanischen Sprachen. Afr. u Übersee, 37, 1, 1952, 7–20. [With considerable reference to **Fula**.]

KLINGENHEBEN, A. Die Diminutiv- und Augmentativklassen des West**ful**. In: Afrikanische Studien Diedrich Westermann zum 80 Gerburtstag gewidmet, ed. J. Lukas. Berlin: Deutsche Akademie der Wissenschaften zu Berlin, Institut für Orientforschung, Nr. 26, 1955, 76-86.
—— Eine neue Nominalklasse des **Fulani**. Z. dtsch. morgenländ. Ges. [Leipzig], 105, 2, 1955, 338-45.
—— Die Präfix-und Suffixkonjugationen des Hamitosemitischen. Mitt. Inst. Orientforsch., 4, 2, 1956, 211-77.
—— Die Inversion im **Ful**. Afr. u. Übersee, 45, 3, 1962, 161-9.
—— Influence of analogy in African languages. J.A.L., 1, 1, 162, 30-42 [incl. reference to **Fula**].
—— 1963. Die Sprache der **Ful** (Dialekt von Adamaua): Grammatik, Texte und Wörteverzeichnis. Pp. xxii+461. Hamburg: J. J. Augustin (Afrikanische Forschungen, I). [Reviewed in Africa, 34, 4, 1964, 390-1, J.A.L. 6, 1, 1967, 81-3 and Archiv Orientälni [Prague] 33, 1965, 116-8.]
*KRAUSE, G. A. 1884. Ein Beitrag zur Kenntnis der **ful**ischen Sprache in Afrika [Sokoto]. Leipzig: Brockhaus (Mitteil der Riebeckschen Niger Expedition).
LABOURET, H. 1955. La langue des **Peuls** ou Foulbé: Lexique français-peul. Pp. 160. Dakar: IFAN (Mém. 41).
LACROIX, P.-F. 1959. Observations sur la Koiné **peule** de Ngaoundéré. Travaux de l'Institut de Linguististique, Faculté des Lettres et Sciences Humaines de l'Université de Paris, Vol. IV.
—— Distribution géographique et sociale des parlers **peul** du Nord-Cameroun. L'Homme [Paris], 2, 3, 1962, 75-101, maps.
—— Observations sur les formes verbales d''habitude' dans les parlers **peuls** de l'Adamawa. Actes du Second Colloque International de Linguistique Négro-Africaine, Université de Dakar, 1963, 39-51.
—— Études **peuls**: état actuel et perspective d'avenir. Rev. École nat. langues orient. [Paris], 1, 1964, 79-93.
—— (ed.) 1965. Poésie **peule** de l'Adamawa. 2 vols. Pp. 645. Paris: Julliard. (Classiques Africains, 3 & 4).
—— Remarques préliminaires à une étude des emprunts arabes en **peul**. Africa, 37, 2, 1967, 188-202.
—— Quelques aspects de la disintegration d'un système classificatoire (**peul** du sud de l'Adamawa). In: La classification nominale dans les langues négro-africaines. Paris: C.N.R.S., 1967, 291-312.
—— Trilingual dictionary, **Fulfulde**-French-English. See UNESCO. 1969.
*LY, D. Coutumes et contes des Toucouleurs du Fouta Toro. Bull. Com. Ét. hist. et sci. A.O.F. [Dakar], 1938.
*MACBRAIR, R. M. 1854. Grammar of the **Fulah** language. Ed. with additions by E. Norris. Pp. 7+95. London.
MAYSSAL, HENRIETTE. Poèmes **foulbé** de la Bénoué. Abbia, 9/10, 1965, 47-90.
*MISCHLICH, A. Über die Herkunft der **Fulbe**, Beilage Haussa. Text in Arabischen Buchstaben. M.S.O.S., 34, 3, 1931, 183-96.
MOHAMADOU, E. Introduction à la littérature **peule** du Nord-Cameron. Abbia, 3, 1963, 66-76.
—— Contes **foulbé** de la Bénoué. Abbia, 9/10, 1965, 11-45.
—— Yeerwa, poème des **peuls** Yillaga de l'Adamawa. Camelang, 1, 1969, 73-111.
—— Les **peuls** du Niger Oriental: groupes ethniques et dialectes [including texts]. Camelang, 2, 1969, 57-93.
—— Trilingual dictionary, **Fulfulde**-French-English. See UNESCO, 1969.
—— et MAYSSAL, HENRIETTE. 1965. Contes et poèmes **foulbé** de la Bénoué, Nord Cameroun. Pp. 84, ill. Yaoundé: Abbia, avec la collaboration de CLE.
*MOLLIEN, G. T. 1820. Voyage dans l'intérieur de l'Afrique. Vol. 2. Vocabulaire des langues iolof, **poule** et serrère. Paris: Courcier.

MONTEIL, V. Contribution à la sociologie des **Peuls** (le Fonds Vieillard de l'IFAN). Bull. IFAN, 25 (B), 3/4, 1963, 351–414, [incl. **Fula** texts and vernacular terms].
MUKAROVSKY, H. G. Vorislamische Gottesnamen im **Ful**. Die Sprache [Wien], 4, 1957.
—— Die Suffixkonjugation im **Ful**. Wiener Z. Kunde Morgenlandes, 53, 3/4, 1957, 161–80.
—— Anlautwechsel, nominale und verbale Formen im Ful. Wiener Z. Kunde Morgenlandes, 58, 1962, 1–23.
—— 1963. Die Grundlagen des Ful und das Mauretanische. Pp. 203. Wien: Herdee and Co.
—— Ful und Hamitentum. Paideuma [Frankfurt a.M.], 13, 1967, 130–42, bibl.
NOYE, RP. D. 1965. Éléments de langue **foulfoulde** (Foulbé du Nord-Cameroun). Pp. 102. Ngaoundere, Cameroun.
—— (n.d.) Humeur et sagesse **peule**. Contes, devinettes et proverbes des Foulbé du Nord-Cameroun. Pp. 118. BP 49, Maroua, Cameroun.
PRESTAT, G. 1953. Cours élémentaire de **fulfulde**. Pp. 125 (ronéo). Paris: Éd. Peyronnet pour le Centre des Hautes Études d'Administration Musulmane.
*REICHARDT, C. A. L. 1859. Three original Fulah pieces in Arabic letters, in Latin transcription, and in English translation. Pp. 61. Berlin.
*—— 1859. Primer in the **Fulah** language [Sierre Leone]. Berlin: Beck.
*—— 1876. Grammar of the **Fulde** language [Sierre Leone]. Pp. xxiii+339. London: C.M.S.
*—— 1878. Vocabulary of the **Fulde** language (Fulde-English, English-Fulde) [Sierre Leone]. Pp. 357. London: C.M.S.
*ROUSSEAU, J. A. Les migrations **foulbés** et la linguistique botanique. Bull. Soc. Ét. camerounaises, 1, 1935, 71–9.
*ROYEN, P. G. Die konsonnantiese Intermutatie in het **Ful**. Festschrift P. W. Schmidt. Anthropos, 1928, 45–60.
SAUVAGEOT, S. et al. Les classes nominales .... (see I. General) [incl. **Fula**].
SAYERS, E. F. In praise of the faith of Futa and a warning to unbelievers—a **Fula** poem with introductory note and translation. Sierra Leone Stud., 13, 1928, 35–53.
SEYDOU, CHRISTIANE. **Majaado Alla gaynaali:** poème en langue **peule** du Foûta-Djalon. Cah. Étud. afr., 6, 4 (24), 1966, 643–81.
—— Essai d'étude stylistique de poèmes **peuls** du Foûta-Djallon. Bull. IFAN, 29 (B), 1/2, 1967, 191–233.
SOW, A. I. Poetic construction in Foûta Djalon. Présence afr. (Eng. ed.), 26/54, 1965, 185–200.
—— Notes sur les procédés poétiques dans la littérature des **Peuls** du Foûta-Djalon. Cah. Étud. afr., 5, 3 (19), 1965, 370–87.
—— Remarques sur les infixes de derivation dans le **Fulfulde** du Foûta-Djalon (Guinée). J.W.A.L., 3, 1, 1966, 13–21.
—— (éd.) 1966. La femme, la vache, la foi: écrivains et poètes du Foûta-Djalon (en **fulfulde** et français). Pp. 375, ill. Paris: Juillard (Classiques africains). [Reviewed in Africa 37. 3, 1967, 368–9.]
—— Trilingual dictionary, **Fulfulde**-French-English. See UNESCO. 1969.
STENNES, L. H. 1961. An introduction to **Fulani** syntax. Pp. 85. Hartford, Connecticut. (Hartford Studies in Linguistics, 2.)
—— 1967. A reference grammar of Adamawa **Fulani**. East Lansing: African Studies Center, Michigan State University. (African Language Monograph No. 8.)
—— 1969. The identification of participants in Adamawa **Fulani**. Ph.D. thesis (unpublished), Hartford, Connecticut.
STOPA, R. The origin of the classification of nouns in **Ful**. Folio orientalia, 2, 1/2, 1960, 89–102.
SWIFT, LLOYD, et al. 1965. **Fula** basic course. Pp. 489. Washington, D.C.: Foreign Service Institute.
*TAYLOR, F. W. Some English words in **Fulani** and Hausa. J. Afr. Soc., 20, 77, 1920, 25–32.
—— 1953. A grammar of the Adamawa dialect of the **Fulani** language. (2nd ed.). Pp. 138. London: O.U.P.

UNESCO. Rapport final sur la réunion d'un groupe d'experts pour l'unification des alphabets des langues nationales, Bamako, 28 fév.–5 mars, 1966. Pp. 40. UNESCO/CLT/BALING/ 13, 15.9.66. French original and English translation. [Mandingue, **Peul**, Tamasheq, Songhay-Zarma, Hausa, Kanuri.]
—— 1969. Trilingual dictionary, **Fulfulde**-French-English. Prepared by D. W. Arnott, P. F. Lacroix, Eldridge Mohamadou, A. I. Sow. Pp. 315. Unesco.
*VIEILLARD, G. Le chant de l'eau et du palmier doum: Poème bucolique du marais nigérien [**Fula**]. Bull. IFAN, 2, 3/4, 1940, 299–315.
*VOHSEN, E. Proben der **Fulah**-Sprache. Z. afr. Spr., 1, 1887–8, 217–37; 3, 1889–90, 296–315.

SECTION II

THE MANDE LANGUAGES

GENERAL

BRADSHAW, A. T. von S. Vestiges of Portuguese in the languages of Sierra Leone. S.L.L.R., 4, 1965, 5–37 [incl. **Mandinka, Susu, Loma, Mende, Kono, Vai, Koranko, Yalunke**].
CALVET, M. J. 1967. La transcription des langues du Sénégal; problèmes théoriques pour la choix d'un alphabet officiel. Avec, en annexe, le Rapport UNESCO sur la réunion d'experts tenue à Bamako en 1966 pour la transcription des langues africaines. Pp. 71. Dakar: CLAD 29 bis, [incl. **Bambara-Malinke**].
*CHRISTALLER, J. G. Die Sprache in dem Negerfreistaat Liberia. Z.A.S., 2, 1888/9, 315–20. [incl. bibl. of **Mande**].
DALBY, D. Language distribution in Sierra Leone. S.L.L.R., 1, 1962, 62–7, map.
HAIR, P. E. H. Ethnolinguistic continuity on the Guinea coast. J. Afr. Hist., 8, 2, 1967, 247–68.
—— An ethnolinguistic inventory of the Upper Guinea coast before 1700. A.L.R., 6, 1967, 32–70 [incl. **Susu, Loko, Mandingo**].
—— An ethnolinguistic inventory of the Lower Guinea coast before 1700. A.L.R., 7, 1968, 47–73, [incl. **Vai, Kono, Mende, Loko**].
HOUIS, M. Le groupe linguistique **mandé**. Notes afr. IFAN, 82, 1959, 38–41, map.
—— Rapport sur les langues du groupe **Mandé**. Actes du Second Colloque International de Linguistique Négro-Africaine, Université de Dakar, 1963, 218–38, bibl.
INNES, G. Genitival phrases in **Mande** languages. A.L.S., 8, 1967, 160–7.
MANESSY, G. Nom et verbe dans les langues mandé. J.A.L., 1, 1, 1962, 57–68 [**Mandingue, Mende, Kpelle, Susu**].
MUKAROVSKY, H. G. Zur Stellung der **Mandé**-sprachen. Anthropos, 61, 3/6, 1966, 679–88.
SHAFER, R. Phonétique comparée du Nigéro-Sénégalien (**Mande**). Bull. IFAN, 21 (B), 1/2, 1959, 179–200.
TASTEVIN, RP. L'appellation '**Mande**'. Notes afr. IFAN, 72, 1956, 124–6.
WEIL, P. M. Language distribution in the Gambia. A.L.R., 7, 1968, 101–6, [incl. **Mandinka, Soninke, Bambara, Dialonke, Koranko**].
WELMERS, W. E. 1958. The **Mande** languages. In: Round-table conference on languages and linguistics. Georgetown Univ. Press. 1958, 9–24.
—— Associative **a** and **ka** in Niger-Congo. Language, 39, 3, 1963, 432–57.
—— Niger-Congo: **Mande**. In: Current trends in linguistics: Vol. 7, Linguistics in Sub-Saharan Africa, ed. Thomas A. Sebeok. Bloomington: Indiana University, 1969.
WILKS, I. The **Mande** loan element in Twi. Ghana Notes & Queries, 4, 1962, 26–8.

1. MANDE TAN

BALLENGHIEN, E. Le système verbo-prédicatif **sonĭke**: parler de Nioro du Sahel. J.W.A.L., 4, 2, 1967, 5–13.

*Bazin, H. Les **Bambara** et leur langue. Anthropos, 1, 1/4, 1906, 681–94.
Beuchelt, E. Die kulturhistorische Entwicklung des **Bambara** zur Verkehrssprache (West-Sudan). Afrika heute [Köln], 10, 1966, 143–7.
*Binger, L.-G. 1886. Essai sur la langue **bambara** parlée dans le Kaarta et dans le Bélédougou, suivi d'un vocabulaire. Pp. vi+134, carte. Paris: Maisonneuve et Leclerc.
Bird, C. S. Determination in **Bambara**. J.W.A.L., 3, 1, 1966, 5–11.
—— Relative clauses in **Bambara**. J.W.A.L., 5, 1, 1968, 35–47.
—— 1968. Aspects of **Bambara** syntax. Thesis. Univ. of California. Ann Arbor, Michigan.
Bradshaw, A. T. von S. Vestiges of Portuguese . . . (see II. General) [incl. **Mandinka, Kono, Vai, Koranko**].
Calvet, M. J. 1967. La transcription des langues du Sénégal . . . (see II. General) [incl. **Bambara-Malinke**].
Brauner, S. Zum System der prosodischen Elemente im **Bambara**. In: Neue afrikanistische Studien, ed. J. Lukas [Hamburg], 1966, 61–8.
Canu, G. 1965. Les systèmes phonologiques des principales langues du Sénégal. Étude comparative. Pp. 44. Dakar: CLAD, No. 13, [incl. **Bambara, Malinke, Soninke**].
Carreira, A. Alguns aspectos da influência da língua **mandinga** na Pajadinca. Bol. cult. Guiné port., 18, 71, 1963, 345–83, map.
Chataigner, A. Les amours de Maammadi et sa mort (Conte **mandingue** de Haute-Gambie (nord Dantilita), récité par Founêké Damfakha, traduit par A. Chataigner). Notes afr. IFAN, 53, 1952, 14–16.
Cloarec-Heiss, France. Essai de phonologie du parler **banda-linda** de Ippy. BSELAF 3.
Daget, J. et al. 1953. La langue **Bozo**. Pp. 277. Koulouba, Soudan: Centre IFAN. (Études soudaniennes, no. 1.)
Dalby, D. The extinct language of **Dama**. S.L.L.R., 2, 1963, 50–4.
—— A survey of the indigenous scripts of Liberia and Sierra Leone: **Vai**, Mende, Loma, Kpelle and Bassa. A.L.S., 8, 1967, 1–51, ill. map.
—— The indigenous scripts of West Africa and Surinam: their inspiration and design. A.L.S., 9, 1968, 156–97.
—— Further indigenous scripts of West Africa: **Manding**, Wolof and Fula alphabets and Yoruba 'holy' writings. A.L.S., 10, 1969, 161–81.
*Dard, J. 1855 (1re éd. 1825). Dictionnaire français-wolof et français-**bambara**, suivi du dictionnaire wolof-français. Pp. 242. Paris: Impr. Royale.
*Delafosse, M. 1901. Essai de manuel pratique de la langue **mandé ou mandingue**. Pp. 304, bibl., carte. Paris: Leroux.
—— 1955. La langue **Mandingue** et ses dialectes (**Malinké, Bambara, Dioula**). 2me vol. Dictionnaire mandingue-français. Pp. xix+857. Paris: Geuthner (Bibliothèque de l'École Nationale des Langues Orientales Vivantes, 15).
*Dembo, C. Chant **mandingue** de Casamance. Notes afr. IFAN, 38, 1948, 22–4.
*Faidherbe, L. L. C. Vocabulaire sarakholé ou **soninke**. Annu. du Sénégal, 1864.
*—— 1864. (1re ed. 1860). Vocabulaire d'environ 1,500 mots français avec leurs correspondants en ouolof de Saint-Louis, en poular (toucouleur) du Fouta, en **soninké** (sarakhollé) de Bakel. Pp. 70. Saint-Louis: Impr. du Gouvt.
*—— 1887. Langues sénégalaises: wolof, arabe-hassania, **soninké**, sérère. Notions grammaticales, vocabulaires et phrases. Pp. 266. Paris: Leroux.
*Fily Dabo Sissoko. Glossaire des mots français passés en **malinké**. Bull. IFAN, 1, 1, 1939, 325–66.
Gamble, D. P. 1955 (1st ed. 1949). Elementary **Mandinka** sentence book. Pp. 35, bibliog. London: Colonial Office, Research Dept.
—— 1956. **Mandinka** reading book (especially printed for European students). Pp. 15. Bathurst: Govt. printer.
—— 1958. **Mandinka** narratives. Pp. 10 (duplicated). Bathurst: Secretariat.
—— 1958 (1st ed. 1954). Medical **Mandinka**. Pp. 4, dupl. London: Colonial Office.
Garnier, P. Le **bambara** le plus pur est-il celui de Ségou? Notes afr. IFAN, 63, 1954, 88–9.

HAIR, P. E. H. Notes on the early study of some West African languages (Susu, Bullom/ Sherbro, Temne, Mende, **Vai** and Yoruba). Bull. IFAN, 23 (B), 3/4, 1961, 683–95, bibl.
—— Notes on the discovery of the **Vai** script, with a bibliography. S.L.L.R., 2, 1963, 36–49.
—— An early seventeenth-century vocabulary of **Vai**. Afr. Stud. 23, 3/4, 1964, 129–39.
—— An ethnolinguistic inventory of the Upper Guinea coast . . . (see II. General) [incl. **Mandingo**].
—— An ethnolinguistic inventory of the Lower Guinea coast . . . (see II. General) [incl. **Vai, Kono**].
HOUIS, M. Les catégories de noms derivés dans un parler **manding**. In: La classification nominale dans les langues négro-africaines. Paris: C.N.R.S., 1967, 99–116.
—— et ZAHAN, DOMINIQUE. Préalables linguistiques d'une 'ethnologie des symboles' [à propos 'La dialectique du verbe chez les **Bambara**' avec réponse de l'auteur]. L'Homme [Paris], 6, 1966, 88–104.
*HUMBLOT, P. Du nom propre et des appellations chez les **Malinké** des vallées du Niandan et du Milo. Bull. Com. Ét. hist. et sci. A.O.F., 1918, 3/4, 519–40; 1919, 7–23, 393–426.
INNES, G. A note on Mende and **Kono** personal names. A.L.R., 5, 1966, 34–8.
JAQUINOD, F. et PROST, A. La langue des Bô ou Bôkâ. Bull. IFAN, 20 (B), 3/4, 1958, 623–35.
LIBERIA UNIVERSITY. 1962. The standard **Vai** script. Pp. 10. African Stud. Program.
LONG, R. W., and DIOMANDE, R. 1968. Basic **Dyula**. Bloomington: Linguistic Circle, Indiana University.
*MACBRAIR, R. M. 1837. A grammar of the **Mandingo** language with vocabularies. Pp. vii+74. London: Wesleyan Methodist Missionary Soc.
MALI, REPUBLIC OF. 1968. Lexique **Bambara** à l'usage des centres d'alpabétisation. Pp. 33. Ministère de l'Éducation Nationale, Éducation de Base, Bamako.
MANESSY, G. Nom et verbe dans les langues Mande. J.A.L., 1, 1, 1962, 57–68, [incl. **Mandingue**].
—— L'alternance consonantique initiale en **manya**, Kpelle, loma, bandi, et mende. J.A.L. 3, 2, 1964, 162–78.
MONTEIL, C. (1871–1949). Vocabulaire **soninké** (parties du corps et noms de parenté). Bull. IFAN, 28 (B), 3/4, 1966, 676–89.
—— Textes **soninké**. Bull. IFAN, 29 (B), 3/4, 1967, 559–98.
—— La légende du Wagadou: texte **soninké** de Malamine Tandyan, retranscrit, traduit et annoté par Abdoulaye Bathily [d'apres Charles Monteil (1871–1949)]. Bull. IFAN, 29, (B), 1/1, 1967, 134–49.
*MONTEL, E. 1887. Éléments de la grammaire **bambara** avec exercices, suivis d'un dictionnaire **bambara**-français. Pp. vii+218. Ngasobil: Mission St. Joseph.
*NORRIS, E. Notes on the **Vei** language and alphabet. J. Roy. Geog. Soc., 20, 1850, 101–13.
PROST, A. La langue des **Blé**. Bull. IFAN, 20 (B), 3, 1968, 1256–70.
ROWLANDS, E. C. 1959. A grammar of Gambian **Mandinka**. Pp. 158. London: School of Oriental & African Studies (obtainable from Luzac).
SPEARS, R. A. 1965. The structure of **Faranah-Maninka**. Ph.D. thesis (unpublished), Indiana University.
—— A note on the tone of **Maninka** substantives. J.A.L., 5, 2, 1966, 113–20.
STEWART, GAIL. Notes on the present-day usage of the **Vai** script in Liberia. A.L.R., 6, 1967, 71–4.
—— and HAIR, P. E. H. A bibliography of the **Vai** language and script. J.W.A.L., 62, 1969, 109–24.
TOKARSKAYA, V. P. 1964. Yazyk Malinke (**Mandingo**) (The **Malinka** language). Pp. 50. Moscow: 'Science' Publishing House.
*TOULOTTE, Mgr. 1897. Essai de grammaire **bambara** (idiome de Ségou). Paris.
UNESCO. Rapport final sur la réunion d'un groupe d'experts pour l'unification des alphabets des langues nationales, Bamako, 28 fév–5 mars, 1966. Pp. 40. UNESCO/CLT/BALING/ 13, 15/9/66. French original and English translation [incl. **Mandingue**].
WEIL, P. M. Language distribution in the Gambia. A.L.R., 7, 1968, 101–6, map [incl. **Mandinka, Soninke, Bambara, Koranko**].

ZAHAN, D. 1963. La dialectique du verbe chez les **Bambara**. Pp. 208. Paris et La Haye: Mouton (École prat. hautes Ét., Monde O.-M. passé et présent, Études, 18).
ZEMP, H. La légende des griots **malinké**. Cah. Étud. afr. 6, 4 (24), 1966, 611–42, bibl.
ZWERNEMANN, J. Zwei Quellen des 17. Jahrhunderts über die **Vai** in Liberia. Samuel Brun und Olfert Dapper. In: Neue afrikanistische Studien, ed. J. Lukas. Hamburg, 1966, 293–319.

2. MANDE FU

BEARTH, T., and ZEMP, H. The phonology of **Dan (Santa)**. J.A.L., 6, 1, 1967, 9–29.
BECKER-DONNER, ETTA. 1965. Die Sprache der **Mano**. Pp. 216, bibl. Wien: Hermann Böhlaus Nachf. (Akad. d. Wiss. Wien, Sitz.-Ber., Philosoph.-hist. Kl., 245, 1).
*BERTHO, J. Quatre dialectes mandé du Nord-Dahomey et de la Nigeria anglaise [**Tienga, Tshanga, Boko de Nikki, Boko de Bussa**]. Bull. IFAN, 13, 4, 1951, 1265–71.
—— La place des dialectes **géré** et **wobé** par rapport aux autres dialectes de la Côte d'Ivoire. Bull. IFAN, 13, 4, 1951, 1272–80.
BRADSHAW, A. T. von S. Vestiges of Portuguese . . . . (see II. General) [incl. **Susu, Loma, Mende, Yalunke**].
*BRUNTON, E. 1802. A grammar and vocabulary of the **Susoo** language. Edinburgh.
BROWN, S. (n.d.) A **Mende** grammar with tones. Pp. 22. Bo: Protectorate Lit. Bureau.
CASTHELAIN, RP. J. 1952. La langue **guerzé**: grammaire et dictionnaire. Pp. 105. Dakar: IFAN (Mém. No. 20).
DALBY, D. An investigation into the **Mende** syllabary of Kisimi Kamara. Sierre Leone Stud., 19, 1966, 119–23, plate.
—— A survey of the indigenous scripts of Liberia and Sierra Leone; Vai, **Mende, Loma, Kpelle**, and Bassa. A.L.S., 8, 1967, 1–51.
—— The indigenous scripts of West Africa and Surinam: their inspiration and design. A.L.S., 9, 1968. 156–97.
DONEUX, J.-L. Notes de travail sur quelques langues de l'Ouest ivoirien. Bull. IFAN, 30 (B), 1, 1968, 248–55 [incl. **Dan**].
*DOUGLIN, P. H. 1887. A reading book in the **Soso** language. Pp. viii+120. London: S.P.C.K.
FRIEDLÄNDER, MARIANNE. Zur Substantivbildung im **Susu**. Mitt. Inst. Orientforschung [Berlin], 12, 3, 1966, 193–8.
HAIR, P. E. H. Notes on the early study of some West African languages (**Susu**, Bullom/Sherbro, Temne, **Mende, Vai** and Yoruba). Bull. IFAN, 23 (B), 3/4, 1961, 683–95, bibl.
—— Bibliography of the **Mende** language. S.L.L.R., 1, 1962, 39–61.
—— **Susu** studies and literature: 1799–1900. S.L.L.R., 4, 1965, 38–53.
—— An ethnolinguistic inventory of the Upper Guinea coast . . . . (see II. General) [incl. **Susu, Loko**].
—— An ethnolinguistic inventory of the Lower Guinea coast . . . . (see II. General) [incl. **Mende, Loko**].
HARRIGAN, W. N. Form, function and distribution of the definite nominal suffix in **Yalunka**. S.L.L.R., 2, 1962, 30–5.
HOUIS, M. Notes lexicologiques sur les rapports du **soso** et des langues mãde-sud du groupe **manabusa**. Bull. IFAN, 16, 3/4, 1954, 391–401.
—— Schèmes et fonctions tonologiques (**sosso**, bobo, **mende**, efik). Bull. IFAN, 18 (B), 3/4, 1956, 335–68.
—— Caractères et possibilités de la langue **Soso** (extrait d'un ouvrage à paraître). Recherches afr., 1, 1962, 3–4.
—— 1963. Étude descriptive de la langue **Susu**. Pp. 83, bibl., carte. Dakar: IFAN (Mém. no. 67).
INNES, G. A note on consonant mutation in **Bandi**. Sierre Leone Stud., 14, 1960, 90–2.
—— 1962. A **Mende** grammar. Pp. viii+151. London: Macmillan.
—— 1963. The structure of sentences in **Mende**. Pp. viii+142. London: S.O.A.S.

INNES, G. Consonant mutation in **Loko**. Mitt. Inst. Orientforsch. [Berlin], 10, 2/3, 1964, 217-26.
—— An outline grammar of **Loko** with texts. A.L.S., 5, 1964, 115-73.
—— A note on **Mende** and Kono personal names. A.L.R., 5, 1966, 34-8.
—— **Mende** in the *Polyglotta Africana*. A.L.R., 6, 1967, 120-7.
—— 1969. A **Mende**-English dictionary. Pp. x+155. London: C.U.P.
*LANG, K. Die Substantivbildung in der **Soso**-Sprache. Bibliotheca Africana, 2, 2, 1927, 285-95.
*LASSORT, RP. P. La langue **Kpèlè**. Études guinéennes [Conakry], 2, 1947, 21-5.
—— 1952. Grammaire **guerzé**. Pp. 198. Dakar: IFAN (Mém. no. 20).
MANESSY, G. Nom et verbe dans les langues mandé. J.A.L., 1, 1, 1962, 57-68. [incl. **Mende, Kpelle, Susu**].
—— Remarques sur la formation du pluriel en **bandi, loma, mende** et **kpelle**. Bull. IFAN, 26 (B), 1/2, 1964, 119-26.
—— Détermination et prédication en **kpelle**. Bull. Soc. Ling. Paris, 59, 1, 1964, 119-24.
—— L'alternance consonantique initiale en manya, **kpelle, loma, bandi**, et **mende**. J.A.L., 3, 2, 1964, 162-78.
MEEUSSEN, A. E. A note on permutation in **Kpele-Mende**. A.L.S., 6, 1965, 112-16.
MILBURN, S. Kisimi Kamara and the **Mende** script. S.L.L.R., 3, 1964, 20-3.
MITCHELL, P. K. A note on the distribution in Sierre Leone of literacy in Arabic, **Mende** and Temne. A.L.R., 7, 1968, 90-100.
MORSE, MARY LYNN. The question of '**Samogo**'. J.A.L., 6, 1, 1967, 61-80.
PROST, A. Les langues mandé-sud du groupe **mana-busa**. Pp. 182, cartes. Dakar: IFAN (Mém. no. 26).
—— Quelques notes sur le Don (**Samogho**). Bull. IFAN, 20 (B), 3/4, 1958, 612-23.
RIVIÈRE, C. A propos de deux contes **soussous**. Notes afr. IFAN, 112, 1966, 122-30.
SADLER, W. 1951. Untangled **Loma**. A course of study of the Loma language of the Western Province Liberia, West Africa. Pp. 465. Baltimore: Board of Foreign Missions.
SANGSTER, LINDA W., and FABER, E. 1969. **Susu** intermediate course. Pp. 242. Bloomington: Indiana University.
SAWYERR, H. A. E. Postpositions and prepositions in the **Mende** language. Sierra Leone Stud., n.s.8, 1957, 209-20.
*SORY, ALMANY, and others. Trois contes **soussou** (avec traduction française). Études guinéennes, 1, 1947, 23-5.
SPEARS, R. A. 1967. Basic course in **Mende**. Pp. vi+571. Evanston: Northwestern University.
—— Tone in **Mende**. J.A.L., 6, 3, 1967, 231-44.
*STRUCK, B. 1911. Die **Boko**-Sprache. Völker-probleme im mittleren Afrika, vorgesichtliche rassen- und sprachgeographische Zusammenhänge auf Grund einer anthropologischen Karte von Aequatorial-Afrika untersucht. Berlin: D. Reimer.
WEIL, P. M. Language distribution in the Gambia. A.L.R., 7, 1968, 101-6, map, [incl. **Dialonke**].
*WELMERS, W. E. New light on consonant change in **Kpelle**. Z. Phonetik u. Sprachwiss., 4, 1/2, 1950, 105-18.
—— The phonology of **Kpelle**. J.A.L., 1, 1, 1962, 69-93.
—— The syntax of emphasis in **Kpelle**. J.W.A.L., 1, 1, 1964, 13-26.
*WESTERMANN, D. Wörterverzeichnis Deutsch-**Kpelle**. Mitt. Sem. Orient. 26/27 (3), 1924, 57-83.

SECTION III

SONGHAI

CLAUZEL, J. Des noms **Songay** dans l'Ahaggar. J.A.L., 1, 1, 1962, 43-44.
DE DIANOUX, H.-J. Les mots d'emprunt d'origine arabe dans la langue **songhay**. Bull. IFAN, 23 (B), 3/4, 1961, 596-606.

Houis, M. Notes sur le **songay**. Bull. IFAN, 20 (B), 1/2, 1958, 225/40.
Prost, A. 1956. La langue **songay** et ses dialectes. Pp. 627, carte. Dakar: IFAN (Mém. no. 47).
—— Mots mossi empruntés au **songay**. Bull. IFAN, 28 (B), 1/2, 1966, 470–5.
*Raffenel, A. J. B. Étude de la langue **Arama**. In: Nouveau voyage dans le pays des nègres, 1856. Raffenel, A.J.B. tome 2, 399–427.
Williamson, Kay. **Songhai** word list (Gao dialect). Res. Notes (Dept. of Ling. and Nigerian languages, Ibadan), 3, 1967, 1–34.

Section IV

THE KRU DIALECTS

Berry, J., and Innes, G. Notes on the phonetics of the **Grebo** language of Liberia. Mitt. Inst. Orientforsch. [Berlin], 5, 2, 1957, 287–98.
*Christaller, J. G. Die Sprache in dem Negerfreistaat Liberia. Z. Afr. Spr., 2, 1888–89, 315–20 [incl. bibl. of **Kru, Grebo**].
Dalby, D. and Hair, P. E. H. "Le langaige de Guynee": a sixteenth century vocabulary from the Pepper Coast. A.L.S., 5, 1964, 174–91 [**Kra**].
Dalby, D. A survey of the indigenous scripts of Liberia and Sierra Leone: Vai, Mende, Loma, Kpelle, and **Bassa**. A.L.S., 8, 1967, 1–51, ill., map.
—— The indigenous scripts of West Africa and Surinam: their inspiration and design. A.L.S., 9, 1968, 156–97.
*Dorsey, J. **Bassa** linguistic notes. Amer. Anthropologist, 2, 1889, 79–80.
Genevray, J. 1952. Éléments d'une monographie d'une division administrative libérienne. Pp. 89–117, la langue **bassa**. Dakar: IFAN (Mém. no. 21).
Grimes, J. E., et al. Several Kru orthographies. Bible Translator, 11, 3, 1960, 111–15.
Hair, P. E. H. An ethnolinguistic inventory of the Lower Guinea Coast before 1700. A.L.R., 7, 1968, 47–73; 8, 1969 [incl. **'Mani', Krã, Bassa, Grebo**].
Hobley, June. A preliminary tonal analysis of the **Bassa** language. J.W.A.L., 1, 2, 1964, 51–5.
—— **Bassa** verbal formations. J.W.A.L., 2, 2, 1965, 39–50.
Innes, G. An outline of the **Grebo** verbal system. A.L.S., 1, 1960, 164–76.
—— Morphological units in **Grebo**. A.L.S., 3, 1962, 84–109.
—— 1966. An introduction to **Grebo**. Pp. 160. London: S.O.A.S. and Kegan Paul.
—— 1967. A **Grebo**-English dictionary. Pp. v+131. London: C.U.P. (West African Language Monographs No. 6).
Monod, Th. Un nouvel alphabet ouest-africain: le **bété** (Côte d'Ivoire), Bull. IFAN, 20 (B), 3/4, 1958, 332–53, ill.
Person, Y. Des Kru en Haute-Volta (**sɛmɛ** ou **siamou** de Orodara). Bull. IFAN, 28 (B), 1/2, 1966, 485–92.
Pichl, W. J. L'écriture **bassa** au Liberia. Bull. IFAN, 28 (B), 1/2, 1966, 481–4.
*Thomann, G. 1905. Essai de manuel de la langue **néouolé** parlée dans la partie occidentale de la Côte d'Ivoire. Pp. viii+198, bibl., carte. Paris: Leroux.
*Wilson, J. L. 1838. A brief grammatical analysis of the **Grebo** language. Cape Palmas.
*—— 1839. Dictionary of the **Grebo** language. Fair Hope, Cape Palmas.

Section V

THE GUR LANGUAGES

GENERAL

Bendor-Samuel, J. Niger-Congo: Gur. In: Current trends in linguistics: Vol. 7, Linguistics in Sub-Saharan Africa, ed. Thomas A. Sebeok. Bloomington: Indiana University, 1970.

*BERTHO, J. Langues voltaïques du Togo-Nord et du Dahomey-Nord. Notes afr. IFAN, 44, 1949, 124–6 [**Bassari, Kokomba, Losso-Nawdem, Moba, Soruba-Kuyobe, Gourma, Somba (Tamberma), Yoabou, Natemba, Tayakon, Pila-Pila, Berba**].

*DELAFOSSE, M. Les langues voltaïques (boucle du Niger). Mém. Soc. Ling. Paris, 16, 1911, 386–95.

DIALLO, D. et LANKOANDE, M. Commission nationale des langues voltaïques. Notes et Docum. voltaïques [Ouagadougou], 2, 2, 1969, 57–9.

KÖHLER, O. Das 'Pferd' in den Gur-Sprachen. Eine sprach-kulturgeographische Studie. Afr. u Übersee, 38, 1954, 93–109.

—— Gur languages in the *Polyglotta Africana*. S.L.L.R., 3, 1964, 65–73 [**More, Yom, Bulea, Gurma, Logba, Kabre, Tem, Sisala, Kasem, Bargu**].

MANESSY, G. Structure de la proposition relative dans quelques langues voltaïques. J.A.L., 2, 3, 1963, 260–7 [**More, Lyele, Moba, Dagara, Lamba, Kabre, Tusya, Mambar, Bwamu**].

—— Les particules affirmatives postverbales dans le group voltaïque. Bull. IFAN, 25 (B), 1/2, 1963, 107–24 [**More, Daghani, Kusaal, Dagara, Lobi, Lamba, Kabre, Kirma, Dogon**].

—— Rapport sur les langues voltaiques. Actes du Second Colloque International de Linguistique Négro-Africaine, Université de Dakar, 1963, 239–66.

—— Adjectifs ephithètes et adjectifs conjoints dans les langues voltaïques. Bull. IFAN, 26 (B), 3–4, 1964, 505–17 [**Gurma, Moba, Mambar, Lyele, Kasem, Kabre, Tem, Kurumfe, Tamari, Sup'ide, Tusyã, Akasele, Tobote, Bwamu, Dagara**].

—— Les substantifs à préfixe et suffixe dans les langues voltaïques. J.A.L., 4, 3, 1965, 170–81; bibl.: 5, 1, 1966, 54–61, [esp. **Gurma** and **Tem**; **Senufo**, '**Banfora**' see V. 1, 3, 6, 7, below].

—— La classification nominale dans les langues voltaïques: observations et hypothèses. Bull. Soc. Ling. Paris, 60, 1, 1965, 180–207, bibl. [covering all sections].

—— Essai de typologie du verbe voltaïque. Bull. Soc. Ling. Paris, 61, 1, 1966, 299–318, bibl., [covering all sections].

—— Remarque sur l'expression de l'injonction directe dans les langues voltaïques. Bull. IFAN, 30 (B), 2, 1968, 642–54, [covering all sections].

PIKE, K. L. 1966. Tagmemic and matrix linguistics applied to selected African languages.... (See GENERAL) [incl. **Kasem, Vagala, Sisala; Dagaari; Bimoba, Basari; Bariba**].

PROST, A. Le verbe dans les langues voltaïques. Actes du Second Colloque International de Linguistique Négro-Africaine, Université de Dakar, 1963, 161–71 [**More, Dagare, Gurmantyema, Mi-gangam, Li-tamari, Moba, Lamba, Mambar, Senar, Tenyer, Win, Kirma, Tyuruma**].

—— Vocabulaires comparés de quatre langues voltaïques du Togo. Bull. IFAN, 26 (B), 1/2, 1964, 212–57 [**Moba, Mi-gangam, Tammari** and **Lamba**, with **Gourmantche**].

—— 1964. Contribution à l'étude des langues voltaïques. Pp. 461, carte. Dakar: IFAN, (Mém. 70). [Reviewed in J.A.L., 5, 2, 1966, 166–7] [**Kirma, Tyuruma, Mambar, Senar, Tenyer, Toussian, Sɛmɛ**].

SWADESH, M. *et al.* A preliminary glottochronology of Gur languages. J.W.A.L., 3, 2, 1966, 27–65, [incl. a 100-word list for 45 Gur languages].

*VON FRANÇOIS. (ed.) Sprachproben aus dem Togoland. Z. afr. Spr., 2, 1888/89, 147–54 [**Gambaga, Kong, Banjauye**].

*WESTERMANN, D. Die Sprachverhältnisse Togos. Evang. Missions-Mag., 1912, 6, 1–13.

ZWERNEMANN, J. Zum Bedeutungsinhalt soziologischer und religiöser Termini in einigen Gur-Sprachen. Afrika u. Übersee, 48, 4, 1964, 284–8. [**Kasena, Lyela, Mosi, Dyan, Grusi, Nuna, Kusase, Mamprusi, Nankane, Lobi, Moba**].

1. SENUFO GROUP

*CHERON, G. Essai sur la langue **minianka**. Bull. Com. Ét. hist. et sci. A.O.F., 1921, no. 4, 560–616.

*Clamens, G. Des noms de personnes en dialecte **tagwana**. Notes afr. IFAN, 46, 1950, 52–4.
*—— Langues secrètes du **Poro**. Notes afr. IFAN, 51, 1951, 93–4.
*—— Anthroponymie **nyarafolo**. Notes afr. IFAN, 52, 1951, 120–2.
—— Essai de grammaire **senufo tagwana**. Bull. IFAN, 14, 4, 1952, 1402–65.
Manessy, G. Structure de la proposition relative . . . (see V. General) [incl. **Tusyã, Mambar**].
—— Adjectifs epithètes . . . (see V. General) [incl. **Mambar, Sup'ide, Tusyã**].
—— Les substantifs . . . (see V. General) [incl. **Senufo, Mambar, (=Minianka), Senar, Tenyer, Toussian, Tagwana, Senadi, Sup'ide**].
—— La classification nominale . . . (see V. General) [incl. **Senadi, Sup'ide, Tusyã**].
—— Essai de typologie du verbe . . . (see V. General) [incl. **Mambar, Sup'ide, Senar, Tenyer, Senadi, Tagwana, Tusya**].
—— Recherches sur la morphologie du verbe **senufo**. Bull. IFAN, 28 (B), 3/4, 1966, 690–722.
—— Remarque sur l'expression de l'injonction . . . (see V. General) [incl. **Senufo, Tusyã**].
Prost, A. Le verbe dans les langues voltaïques . . . (see V. General) [incl. **Mambar, Senar, Tenyer, Win**].
—— 1964. Contribution à l'étude des langues voltaïques . . . (see V. General) [incl. **Mambar, Senar, Tenyer, Toussian**].

2. KULANGO

3. LOBI-DOGON

*Arnaud, R. Notes sur les Montagnards Habé des cercles de Bandiagara et de Hombori. Rev. Ethn. et Trad. pop. II (1921), 241–314, [with important vocabulary of **Dogon** dialects].
Calame-Griaule, Geneviève. Diversité linguistique et organisation sociale chez les **Dogon** du Soudan français. Notes afr. IFAN, 55, 1952, 77–9.
—— Les dialectes **dogon**. Africa, 26, 1, 1956, 62–72, map.
—— Le verbe **dogon**. Actes du Second Colloque International de Linguistique Négro-Africaine, Université de Dakar, 1963, 99–110.
—— Syntaxe des particules 'subordinatives' en **Dogon**. J.A.L., 2, 3, 1963, 268–71.
—— 1966. Ethnologie et langage: la parole chez les **Dogon**. Pp. 589, bibl., ill. Paris: Gallimard (Bibl. des Sci. humaines).
—— Essai d'étude stylistique d'un texte **dogon**. J.W.A.L., 4, 1, 1967, 15–24.
—— Dictionnaire **dogon** (dialecte tɔrɔ): langue et civilisation. Paris, Klincksieck, 1968. Pp. xlii+333, ill., carte.
Cuenot, J. Essai de grammaire **bobo**-oulé (dialecte de Massala). Bull. IFAN, 14, 3, 1952, 996–1045.
Di Dio, F. 1967. Les **Dogon**: les chants de la vie; le rituel funéraire (avant-propos par G. Dieterlen), Pp. 12, ill., et disque OCR 33. Paris: Office de la Coopération radio-phonique (OCORA) [Nouvelle impr. des disques SOR 1 te 2.]
*Haillot, J. Étude sur la langue **dian**. Bull. Com. Et. hist. et sci. A.O.F., 1920, 3, 348–80.
Houis, M. Schemes et fonctions tonologiques (sosso, **bobo**, mende, efik). Bull. IFAN, 18 (B), 3/4, 1956, 335–68.
*Labouret, H. Nos connaissances relatives aux **Bobos** et à leurs parlers. In: Les Bobo: la vie sociale, by J. Cremer. Paris: Geuthner, 1924, xxi–xxx.
—— 1958. Nouvelles notes sur les tribus du rameau **lobi**, leurs migrations, leur évolution, leurs parlers et ceux de leurs voisins. Pp. 295, Dakar: IFAN (Mém. 54).
Lamothe, Rp. C. Esquisse du système verbal **lobi**. Documents Linguistiques No. 2. Université de Dakar s.a. (roneoed).
—— 1966. Esquisse du système grammatical **lobi**. Pp. 163, bibl., carte. Paris: C.N.R.S.; Ouagadougou, CVRS. (Recherches voltaïques, 4.)
Manessy, G. 1960. La morphologie du nom en **Bwamu** (**bobo**-oulé), dialecte de Bondoukuy. Pp. 318. Université de Dakar (Publications de la Section de Langues et Littératures, 4).
—— Structure de la proposition relative . . . (see V. General) [incl. **Bwamu**].

MANESSY, G. Les particules affirmatives . . . (see V. General) [incl. **Lobi, Dogon, Kirma**].
—— Adjectifs epithètes . . . (see V. General) [incl. **Bwamu**].
—— Les substantifs . . . (see V. General) [incl. **Tyurama, Kirma**].
—— La classification nominale . . . (see V. General) [incl. **Bwamu, Kirma**].
—— Essai de typologie du verbe . . . (see V. General) [incl. **Lobi, Kirma, Tyurama**].
—— Remarque sur l'expression de l'injonction . . . (see V. General) [incl. **Bwamu, Lobi, Kirma, Tyurama**].
PROST, A. Le verbe dans les langues voltaïques . . . (see V. General) [incl. **Kirma, Tyurama**].
—— 1964. Contribution à l'étude des langues voltaïques . . . (see V. General) [incl. **Kirma, Tyurama, Sεmε** (=Siamou)].
ZWERNEMANN, J. Zum Bedeutungsinhalt . . . (see V. General) [incl. **Dyan, Lobi**].

4. GRUSI

BENDOR-SAMUEL, J. T. The **Grusi** sub-group of the Gur languages. J.W.A.L., 2, 1, 1965, 47–55.
BERGMAN, R., and GRAY. Collected field reports on the phonology of **Tampulma**. Legon: Inst. Afr. Stud. (Collected Language Notes Series No. 9).
BON, G., et NICOLAS, F. 1953. I. Grammaire l'**élé**, par G. Bon; II. Glossaire l'**élé**-français, par F. Nicolas. Pp. 453, bibl. ill. carte. Dakar: IFAN (Mém. 24).
CALLOW, J. C. **Kasem** nominals—a study in analyses. J.W.A.L., 2, 1, 1965, 29–36.
—— Nominal and verbal group matrices for **Kasem**. In: Tagmemic and matrix linguistics applied to selected African languages, K. L. Pike. Ann Arbor, 1966, 197–205 (Appendix V).
—— A hierarchical study of neutralisation in **Kasem**. Journal of Linguistics, 1968, 33–45.
—— Collected field reports on the phonology of **Kasem**. Legon: Inst. Afr. Stud. (Collected Language Notes Series No. 1).
CALLOW, KATHLEEN. Preliminary notes on serial constructions in **Kasem**. In: Tagmemic and matrix linguistics applied to selected African languages, K. L. Pike. Ann Arbor, 1966, 182–6 (Appendix II).
*CHRISTALLER, J. G. Sprachproben vom Sudan zwischen Asante und Mittel-Niger. Z.A.S., 3, 1889–90, 107–32 [incl. **Lele, Binyinu, Kasima, Sisai (Isala), Tšaña**].
CROUCH, M., and SMILES, N. Collected field reports on the phonogy of **Vagala**. Legon: Inst. Afr. Stud. (Collected Language Notes Series No. 4).
MANESSY, G. Structure de la proposition relative . . . (see V. General) [incl. **Lyele**].
—— Adjectifs epithètes . . . (see V. General) [incl. **Lyele, Kasem, Kurumfe**].
—— La classification nominale . . . (see V. General) [incl. **Lyele, Kasem, Kurumfe**].
—— Essai de typologie du verbe . . . (see V. General) [incl. **Lyele, Nuna, Kasem, Sisala**].
—— Évolution de la classification nominale dans les langues **gurunsi** (groupe voltaïque). In: La classification nominale dans les langues négro-africaines. Paris: C.N.R.S., 1967, 207–24.
—— Remarque sur l'expression de l'injonction . . . (see V. General) [incl. **Sisala, Lyele, Kasem, Nuna**].
NICOLAS, F.-J. Les surnoms-devises des **L'éla** de la Haute-Volta. Anthropos, 45, 1/3, 1950, 81–118; 49, 1/2, 1954, 82–102, ill., carte.
—— Un texte des **L'éla** de la Haute-Volte (A.O.F.). Afr. u. Übersee, 36, 4, 1952, 163–72.
—— Sept contes des **L'éla** de la Haute-Volta. Anthropos, 47, 1/2, 1952, 80–94.
—— Mythes et êtres mythiques des **L'éla** de la Haute-Volta. Bull. IFAN, 14, 4, 1952, 1353–84, carte.
—— Onomastique personnelle des **L'éla** de la Haute-Volta. Bull. IFAN. 15, 2, 1953, 818–47.
—— Un conte à refrain chanté, des **L'éla** de la Haute-Volta. Anthropos, 48, 1/2, 1953, 158–70, ill.
—— Enigmes des **L'éla** de la Haute Volta (A.O.F.). Anthropos, 49, 5/6, 1954, 1013–40.
ROWLAND, R. 1966. A short dictionary of **Isaalang**. Pp. vi+42. Legon: Inst. of Linguistics.
—— **Sissala** noun groups. J.W.A.L., 3, 1, 1966, 23–8.

ROWLAND, R., and MURIEL. Collected field reports on the phonology of **Sisala**. Legon: Inst. Afr. Stud. (Collected Language Notes Series No. 2).
SCHWEEGER-HEFEL, ANNEMARIE et MUKAROVSKY, H. G. Notes préliminaires sur la langue des **Kurumba** (Haute-Volta). Arch. f. Völkerkde. [Wien]. 16, 1961, 177–97.
ZWERNEMANN, J. Untersuchungen zur Sprache der **Kasena**. Afr. u. Übersee, 41, 1/2, 1957, 3–26; 41, 3, 1957, 97–116.
—— Notizen über das Verbum des **Nuna**. Afr. u. Übersee, 45, 4, 1961, 258–71.
—— Remarques préliminaires sur le verbe du **kasem** et du **nuna**. Actes du Second Colloque International de Linguistique Négro-Africaine, Université de Dakar, 1963, 191–9.
—— Personennamen des **Kasena**. Afr. u. Übersee, 47, 1/2, 1963, 133–142.
—— Zum Bedeutungsinhalt soziologischer und religiöser Termini in einigen **Gur**-Sprachen. Afrika u. Übersee, 48, 4. 1964. 284–8 [incl. **Kasena, Lyela, Grusi, Nuna**].
—— **Kasem** dialects in the *Polyglotta Africana*. A.L.R., 6, 1967, 128–52.
—— Ein **'Gurunsi'**-Vokabular aus Bahia. Tribus [Stuttgart], 17, 1968, 147–56.

5. MOSSI

ALEXANDRE, RP. 1953. La langue **moré**. Tomes I et II. Pp. 407, 506. Dakar: IFAN (Mém. 34).
*ARNOULD, C. L'origine et les sens des prénoms en **'moré'**. Marches colon. 5, 194, 1949, 1656–7; 195, 1949, p. 1706.
*BERTHO, J. Langues voltaïques du Togo-Nord . . . (see V. General) [incl. **Losso-Nawdem**].
CANU, G. Les classes nominales en **moːrē** (dialecte de Ouagadougou). In: La classification nominale dans les langues négro-africaines. Paris: C.N.R.S., 1967, 175–206.
—— Remarques sur quelques emprunts lexicaux en **Mòːre** (dialecte de Ouagadougou). J.W.A.L., 5, 1, 1968, 25–34, bibl.
—— 1969. Contes **mossi** actuels: étude ethnolinguistique. Pp. 361, bibl., carte. Dakar: IFAN. (Mém. 82).
*FROELICH, J. C. Notes sur les **Naoudeba** du Nord-togo. Bull. IFAN, 12, 1, 1950, 102–21.
GIRAULT, L. Le verbe en **dagara** et les familles de verbes dérivés. Actes du Second Colloque International de Linguistique Négro-Africaine, Université de Dakar, 1963, 172–81.
—— Note sur la particule postverbale **na** en **dagara**. Bull. IFAN, 26 (B), 3/4, 1964, 499–504.
—— 1964. Notes sur la langue **dagara**. Pp. 11. Dakar: IFAN (polygraphié).
HOUIS, M. Principes d'orthographe du **more**. Notes afr. IFAN, 86, 1960, 52–5.
—— 1963. Les noms individuels chez les **Mosi**. Pp. 141, bibl. Dakar: IFAN (Initiations et études afr. 12).
KENNEDY, J. Collected field reports on the phonology of **Dagaari**. Legon: Inst. Afr. Stud. (Collected Language Notes Series No. 6).
LEHR, MARIANNE et al. 1966. **More** basic course. Pp. xxxix+340. Washington, D.C. Foreign Service Inst.
KÖHLER, O. Gur languages in the *Polyglotta Africana* . . . (see V. General) [incl. **More, Bulea, Sisala, Kasem**].
MANESSY, G. Structure de la proposition relative . . . (see V. General) [incl. **More, Dagara**].
—— Les particules affirmatives . . . (see V. General) [incl. **More, Dagbane, Kusaal, Dagara**].
—— Adjectifs epithètes . . . (see V. General) [incl. **Dagara**].
—— La classification nominale . . . (see V. General) [incl. **More, Dagbane, Dagara**].
—— Essai de typologie du verbe voltaïque . . . (see V. General) [incl. **More, Nandem, Dagbane, Dagara**].
—— Remarque sur l'expression de l'injonction . . . (see V. General) [incl. **More, Dagara, Dagbane, Gurenne, Naudem**].
*MERCIER, P. Note sur les **Pila-Pila** et les Taneka. Ét. dahoméennes, 3, 1950, 39–71.
NARE, L. Principes d'orthographe de la langue **moorē**. Notes et Docum. voltaïques [Ouagadougou], 2, 1, 1968, 4–21.
PÈRES BLANCS (ed.). 1925. Syllabaire **mossi**. Pp. 16. Alger: Maison Carrée.

PROST, A. 1961. Grammaire **Moba**. Mission de Dapanyo. (roneoed).
—— Le verbe dans les langues voltaïques . . . (see V. General) [incl. **More, Dagara**].
—— Notes sur le **naudem** du Togo: rapports entre le naudem et le **mõre**. Bull. IFAN, 28 (B), 1/2, 1966, 433–69.
—— Mots **mossi** empruntés au Songay. Bull. IFAN, 28 (B), 1/2, 1966, 470–5.
—— et GIRAULT, L. 1958. Abrégé de la langue **dagara**. Grammaire et dictionnaire. Diocèse de Bobo-Dioulasso.
RAPP, E. L. Orthography of **Dagomba**. Africa, 9, 1936, 410–11.
—— 1966. Die **Gurenne**-Sprache in Nordghana. 1. Einführung in das **Gurenne**, Sprichwörter der **Gurense**. 2. Wörterbuch **Gurenne**-Deutsch. Pp. 240. Leipzig: VEB Verlag Enzyklopädie (Lehrbücher Studium orient. u. afr. Sprachen, 11). [Reviewed in Afr. u. Übersee, 51, 1968, 72.]
SOCQUET (Mgr.) 1952. Manuel-grammaire **mossi**. Pp. 87. Dakar: IFAN (Initiations afr., no. 4).
SPRATT, D., and N. Collected field reports on the phonology of **Kusal**. Legon: Inst. of Afr. Stud. (Collected Language Notes Series No. 10).
—— Collected field reports on the Grammar of **Kusal**. Legon: Inst. of Afr. Stud. (Collected language Notes Series).
STREVENS, P. D. Konkomba or **Dagomba**? (A linguistic corollary to *History and social organisation* by D. Tait). Trans. Gold Coast & Togoland Hist. Soc., 1, 5, 1955, 211–16.
*WESTERMANN, D. Die **Mossi**-Sprachengruppe im westlichen Sudan. Anthropos, 8, 1913, 467–506, 810–30.
WILSON, W. A. A. Relative constructions in **Dagbani**. J.A.L., 2, 2, 1963, 139–44.
—— Problems of analysis in the **Dagbani** verb. Actes du Second Colloque International de Linguistique Négro-Africaine, Université de Dakar, 1963, 200–3.
—— External tonal sandhi in **Dagbani**. A.L.S., 11, 1970, 405–16.
—— and BENDOR-SAMUEL, J. T. The phonology of the nominal in **Dagbani**. Bulletin of the Institute of African Studies, [Legon], 1, 1965, 1–46.
ZWERNEMANN, J. Zum Bedeutungsinhalt . . . (see V. General) [incl. **Mosi, Kusase, Mampruse, Nankane**].

6. GURMA

ABBOTT, M., and COX, M. Collected field reports on the phonology of **Basari**. Legon: Inst. Afr. Stud. (Collected Language Notes Series No. 5).
BENDOR-SAMUEL, J. T. Problems in the analysis of sentences and clauses in **Bimoba**. Word, 21, 3, 1965, 452–62.
CARTRY, M. Bibliographie des **Gourmantché**. Notes et Docum. voltaïques [Ouagadougou], 1, 3, 1968, 28–42.
CHANTOUX, A. G. *et al.* 1968. Grammaire gourmantché. Pp. 160. Dakar: IFAN. (Initiations et Études africaines, 23.)
JACOBS, GILLIAN. The structure of the verbal clause in **Bimoba**. J.W.A.L., 3, 1, 1966, 47–53.
—— **Bimoba** syntax. Legon: Inst. of Afr. Stud. (Collected Language Notes Series).
KÖHLER, O. Gur languages in the *Polyglotta Africana* . . . (see V. General) [incl. **Gurma, Yom**].
MANESSY, G. Structure de la proposition relative . . . (see V. General) [incl. **Moba**].
—— Adjectifs epithètes . . . (see V. General) [incl. **Gurma, Moba, Tamari, Akasele, Tobote**].
—— Les substantifs . . . (see V. General) [incl. **Gurma, Akasele, Tobote, Tyan, Moba, Tamari, Ngangam, Pila-Pila**].
—— La classification nominale . . . (see V. General) [incl. **Gurma, Moba, Ngangam, Tamari**].
—— Essai de typologie du verbe . . . (see V. General) [incl. **Gurma, Moba, Ngangam Tamari**].
—— Remarque sur l'expression de l'injonction . . . (see V. General) [incl. **Gurma, Moba, Tamari, Ngangam, Kasele**].

PIKE, K. L., and JACOBS, GILLIAN. Matrix permutation as a heuristic device in the analysis of the **Bimoba** verb. Lingua, 21, 1968, 321-45.
PROST, A. Les classes nominales en **Bassari-Tobote**. J.A.L., 2, 3, 1964, 260-7.
—— La verbe dans les langues voltaïques . . . (see V. General) [incl. **Gourmantyema, Mi-gangam, Li-tamari, Moba**].
—— Vocabulaires comparés . . . (see V. General) [incl. **Moba, Mi-gangam, Tammari,** with **Gourmantché**].
—— 1964. **Li-tamari**, langue des **Tamberma** du Togo. Pp. 55. Dakar: IFAN (polygraphié). (Université de Dakar, Documents Linguistiques No. 6).
—— **Mi-Gangam**. Dakar: Université de Dakar (Documents Linguistiques No. 7).
—— La langue **gurma** dans la *Polyglotta Africana*. S.L.L.R., 5, 1966, 134-8.
STEELE, MARY, and WEED, GRETCHEN. 1966. Collected field reports on the phonology of **Konkomba**. Pp. 77. Legon: Inst. Afr. Stud. (Collected Language Notes No. 3).
STREVENS, P. D. **Konkomba** or Dagomba? (A linguistic corollary to *History and social organisation* (by D. Tait). Trans. Gold Coast & Togoland Hist. Soc., 1, 5, 1955, 211-16.
TAIT, D. **Konkomba** nominal classes, with a phonetic commentary by P. D. Strevens. Africa, 24, 2, 1954, 130-48.
TERSIS, N. Essai pour une phonologie du **gurma** parlé a Kpana (Nord-Togo). Lexique **gurma**-français. Paris: BSELAF No. 4.
ZWERNEMANN, J. Versuch einer Analyse der nominalen Klassifizierung in einigen Gur-Sprachen. In: La classification nominale dans les langues négro-africaines. Paris: C.N.R.S., 1967, 75-98 [**Gurma, Gangam, Tamberma, Tobote, Konkomba**].
—— Zum Bedentungsinhalt . . . (see V. General) [incl. **Moba**].

7. TEM

BERTHO, J. Les dialectes du moyen-Togo. Bull. IFAN, 14, 3, 1952, 1046-1107 [incl. **Ntribō**].
*BRUNGARD, RP. 1937. Grammaire et dictionnaire **kabré**. Imp. Polyglotte, N.D. de la Providence.
DELORD, J. 1964. Morphologie abrégée du **kabrè** (au Togo). Pp. 57. Dakar: IFAN. (polygraphié.).
—— Nasale preposée dans les noms **kabrè**. Bull. IFAN, 28 (B), 1/2, 1966, 476-80.
—— Sur le **kabrè** du Togo; jeux de tons. Bull. IFAN, 30 (B), 1, 1968, 256-68.
—— Le **Kaure** de la *Polyglotta Africana* et le Kabrè d'aujourd'hui. A.L.R., 7, 1968, 114-39.
—— La transcription du **kabrè**. Docum. Centre Étud. et Recherches kara [Togo], 3, 1968, 56-60.
MANESSY, G. Structure de la proposition relative . . . (see V. General) [incl. **Lamba, Kabre**].
—— Les particules affirmatives . . . (see V. General) [incl. **Lamba, Kabre**].
—— Adjectifs epithètes . . . (see V. General) [incl. **Kabre, Tem**].
—— Les substantifs . . . (see V. General) [incl. **Kabre, Tem, Lamba, Câla, Delo, Bagó, Lugba (Dompago)**].
—— La classification nominale . . . (see V. General) [incl. **Kabre, Lamba**].
—— Essai de typologie du verbe . . . (see V. General) [incl. **Tem. Lamba, Kabre, Delo**].
—— Le verbe dans les langues du groupe **tem**: essai d'interprétation générique. Afrika u. Übersee, 49, 4, 1966, 237-56, bibl. [incl. **Tem, Kabre, Lamba, Dompago, Delo, Câla, Bagó**].
—— Remarque sur l'expression de l'injonction . . . (see V. General) [incl. **Tem, Lamba, Kabre**].
PROST, A. Le verbe dans les langues voltaïques . . . (see V. General) [incl. **Lamba**].
—— Vocabulaires comparés . . . (see V. General) [incl. **Lamba**].
—— 1964. Le **lamba**, dialecte des Lambadu Kande au Togo. Pp. 79. Dakar: IFAN (polygraphié).

8. BARGU

HADDOCK, N. L. The tones of **Bariba**. Phonetics, 3, 1959, 90-4.

MANESSY, G. Essai de typologie du verbe . . . (see V. General) [incl. **Bariba**].
—— Remarque sur l'expression de l'injonction . . . (see V. General) [incl. **Bariba**].
WELMERS, W. E. Notes on the structure of **Bariba**. Language, 28, 1, 1952, 82–103.
*WOLF, L. Zahlen aus der **Barbar**-Sprache. Z. Afr. Spr., 3, 1889/90, 295.

SECTION VI

THE KWA LANGUAGES

GENERAL

*CADENAT, J. et PARAISO, F. Noms vernaculaires des principales formes d'animaux marins et des lagunes du Togo et du Dahomey. Notes afr. IFAN, 49, 1951, 24–9, ill., [incl. **Keta, Ewe, Mina, Fon, Nago, Toffin, Pedah, Pia, Goun**].
*CHRISTALLER, J. G. Die Sprachen des Togogebiets in kurzer allgemeiner Übersicht. Z. afr. u. ocean. Spr., 1, 1895, 5–8, [incl. bibl. for: **Ephe, Fõ, Ogunu, Aneho, Tshi (Asante u. Fante) Guan, Gã** mit **Adaṅme**].
COKER, H. E. 1954. Grammar of African names: an outline guide to the study and appreciation of African names selected from **Akan** (Gold Coast), **Yoruba, Ibo, Ijaw**, and **Efik-Ibibio** language groups. Pp. 36. Lagos: Techno-Literary Works.
*FUNKE, E. Der Gottesname in den Togosprachen. Arch. f. Anthrop., n.F. 15, 3, 1917, 161–3.
HAIR, P. E. H. An ethnolinguistic inventory of the Lower Guinea Coast before 1700. A.L.R., 7, 1968, 47–73, [incl. **Akan, Gã-Adaṇme, Ewe, Yoruba, Edo**].
HINTZE, URSULA. 1959. Bibliographie der **Kwa**-Sprachen und der Sprachen der Togo-Restvölker. Pp. 102, maps. Berlin: Akademie-Verlag (Dtsch. Akad. Wiss., Inst. Orientforsch., Veröffentl. 42).
STEWART, J. M. Niger-Congo, Kwa. In: Current trends in Linguistics: Vol. 7, Linguistics in Sub-Saharan Africa, ed. Thomas A. Sebeok. Bloomington: Indiana University, 1970.
*WESTERMANN, D. H. Die Sprachverhältnisse Togos. Pp. 13. Evang. Missions-Mag., 1912, No. 6.

1. THE 'LAGOON' GROUP

VOGLER, P. Esquisse d'une phonologie de l'**ébrié**. Annales de l'Université d'Abidjan, H, 1, 1, 1968, 60–5.

2. AKAN GROUP

(a) GENERAL

BERRY, J. The **Akan** languages. In: The Akan and Gã-Adangme peoples of the Gold Coast, Madeline Manoukian (Ethnographic Survey of Africa. Western Africa, Part I). London: International African Institute, 1950.
—— 1952. Structural affinities in the Volta River languages and their significance for linguistic classification. Ph.D. theses (unpublished). London: S.O.A.S.
—— Sociolinguistic Research in Africa: The Madina Project, Ghana. In: Expanding horizons in African Studies. Evanston: Northwestern University Press, 1969.
—— The Madina Project, Ghana: Language attitudes in Madina. In: Proceedings of the Seminar on the Social Implications of Multi-lingualism in Eastern Africa, Dar-es-Salaam, 1969.
MATSON, J. N. History in **Akan** words. Trans. Gold Coast and Togoland Hist. Soc. [Achimota], 2, 2, 1956, 63–72.
NKETIA, J. H. K. 1955. Funeral dirges of the **Akan** people (Texts in original and translation). Pp. 296. Achimota: University College of the Gold Coast, Dept. of Sociology. [**Twi, Fante**].
—— 1963. Folk songs of Ghana. Pp. x+205, Legon: Univ. of Ghana (and O.U.P.) [Reviewed in Afr. u. Übersee, 47, 1963, 301–3.]

SAUNDERS, G. F. T. **Akan** vocabulary of diseases. Mitt. Inst. Orientforsch., 4, 1, 1956, 109-19.
STEWART, J. M. **Akan** history: some linguistic evidence. Ghana Notes and Queries, 9, 1966, 54-8.
—— Comparative study of the **Volta-Comoe** languages. Research Rev. (Ghana), 2, 2, 1966, 41-7. .
TAYLOR, C. J. Some **Akan** names. Nigerian field, 18, 1, 1953, 34-7.

(b) TWI-FANTE

*AKROFI, C. A., and WATT, J. A. Notes on **Twi** spelling in the new script. Teachers' J., 5, 3, 1933, 212-16.
*AKROFI, C. A., and RAPP, E. L. 1938. A **Twi** spelling book. Pp. 110. Accra: Govt. Printing Office.
AKROFI, C. A. 1963 (2nd ed.) Twi kasa mmare [**Twi** grammar in Twi]. Pp. xiv+110. Accra: Longmans.
*BARTELS, F. L. 1944 (1st ed. 1942) **Fante** word list with rules of spelling. Pp. 84. Cape Coast: Methodist Book Depot.
*BARTELS, F. L., and ANNOBIL, J. A. 1946. A **Fante** grammar of function (Stages 1, 2, and 3). Pp. 182. Cape Coast: Methodist Book Dept.
*BARTOLOME, A. 1917 (2nd ed.) **Fanti**-English method. Cape Coast: Catholic Press.
*BELLON, I. Personen- und Ortsnamen der **Tschi**-Neger. Mitt. Sem. orient. Spr., 19 (3), 1916, 129-67.
—— 1955 (revised ed.). **Twi** lessons for beginners: including a grammatical guide and numerous idioms and phrases. Pp. xv+74. Kumasi: Basel Mission Book Depot.
BERRY, J. A note on **Twi** accents. Afrikanistische Studien, ed. J. Lukas. Hamburg, 1955, 295-8.
—— Vowel harmony in **Twi**. Bull. S.O.A.S., 19, 1957, 124-30.
—— 1960. An English-**Twi-Asante-Fante** dictionary (for use in Ghana schools). Pp. 160. London: Macmillan.
BERTHO, J. Les dialectes du Moyen-Togo. Bull. IFAN, 14, 3, 1952, 1046-1107, [incl. **Twi**].
BOADI, L. Palatality as a factor in **Twi** vowel harmony. J.A.L., 2, 2, 1963, 133-8.
—— Some **Twi** phrase structure rules. J.W.A.L., 2, 1, 1965, 37-46.
—— 1966. The syntax of the **Twi** verb. Ph.D. thesis (unpublished). London: S.O.A.S.
—— Comparative setences in **Twi-Fante**. J.W.A.L., 3, 1, 1966, 39-46.
—— Some aspects of **Akan** deep syntax. J.W.A.L., 5, 2, 1968, 83-90.
*BROOKING, R. 1843. Nucleus of a grammar of the **Fanti** language, with a vocabulary. Pp. 24.
BROSNAHAN, L. F. A fifteenth-century word list. J.W.A.L., 2, 2, 1965, 5.
*BROWN, J. P. 1913. **Mfantsi** grammar. Pp. 72. Cape Coast: Wesleyan Book Depot.
*CANNELL, W. M. 1886. A concise **Fanti**-English dictionary. London.
*CARR, D. L., and BROWN, J. P. 1868. **Mfantsi** grammar. Cape Coast.
*CHRISTALLER, J. G. et al. 1874. A dictionary, English, **Tshi** (Asante) Akra. Pp. 275. Basel: Evangelical Missionary Society.
DALBY, D., and HAIR, P. E. H. A further note on the **Mina** vocabulary of 1479-80. J.W.A.L., 5, 2, 1968. 129-31. [cf. HAIR, P. E. H. below.]
DOLPHYNE, FLORENCE. 1965. The phonetics and phonology of the verbal piece in the Asante dialect of **Twi**. Ph.D. thesis (unpublished). London: S.O.A.S.
—— A phonological analysis of **Twi** vowels. J.W.A.L., 4, 1, 1967, 83-9.
*ELLIS, A. B. 1894. The Yoruba-speaking peoples of the slave coast of West Africa, their religion, manners, customs, laws, languages, etc. with an appendix containing a comparison of the **Tshi**, Ga, Ewe and Yoruba languages. Pp. 402. London: Chapman and Hall.
FROMKIN, VICTORIA. On system-structure phonology. Language, 41, 1965, 601-9 [**Twi**].
GHANA. Bureau of Ghana Languages. 1962. The writing of **Akan**. Pp. 22. Accra, P.O. Box 3255.

SUPPLEMENTARY BIBLIOGRAPHY

*GROH, B. Sprachproben aus zwölf Sprachen des Togohinterlandes. Mitt. Sem. orient. Spr., 14 (3), 1911, 227–39, [incl. **Twi**].
HAIR, P. E. H. A note on de la Fosse's **'Mina'** vocabulary of 1479–80. J.W.A.L., 3, 1, 1966, 55–7.
—— An ethnolinguistic inventory . . . (see VI. General) [incl. **Akan** (Twi-Fante-Asante)].
*HERMAN, A. 1939. A short **Twi** grammar with English-Twi-French vocabulary. Pp. 48.
*MASON, C. I., and BILSON, E. C. 1936. First stage in **Fante** reading. Pp. 51, ill. Accra: Achimota Press.
*METHODIST BOOK DEPT. 1950. **Twi** grammar of function. Pp. 191. Cape Coast.
—— 1955. Mfantse nkasafua nkyerekyerease [Interim **Fante**-English dictionary]. Pp. 68. Cape Coast.
*MOHR, A. TH. 1909 (2nd ed.). A dictionary English–**Twi**. Pp. xvi+247. Basel: Basel Missionary Society.
MUKAROVSKY, H. G. The comparative method applied to **Twi**. Afrika u. Übersee, 49, 4, 1966, 256–69.
*RAPP, E. L. (ed.). 1934. Five hundred **Twi** proverbs (collected by J. J. Adaye). Pp. 12. Akropong, Akwapem: Sika Mpoano.
—— Zur Ausbreitung einer westafrikanischen Stammessprache (das **Twi**). Afrikanistische Studien, ed. J. Lukas. Hamburg, 1955, 220–30.
*RATTRAY, R. S. 1916. **Ashanti** proverbs: the primitive ethics of a savage people; translated from the original with grammatical and anthropological notes. Pp. 190. Oxford: Clarendon Press.
*—— 1930. Akan-**Ashanti** folk-tales (in **Twi** with English translation). Pp. xx+275, ill. Oxford: Clarendon Press.
REDDEN, J. E. et al. 1963. **Twi** basic course. Pp. xvi+224. Washington, D.C., Foreign Service Inst.
*RIIS, H. N. 1853. Elemente des **Akwapim** Dialekts der Odschi-Sprache. Pp. xviii+322. Basel: Bahnmeier.
*—— 1854. Grammatical outline and vocabulary of the Oji language, with special reference to the **Akwapim** dialect; together with a collection of proverbs of the natives. Pp. viii+276. Basel.
*RUSSELL, J. D. 1910. **Fanti**-English dictionary. Pp. 193. Cape Coast: Wesleyan Book Depot.
*SALISBURY, E. E. On the **Fanti** dialect. J.A.O.S., 1849, 378 ff.
SCHACHTER, P. Phonetic similarity in tonemic analysis, with notes on the tone system of Akwapim **Twi**. Language, 37, 2, 1961, 231–8.
—— Natural assimilation rules in **Akan**. I.J.A.L., 35, 4, 1969, 342–55.
—— and FROMKIN, VICTORIA. 1968. A phonology of Akan: **Akuapem, Asante** and **Fante**. Pp. 268, Los Angeles: U.C.L.A. (Working papers in Phonetics, No. 9.)
STEWART, J. M. 1962. An analysis of the structures of the **Fante** verb with special reference to tone and glottalisation. Ph.D. thesis (unpublished). London: S.O.A.S.
—— **Twi** tenses in the negative. Actes du Second Colloque International de Linguistique Négro-Africaine, Université de Dakar, 1963, 182–9.
—— Some restrictions on objects in **Twi**. J.A.L., 2, 2, 1963, 145–9.
—— 1964. The typology of the **Twi** tone system (with comments by P. Schachter and W. E. Welmers). Pp. 1–67. Accra: Inst. Afr. Stud.
—— Asante **Twi** in the *Polyglotta Africana*. S.L.L.R., 5, 1966, 111–15.
—— A note on **Akan**-centred linguistic acculturation. Research Rev. (Inst. Afr. Stud., Legon), 3, 2, 1967, 66–73.
—— Tongue root position in **Akan** vowel harmony. Phonetica, 16, 1967, 185–204.
—— Drills for indicative tenses of the **Ashanti** verb. Legon: Inst. Afr. Studies.
—— Tongue root position in the **Volta-Comoe** languages and its significance for the reconstruction of the original Bantu vowel sounds. A.L.S., 11, 1970, 340–50.
*VON FRANÇOIS (ed.). Sprachproben aus dem Togoland. Z. afr. Spr., 2, 1888/89, 147–54 [incl. **Asante**].

WHITTAKER, K. C. 1968. The aspects of the **Akan** verb—their forms and uses (with special reference to the **Fante** dialect). Ph.D. thesis (unpublished). London.
WILKS, I. The Mande loan element in **Twi**. Ghana Notes and Queries, 4, 1962, 26–8.
*WOHLGEMUTH, N. Ein **Fante**-Tiermärchen. Ethnos, 5, 1936, 128–32.

(c) ANYI-BAULE

BERRY, J. Some notes on the phonology of the **Nzema** and **Ahanta** dialects. Bull. S.O.A.S. 17, 1, 1955, 160–5.
—— Consonant mutation in **Nzema**. Mitt. Inst. Orientforsch., 3, 2, 1955, 264–71.
CHINEBUAH, I. K. The category of number in **Nzema**. J.A.L., 2, 3, 1963, 244–59.
—— 1963. A phonetic and phonological study of the nominal piece in **Nzema**, based on the candidate's own pronunciation. M.A. thesis (unpublished). London: S.O.A.S.
DOLEZAL, E. **Baule**, Sprache eines Negervolkes an der Elfenbeinküste. Sprache [Wien], 4, 1958, 178–97.
*GROH, B. Sprachproben aus zwölf Sprachen des Togohinterlandes. Mitt. Sem. orient. Spr., 14 (3), 1911, 227–39, [incl. **Tschokossi Mangu**].
GROSS, M. Essai pour une phonologie du **baule**. Paris: SELAF (No. 2).
GROTTANELLI, V. L. **Nzema** proverbs. Afr. u. Übersee, 42, 1, 1958, 17–26.
HINTZE, URSULA. Die sprachliche Stellung des **Anufo (Cokosi)**: Ein Beitrag zur Gliederung der Akan-Sprachen. Mitt. Inst. Orientforsch., 1, 1, 1953, 151–77.
*JEAND'HEUR, F. 1893. Vocabulaire français-**agni**. Paris.
*KOUADIO, N' J. Le nom chez les **Baoulés**. Notes afr. IFAN, 20, 1943, 11–12.
MIEGE, J. Notes de toponymie **baoulé**. Ét. éburnéennes, 3, 1954, 131–40.
PROST, A. 1964. La langue des **Anufom** de Sansanné Mango (Togo). Pp. 80. (polygraphié). Dakar: IFAN.
ROGGERO, J., et VOGLER, P. [n.d.] Comparaisons des sons du **baoulé** et du français accompagnée de quelques indications de phonétique générale et de phonétique corrective. Univ. d'Abidjan, Inst. de Ling. Appl.
STANFORD, R. Collected field reports on the grammar and phonology of **Chakosi**. Legon: Inst. of Afr. Stud. (Collected Language Notes Series No. 11).
STEWART, J. M. Notes on **Baule** phonology. Bull. S.O.A.S., 18, 2, 1956, 353–65.
VOGLER, P. Esquisse d'une phonologie du **baoulé**. Annales de l'Université d'Abidjan, H-1, 1, 1968, 5–17.
—— Corpus **baoulé**. Ann. Univ. Abijdan, H, 1, 1, 1968, 18–45.
—— Trente dictons **baoulés**. Ann. Univ. Abidjan, H, 1, 1, 1968, 46–9.

—— Les emprunts français du **baoulé**. Ann. Univ. Abidjan, H, 1, 1, 1968, 50–9.

(d) GUANG

BERRY, J. The **Guang** group. In: Tribes of the Northern Territories of the Gold Coast, Madeline Manoukian (Ethnographic Survey of Africa. Western Africa, Part V). London: International African Institute, 1951.
*BERTHO, J. Trois îlots linguistiques du Moyen-Dahomey: le **Tshummbuli**, le **Bazantché** et le **Basila**. Bull. IFAN, 13, 1951, 872–92.
—— Les dialectes du Moyen-Togo. Bull. IFAN, 14, 3, 1952, 1046–1107, [incl. **Gbanya, Tshimboro, Tshummbuli, Nawuri, Atyuti, Kratshi, Nkunya**].
CORNEVIN, R. Contribution à l'étude des populations parlant des langues **gouang** au Togo et au Dahomey. J.A.L., 3, 3, 1964, 226–30.
FRAJZYNGIER, Z. Note on **Awutu** printings. Africana Bull. [Warsaw], 6, 1967, 67–71.
—— An analysis of the **Awutu** verb. Africana Bull. [Warsaw], 8, 1968, 85–115.
GOODY, J. R. Ethnological notes on the distribution of the **Guang** languages. J.A.L., 2, 3, 1963, 173–89.

PAINTER, C. The distribution of **Guang** in Ghana, and a statistical pre-testing on twenty-five idiolects. J.W.A.L., 4, 1, 1967, 25–78, bibl., maps.
—— The **Guang** and West African historical reconstruction. Ghana notes and queries, 9, 1966, 58–66.
—— 1969. A phonological study of **Gonja**, with special reference to the operation of tone in the grammatical hierarchy. Ph.D. thesis (unpublished). London.
PILSZCZIKOWA, N. Some preliminary notes on Lɛtɛ grammar (dialect of **Guang**). Africana Bull. [Warsaw], 3, 1965, 67–108.
*PLEHN, R., ed. SEIDEL, A. Beiträge zur kenntnis der Sprachen in Togo. Z. afr. u. ocean Spr., 4, 1898, 201–86, [incl. **Nkunya**].
*RAPP, E. L. Sprichwörter der Kyerepon von Apriade. (**Guang** Studien, 1.) Mitt. Ausland-Hochschule, 42 (3), 1939, 127–58.
—— Sprachproben der wichtigsten **Guang**-Dialekte. Z. Phonetik u. allg. Sprachwiss., 10, 1957, 153–62.
—— The **Gonja** language (**Guang**-Studien II). Mitt. Inst. Orientforsch., 5, 2, 1957, 235–86.
REINEKE, BRIGITTE. Die nominale Struktur des **Nkunya**. Mitt. Inst. Orientforsch., 12, 3, 1966, 209–19.
RYTZ, O. (ed.) **Gonja** proverbs. Legon: Inst. Afr. Stud.
STEWART, J. M. 1966. **Awutu, Larteh, Nkonya**, and **Krachi** with glosses in English and Twi. Legon: Inst. Afr. Stud. (Comparative African Wordlists Series No. 1.)

3. GÃ-ADANGME GROUP

APRONTI, E. O. 1967. A phonetic and phonological study of the nominal piece in **Adangme**. Ph.D. thesis (unpublished). London: S.O.A.S.
*ARMSTRONG, M. 1931. A new **Gã** reader. Pp. 46. London: O.U.P.
*BANNERMAN, C. J. 1948 (1st ed. 1944). **Gã** grammar of function. Pp. 168. Cape Coast: Methodist Book Depot.
*BERRY, J. A **Gã** folk tale. Bull. S.O.A.S., 12, 2, 1948, 409–16.
—— The **Gã-Adangme** dialects. In: The Akan and Gã-Adangme peoples . . . . (see VI. 2, General).
*—— 1951. The pronunciation of **Gã**. Pp. 24. Cambridge: Heffer.
—— Some notes on the pronunciation of the Krobo dialect of **Adangme**. Mitt. Inst. Orientforsch., 5, 3, 1957, 418–31.
—— Some preliminary notes on **Ada** personal nomenclature. A.L.S., 1, 1960, 177–84.
—— and KOTEI, N. A. 1969. An introductory course in **Gã**. Pp. ii+148. Washington: US Dept. of Health, Education and Welfare. [Final report of Research project No. 070811, at Northwestern University, Evanston, Ill.].
*CHRISTALLER, J. G. et al. 1874. A dictionary, English, Tshi (Asante), **Akra**. Pp. 275. Basel: Evangelical Missionary Society.
*CHRISTALLER, J. G. 1892. Primer of the **Gã** or Akra language.
*ELLIS, A. B. 1894. The Yoruba-speaking peoples of the slave coast of West Africa, their religion, manners, customs, laws, languages, etc. With an appendix containing a comparison of the Tshi, Ga, Ewe and Yoruba languages. Pp. 402. London: Chapman and Hall.
*FLEISCHER, C. F. 1924. (1st ed. 1912). A new **Gã**-English method. Pp. vii+183. Oxford.
*GÃ SOCIETY. 1946 (3rd ed.). **Gã** word list with rules of spelling. Pp. 55. Cape Coast.
HAIR, P. E. H. An ethnolinguistic inventory . . . . (see VI. General) [incl. **Gã-Adangme**].
*HANSON, A. W. On the grammatical principles of the **Gha** (Accra) language. J. Ethnol. Soc., 4, 1856, 84–97.
*JOHNSON, H., and CHRISTALLER, J. G. 1886. Vocabularies of the Niger and Gold Coast, West Africa [including **Gã**]. Pp. iv+34. London: S.P.C.K.
KOTEI, N. A. A description of modern spoken **Gã**, with particular reference to tone and intonation. Ph.D. thesis (unpublished). Evanston: Northwestern University, 1969.

KROPP, MARY E. The morphology of the **Adangme** verb complex. J.A.L., 3, 1, 1964, 80–95.
—— The morphology of the **Gã** aspect system. J.A.L., 5, 2, 1966, 121–7.
—— An analysis of the consonant system of **Gã**. J.W.A.L., 1968, 59–61.
—— 1968. **Gã, Adangme** and Ewe (Lomé) with English gloss. Legon: Inst. Afr. Stud. Ghana. (Comparative African Wordlists Series No. 2).
—— 1968. A comparative study of **Gã** and **Adangme** with special reference to the verbal system. Ph.D. thesis (unpublished). London: S.O.A.S.
OKUNOR, V. Tone in the **Gã** verb. Legon: Inst. Afr. Stud.
PUPLAMPU, D. A. 1952. An **Adangme** script (Adangme teachers' handbooks, no. 1). Pp. 20. London: Macmillan.
—— 1953. **Adangme** manner of speech: a study of the Adangme language, parts 1 and 2. Pp. 112. London: Macmillan.
WERTZ, F. **Gã**-English dictionary. 9 vols. (In library of Ghana Univ. Photostat copy at School Orient. & Afr. Stud. London).

4. EWE

ADALI-MORTTY, G. **Ewe** poetry. Ɔkyeame. I, 1, 1961, 49–52.
*ADANDE, A. Javanais chez les Gû de Porto-Novo. Notes afr. IFAN, 24, 1944, 10–11.
*ALAPINI, J. Notes sur les chansons **dahoméennes**. Educ. Afr., 28, 102/3, 1939, 25–31.
*—— c. 1950. Le petit **dahoméen**: Grammaire-vocabulaire; Lexique en langue du Dahomey. Pp. 284. Avignon: Presses Universelles.
ANSRE, G. 1961. The tonal structure of **Ewe**. Pp. 86. Hartford, Connecticut. (Hartford Studies in Linguistics, 1.)
—— Reduplication in **Ewe**. J.A.L., 2, 2, 1963, 128–32.
—— The tones of **Ewe** verbals. Actes du Second Colloque International de Linguistique Négro-Africaine, Université de Dakar, 1963, 112–17.
—— The verbid—a caveat to 'serial verbs'. J.W.A.L., 3, 1, 1966, 29–32, [**Ewe**].
—— 1966. The grammatical units of **Ewe**. A study of their structure, classes and systems. Ph.D. thesis (unpublished). London: S.O.A.S.
BAËTA, L. 1962. Míafe gbe agbalẽ gbãto [**Ewe** grammar], pp. 168. London: Macmillan.
*BERRY, J. 1951. The pronunciation of **Ewe**. Pp. 28. Cambridge: Heffer.
—— Language. In: The **Ewe**-speaking people of Togoland and the Gold Coast, Madeline Manoukian (Ethnographic Survey of Africa. Western Africa, Part VI). London: International African Institute, 1952.
*BLASER, W. Die Bedeutungsbildung auf der Struktur 'gebogen' und 'zusammen' in der **Ewe**-Sprache. Arch. ges. Psychol., 103, 1939, 353–412.
*BONNAVENTURE, A. 1895. Éléments de grammaire de la langue **fon** ou dahoméenne, suivie d'un vocabulaire et d'un recueil de conversations. Pp. 72. Paris: Lavauzelle.
*BÜRGI, E. 1894. Übungen in der **Evhe**sprache. Bremen.
*—— 1897. Kurzgefasste Grammatik der **Ewe**-Sprache. Bremen.
*COURDIOUX, PH.-E. 1879. Dictionnaire abrégé de la langue **fongbe** ou dahoméenne. Pp. 43. Paris.
*CZERMAK, W. 1924. Zur Sprache der **Ewe**-Neger (ein Beitrag zur Seelenkunde). Pp. 39. Innsbruck: F. Rauch (Supplementa africana,1).
DA CRUZ, G. Essai de petit vocabulaire français-**fongbe**. Et. dahoméennes, 11, 1954, 15–19.
—— Petit recueil des pseudonymes (population **Fon**, région d'Abomey). Ét. dahoméennes, 15, 1956, 3–34.
*DREXEL, A. Der **Ewe**-Typus in seiner systematischen Eigenart und in seiner sprachgesichtlichen Stellung. Bibliotheca africana, 4, 2, 1931, 31–41.
DUJARIER, M. 1967. Manuel progressif de conversation en langue **fon**. [See p. 63, J.W.A.L., 5, 1, 1968.]
*ELLIS, A. B. 1894. The Yoruba-speaking peoples of the slave coast of West Africa, their religion, manners, customs, laws, languages, etc. with an appendix containing a comparison of the Tshi, Ga, **Ewe** and Yoruba languages. Pp. 402. London: Chapman and Hall.

*EWEN, J. 1906. Grammatikalische Elemente von südwest Togo. Lomé.
FEYER, U. Ein Beitrag zur Lautlehre des Gũ-Dialektes der Ewesprache. Afrikanistische Studien, ed. J. Lukas, Hamburg, 1955, 405–16.
*FUNKE, E. Die Stellung der Haussasprache unter den Sprachen Togos. Mitt. Sem. orient Spr., 19 (3), 1916, 116–28, [incl. Ewe].
HAIR, P. E. H. An ethnolinguistic inventory . . . (see VI. General) [incl. Ewe].
*HEINITZ, W. Ein Beitrag zur Reproduktion des musikalischen Elements in der Ewe-Sprache. Vox, 2, 1916, 83 ff.
*HENRICI, E. 1906. (1st ed. 1891). Lehrbuch der Ephe-Sprache: Anlo, Anecho und Dahome Mundart, mit Glossar. Pp. xxi+176, map. Stuttgart: Berlin.
*HERMAN, A. 1939. A short Ewe grammar with English-Ewe-French vocabulary. Pp. 48.
HÖFTMANN, H. Möglichkeiten zur Wiedergabe europäischer Begriffe im Ewe. Veröff. Mus. Völkerkde. Leipzig, 11, 1961, 276–84.
JOHNSON, G. K. Un problème de terminologie: le mot ewe/eve/ du bas Togo dans la classification des langues négro-africaines. Ét. togolaises [Lomé], 1, 1, 1965, 38–50, bibl. carte.
—— Morphologie des nominaux dans la langue gẽ ou gẽgbe (minapopo) du bas Togo. Ét. togolaises [Lomé], 1, 1, 1965, 51–61.
—— 'Mawu' ou 'Dieu' chez les Gẽ-Mina du bas Togo par le patronyme. Ét. togolaises [Lomé], 1, 1, 1965, 74–87.
*JOULORD, J. 1907. Manuel français-dahoméen: grammaire, phrases usuelles, vocabulaires. Pp. 220. Lyon: Paquet.
*KNÜSLI, A. 1892. Deutsch-Ewe Wörterbuch. Bremen.
KROPP, MARY E. The Adampe and Anfue dialects of Ewe in the Polyglotta Africana. S.L.L.R. 5, 1966, 116–21.
—— 1966. Gã, Adangme and Ewe (Lomé) with English glosses. Legon: Inst. Afr. Stud. (Comparative African Wordlist Series No. 2).
*MEINHOF, C. Theoretische und empirische Tonhöhe in Ewe. Vox, 2, 1916, 2 ff.
*MILLER, FR. Folkloristische Ewhetexte (Gẽ-Dialekt). Globus, 79, 1, 1901, 45–6.
*POTAKEY, F. K. Notes on Ewe writing. Teachers' J., 8, 3, 1936.
*—— Diacritical marks used in Ewe writing. Teachers' J., 9, 2, 1937, 128–30.
—— and CHAPMAN, D. A. 1944. Ewe spelling. Pp. 11. Gold Coast: Achimota Press (Ewe Studies, 2).
*RHODES, J. 1904. Anglo-Franco Dahomian grammar and vocabulary. Pp. 44. Colwyn Bay.
ROUGET, G. Une chante-fable d'un signe divinatoire (Dahomey) (Gũ). J.A.L., 1, 3, 1962, 273–92.
—— Le problème du 'ton moyen' en Gũ. J.A.L., 2, 3, 1963, 218–21.
—— Tons de la langue, en Gun (Dahomey) et tons du tambour. Rev. Musicol., 50, 1964, 3–29.
—— Analyse des tons du gũ (Dahomey) par le 'détecteur de mélodie' de l'Institut de Phonétique de Grenoble: rapport d'expériences. Langage et Comportement, 1, 1965, 31–48.
SAULNIER, P. Noms patronymiques derivés du SE [Goun, Fon] Ét. dahoméennes, 12, 1, 1968, 23–37.
*SCHLEGEL, J. B. 1857. Schlüssel zur Ewe-Sprache. Pp. 328. Stuttgart: Steinkopf.
*SCHOBER, R. Die semantische Gestalt des Ewe. Anthropos, 28, 5/6, 1933, 621–32.
*—— (Tr.) Die fünfte Lagune [Toko atolia (Ewe drama) by F. K. Fiawoo, with German translation]. Mitt. Ausland-Hochschule, 40 (3), 1937, 1–127.
SMITH, N. V. Tone in Ewe. In: M.I.T. Research Lab. of Electronics, Quarterly Progress Report 88, 1968. Cambridge, Mass.: Mass. Institute of Technology.
SPRIGGE, R. G. S. A song from Eweland's Adangbe: notes and queries. Ghana Notes and Queries, 10, 1968, 23–8.
VON ESSEN, O. Zur Phonetik des vollstimmhaften und endstimmhaften Velarlabialen in des Ewesprache. Z. f. Phonetik, 12, 1/4, 1959, 23–6.
WARBURTON, ? et al. 1969. Ewe basic course. Bloomington: Indiana University Linguistic Circle.

WESTERMANN, D. 1954 (revised ed.). Wörterbuch der **Ewe**-Sprache. Pp. 796. Berlin: Akademie-Verlag (Dtsche Akad. Wiss. Berlin, Inst. Orientforsch., Veröffentl. 8). [Reviewed in Afr. u. Übersee, 39, 1954/5, 193–5.]
—— Texte in der Gĕ-Mundart des **Ewe**. Afr. u. Übersee, 39, 1, 1954, 1–5.
—— 1961 (1st ed. 1939). Die **Ewe**-Sprache in Togo: eine praktische Einführung (2. berichtige Auflage von E. Kähler-Meyer). Pp. x+95. Berlin: De Gruyter (Lehrb. Seminars orient. Sprachen Univ. Bonn, N.F., 1). [Reviewed in Afr. u. Übersee, 45, 1961, 226.]
WIEGRABE, P. **Ewe**lieder. Afr. u. Übersee, 37, 3, 1953, 99–108; 38, 1, 1953/4, 17–26; 3, 113–20; 4, 155–64.

5. YORUBA (incl. Itsekiri, Igala)

ABRAHAM, R. C. 1958. Dictionary of modern **Yoruba**. Pp. 776, ill. University of London Press.
*ADEYEMI, M. C. and LATUNDE, S. Y. 1933. **Yoruba** composition. Ondo.
AJAO, D. O. Orin idagbere (a **Yoruba** dirge). Odù, 3, 1956, 33–4.
AJAYI, J. F. A. How **Yoruba** was reduced to writing. Odù, 8, 1960, 49–58.
AJIBQLA, J. O. 1962 (1st impression 1947). Owe Yoruba (**Yoruba** proverbs with English translations). Pp. 83. London and Ibadan: O.U.P.
*AKINTAN, E. A. 1931. Dictionary of the **Yoruba** language. Parts 1 and 2. Lagos: C.M.S. Bookshop.
*—— 1943. Second steps in **Yoruba** composition. Pp. 50. Lagos: Alebiosu Press.
*—— 1947. English translation of **Yoruba** phrases and proverbs. Pp. 50. Lagos: Alebiosu Press.
AKINWUNMI, M. A. 1960. **Yoruba** language simplified. Pp. 48. Brooklyn, Akinwumi Enterprises. (A Library of African Cultures.)
ALOYADE, B. A preliminary bibliography of Nigerian languages: Part One—Hausa, **Yoruba** and Igbo. Special supplement, African Notes [Ibadan], 5, 1, 1968, xii–xxi.
ARMSTRONG, R. G. The **Igala**: Language. In: Peoples of the Niger-Benue confluence (Ethnographic survey of Africa, Western Africa, Part X). London: International African Institute, 1955.
—— 1962. **Yoruba** numerals. Pp. 36. O.U.P. (Nigerian Social and Economic Studies, No. 1.) [Reviewed in Afr. u. Übersee, 47, 1963, 143.]
—— Comparative word lists of two dialects of **Yoruba** with **Igala**. J.W.A.L., 2, 2, 1965, 51–78.
—— et al. (transcr., tr. and ed.) Ekiti traditional dirge of Lt. Colonel Adekunle Fajuyi's funeral. African Notes [Ibadan], 5, 2, 1969, 63–94.
ASHIWAJU, M. 1967. Lehrbuch der **Yoruba**-Sprache. Pp. 139. Leipzig: VEB Verlag Enzyklopädie.
AWOBULUYI, A. O. Vowel and consonant harmony in **Yoruba**. J.A.L., 6, 1, 1967, 1–8.
—— 1967. Studies in the syntax of the standard **Yoruba** verb. Ph.D. thesis (unpublished). New York: Columbia University.
—— and BAMGBOṢE, A. Two views of vowel harmony in **Yoruba**. J.A.L., 6, 3, 1967, 274–7.
*BABALQLA, A. **Yoruba** oral poetry. W. Afr. Rev., 22, 281, 1951, 130–1.
—— Three **Yoruba** poems. Odù, 2, 1955, 36–8.
—— 1962. Iwe ede **Yoruba**. Parts I and II. Longmans of Nigeria.
—— The characteristic features of outer form of **Yoruba** ijala chants. Odù, N.S. 1, 1, 1964, 33–44; 1, 2, 1965, 47–77.
—— 1966. The content and form of **Yoruba** ijala. Pp. xiv+396, bibl. Oxford: Clarendon Press. (Oxford Lib. Afr. Lit.)
—— and ODUNSI, A. O. **Yoruba** poems. Odù, 8, 1960, 67–9.
BAMGBOṢE, A. The structure of the **Yoruba** predicator. Actes du Second Colloque International de Linguistique Négro-Africaine, Université de Dakar, 1963, 119–26.
—— Verb-nominal collocations in **Yoruba**: a problem of syntactic analysis. J.W.A.L., 1, 2, 1964, 27–32.
—— Assimilation and contraction in **Yoruba**. J.W.A.L., 2, 1, 1965, 21–7.

BAMGBOṢE, A. 1965. **Yoruba** orthography: a linguistic appraisal with suggestions for reform. Pp. 33. Ibadan: Univ. Press.
—— The assimilated low tone in **Yoruba**. Lingua, 14, 1, 1965, 1–13.
—— 1966. A grammar of **Yoruba**. Pp. xii+175. bibl. London: Cambridge Univ. Press. (W. Afr. language monograph series, 5.) [Reviewed in J.A.L., 6, 1, 1967, 89–98 and Bull. S.O.A.S., 30, 3, 1967, 736–7.]
—— Vowel harmony in **Yoruba**. J.A.L., 6, 3, 1967, 268–73.
—— The form of **Yoruba** proverbs. Odù, 4, 2, 1968, 74–86.
—— **Yoruba**. In: Twelve Nigerian Languages, ed. Elizabeth Dunstan. London: Longmans, 1969, 163–72.
—— Word play in **Yoruba** poetry. I.J.A.L., 36, 2, 1970.
BANJO, A. 1969. A contrastive study of aspects of the syntactic and lexical rules of English and **Yoruba**. Ph.D. thesis (unpublished). Ibadan.
*BANJO, S. A. The teaching of **Yoruba** in the secondary schools of Nigeria. Nigeria, 13, 1938, 58–69.
*BASCOM, W. R. Literary style in **Yoruba** riddles. J. Amer. Folklore, 62, 243, 1949, 1–16.
—— 1969. Ifa Divination [**Yoruba**]. Pp. xii+575, 15 plates. Bloomington: University of Indiana Press.
*BEECROFT, W. S. 1914. **Yoruba** grammar and composition. Pp. 95. London: Kegan Paul.
BERTHO, J. Aperçu d'ehsemble sur les dialectes de l'Ouest de la Nigéria. Bull. IFAN, 14, 1, 1952, 259–71, [incl. **Yoruba**].
*BOWEN, T. J. 1858. A grammar and dictionary of the **Yoruba** language, with an introductory description of the country and people. Pp. xxi+136. Washington: Smithsonian Institution.
BRADSHAW, A. T. von S. A list of **Yoruba** words in Krio. S.L.L.R., 5, 1966, 61–71.
CABRERA, L. 1957. Anago-vocabulario lucumi (el **Yoruba** que se habla en Cuba). La Habana.
CARNOCHAN, J. Pitch, tone and intonation in **Yoruba**. In: In Honour of Daniel Jones, ed. Abercrombie and others. Longmans, 1964, 397–406.
*CHURCH MISSIONARY SOCIETY. 1931. **Yoruba** names and salutations. Lagos: C.M.S.
COLLIER, F. S. **Yoruba** hunters' salutes. Nigerian Field, 18, 2, 1953, 52–67, ill.
*COOMBER, A. G. 1867. **Igara** primer. Pp. 26. London: C.M.S.
*CROWTHER, S. A. 1843. A dictionary of the **Yoruba** language.
*—— 1852. A grammar and vocabulary of the **Yoruba** language. Pp. v+18, vii+291. London: Seeley, Service.
DALBY, D. Further indigenous scripts of West Africa: Manding, Wolof and Fula alphabets and **Yoruba** 'holy' writings. A.L.S., 10, 1969, 161–81.
DA SILVA, E. N. 1958. Introdução ao estudo gramatical da língua **Yoruba**. Bahia.
*D'AVEZAC. Esquisse grammaticale de la langue **yéboue**. Mém. Soc. ethnol., 1, 2, 1841–5.
DELANO, I. O. 1958. Atúmọ̀ ede Yoruba. A short **Yoruba** grammar and dictionary. Pp. 209, map. London: O.U.P.
—— 1958. Owe l'ẹsin ọrọ—Yoruba proverbs. Pp. xi+154. Ibadan: O.U.P.
—— 1960. Agbeka ọrọ Yoruba: appropriate words and expressions in **Yoruba**. Pp. 160. London: O.U.P.
—— 1965. A modern **Yoruba** grammar. London: Nelson.
—— 1969. A dictionary of **Yoruba** monosyllabic verbs. 2 vols. Pp. vi+469, 458. Ife: Inst. of Afr. Stud., University of Ife.
*ELLIS, A. B. 1894. The Yoruba-speaking peoples of the slave coast of West Africa, their religions, manners, customs, laws, languages, etc. with an appendix containing a comparison of the Tshi, Ga, Ewe and **Yoruba** languages. Pp. 402, London: Chapman and Hall.
FRESCO, E. M. Two dialects of **Igálá**, and **Yorùbá**: some comparisons. Research Notes [Ibadan], 4, 1968, 32–46.
—— A folktale in the Ketu dialect of **Yoruba**. African Notes [Ibadan], 5, 1, 1968, 38–60.
—— The tones of the **Yoruba** and **Igala** disyllabic noun prefix. J.W.A.L., 6, 1, 1969, 31–4.

*Gouzien, P. 1899. Manuel franco-**yoruba** de conversation spécialement à l'usage du médecin. Contribution à l'étude des dialectes du Dahomey. Pp. viii+64. Paris: Challamel.

Hair, P. E. H. Notes on the early study of some West African languages (Susu, Bullom/Sherbro, Temne, Mende, Vai and **Yoruba**). Bull. IFAN, 23 (B), 3/4, 1961, 683–95.

—— An ethnolinguistic inventory . . . (see VI. General) [incl. **Yoruba**].

Heidt, K. M. 1954. Laut und Ton in **Yoruba**. Phil. F. thesis, Hamburg.

Ịkọ, A. (n.d.) Yoruba proverbs. Pp. 91. Ibadan: Ayọrinde Printing Works.

*Jacquot. 1880. Étude sur la langue nago ou **Yoruba**. Lyon.

*Johnson, S. The **Yoruba** language. In: The history of the Yorubas. Lagos: C.M.S., 1921.

Kirk-Greene, A. H. M. The linguistic statistics of Northern Nigeria: a tentative presentation. A.L.R., 6, 1967, 75–101. [Kanuri, Tiv, Nupe, **Yoruba**, Hausa, Fulani and other languages.]

Kubik, G. Àlọ́—**Yoruba** story songs. Afr. Music [Jo'burg], 4, 2, 1968, 10–32.

Ladipo, D. Ọba ko so (The king did not hang). Selections. Transcription and translation by R. G. Armstrong and R. L. Awujoola. Ibadan: Inst. of Afr. Stud. (Occ. Publ. 3).

—— et al. Ọba ko so (complete text and translation). Ibadan: Inst. of Afr. Stud. (Occ. Publ. 10).

Laloum, Cl. et Rouget, G. La musique de deux chants liturgiques **yoruba**. J. Soc. Africanistes, 35, 1, 1965, 109–39 [avec disque].

*Language studies in **Yoruba**. 1914. Pp. 105. Lagos: C.M.S. Bookshop.

Lașebikan, E. L. Tone in **Yoruba** poetry. Odù, 2, 1955, 35–6.

—— The tonal structure of **Yoruba** poetry. Présence afr. n.s. 8/10, 1956, 43–50.

—— 1958. Learning **Yoruba**. Pp. 81. London: O.U.P.

*Lloyd James, A. The tones of **Yoruba**. Bull. S.O.A.S., 3, 1923–25, 119–28.

Lucas, O. 1965. The **Yoruba** language: its structure and relationship to other languages. The author.

*Lyon: Société des Missions africaines. 1908. Guide pratique de conversation en français, anglais, et **yoruba** ou nago, (par C.B. et L.B.). Pp. 126.

*Mann, A. C. Eine geschichtliche Sage aus der Zeit der Ersten Niederlassungen der Egba, ein Stamm der **Yoruba**-Nation, West Afrika. Z. afr. Spr., 2, 1888-89, 209–19 [incl. bibl.].

Mukarovsky, H. G. Some reflexions on a Nigerian class language. Wiener völkerkdl. Mitt., 6, 1/4, 1963, 65–83, [incl. vocab. of **Yoruba**].

Odunuga, O. 1965. Sopostevitelny analiz sintaksicheskoi struktury prostovo predlozheniya v yazyke **Yoruba** i v russkom yazyke [Comparative analysis of the syntactical structure of the simple sentence in the Yoruba and Russian languages]. Moscow. Patrice Lumumba Friendship University.

—— 1966. Vido-vremennaya sistema v yazyke **Yoruba** v sopostavlenii s vido-vremennoi sistemoi v russkom yazyke [The tense/aspect system in the Yoruba language in comparison with that of Russian]. Moscow. Patrice Lumumba Friendship University (mimeographed).

Ogunmola, K. et al. The palmwine drinkard (complete text and translation). Ibadan: Inst. of Afr. Stud. (Occ. Publ. 11).

Oke, D. O. 1969. A grammatical study of the Yoruba verb system. D.Phil. thesis (unpublished). University of York.

Olayemi, V. Forms of the song in **Yoruba** folktales. African notes [Ibadan], 5, 1, 1968, 25–32.

*Olmsted, D. L. The phonemes of **Yoruba**. Word, 7, 1951, 245–9.

*—— Comparative notes on **Yoruba** and Lucumi. Language, 29, 1953, 157–64.

Opubor, A. E. **Itsekiri**. In: Twelve Nigerian languages, ed. Elizabeth Dunstan. London: Longmans, 1969, 125–32.

Philips, E. 1953. **Yoruba** music (African): fusion of speech and music. Pp. 58. Johannesburg: African Music Society.

*Rambaud, J. B. Des rapports de la langue **yoruba** avec les langues de la famille mandé. Bull. Soc. Ling. Paris, 4, 1897.

Report of the **Yoruba** orthography committee, 1967. Ibadan: Govt. Printer.

Rowlands, E. C. Types of word junction in **Yoruba**. Bull. S.O.A.S., 16, 2, 1954, 376–88.
—— The mid tone in **Yoruba**. Afrikanische Studien, ed. J. Lukas [Hamburg] Hamburg, 1955, 333–6.
—— Some features of nasalised vowels in **Yoruba**. Akten des 24 International Orientalisten-Kongresses, Munich, 1957, 719–21.
—— **Yoruba** and English: a problem of coexistence. A.L.S., 4, 1963, 208–14.
—— **Yoruba** dialects in the Polyglotta Africana. S.L.L.R., 4, 1965, 103–8.
—— The illustration of a **Yoruba** proverb. J. Folklore Inst. [Bloomington, Ind.], 4, 2/3, 1967, 250–64.
—— 1969. Teach yourself **Yoruba**. Pp. vi+276, London: English Univ. Press.
—— Ideophones in **Yoruba**. A.L.S., 11, 1970, 289–97.
Salami, A. 1965–6. A phonetic and phonological study of **Yoruba** personal names. M.A. thesis (unpublished). London: S.O.A.S.
—— 1969. English loan-words in **Yoruba**. Ph.D. thesis (unpublished). London.
Siertsema, Bertha. Some notes on **Yoruba** phonetics and spelling. Bull. IFAN, 20 (B), 3/4, 1958, 576–92.
—— Problems of phonemic interpretation I: nasalised sounds in **Yoruba**. Lingua, 7, 1958, 356–66.
—— Problems of phonemic interpretation II: long vowels in a tone language. Lingua, 8, 1959, 42–64 [**Yoruba**].
—— Stress and tone in **Yoruba** word composition. Lingua, 8, 1959, 385–402.
—— Three **Yoruba** dictionaries. Bull. IFAN, 21 (B), 3–4, 1959, 572–8.
*Sowande, E. J. et al. 1911. English-**Yoruba** dictionary. Lagos: C.M.S. Bookshop.
*Sowande, E. J. et al. 1950 (1st ed. 1913). A dictionary of the **Yoruba** language. Pp. 218+243. London: O.U.P.
Sowande, F. Three **Yoruba** songs. Odù, 3, 1956, 36–40.
Stevick, E. W. Pitch and duration in two **Yoruba** idiolects. J.A.L., 4, 2, 1965, 85–101.
—— and Aremu, O. 1963. **Yoruba** basic course. Pp. xxxviii+343. Washington, D.C.; Foreign Service Inst.
*Struck, B. Linguistic bibliography of Northern Nigeria [with notes on the **Yoruba** dialects]. J. Afr. Soc., 4, 47–61, 1911, 213–30.
*Tidjani, A. S. Le nom **yoruba** (Dahomey). Notes afr. IFAN, 26, 1945, 19–21.
Ward, Ida C. 1952. Introduction to the **Yoruba** language. Pp. 255. Cambridge: W. Heffer.
Williamson, Kay. Some food plant names in the Niger Delta. I.J.A.L., 36, 2, 1970 [incl. **Itsekiri**].
Wolff, H. Sub-system typologies and area linguistics. Anth. Ling., 1, 7, 1959, 1–88 [incl. **Itsekiri**].
—— Niger-delta languages I: classification. Anth. Ling. 1, 8, 1959, 32–53 [incl. **Itsekiri**].
—— **Rárà**: A **Yoruba** chant. J.A.L., 1, 1, 1962, 45–56.
—— 1963. Beginning **Yoruba**. East Lansing: Michigan State University.
—— 1964. Second year **Yoruba**. East Lansing: Michigan State University.
*Wood, J. B. 1879. Notes on the construction of the **Yoruba** language. Pp. 47. Exeter.
Yakovleva, V. K. 1963. Yazyk **Yoruba** [The Yoruba language]. Moscow Akademia Nauk. USSR, Institut Narodov Azii.

6. NUPE GROUP

Bertho, J. Aperçu d'ensemble sur les dialectes de l'ouest de la Nigéria. Bull. IFAN, 14, 1, 1952, 259–71 [incl. **Nupe**-Gwari].
*Crowther, S. 1864. Grammar and vocabulary of the **Nupe** language. London: C.M.S.
Gregersen, E. A. Linguistic seriation as a dating device for loanwords, with special reference to West Africa. A.L.R., 6, 1967, 102–8. [Hausa, **Nupe** and Kanuri].
Kirk-Greene, A. H. M. The linguistic statistics of Northern Nigeria: a tentative presentation A.L.R., 6, 1967, 75–101. [Kanuri, Tiv, **Nupe**, Yoruba, Hausa, Fulani and other languages].

LADEFOGED, P. **Igbirra** notes and word-list. J.W.A.L., 1, 1, 1964, 27–37.
NADEL, S. F. Morality and language among the **Nupe**. Man, 54, 77, 1954, 55–7, ill.
SMITH, N. V. The phonology of **Nupe**. J.A.L., 6, 2, 1967, 153–69.
—— 1967. An outline grammar of **Nupe**. London: S.O.A.S. [Reviewed in Lingua, 22, 1969, 303–9.]
—— The verb in **Nupe**. A.L.S., 10, 1969, 90–160.
—— **Nupe**. In: Twelve Nigerian languages, ed. Elizabeth Dunstan. London: Longmans, 1969, 133–41.
—— Repetition of the verb in **Nupe**. A.L.S., 11, 1970, 319–39.
WOLFF, H. Sub-system typologies and area linguistics. Anth. Ling. 1, 7, 1959, 1–88 [incl. **Nupe, Igbira**].

7. BINI GROUP

BRADBURY, R. E. Comparative **Edo** word lists. Research notes [Ibadan], 4, 1968. [**Urhobo, Bini, Ishan, Uneme-Etuna, Ikpeshi, Ososo, Ibilo, Ugbosi, Somorika, Otuɔ**, and introduction on classification of **Edo** by Kay Williamson.]
CLARK, D. J. 1969. A grammatical study of **Ekpeye**. Ph.D. thesis (unpublished). London: S.O.A.S.
*EDEGBE, J. E. 1935. Emwe ebo keube **Edo** [English and Edo syntax]. Lagos: C.M.S. Bookshop.
EGHAREVBA, J. U. 1953 (2nd ed.). Ozedu-interpreter. Pp. 24. Benin: Author.
HAIR, P. E. H. An ethnolinguistic inventory . . . . (see VI. General) [incl. **Edo**].
HUBBARD, J. [n.d.] The **Sobo** of the Niger delta. Zaria: Gaskiya.
KELLY, J. Vowel patterns in the **Urhobo** noun. J.W.A.L., 6, 1, 1969, 27–30.
—— **Urhobo** in the *Polyglotta Africana*. A.L.R., 7, 1968, 107–13.
—— **Urhobo**. In: Twelve Nigerian languages, ed. Elizabeth Dunstan. London: Longmans, 1969, 153–61.
LAVER, J. A preliminary phonology of the Ayele dialect of **Esako**. J.W.A.L., 4, 2, 1967, 53–6.
—— **Etsako**. In: Twelve Nigerian languages, ed. Elizabeth Dunstan. London: Longmans, 1969, 47–56.
MAFENI, B. Ogbéí Avọ Ụ́wụ́zụ̀ (an **Isoko** tortoise story), Research Notes [Ibadan], 2, 1–2, 1969.
—— **Isoko**. In: Twelve Nigerian languages, ed. Elizabeth Dunstan. London: Longmans, 1969, 115–24.
MUNRO, D. English-**Edo** word-list: an index to Melzian's Bini-English Dictionary. Ibadan: Inst. of Afr. Stud. (Occ. Publ. 7).
*TALBOT, P. A. The linguistic situation in the western parts of the Niger delta. Africa, 6, 3, 1933, 331–2.
THOMAS, ELAINE. Preliminary paradigm of some **Degema** independent clauses. In: Tagmemic and matrix linguistics applied to selected African languages, K. L. Pike. Ann Arbor, 1966, 187–91 (Appendix III).
—— 1969. A grammatical description of the **Engenni** language. Ph.D. thesis (unpublished). London: S.O.A.S.
—— and WILLIAMSON, KAY. 1967. Word-lists of Delta Edo: **Epie, Engenni, Degema**. Ibadan: Inst. Afr. Stud. (Occ. Publ. 8).
*THOMAS, N. W. Notes on **Kukuruku**. Man, 17, 32, 1917, 43–5.
*WELCH, J. W. The linguistic situation in the western parts of the Niger delta. Africa, 6, 2, 1933, 220–2.
WESCOTT, R. W. Problems in linguistic anthropology [based on **Bini**]. W. Afr. Inst. Soc. & Econ. Res., Ann. Conf. Mar. 1956, 138–44.
—— The metalinguistics of **Bini**: a West African language. Anth. Ling., 2, 6, 1960, 19–21.
—— 1962–3. A **Bini** grammar. 1. Phonology. 2. Morphology. 3. Lexemics. Pp. 119, 34, 168. New Haven, Conn.: Bartlett Hofman.
—— Speech-tempo and the phonemics of **Bini**. J.A.L., 4, 3, 1965, 182–90.

WILLIAMSON, KAY. Languages of the Niger Delta. Nigeria Mag. [Lagos], 97, 1968, 124–30, bibl., map.
—— Some food plant names in the Niger Delta. I.J.A.L., 36, 2, 1970 [incl. **Delta Edo, Urhobo**].
WOLFF, H. Sub-system typologies and area linguistics. Anth. Ling. 1, 7, 1959, 1–88 [incl. **Atisa, Bini, Ishan, Esako, Urhobo, Isoko**].
—— Niger-delta languages I: classification. Anth. Ling., 1, 8, 1959, 32–53, [incl. **Edo**].

8. IGBO (incl. Izi)

ABRAHAM, R. C. 1967. The principles of **Ibo**. Ibadan: Inst. of Afr. Stud. Occ. publ. 4.
*ADAMS, R. F. G., and OGUGMANA, T. K. 1932. Olu **Igbo**. Pp. 64. London: Brown.
*AKWUKWO-OGUGU. 1912. Umòn **Ibo** primer prepared by Archdeacon T. J. Dennis. Pp. 64. London: C.M.S.
ALOYADE, B. A preliminary bibliography of Nigerian languages: Part One—Hausa, Yoruba and **Igbo**. Special supplement, African Notes [Ibadan], 5, 1, 1968, xxi–xxvi.
ARMSTRONG, R. G. 1967. A comparative word-list of five **Igbo** dialects. Ibadan: Inst. of Afr. Stud. (Occ. Publ. 5).
BENDOR-SAMUEL, J. T. Verb clusters in **Izi**. J.W.A.L., 5, 2, 1968, 119–27.
—— and MEIER, INGE. Some contrasting features of the **Izi** verbal system. J.A.L., 6, 1, 1967, 30–41.
CARNOCHAN, J. Vowel harmony in **Igbo**. A.L.S., 1, 1960, 155–63.
—— Pitch, tone and intonation in **Igbo** grammar. Proceedings of the Fourth International Congress of Phonetic Sciences. Helsinki, 1961. Mouton, 547–54.
—— The category of number in **Igbo** grammar. A.L.S., 3, 1962, 110–15.
—— Towards a syntax for **Igbo**. J.A.L., 2, 3, 1963, 222–6.
—— Word classes—**Igbo**. Lingua, 17, 1/2, 1967, 1–23.
—— and IWUCHUKU, B. 1963. An **Igbo** revision course. Pp. xvii+168. O.U.P.
CARREL, P. L. G. 1966. A transformational grammar of **Igbo**. Ph.D. thesis (unpublished). Univ. of Texas.
*CHURCH MISSIONARY SOCIETY. 1924. English-**Ibo** phrase book. Pp. 42. Onitsha: C.M.S.
*CORREIA, J. A. Vocables réligieux et philosophiques des peuples **Ibos**. Bibl. Africana, 1, 1924, 104–13.
*CROW, H. 1790. Ein Kleines Vokabular English-**Eboe** würde vom Captain Crow während seines Aufenthaltes als Sklavenhändler in etwa 10 Jahren (von 1790 ab) in Bonny aufgenommen.
*CROWTHER, S. A. 1857 (reprinted 1859). Isoama-**Ibo** primer. Pp. 17. London: C.M.S.
*—— 1882. Vocabulary of the **Ibo** language. (Part 1. Ibo-English.) Pp. viii+109. London: S.P.C.K. (Part 2, English-Ibo, is by J. F. Schön.)
*DENNIS, T. J. et al. 1923. Dictionary of the **Ibo** language, English-Ibo. Pp. 189. Lagos: C.M.S. Bookshop.
DUNSTAN, ELIZABETH, and IGWE, G. E. Two views of the phonology of the Ọ̀hụ̀hụ̀ dialect of **Igbo**. J.W.A.L., 3, 2, 1966, 71–5.
*GANOT, A. 1899. Grammaire **Ibo** [with French-Ibo and Ibo-French vocabulary]. Pp. 209. Onitsha: Niger Catholic Mission.
*—— 1904. English, **Ibo** and French dictionary. Pp. 306. Salzburg, Austria: Missionary Printing Office of the Sodality of St. Peter Claver.
*GREEN, MARGARET M. The present linguistic situation in **Ibo** country. Africa, 9, 4, 1936, 508–23.
—— Sayings of the ọkọnkọ society of the **Igbo**-speaking people. Bull. S.O.A.S., 21, 1, 1958, 157–73.
—— Suffixes in **Igbo**. A.L.S., 5, 1964, 92–114.
—— **Igbo** dialects in the *Polyglotta Africana*. A.L.R., 6, 1967, 111–19.
—— and ỌNWỤAMAEGBU, M. O. (ed.) 1962. Akukọ ife nke ndi Igbo. Stories in the official **Igbo** orthography. O.U.P.

SUPPLEMENTARY BIBLIOGRAPHY

*GREEN, MARGARET M. and IGWE, G. E. 1963. A descriptive grammar of **Igbo**. Pp. xiv+236. Berlin: Akademie-Verlag (Veröff. Inst. Orientforsch., 3). [Reviewed in B.S.O.A.S., 28, 3, 1965, 668–9.]

—— 1966. Introductory **Igbo** language course for non-Igbo speakers [incl. tape]. London: Methodist Missionary Society (suppliers).

IGWE, G. E., and GREEN, MARGARET M. 1964. A short **Igbo** grammar. Pp. viii+60. London: O.U.P.

—— 1967. **Igbo** language course [Expansion of above]. 1. Igbo language study. 2. Igbo dialogues and stories. Pp. 159, 70. Ibadan: O.U.P. [Tapes available from publisher.]

JEFFREYS, M. D. W. Some **Ibo** proverbs. Folk-lore, 67, Sept. 1956, 168–9.

KELLY, B. J. 1954. An introduction to Onitsha **Igbo**. Pp. 63. London: Macmillan.

MEIER, P. E. The relative clause in **Izi**. J.W.A.L., 6, 1, 1969, 35–50.

MUKAROVSKY, H. G. Some reflexions on a Nigerian class language. Wiener völkerkdl. Mitt., 6, 1/4, 1963, 65–83, [incl. vocab. of **Ibo**].

MÜLLER, F. Die **Ibo**-Sprache. In: Grundriss der Sprachenwissenschaft [Vienna], 1-2, 1877, 115–25.

OGBALU, F. C. 1952. An investigation into the new **Ibo** orthography, with the help of D. C. Erinne. Pp. 78. Port Harcourt: Goodwill Press.

—— 1959. **Igbo**-English dictionary. Pp. 49. Port Harcourt: African Lit. Bureau.

—— 1961. Ilu Igbo (The book of **Igbo** proverbs). Pp. 162. Onitsha: University Publishing Company.

—— 1962. Ọkọwa-okwu. **Igbo**-English—English-Igbo dictionary. Pp. 166. Onitsha: University Publishing Company.

OKASA, A. 1966. **Igbo** lessons for non-Igbos (Onitsha dialect) [Based on Green & Igwe grammar]. Asaba: Rural Training Centre.

OKONYIA, C. 1962. **Igbo** grammar and composition. Pp. 113. Onitsha: Etudo Ltd.

ONUORAH. The compromise in **Igbo** orthography controversy. Onuorah (Onitsha), 1, 1, 1956, 1–2.

ONWU Committee. 1961. The official **Igbo** orthography as recommended by the Onwu Committee in 1961 [with notes on script and spelling for teachers].

*PARKINSON, J. Note on the Asaba people (**Ibos**) of the Niger. J. Roy. Anthrop. Inst., 26, 1906, 312–24.

*SCHÖN, J. F. 1861. Oku-Ibo: grammatical elements of the **Ibo** language. London.

*—— 1883. Vocabulary of the **Ibo** language. (Part 2. English-Ibo.) Pp. 90. London: S.P.C.K. [Part 1, Ibo-English, is by S. A. Crowther.]

*SMITH, S. R. 1923. Dictionary of the **Ibo** language. English-Ibo. Pp. vii+189. Lagos: C.M.S. Bookshop.

*SPENCER, J. 1901 (1st ed. 1892). An elementary grammar of the **Ibo** language. Pp. vi+52. London: S.P.C.K.

*—— 1924 (1st ed. 1916). An elementary grammar of the **Ibo** language, revised by T. J. Dennis. Pp. viii+116. London: S.P.C.K.

SWIFT, L. B., et al. 1962. **Igbo** basic course. Pp. xiv+498. Washington, D.C.: Foreign Service Inst.

*THOMAS, N. W. Tones in **Ibo**. Man, 15, 21, 1915, 36–8.

*UDOH, Mrs. A. I. and the **Ibo** Translation Bureau, S. Nigeria. 1932. Emo íle omomo mbo dana ogogo akwokwo (First primer). Lagos: C.M.S. Bookshop.

*WARD, IDA C. A linguistic tour in Southern Nigeria. Certain problems re-stated. Africa, 8, 1935, 90–7.

WELMERS, BEATRICE F., and W. E. 1968. **Igbo**: a learner's dictionary. Pp. x+397. Los Angeles: Afr. Stud. Center.

—— Noun modifiers in **Igbo**. I.J.A.L., 35, 4, 1969, 315–22.

WESTCOTT, R. W. **Ibo** phasis. Anthrop. Ling. [Bloomington, Indiana], 5, 2, 1963, 6–8, bibl.

WILLIAMSON, KAY. The status of /e/ in Onitsha **Igbo**. J.W.A.L., 3, 2, 1966, 67–9.

—— (ed.) 1968. Ika and Ụkwụani. Ibadan: Inst. of Afr. Studies.

WILLIAMSON, KAY. **Igbo.** In: Twelve Nigerian languages, ed. Elizabeth Dunstan. London: Longmans, 1969, 85–96.
*ZAPPA, C. 1907. Essai de dictionnaire Français-**Ibo** ou Français-**Ika**. Lyon: Société des Missions africaines.

SECTION VII

CLASS LANGUAGES

(a) TOGOLAND

*BERTHO, J. Trois îlots linguistiques du Moyen-Dahomey: le Tshummbuli, le Bazantché, et le **Basila**. Bull. IFAN, 13, 1951, 872–92.
—— Les dialectes du Moyen-Togo. Bull. IFAN, 14, 3, 1952, 1046–1107, [incl. **Akebu, Logba, Adélé, Lelemi-Lefana, Bowuri, Lolobi-Akpafu, Sătrokofi, Likpe, Avatime, Tafi, Nyăgbõ, Ahlõ, Akposo, Bashila**].
*CHRISTALLER, J. G. Die Sprachen des Togogebiets in kurzer allgemeiner Übersicht. Z. afr. u. ocean. Spr., 1, 1895, 5–8 [incl. bibl. for **Avatime**].
*—— Die **Adele**sprache im Togogebiet. Z. afr. u. ocean. Spr., 1, 1895, 16–33.
*—— Sprachproben vom Sudan zwischen Asante und Mittel-Niger (specimens of some Sudan languages). Z.A.S., 3, 1889–90, 107–32 [incl. **Avatime**].
DEBRUNNER, H. W. Vergessene Sprachen und Tricksprachen bei den Togorestvölkern. Afrika u. Übersee, 46, 1962, 109–17 [incl. **Nyangbo, Teteman (Lelemi-Lefana), Lolobi-Akpafu, Bowiri, Simai, Sitobi, Siko**].
*FUNKE, E. Die Stellung der Haussasprache unter den Sprachen **Togos**. Mitt. Sem. orient. Spr., 19 (3), 1916, 116–28, [incl. **Avatime**].
*—— Der Gottesname in den Togosprachen. Arch. f. Anthrop., n.F. 15, 3, 1917, 161–3.
*—— Original Texte aus den Klassensprachen in Mitteltogo. Z. Eingeb.-Spr., 10, 4, 1919–20, 261–313 [**Lipke, Akpafu, Akposo, Lefana, Avatime**].
HEINE, B. 1968. Die Verbreitung und Gliederung der Togorestsprachen. Pp. 311. Berlin: Dietrich Reimer. Kölner Beitrage (zur Afrikanistik, I), bibl., maps. [**Basila, Balemi, Logba, Adele, Lipke, Santrakofi, Akpafu-Lolobi, Avatime, Nyangbo-Tafi, Bowili, Ahlõ, Kposo, Kebu, Animere**.] [Reviewed in Africa, 40, 1, 1970, 95–6.]
HINTZE, U. 1959. Bibliographie der Kwa-Sprachen und der Sprachen der Togo-Restvölker. Berlin.
HÖFTMANN, HILDEGARD. Zur Grammatik des **Bowiri** (Voltaregion, Ghana). Mitt. Inst. Orientforsch., 12, 3, 1966, 199–207.
—— Die Nominalklassen im **Lelemi**. In: Neue afrikanistische Studien, ed. J. Lukas. Hamburg, 1966, 100–8.
*PLEHN, R. (ed. SEIDEL). Beiträge zur Kenntnis der Sprachen in Togo. Z. afr. u. ocean. Spr., 4, 1898, 201–86, [incl. **Avatime, Logba, Nyambo, Tafi, Ḷórada, Boviri, Akpafu, Santrekofi, Likpe, Aχolo, Akposo, Kebu, Atakpame, Boro**; Fetischsprache vom **Agu, Gbelle, Muatše**].
*WESTERMANN, D. H. Sprachstudien aus dem Gebiet der Sud.insprachen. I. Die **Lefana**sprache in Togo. Mitt. Sem. orient. Spr., 13, (3), 1910, 39–72.
*—— Die Sprachverhältnisse Togos. Pp. 13. Evang. Missions-Mag., 1912, No. 6.
*—— Vier Sprachen aus Mittel-togo. **Likpe, Bowili, Akpafu** und **Adele**, nebst einigen Resten der **Boro**sprache. Nach Aufnahmen von E. Funke und A. Mischlich. Mitt. Sem. orient. Spr., 23/25 (3), 1922, 1–59.
—— Die Togo-Restvölker und ihre Sprachen. Tribus, n.F. 4/5, 1954–5 (1956), 63–8 [alternative names of 19 languages].

(b) NIGERIA

GENERAL

VOORHOEVE, J., and DE WOLF, P. P. (ed.) 1969. **Benue-Congo** noun class systems. Pp. 198. West Afr. Ling. Soc. and Afrika Studie Centrum, University of Leiden.

WILLIAMSON, KAY. The **Benue-Congo** languages and Ijọ. In: Current trends in linguistics: Vol. 7, Linguistics in Sub-Saharan Africa. Bloomington: Indiana University, 1970.

—— and SHIMIZU, K. (ed.) 1968. **Benue-Congo** comparative word-list. Vol. 1. Pp. xxxiii + 233. Ibadan: West Afr. Ling. Soc.

1. CLASS LANGUAGES OF NORTHERN NIGERIA

(ANON.) Grammar of the **Tula** language. (N.P. Nigeria), by a missionary. Afr. u. Übersee, 39, 3, 1955, 101–18; 4, 149–68.

ARMSTRONG, R. G. A few more words of **Eloyi**, J.W.A.L., 1, 2, 1964, 60. [cf. MACKAY, H. D. below.]

BOUQUIAUX, L. A propos de numération: l'emploi du système décimal et du système duodécimal dans la langue **Birom** (Nigéria septentrional) Afr. Linguistica [Tervuren], Annales No. 42, 1962, 7–10.

—— Textes **birom** (Nigeria septentrional). Afr. Linguistica [Tervuren], Annales No. 42, 1962, 11–30.

—— A word list of **Aten** (Ganawuri). J.W.A.L., 1, 2, 1964, 5–25.

—— Le système des classes nominales dans quelques langues (**birom, ganawuri, anaguta, irigwe, kaje, rukuba**) appartenant au groupe 'Plateau' (Nigéria central) de la sous-famille Benoué-Congo. In: La classification nominale dans les langues négro-africaines. Paris: C.N.R.S., 1967, 133–56.

BRISTOW, W. M. Some notes on the **Jarawa** people near Jos, Plateau Province, Nigeria. Afr. u. Übersee, 37, 1952–3, 61–4.

—— **Birom** texts (Plateau Province, near Jos). Afr. u. Übersee, 37, 4, 1953, 145–50.

GERHARDT, L. Analytische und vergleichende Untersuchungen zu einigen zentralnigerianischen Klassensprachen. Afr u. Übersee, 51, 3, 1968, 161–98; 52, 1969, 23–57, 125–43, 207–42; 53, 1, 1969, 45–65. [**Kagoro, Kaje, Iregwe, Jarawa, Birom**.]

—— Über sprachliche Beziehungen auf dem zentralnigerianischen Plateau. In: Kongressbericht des 17. Deutschen Orientalistentages. Wiesbaden, 1970.

*HARRIS, P. G. Notes on the **Reshe** language. Afr. Stud., 5, 4, 1946, 221–42.

HOFFMANN, C. H. Zur Sprache der **Cibak**. Afrikanistische Studien, ed. J. Lukas. Berlin: Akademie-Verlag, 1955, 118–46.

—— The noun class system of central **Kambari**. J.A.L., 2, 2, 1963, 160–9.

—— A word-list of central **Kambari**. J.W.A.L., 2, 2, 1965, 7–31.

—— An outline of the **Dakarkari** noun class system and the relation between prefix and suffix noun class systems. In: La classification nominale dans les langues négro-africaines. Paris: C.N.R.S., 1967, 237–59.

JUNGRAITHMAYR, H. Class languages of Tangale-Waja District. Afr. u. Übersee, 52, 3/4, 1969, 161–206 [**Longuda, Waja, Tula, Cham, Dadiya, Awak, Burak**].

LUKAS, J., and WILLMS, A. Outline of the language of the **Jarawa** in Northern Nigeria (Plateau Province). Afr. u. Übersee, 45, 1/2, 1961, 1–66.

MACKAY, H. D. A word-list of **Eloyi**. J.W.A.L., 1, 1, 1964, 5–12.

MUKAROVSKY, H. G. Some reflexions on a Nigerian class language. Wiener Völkerkdl. Mitt., 6, 1/4, 1963, 65–83 ['**Jarawa**'].

ROWLANDS, E. C. Notes on some class languages of Northern Nigeria. A.L.S., 3, 1962, 71–83 [incl. dialects of **Dakarkari, Duka, Kambari, Kamuku**].

WOLFF, H. Sub-system typologies and area linguistics. Anth. Ling., 1, 7, 1959, 1–88 [incl. **Birom, 'Jarawa', Yergam, Fyam**].

—— Noun classes and concord in **Berom**. Actes du Second Colloque International de Linguistique Négro-Africaine. Univ. de Dakar, 1963, 86–96.

2. TIV

ARNOTT, D. W. The classification of verbs in **Tiv**. Bull. S.O.A.S., 21, 1, 1958, 111–33.
—— Downstep in the **Tiv** verbal system. A.L.S., 5, 1964, 34–51.
—— Some reflections on the content of individual classes in Fula and **Tiv**. In: La classification nominale dans les langues négro-africaines. Paris: C.N.R.S., 1967, 45–74.
—— **Tiv**. In: Twelve Nigerian languages, ed. Elizabeth Dunstan. London: Longmans, 1969, 143–51.
KIRK-GREENE, A. H. M. The linguistic statistics of Northern Nigeria: a tentative presentation A.L.R., 6, 1967, 75–101. [Kanuri, **Tiv**, Nupe, Yoruba, Hausa, Fulani and other languages.]
TERPSTRA, G. English-**Tiv** dictionary. Ibadan: Inst. of Afr. Stud. (Occ. Publ. 13).

3. EKOI

BYSTRÖM, K. Notes on the Ekparabong Clan. Orientalia Suecana, 3, 1954, 3–26.
CRABB, D. W. 1965. **Ekoid** Bantu languages of Ogoja. 1. Introduction, phonology and comparative vocabulary. Pp. xii+108, bibl. London: C.U.P. (W. Afr. language monograph series, 4).
—— The dia-phonemic principle in field work (**Ekoi** investigation). S.L.L.R., 4, 1965, 91–4.
—— Emergent diphthongs in three **Ekoid** Bantu languages. I.J.A.L., 36, 2, 1970.
EDMONDSON, EILEEN. Nouns of **Etung** classified by their singular-plural prefix pairs. In: Tagmemic and matrix linguistics applied to selected African languages, K. L. Pike. Ann Arbor, 1966, 206–26 (Appendix VI).
EDMONDSON, T. Preliminary description of some verb structures in **Etung**. In: Tagmemic and matrix linguistics applied to selected African languages, K. L. Pike. Ann Arbor, 1966, 227–44 (Appendix VII).
EDMONDSON, T., and BENDOR-SAMUEL, J. T. Tone paterns of **Etung**. J.A.L., 5, 1, 1966, 1–6.
*GOLDIE, H. 1874. Efik dictionary (see VIII, 1. Ibibio-Efik). [Introduction pp. xliii–xlviii contains vocabulaires of languages which may belong to this group.]
*JEFFREYS, M. D. W. A note on the **Ekoi** language. Z. Eingeb.-Spr., 35, 1950, 260–3.
PIKE, K. L. Tagmemic and matrix linguistics ... (see General) [incl. **Bette, Etung**].
*TALBOT, P. A. 1912. In the shadow of the bush [includes vocabularies of **Ekoi** and other languages of this group]. London: Heinemann.
*—— 1926. The peoples of Southern Nigeria. Vol. IV, Chap. 3, The languages. London: O.U.P.

4. IJO (Perhaps to be classified under Section VI, Kwa)

ẸFẸBQ, L. A. 1967. **Nembe** language made easy. Ibadan: Inst. of Afr. Stud. (Occ. Publ. 6).
FREEMAN, R. A., and WILLIAMSON, KAY. **Ijọ** proverbs. Research Notes [Ibadan], 1, 1967, 1–11.
HAIR, P. E. H. An ethnolinguistic inventory of the Lower Guinea Coast before 1700. A.L.R., 7, 1968, 47–73 [incl. **Ijɔ**].
KALIAI, M. H. I. 1964. **Nembe**-English dictionary. 2 vols. Pp. xii+267, 30s. Ibadan: Inst. of Afr. Stud.
ROWLANDS, E. C. Tone and intonation systems in Brass-Nembe **Ijaw**. A.L.S., 1, 1960, 137–54.
*TEPOWA, A. Notes on the (**Nembe**) Brass language. J. Afr. Soc., 4, 13, 1904, 117–33.
WILLIAMSON, KAY. The syntax of verbs of motion in **Ijọ**. J.A.L., 2, 2, 1963, 150–4.
—— 1965. A grammar of the Kolokuma dialect of **Ijọ**. Pp. vii+127. London: C.U.P. (West African languages monograph series, 2).
—— **Ijọ** dialects in the *Polyglotta Africana*. S.L.L.R., 5, 1966, 122–33, map.
—— Deep and surface structure in tone languages [with illustrations from **Ijọ**]. J.W.A.L., 5, 2, 1968, 77–82.
—— **Ijọ** [Kalabari, Kolokuma and Nembe]. In: Twelve Nigerian languages, ed. Elizabeth Dunstan. London: Longmans, 1969, 97–114.

WILLIAMSON, KAY. Some food plant names in the Niger Delta. I.J.A.L., 36, 2, 1970.
—— The Benue-Congo languages and **Ijo** . . . (see VII (b) General).
WOLFF, H. Sub-system typologies and area linguistics. Anth. Ling., 1, 7, 1959, 1-88 [incl. **Akassa, Ijo**].
—— Niger-delta languages I: classification. Anth. Ling., 1, 8, 1959, 32-53 [incl. **Ijo**].

5. OTHER

BAMGBOṢE, A. Nominal classes in **Mbe**. Afr. u. Übersee, 49, 1, 1966, 32-53.
—— Tense/aspect forms in **Mbe**. Research Notes [Ibadan], 1, 1967, 12-20.
—— Verbal classes in **Mbe**. Afr. u. Übersee, 50, 3, 1967, 173-93.
—— Notes on the phonology of **Mbe**. J.W.A.L., 4, 1, 1967, 5-11.
BARNWELL, KATHLEEN. Notes on the **Mbembe** clause system—a preliminary analysis. In: Tagmemic and matrix linguistics applied to selected African languages. K. L. Pike. Ann Arbor, 1966, 156-81 (Appendix I).
—— The noun class system in **Mbembe**. J.W.A.L., 6, 1, 1969, 51-8.
COOK, T. L. Notes on **Kòhûmónò** phonology. Research Notes [Ibadan], 2, 3, 1969.
KIRK-GREENE, A. H. M. The linguistic statistics of Northern Nigeria: a tentative presentation. A.L.R., 6, 1967, 75-101 [Kanuri, Tiv, Nupe, Yoruba, Hausa, Fulani and **other languages**].
PIKE, K. L. Tagmemic and matrix linguistics . . . (see General) [incl. **Agbo, Mbembe**].
REVILL, P. M. Preliminary report on paralinguistics in **Mbembe** (E. Nigeria). In: Tagmemic and matrix linguistics applied to selected African languages, K. L. Pike. Ann Arbor, 1966, 245-54 (Appendix VIII).
SPREDA, K. and JANICE. An interim workshop report on the phonological data of **Agbo**. In: Tagmemic and matrix linguistics applied to selected African languages. K. L. Pike. Ann Arbor, 1966, 255-84 (Appendix IX).
STANFORD, R. 1967. The **Bekwarra** language of Nigeria—a grammatical description. Ph.D. thesis (unpublished). London: S.O.A.S.
STANFORD, R., and L. 1969. The phonology of **Bekwarra**. Zaria: Inst. of Ling. and Ahmadu Bello Univ. Dept. of Lang. (Studies in Nigerian languages, No. 1.)
WINSTON, F. D. D. The nominal class system of **Lokə**. A.L.S., 3, 1962, 49-70.
—— Nigerian Cross River languages in the *Polyglotta Africana*. S.L.L.R., 3, 1964, 74-82; 4, 1965, 122-8.

(c) CAMEROONS

*ANKERMANN, B. Koelles **Mbe**-Sprache. Mitt. Sem. orient. Spr., 30 (3), 1927, 1-4.
BOT BA NJOCK, H. M. Le problème linguistique au Cameroun. Afr. et Asie [Paris], 73, 1966, 3-13.
CLEMENT, N. Lore and learning in **Mankon** tongue, Bamenda, W. Cameroon. Abbia, 9/10, 1965, 147-61.
*CRAWFORD, O. G. S. The writing of Njoya (Sultan Njoya's ideographic script for the **Bamoun** language). Antiquity, 9, 1936, 435-42, ill.
DALBY, D. The indigenous scripts of West Africa and Surinam: their inspiration and design. A.L.S., 9, 1968, 156-97 [incl. **Bamum** and **Bagam** scripts].
DELAFOSSE, M. Naissance et évolution d'un système d'écriture de création contemporaine. Rev. Ethnog. et Trad. populaires, 3, 9, 1922, 11-36 [**Bamoun**].
*DINKELACKER, E. Über Ortsnamen in Kamerun. Mitt. dtsch. Schutzgeb., 15, 1902, 173-80.
*DUGAST, IDELETTE. La langue secrète du Sultan Njoya. Ét. camerounaises, 3, 31/32, 1950, 231-60 [**Bamam**].
*—— Petit vocabulaire **bandem**. Ét. camerounaises, 4, 33/34, 1951, 60-6.
*—— et JEFFREYS, M. D. W. 1950. L'écriture des **Bamum**, sa naissance, son évolution, sa valeur phonétique, son utilisation. Pp. 109, bibl., ill., carte. Douala: Mém. IFAN (Sér. Populations, 4).

DUNSTAN, ELIZABETH. Conjugation in **Ngwe**. J.A.L., 2, 3, 1963, 235-43.
—— Towards a phonology of **Ngwe**. J.W.A.L., 1, 1, 1964, 39-42.
—— Tone on disyllabic nouns in **Ngwe**. J.W.A.L., 3, 1, 1966, 33-8.
—— 1966. Tone and concord in **Ngwe** nominals. Ph.D. thesis (unpublished). London: S.O.A.S.
—— Two **Ngwe** folktales. Research Notes [Ibadan], 1, 1967, 21-4.
FONLON, B. The language problem in Cameroon. Abbia, 22, 1969, 5-40.
*GENGENBACH, K. Märchen in der **Nyang**-Sprache. Z. Eingeb.-Spr., 29, 1, 1938, 1-37; 2, 1939, 119-45; 3, 216-33.
HAUDRICOURT, A. G. et THOMAS, J. M.-C. 1967. Le notation des langues: phonétique et phonologie. Pp. 166+2 discs. Paris: Inst. Géog. nat. et inst. d'ethn. [disc 2 includes **Bamiléké**].
*ITTMANN, J. **Nyang**-Märchen. Z. Eingeb.-Spr., 22, 1, 1931-32, 47-67.
*—— Sprichwörter der **Nyang**. Z. Eingeb.-Spr., 22, 2, 1932, 120-55; 3, 215-30; 4, 281-312.
*—— **Kenyan**, die Sprache der Nyang. Z. Eingeb.-Spr., 26, 1, 1935-36, 2-35; 2, 17-192; 3, 174-202; 4, 272-300.
*JEFFREYS, M. D. W. The death of a dialect (**Gbedegi**, British Cameroons—Bamenda division). Afr. Stud., 4, 1, 1945, 37-40.
—— The alphabet of Njoya. W. Afr. Rev., 23, 296, 1952, 428-30, 433.
KÄHLER-MEYER, EMMI. Sprachproben aus der Landschaft **Mbembe** im Bezirk Bamenda, Kamerun. Afr. u. Übersee, 37, 3, 1953, 109-18, map; 4, 151-82.
—— Beobachtungen am Konsonantenbestand der **Graslandsprachen** von Kamerun. Afr. u. Übersee, 39, 1, 1954, 7-18.
*MALCOLM, L. W. G. Short notes on the numerals of the **Eghap** and **Bali** tribes. Man, 20, 47, 1920, 89-91.
*—— Short notes on the syllabic writing of the **Eghap**, Central Cameroons. J. Afr. Soc., 20, 78, 1921, 127-9, bibl.
*—— Short notes on the personal names of the **Eghap**, Central Cameroons. J. Afr. Soc., 24, 93, 1924, 34-8.
*MEYER, EMMI. Das Problem der Verkehrssprachen von Tropisch-Afrika, insbes. von Kamerun. Mitt. geog. Ges. Hamburg, 48, 1944, 253-88.
NICOLAS, J. P. Couverture linguistique du pays dit **'Bamileke'**: présentation de deux cartes nouvelles de répartition. Bull. IFAN, 15, 4, 1953, 1633-41, cartes.
PAUVERT, J. 1953. Le problème de la lecture publique et de la culture populaire au Cameroun. Pp. ii+50. Annexe no. 1, Bibliographie; no. 2, Principales langues parlées au Cameroun. Yaoundé: Bureau d'Éduc. de Base et d'Éduc. des Adultes.
RICHARDSON, I. 1957. Linguistic survey of the Northern Bantu borderland. Vol. II. Pp. 95. London: O.U.P. for Int. Afr. Inst. [Reviewed in Afrika und Übersee, 43, 1959, 69-72.]
—— Some problems of language classification with particular reference to the North-West Bantu borderland. Africa, 25, 2, 1955, 161-9, map.
SCHMITT, A. 1963. Die **Bamum**-Schrift. 1. Text 2. Tebellen. 3. Urkunder. 3 vols. Leipzig: O. Harrassowitz.
STOLL, A. 1955. La tonétique des langues bantu et semi-bantu du Cameroun. Pp. 173, bibl. Douala: Centre IFAN Cameroun (Mém., 4). [incl. **Bafang, Ndoka, Dschang, Bandjoun, Bali, Bangante, Bamum**].
TAYOUMO, J. Notes sur le possessif en **bamendjou**. Camelang, 1, 1969, 58-72.
TISCHHAUSER, G. Kurze Worliste der Sprache von Bebedjato in der Landschaft **Mbembe**, Kamerun. Afr. u. Übersee, 38, 2, 1954, 69-72.
*VAN GENNEP, A. Une nouvelle écriture nègre: sa portée théorique. Rev. Ét. ethnog. et sociol., 1, 1908, 129-39 [**Bamum**].
VOORHOEVE, J. La classification nominale dans le **Bangangté**. J.A.L., 2, 3, 1963, 206-9.
—— The structure of the morpheme in Bamiléké. [**Bangangté**]. Lingua, 13, 4, 1965, 319-34.
—— Personal pronouns in Bamiléké. Lingua, 17, 4, 1967, 421-30 [**Bangangté**].
—— Noun classes in Bamiléké. Lingua, 21, 1968, 584-93 [**Ngwe, Bandjoun, Bangangté**].

VOORHOEVE, J. and DE WOLF, P. P. (ed.) 1969. **Benue-Congo** noun class systems. Pp. 198. West Afr. Ling. Soc. and Afrika Studie Centrum, Univ. of Leiden.

WILLIAMSON, KAY. The **Benue-Congo** languages and Ịjọ. In: Current trends in linguistics: Vol. 7, Linguistics in Sub-Saharan Africa. Bloomington: Indiana University. 1970.

—— and SHIMIZU, K. (ed.) 1968. **Benue-Congo** comparative word-list. Vol. I. Pp. xxxiii+233. Ibadan: West Afr. Ling. Soc.

SECTION VIII

NON-CLASS LANGUAGES

1. IBIBIO-EFIK

*ADAMS, R. F. G. Obɛri ɔkaimɛ: a new African language and script [Texts and tr. into **Efik** and English.] Africa, 17, 1, 1947, 24–34.

—— 1952, 1953 (3rd ed.). English-**Efik** dictionary. Efik-English dictionary. 2 vols. Pp. 161, 279. Liverpool: Philip.

AKPAYUN, O. A. 1962. A study of **Efik** for schools and colleges. Pp. viii+127. London: Nelson. [The greater part is written in Efik.]

BROSNAHAN, L. F. Outlines of the phonology of the Gokana dialect of **Ogoni**. J.W.A.L., 1, 1, 1964, 43–8.

—— A word-list of the Gokana dialect of **Ogoni**. J.W.A.L., 4, 2, 1967, 43–52.

COOK, T. L. **Efik**. In: Twelve Nigerian languages, ed. Elizabeth Dunstan. London: Longmans, 1969, 35–46.

—— and KOKO EYƆ ÌTA. 1969. The pronunciation of **Efik** for speakers of English. Pp. xxviii+204+7. Bloomington: Intensive Language Training Center, Indiana University.

DALBY, D. The indigenous scripts of West Africa and Surinam: their inspiration and design. A.L.S., 9, 1968, 156–97 [incl. Obɛri ɔkaimɛ and Nsibidi scripts].

ESSIEN, U., and COOK, T. L. 1966. A brief introduction to **Efik**. Enugu: U.S. Peace Corps.

HAIR, P. E. H. An ethnolinguistic inventory of the Lower Guinea Coast before 1700. A.L.R., 7, 1968, 47–73 [incl. **Ibibio**].

HOUIS, M. Schèmes et fonctions tonologiques (Sosso, Bobo, Mende, **Efik**). Bull. IFAN, 18 (B), 3/4, 1956, 335–68.

MUKAROVSKY, H. G. Some reflexions on a Nigerian class language. Wiener völkerkdl. Mitt., 6, 1/4, 1963, 65–83 [incl. vocab. of **Efik**].

SIMMONS, D. C. Specimens of **Efik** folklore. Folklore, 66, 1955, 417–24.

—— Erotic **Ibibio** tone riddles. Man, 56, 78, 1956, 79–82.

—— **Oron** verb morphology. Africa, 26, 3, 1956, 250–64.

—— **Efik** riddles. Nigerian Field, 21, 4, 1956, 168–71.

—— **Ibibio** verb morphology. Afr. Stud., 16, 1, 1957, 1–19.

—— **Ibibio** topical ballads. Man, 60. 70, 1960, 58–9.

—— Tonal rhyme in **Efik** poetry. Anth. Ling., 2, 6, 1960, 1–10.

—— **Ibibio** tone riddles. Nigerian Field, 25, 3, 1960, 132–4.

—— **Oron** noun morphology. J.W.A.L., 2, 2, 1965, 33–7.

*WADDELL, H. M. 1849. A vocabulary of the **Efik** or Old Calabar language, with prayers and lessons. [2nd ed. rev. and enlarged]. Pp. vi+88. Edinburgh.

WELMERS, W. E. **Efik** grammar. Ibadan: Inst. of Afr. Stud. (Occ. Publ. 12).

WILLIAMSON, KAY. Some food plant names in the Niger Delta. I.J.A.L., 36, 2, 1970 [incl. **Ogoni**].

WINSTON, F. D. D. The 'mid tone' in **Efik**. A.L.S., 1, 1960, 185–92.

—— Nigerian Cross River languages in the *Polyglotta Africana*. S.L.L.R., 3, 1964, 74–82; 4, 1965, 122–8.

—— Some Bantu-like features of **Efik** structure. A.L.S., 11, 1970, 417–35.

WOLFF, H. Sub-system typologies and area linguistics. Anth. Ling., 1, 7, 1959, 1–88 [incl. **Abua, Ogbia, Odual, Kana, Gokana, Eleme**].
—— Niger-delta languages I: classification. Anth. Ling., 1, 8, 1959, 32–53 [incl. **Ogoni, Abuan**].
—— Synopsis of the **Ogoni** languages. J. A.L., 3, 1, 1964, 38–51.

2. OTHER LANGUAGES

ARMSTRONG, R. G. The Idoma-speaking peoples: language (incl. **Idoma, Iyala, Etulo, Afu, Egede, Akweya-Yachi, Utonkon-Effium**). In: Peoples of the Niger-Benue confluence (Ethnographic survey of Africa, Western Africa, Part X). London: International African Institute, 1955, 91–3, 128, 134–5, 136, 141, 148, 151.
—— The subjunctive in **Idoma**. J.A.L., 2, 2, 1963, 155–9.
—— The **Idoma** verb. Actes du Second Colloque International de Linguistique Négro-Africaine, Univ. de Dakar, 1963, 127–57.
—— Notes on **Etulo**. J.W.A.L., 1, 2, 1964, 57–60.
—— **Yala** (Ikom): a terraced-level language with three tones. J.W.A.L., 5, 1, 1968, 49–58, bibl.
*BAUDELAIRE, H. La numération de 1 à 10 dans les dialectes habé de Garoua, Guider, Poli et Rey Bouba. Bull. Soc. Ét. camerounaises, 5, 1944, 23–31 [incl. **Depa, Duru, Doayo, Fali, Galké, Kali, Laka, Mambay, Mbum, Mon-Non, Mundang, Panon, Sari**].
FLØTTUM, S. 1957. **Mbum**-English vocabulary. Pp. 70. Tibati, Cameroun: Mission Protestante Norvégienne.
HAGEGE, C. (n.d.) Description phonologique du **mbum**. BSELAF, No. 5, Paris.
—— La traduction des écritures en langue **mbum**. J.W.A.L., 5, 1, 1968, 97–106.
*JUDD, A. S. Notes on the language of the **Arago** or Alago tribe of Nigeria. J. Afr. Soc., 23, 89, 1923, 30–8.
†JUNGRAITHMAYR, H. On the ambiguous position of the **Angas**. J.A.L., 2, 3, 1963, 272–8.
†—— Texte und Sprichwörter im **Angas** von Kabwir (Nordnigerien). Afr. u. Übersee, 48, 1, 1964, 17–35; 2, 1965, 114–27.
†—— Die Sprache der **Sura** (Maghavul) in Nordnigerien. Afr. u. Übersee, 47, 1/2, 1964, 8–89; 3-4, 204–20.
†—— Internal A in **Ron** plurals. J.A.L., 4, 2, 1965, 102–7.
†—— Materialen zur Kenntnis des **Chip, Montol, Gerka** und **Burrum** (Südplateau, Nordnigerien). Afr. u. Übersee, 48, 3, 1965, 161–81.
†—— Die Laryngale h und ' im **Scha** (Süd-Plateau, Nordnigerien). Afr. u. Übersee, 49, 3, 1966, 169–73.
†—— Zur Bildung der Aspekstämme in den **Ron**-Sprachen. In: Neue afrikanistische Studien, ed. J. Lukas. Hamburg, 1966, 117–25.
†—— The Hamito-Semitic present-habitative verb stem in **Ron** and Mubi. J.W.A.L., 5, 2, 1968, 71–6.
†—— A comparative word-list of the **Ron** languages (Southern Plateau, Northern Nigeria). Africana Marburgensia, 1, 2, 1968, 3–12.
†—— Hausa, **Ron, Angas**: a comparative analysis of their 'aspect' systems. Afr. u. Übersee, 52, 1, 1968, 15–22.
†—— Ancient Hamito-Semitic remnants in the Central Sudan. A.L.R., 7, 1968, 16–22, [Ron languages (**Fyer, Bokkos, Daffo-Butwra, Sha, Kulere**)].
LACROIX, P. F. Note sur la langue **galke** (^{n}dáí). J.A.L., 1, 2, 1962, 94–121, map.
MUKAROVSKY, H. G. Some reflexions on a Nigerian class language. Wiener völkerkdl. Mitt., 6, 1/4, 1963, 65–83 [incl. vocab. of **Idoma**].
NETTING, R. A word-list of **Kofyar** [N. Nigeria]. Research Notes [Ibadan], 2, 1967, 1–36.
PERRIN, M. J., and HILL, M. V. 1969. **Mambila** (parler d'Atta): description phonologique. Univ. Féd. de Cameroun, Section de Ling. Appl. and Inst. of Ling.
*VON DUISBURG, A. Untersuchungen über die **Mbum**-Sprache in Adamaua. Mitt. Sem. orient. Spr., 28 (3), 1925, 132–74.

WOLFF, H. Sub-system typologies and area linguistics. Anth. Ling., 1, 7, 1959, 1–88 [incl. **Idoma, Angas, Sura, Ankwe, Chamba, Mumuye, Jukun**].

† These items would probably be more appropriately included in Section X, but are listed here since the languages appear in Chapter VIII of the Handbook.

Section IX

THE CHADIC LANGUAGES

(This section covers only the languages listed as Chadic in Section IX of the Handbook. Those included in Greenberg's 'Chad languages', but classified in the Handbook as Chado-Hamitic, are covered by Section X below.)

*BAUDELAIRE, H. La numération de 1 à 10 dans les dialectes Habe de Garoua, Guider, Poli et Rey Bouba. Bull. Soc. Ét. camerounaises, 5, 1944, 23–31 [incl. **Bata, Gidar, Gude, Gujuguju, Njeny**].

BÜCHNER, H. Vokabulare der Sprachen in und um **Gava** (Nordnigerien). Afr. u. Übersee, 48, 1, 1964, 36–45.

CARNOCHAN, J. The coming of the Fulani: a **Bachama** oral tradition. Bull. S.O.A.S., 30, 3, 1967, 622–33, map.

—— Grammatical categories of the verbal piece in **Bachama**. A.L.S., 11, 1970, 81–112.

*DAUZATS, A. Quelques notes de toponymie du Nord-Cameroun. Bull. Soc. Ét. camerounaises, 4, 1943, 47–60 [incl. **Guiziga, Mandara**].

HODGE, C. T. Afroasiatic pronoun problems. I.J.A.L., 35, 4, 1969, 366–76 [incl. reference to **Margi**].

HOFFMANN, C. F. 1955. Untersuchungen zur Struktur und sprachlichen Stellung des **Bura**. Dissertation, Hamburg.

—— Zur Sprache der **Cibak**. Afrikanistische Studien, ed. J. Lukas. Hamburg, 1955, 118–46.

—— 1963. A grammar of the **Margi** language. Pp. viii+287. London: O.U.P. for Int. Afr. Inst. [Reviewed in J.A.L., 3, 3, 1964, 306–8.]

—— A **Higi** folktale. Research Notes [Ibadan], 1, 1967, 29–34.

KIRK-GREENE, A. H. M. The linguistic statistics of Northern Nigeria: a tentative presentation. A.L.R., 6, 1967, 75–101.

LAVER, J. D. M. Some observations on alveolar and dental consonant-articulations in **Higi**. J.W.A.L., 2, 1, 1965, 59–61, ill.

*LUKAS, J. Wandala-Gruppe. 27. **Wandala**. In: Zentralsudanische Studien, 1937, 115–126.

—— Das **Hitkalanci**, eine Sprache um Gwoza (Nordostnigerie .). Afr. u. Übersee, 48, 2, 1965, 81–114.

—— Nunation in afrikanischen Sprachen. Anthropos, 63, 1968, 97–114 [incl. **Matakam**].

—— 1970. Studien zur Sprache der **Gisiga** (Nordkamerun). Pp. 250. Hamburg (Afrikanistische Forschungen Band IV).

MIRT, H. Zur Phonologie des **Mandara**. In: Verhandlungsberichte des XVII. Deutschen Orientalistentages. Wiesbaden, 1970.

—— Zur Morphologie des Verbalcomplexes im **Mandara**. Afr. u. Übersee, 53, 1970.

MOUCHET, J. Vocabulaires comparatifs de sept parlers du Nord-Cameroun. Ét. camerounaises, 6, 41/42, 1953, 137–205, carte [**Matakam, Mofu, Mboku, Hurza, Uzam, Mada, Zəlgwa**].

—— Grammaire et vocabulaire comparés du dialecte **Daba** (région de Guider, Nord Cameroun). Maroua, N. Cameroun: Mouchet.

—— 1967. Le parler **daba**: esquisse grammaticale précédée d'une note sur l'ethnie daba, suivie de lexiques daba-français et français-daba. Pp. 226, bibl., map. Yaoundé (Recherches et Ét. camerounaises, 10).

NEWMAN, P. A word-list of **Tera**. J.W.A.L., 1, 2, 1964, 33–50.
—— A brief note on the **Maha** language. J.W.A.L., 2, 1, 1965, 57–8.
—— Ideophones from a syntactic point of view [Hausa and **Tera**]. J.W.A.L., 5, 2, 1968, 107–17.
—— and MA, ROXANA. Comparative **Chadic**: phonology and lexicon. J.A.L., 5, 3, 1966, 218–51, bibl., map.
PASCAL, A. Conte **daba** (dialecte de Mandama). Camelang [Yaounde], 2, 1969, 12–24.
RAPP, E. L. Pronomen and Verbum in **Glavda** und **Yaghwatadaxa** in den nordwestlichen Mandarabergen Nordostnigeriens. In: Neue afrikanistische Studien, ed. J. Lukas. Hamburg, 1966, 208–17, bibl.
—— and BENZING, BRIGITTA. 1968. Dictionary of the **Glavdá** language. Pp. 131. Frankfurt a. M.: Bible Soc.
—— and MÜHLE, CHRISTRAUD. 1969. Dictionary of the **Glavdá** language. Part 2. English-Glavdi. Pp. 133–220. Frankfurt a. M.: Bible Society.
SCHEYTT, W. Proben der Sprache der **Yaghwatadaxa** in Gavva (Nordostnigerien) [introd. by J. Lukas]. Afr. u. Übersee, 50, 1/2, 1967, 4–34.
TERRY, R. R. Chadic. In: Current trends in linguistics: Vol. 7, Linguistics in Sub-Saharan Africa, ed. Thomas A. Sebeok. Bloomington: Indiana University, 1970. [Covers both the Chadic and Chado-Hamitic sections of the Handbook.]
WOLFF, H. Sub-system typologies and area linguistics. Anth. Ling., 1, 7, 1959, 1–88 [incl. **Bura-Pabir, Margi, Kilba, Higi, Bachama**].

SECTION X

THE CHADO-HAMITIC LANGUAGES

GENERAL

JUNGRAITHMAYR, H. Zum Bau der Aspekte im Westtschadohamitischen. Z.D.M.G., 116/2, 1966, 227–34.
TERRY, R. R. Chadic. In: Current trends in linguistics: Vol. 7, Linguistics in Sub-Saharan Africa, ed. Thomas A. Sebeok. Bloomington: Indiana University, 1970, [incl. Chado-Hamitic languages].
NEWMAN, P., and MA, ROXANA. Comparative Chadic: phonology and lexicon. J.A.L., 5, 3, 1966, 218–51, bibl., map [incl. Chado-Hamitic languages].

1. HAUSA

ABRAHAM, R. C. 1959. The language of the **Hausa** people. Pp. xii+236. London: University of London Press.
—— 1959. Hausa literature and the **Hausa** sound system. Pp. 186. University of London Press.
ALOYADE, B. A preliminary bibliography of Nigerian languages: Part one—**Hausa**, Yoruba and Igbo. African Notes [Ibadan], 5, 1, 1968, special supplement, i–xxvi.
AMES, D. W. 1968. The music of Nigeria: **Hausa** music, records 1 and 2 [commentary in English, French, German]. Pp. 8, 9, ill., w. records BM 30 L 2306, 2307. Kassel: Barenreiter-Musicaphon. (Unesco collection: an anthology of African music, 6 and 7.)
ARNOTT, D. W. 'The song of the rains': a **Hausa** poem by Na'ibi S. Wali. A.L.S., 9, 1968, 120–47.
*BAIKIE, W. B. 1861. Observations on the **Háusa** and Fulfúlde languages. Pp. 29. London.
*BARTH, H. Vocabularies of the **Hausa** and Emghedesia languages. J. Roy. Geog. Soc., 21, 1851.

*Basset, R. Contes **haoussas**. Mélusine, 3, 19, 1886, 441–5.
*—— 1898, 1902, 1909. Rapport sur les études berbères et **haoussa**, 1891–7, 1897–1902, 1902–08. 3 vols. Paris.
Brauner, S. Bemerkungen zum entlehnten Wortschatz des **Hausa**. Mitt. Inst. Orientforschung, 10, 1964, 103–7.
—— and Ashiwaju, M. 1965. Lehrbuch der **Hausa**-Sprache. Pp. 177. Leipzig: VEB Verlag Enzyklopädie (Lehrbücher Studium orient. u. afr. Sprachen, 10). [Reviewed in Africa, 37, 2, 1967, 248.]
*Brooks, W. H., and Nott, L. H. (tr.) 1903. Baru na Abubuan **Hausa** [by Ibrahim], with translation, vocabulary and notes. Pp. 56. London: O.U.P.
Campbell, M. J. 1964. A word list of government and local government terms: English-**Hausa**. Pp. 23. Zaria: Ahmadu Bello Univ.
*Carnochan, J. Gemination in **Hausa**. In: Studies in linguistic analysis (special volume of the Philological Society). Oxford: Blackwell, 1957, 149–81.
—— Glottalization in **Hausa**. In: Transactions of the Philological Society. Oxford: Blackwell, 1962, 78–109.
*Charlton, Capt. 1908. A **Hausa** reading book, containing a collection of texts . . . with transliterations. Pp. 83 +45. London: O.U.P.
*Cohen, M. La question de la parenté du **Haoussa** (Soudan Français). GLECS, 2, 1934, 1–3.
*Crabtree, W. A. The Ntu element in **Hausa**. Bibliotheca africana, 2, 1, 1926, 208–28.
Dalby, D. The noun *gàrii* in **Hausa**: a semantic study. J.A.L., 3, 3, 1964, 273–305.
*Dirr, A. 1895. Manuel pratique de la langue **haoussa**, langue commerciale du Soudan, avec exercices gradués, d'un vocabulaire haoussa-français et d'un vocabulaire systématique. Pp. ii +140. Paris: Leroux.
*Edgar, F. Litafi na Tatsuniyoy na **Hausa**. 1911. 3 vols. Pp. xviii +435; xvi +463; xvi +464. Belfast: W. Erskine Mayne.
El-Masri, F. H., et al. Sifofin Shehu: an autobiography and character study of 'Uthmān b. Fūdi in verse. Research Bull. [Centre Arabic Doc., Ibadan], 2, 1, 1966, 1–36.
*Feyer, Ursula. **Haussa** als Verkehrssprache. Z. Phonetik u. Sprachwiss, 1, 3, 1947, 108–29
Fichman, V. S. Materialy k izuceniju glagola v jazyke **Hausa**. [Materials for the analysis of the Hausa verb.] Afrikanskij etnogr. sbornik [Moscow], 5, 1963, 222–58.
Frajzyngier, Z. An analysis of intensive forms in **Hausa** verbs. Rocznik orientalistyczny [Warsaw], 29, 2, 1965, 31–51. [See: Africana Bull., 5, 1966, 164–5.]
Galadanci, M. K. M. 1969. The simple nominal phrase in **Hausa**. Ph.D. thesis (unpublished). London: S.O.A.S.
*Galtier, Le pronom-affixe de la première personne du singulier en **Haoussa**. Actes 11e Congr. Orientalistes 1898, 1899, sect. 5, 209–13.
Gidley, C. G. B. *Mantanfas*—a study in oral tradition. A.L.S., 6, 1965, 32–51.
—— *'Yankamanci*: the craft of the **Hausa** comedians. A.L.S., 8, 1967, 52–81, ill.
—— *Maiwutsiya*: the comet myth among the **Hausa**. A.L.S., 11, 1970, 183–90.
Goerner, Margaret, et al. 1966. Two essays on Arabic loan words in **Hausa**. Pp. ii +32. Zaria: Ahmadu Bello Univ. Dept. of Languages. (Occ. Pap. 7.)
Gouffé, C. Observations sur le degré causatif dans un parler **haoussa** du Niger. J.A.L., 1, 2, 1962, 182–200.
—— La lexicographie du **Haoussa** et le préalable phonologique. J.A.L., 4, 3, 1965, 191–210.
—— A propos de la phrase relative et de la phrase nominale en berbère et en **haoussa**. GLECS, 10, 1963–6, 35–54.
—— Noms d'objets 'ronds' en **haoussa**. GLECS, 10, 1963–6, 104–13.
—— Les problèmes de l'aspect en **haoussa**. GLECS, 10, 1963–6, 151–65; 11, 1966/7, 29–67, bibl.
—— 'Manger' et 'boire' en **haoussa**. Rev. École nat. langues orient. [Paris], 3, 1966, 77–111.
—— Problèmes de toponymie **haoussa**: les noms de villages de la région de Maradi (République du Niger). Rev. int. onomastique [Paris], 19, 2, 1967, 95–127.
—— A propos de la notation des tons en **haoussa**. Bull. IFAN, 29 (B), 3/4, 1967, p. 922.

GOUFFÉ, C. Deux notes grammaticales sur le parler **haoussa** de Dogondoutchi (République du Niger). Afr. u. Übersee, 52, 1, 1968-9, 1-14.
*GOWERS, W. F. 1919 (revised ed. 1930). Notes on Muhammadan law in Northern Nigeria (being extracts mainly from the Risalah of Abu Muhammadu ibn Abu Zayd, translated into **Hausa**). Pp. 32. Lagos: Govt. Printer.
*GREENBERG, J. H. Some problems in **Hausa** phonology. Language, 17, 1941, 316-23.
*—— Arabic loanwords in **Hausa**. Word [New York], 3, 1/2, 1947, 86-97.
—— Linguistic evidence for the influence of the Kanuri on the **Hausa**. J. Afr. Hist., 1, 2, 1960, 205-212.
—— An Afro-Asiatic pattern of gender and number agreement. J.A.O.S., 80, 1960, 317 ff.
GREGERSEN, E. A. Some competing analyses in **Hausa**. J.A.L., 6, 1, 1967, 42-57.
—— Linguistic seriation as a dating device for loanwords, with special reference to West Africa. A.L.R., 6, 1967, 102-8.
—— The palatal consonants in **Hausa**: internal reconstruction and historical inference. J.A.L., 6, 2, 1967, 170-84.
*HARRIS, P. G. Some conventional **Hausa** names. Man, 31, 265, 1931, 272-4.
HAUDRICOURT, A. G., et THOMAS, JACQUELINE, M.-C. 1967. La notation des langues: phonetique et phonologie. Paris, Institut Géographique National et Institut d'Ethnologie. Pp. v+166, bibl. [avec disques 31-4), [incl. **Hausa**].
HISKETT, M. The 'Song of Bagauda': a **Hausa** king list and homily in verse. Bull. S.O.A.S., 27, 3, 1964, 540-67; 28, 1, 1965, 112-35; 28, 2, 1965, 363-85.
—— The historical background to the naturalization of Arabic loan-words in **Hausa**. A.L.S., 6, 1965, 20-6.
—— The Arab star calendar and planetary system in **Hausa** verse. Bull. S.O.A.S., 30, 1, 1967, 158-76.
—— **Hausa**. iii Hausa Literature. In: Encyclopedia of Islam (new edition). Leiden: Brill, 280-3.
—— 1969. **Hausa** Islamic verse: its sources and development prior to 1920. Ph.D. thesis (unpublished). London: S.O.A.S.
—— Mamman Konni: an eccentric poet and holy man from Bodinga. A.L.S., 11, 1970, 211-29.
*HODGE, C. T. Morphene alternants and the noun phrase in **Hausa**. Language, 21, 2, 1945, 87-91.
*—— 1947. An outline of **Hausa** grammar. Pp. 61. Suppl. to Language, J. Ling. Soc. Amer.
—— **Hausa**-Egyptian establishment. Anthr. Ling., 8, 1, 1966, 40-57.
—— Afroasiatic pronoun problems. I.J.A.L., 35, 4, 1969, 366-76 [incl. reference to **Hausa**].
—— and HAUSE, HELEN E. **Hausa** tone. J.A.O.S., 64, 2, 1944, 51-2.
—— and UMARU, I. 1963. **Hausa** basic course. Pp. xx+399. Washington, D.C.: Foreign service Inst.
HOFFMANN, C., and SCHACHTER, P. **Hausa**. In: Twelve Nigerian languages, ed. Elizabeth Dunstan. London: Longmans, 1969, 73-84.
HOFFMANN, INGE. Das Verhältnis der Langvokale zu den Kurzvokalen im **Hausa**. Afr. u. Übersee, 48, 3, 1965, 202-11.
HOWEIDY, A. 1953. Concise **Hausa** grammar. Pp. xii+232. Wheatley, Oxford: G. Ronald.
HUGOT, P. 1957 (1er éd. 1953). Cours élémentaire de **hausa**. Pp. 77 (roneo). Paris: Éd. Peyronnet pour le Centre des Hautes Études d'Administration Musulmane (Langues et dialectes d'Outre-Mer, 1).
JUNGRAITHMAYR, H. **Hausa**, Ron, Angas: a comparative analysis of their 'aspect' systems. Afr. u. Übersee, 52, 1, 1968, 15-22.
KAPELINSKI, F. J. 1965. Observations on phonetic interference in learning English and French in Nigeria. Pp. 15. Zaria: Ahmadu Bello Univ. Department of Languages (Occ. Pap. 4).
KING, A. V. A *boòrií* liturgy from Katsina (introduction and *Kíráarìi* texts). A.L.S., 7, 1966, 105-25; 7 (suppl.), 1967, 1-157.

KING, A. V. 1969. Music at the Court of Katsina—*gángúnaà* and *kàakàakíi*. Ph.D. thesis (unpublished). London: S.O.A.S.
—— and IBRAHIM, R. 'The song of the rains': metric values in performance. A.L.S., 9, 1968, 148–55.
KIRK-GREENE, A. H. M. Neologisms in **Hausa**: a sociological approach. Africa, 33, 1, 1963, 25–44.
—— A preliminary survey of neologisms in **Hausa**. Actes du Second Colloque International de Linguistique Négro-Africaine, Université de Dakar, 1963, 204–9.
—— The **Hausa** language board. Afr. u. Übersee, 47, 1964, 187–203.
—— 1964. A preliminary inquiry into **Hausa** onomatology: three studies in the origins of personal, title and place names. Pp. iv+56. Zaria: Inst. of Admin., in cooperation with Graduate School of Public and Int. Affairs, Univ. Pittsburgh, and U.S. Agency for Int. Development.
—— 1966. (tr. and annotated). **Hausa** ba dabo ba ne: a collection of 500 proverbs. Pp. xv+84. Ibadan: O.U.P.
—— The vocabulary and determinants of schoolboy slang in Northern Nigeria. [Frequent reference to **Hausa**.] J.A.L., 5, 1, 1966, 7–33.
—— The linguistic statistics of Northern Nigeria: a tentative presentation. A.L.R., 6, 1967, 75–101 [incl. **Hausa**].
—— The meaning of place names in Hausaland. Bull. IFAN, 31 (B), 1, 1969, 264–78.
—— and ALIYU, Y. 1967. A modern **Hausa** reader. Pp. 143. London: Univ. London Press.
KORSHUNOVA, G. P. Prilagatel'nyye yazyka Khausa [**Hausa** adjectives]. Narody Azii i Afriki [Moscow], 1, 1966, 129–32.
KRAFT, C. H. 1963. A study of **Hausa** syntax. 3 vols. 1 Structure. 2. Function words. 3. Texts. Hartford Seminary Foundation, Dept. of Linguistics.
—— A new study of **Hausa** syntax. J.A.L., 3, 1, 1964, 66–74.
—— The morpheme *nà* in relation to a broader classification of **Hausa** verbals. J.A.L., 3, 3, 1964, 231–40.
—— and ABUBAKAR, S. 1965. An introduction to spoken **Hausa**. Pp. 408, also tape and workbook. Michigan State Univ., Afr. Studies Center. [Reviewed in Afr. Stud., Bull., 9, 1, 1966, p. 90.]
KRIEGER, K. Aus dem Leben eines **Hausa**. In: Neue afrikanistische Studien, ed. J. Lukas. Hamburg, 1966, 166–72.
LAPTUKHIN, V. V. 1965. O nekotorikh razlichiakh v sovremennoi leksike dialektov **Hausa** Nigerii i Nigeru [On some differences in modern vocabulary of the dialects of the Hausa language in Nigeria and Niger]. Afrikanskaya Filologia, Moscow State University.
*LE ROUX, J. M. 1886. Essai de dictionnaire français-**haoussa** et haoussa-français, précédé d'un essai de grammaire de la langue haoussa parlée par les nègres du Soudan. Pp. xiv+330. Alger: Jourdan.
LESLAU, W. A prefix ḥ in Egyptian, modern South Arabian and **Hausa**. Africa, 32, 1, 1962, 65–8.
*LIPPERT, J. Sudanica. Die Monatsnamen in der **Haussa**sprache. Mitt. Sem. orient. Spr., 3 (3), 1900, 198–207.
*—— **Haussa**-Märchen. Mitt. Sem. orient. Spr., 8 (3), 1905, 223–50.
*—— Über die Stellung der **Haussa**sprache unter den afrikanischen Sprachgruppen. Mitt. Sem. orient. Spr., 9 (3), 1906, 334–44.
LUKAS, J. Über die Verwendung der Partikel *sai* im **Haussa**. Afrikanistische Studien, ed. J. Lukas. Hamburg, 1955, 108–17.
—— Der II. Stamm des Verbums im **Hausa**. Afr. u. Übersee, 47, 3/4, 1964, 162–86.
—— **Hausa**, eine umfassende Verkehrssprache für Westafrika. Neues Afr., 6, 8, 1964, 275–9.
—— Nunation in afrikanischen Sprachen. Anthropos, 63, 1968, 97–114 (incl. **Hausa**).
*MACDONELL, I. H. 1943. Notes on colloquial **Hausa** for beginners. Pp. 42. Gold Coast: Govt. Printer.

*Marre, E. C. 1901. Die Sprache der **Hausa**. Grammatik, Übungen und Chrestomathie, sowie hausanisch-deutsches und deutsch-hausanisches Wörterverzeichnis. Pp. x+176. Wien: Hartleben.

Maxwell, J. L., and Forshey, E. M. 1966. Yau da gobe: a **Hausa** grammar for beginners. Pp. 192. Jos: Sudan Interior Mission.

Meinhof, C. **Hausa**. In: Die Sprachen d. Hamiten, 1912, 58–86.

*—— Ein magisches Quadrat auf einem **Haussa**-Amulett. Z. Eingeb.-Spr., 14, 1924, 224–6, 315.

*Merrick, G. 1905. **Hausa** proverbs. Pp. viii+113. London: Kegan Paul.

*—— Notes on **Hausa** and Pidgin English. J. Afr. Soc., 8, 31, 1909, 303–7.

*Miller, W. R. 1907. **Hausa**-English vocabulary.

*Mischlich, A. Über Sitten und Gebrauche der **Hausa**. M.S.O.S., 11, 1908.

*—— 1914. Metoula-Sprachführer. **Hausa**. Pp. 112. Berlin: Langenscheidt. [Details of original entry amended.]

*—— Religiöse und weltliche Gesänge der Mohammedaner aus dem Sudan [von Imam Umaru]. Afrika [Berlin], 2, 3, 1942, 129–98.

Muhammad, L. Comments on John N. Paden's 'A survey of Kano **Hausa** poetry'. Kano Studies, 2, 1966, 44–52.

—— 1968. **Hausa** in the modern world. Pp. vii+38. Zaria: Ahmadu Bello University, Dept. of Languages (Occ. Pap. 8).

Murphy, J. D. 1969. An inductive reader of newspaper **Hausa**. Bloomington: Indiana Univ. Ling. Circle.

*Newman, F. W. 1843. Remarks on the **Hausa** language, based upon the vocabulary of the same, with grammatical elements, by the Rev. J. F. Schoen.

Newman, P. Ideophones from a syntactic point of view (**Hausa** and Tera). J.W.A.L., 5, 2, 1968, 107–17.

—— Feminine plurals in Hausa: a case of syntactic overcorrection. J.A.L., 6, 3, 1967, 245–8.

Nuttall, Christine E. 1956. Phonological interference of **Hausa** with English. Pp. iv+23. Zaria: Ahmadu Bello Univ. Dept. of Languages (Occ. Pap. 5).

Ol'derogge, D. A. Hamitskaya problema v afrikanistike [Hamitic problems in Africanist studies]. Sovietskaya Etnografia, 3, 1949, 156–70.

—— 1954. Jazyk Khausa [A **Hausa** grammar and reader with a Hausa-Russian vocabulary]. Pp. 170, endpaper maps. Leningrad: Leningradsky Gosudarstvenn'y Ordena Lenina Universitet.

—— 1963. Khausa-russkiy Slovar' [**Hausa**-Russian dictionary]. Pp. 460. Moscow: State publ. house of for. and nat. dictionaries.

Osnickaja, N. A. Imennoje slovoobrazovanije v jazyke Khausa [Noun-formation in the **Hausa** language]. Afrikanskij etnogr. sbornik [Moscow], 4, 1962, 221 ff.

Paden, J. N. A survey of Kano **Hausa** poetry. Kano Studies, 1, 1965, 33–39.

—— Letter of reply to L. Muhammad's comments on 'Kano **Hausa** poetry'. Kano Studies, 2, 1966, 53–5.

—— Language problems of national integration in Nigeria: the special position of **Hausa**. In: Language problems of developing nations, Fishman, J. A., et al. New York, 1968, 199–213.

Parsons, F. W. The 'mutable' verb in **Hausa**. In: Atken des XXIII Internationalen Orientalisten-Kongresses, Cambridge, 1954.

—— Abstract nouns of sensory quality and their derivatives in **Hausa**. Afrikanistische Studien, ed. J. Lukas. Hamburg, 1955, 373–404.

—— Case in **Hausa**. In: Akten des XXIV. Internationalen Orientalisten-Kongresses, Munich, 1957. Wiesbaden: Franz Steiner, 1959, 707–10.

—— 1960. Tsarin laifuffuka da hukuncinsu, 1959. (**Hausa** translation of the Penal Code of Northern Nigeria, with translator's preface.) Pp. 151. Kaduna: Govt. Printer.

—— The verbal system in **Hausa**. Afr. u. Übersee, 44, 1, 1960, 1–36.

—— An introduction to gender in **Hausa**. A.L.S., 1, 1960, 117–36.

PARSONS, F. W. The operation of gender in **Hausa**: the personal pronouns and genitive copula. A.L.S., 2, 1961, 100–24.
—— Some observations on the contact between **Hausa** and English. In: Symposium on Multingualism, Brazzaville, 1962. CCTA/CSA publication No. 87, 197–204.
—— Further observations on the 'causative' grade of the verb in **Hausa**. J.A.L., 1, 3, 1962, 253–72.
—— 1962. Hanyar tafiyad da hukuncin laifi. (**Hausa** translation of the Criminal Procedure Code of Northern Nigeria, with translator's preface.) Pp. xiii+159. Kaduna: Govt. Printer.
—— The operation of gender in **Hausa**: stabilizer, dependent nominals and qualifiers. A.L.S., 4, 1963, 166–207.
—— **Hausa**. ii. Language. In: Encyclopedia of Islam (new edition). Leiden: Brill, 278–80.
—— Is Hausa really a Chadic language? Some problems of comparative phonology. A.L.S., 11, 1970, 272–88.
PILSZCZIKOWA, NINA. 1957. System czasownikowy języka **Hausa**. Stosunki między kategoriami aspektu i czasu [The verbal system of Hausa. Polish text with English summary.] Pp. 104. Warsaw: Polska Akademia Nauk.
—— Glagol'naya sistema yazyka **Hausa** [The verbal system of the Hausa language. In Russian with English summary]. Pp. 103. Warsaw.
—— Contribution à l'étude des rapports entre le **haoussa** et les autres langues du groupe nigéro-tchadien. Rocznik Orientalistyczny [Warsaw], 22, 2, 1958, 76–99. [French summary in Africana Bull. (Warsaw), 1, 1964, 204–5.]
—— Les verbes auxiliaires en **haoussa**. Rocznik Orientalistyczny, 23, 2, 1960, 101–118.
—— Le **haoussa** et le chamito-sémitique à la lumière de l'*Essai Comparatif* de Marcel Cohen. Rocznik Orientalistyczny [Warsaw], 24, 1, 1960, 126–76. [French summary in Africana Bull. (Warsaw), 1, 1964, p. 206].
*PRIETZE, R. Sprichwörter der **Hausa**. Z. afr. u. ocean. Spr., 6, 1902, 248–53.
*—— Tiermärchen der **Hausse**. Z.f. Ethnol., 39, 1907, 916–39 [with German translation].
*—— 1916. **Haussa** Sänger. Pp. 69. Göttingen: W. F. Kastner.
PUGAC, Z. L. Istorija izucenija jazyka chausa [The history of research in the **Hausa** language]. Afrikanskij etnograf. sbornik, [Moscow-Leningrad], 5, 1963, 200–22.
*RAT, J. N. 1889. The elements of the **Hausa** language, or a short introductory grammar in that language. Pp. vi+60. London: Waterlow.
*ROBINSON, C. H. The work of the **Hausa** Association. J. Manchester Geog. Soc., 12, 1896, 60–4, map.
*—— 1896. Specimens of **Hausa** literature. Pp. xix+112+106. Cambridge: Univ. Press.
RÖSSLER, O. Die lexikalischen Beziehungen des Hausa und die afrikanische Lautverschiebung. Africana Marburgensia, 2, 2, 1969, 17–21.
SCHACHTER, P. A generative account of **Hausa** *ne/ce*. J.A.L., 5, 1, 1966, 34–53.
*SCHÖN, J. F. Grammatical sketch of the **Hausa** language. J. Roy. Asiat. Soc., 14, 2, 1842.
*—— 1843. Vocabulary of the **Haussa** language (English-Haussa and Haussa-English), phrases and specimens of translations, with the grammatical elements of the Haussa language. Pp. v+190. London: C.M.S.
*—— 1857. A primer of the **Hausa** language. Pp. 53+46. Berlin: Unger.
*—— 1862. Grammar of the **Hausa** language. Pp. 234. London: C.M.H.
G *—— 1876. Dictionary of the **Hausa** language. Part 1. Hausa-English. Part 2. English-Hausa. With appendices of Hausa literature. Pp. 281+142+xxxiv. London: C.M.H.
*—— 1877. **Hausa** reading book, with the rudiments of grammar and vocabularies, and traveller's vade mecum. Pp. 103+xxxiv. London: C.M.H.
*—— (tr.). 1885. Magána **Hausa**: native literature, proverbs, tales, fables and historical fragments in the Hausa language. Pp. xx+288. London: S.P.C.K.
*—— 1888. Appendix to the Dictionary of the **Hausa** language, Hausa-English part, with additions of Hausa literature. Pp. 206. London: C.M.H.

*SEIDEL, A. 1906. Die **Haussa**sprache. Grammatik (deutsch) und systematisch geordnetes Wörterbuch: Haussa-deutsch-französisch-englisch. (Text in German, French and English.) Pp. xvi+290. Heidelberg: J. Groos (Lehrbücher Methode Gaspey-Otto-Sauer).

*—— 1907. **Hausa** language. Grammar and vocabulary. London: Nutt.

SHCHEGLOV, Y. K. Iz morfologii yazyka Khausa (obrazovaniye mnozhestvennogo chisla imen) [Some points of **Hausa** morphology (the structure of the plural forms of nouns)]. Narody Azii i Afriki, 3, 1965, 122–32.

—— Logichesky subjekt i predikat i sposoby ikh vydelenya v yazyke khause [The logical subject and predicate and their delimitation in the **Hausa** language]. Afrikanskaya Filologiya [ed. N. V. Okhotina, Moscow], 1965, 103–17.

SKINNER, (A.) N. 1959. Kamus na Hausa da Turanci [**Hausa**-English pocket dictionary]. Pp. x+69. Zaria: Norla; London: Longmans.

—— 1965. Kamus na Turanci da **Hausa** [English-Hausa dictionary]. Pp. viii+191. Zaria: Hausa Language Board and Gaskiya.

—— **Hausa** pronoun forms: a test case. J.W.A.L., 4, 1, 1967, 79–81.

—— The **Hausa** particle *àmmā*: an etymological note. J.A.L., 6, 2, 1967, 146–52.

—— 1968. (1st edition 1958). **Hausa** for beginners. Pp. 76. University of London Press.

—— The origin of the name '**Hausa**'. Africa, 38, 3, 1968, 253–7.

—— 1968. **Hausa** readings: selections from Edgar's *Tatsuniyoyi*. Pp. xxi+279. Madison: Univ. of Winsconsin Press for Dept. of African Languages and Literature.

—— (tr. and ed.) 1969. **Hausa** tales and traditions. [An English translation of *Tatsuniyoyi na Hausa*, originally compiled by F. Edgar; q.v.] Vol. I. Pp. xxxiv+440. London: Cass.

SMIRNOVA, M. A. 1960. Jazyk Chaussa [The **Hausa** language]. Moscow.

SÖLKEN, H. Die Geschichte von Kabi nach Imam Umari (1. Teil). Mitt. Inst. Orientforsch. [Berlin], 7, 1, 1959, 123–62.

*STUMME, H. Metrische Fragen auf dem Gebiete der berberischen und **haussa**nischen Poesie. Verhandl. 13. Orient.-Kongress (1902), 1904, 351–3.

*TAYLOR, F. W. Some English words in Fulani and **Hausa**. J. Afr. Soc., 20, 77, 1920, 25–32.

*—— **Hausa** and the late Canon C. H. Robinson (1861–1925). J. Afr. Soc., 27, 102, 1927, 145–59.

*—— The orthography of African languages, with special reference to **Hausa** and Fulani. J. Afr. Soc., 28, 100, 1929, 241–52.

—— 1959 (2nd rev. ed.; 1st ed. 1923). A practical **Hausa** grammar. Pp. 178. London: O.U.P. [Reviewed in Afr. u. Übersee, 43, 1959, 313–14.]

*—— and WEBB, A. G. G. 1932. Labarun al'adun Hausawa da zantatukansu. Accounts and conversations describing certain customs of the Hausas [in **Hausa** and English]. Pp. xii+226. London: O.U.P.

UNESCO. Rapport final sur la réunion d'un groupe d'experts pour l'unification des alphabets des langues nationales, Bamako, 28 fev.–5 mars, 1966. Pp. 40. UNESCO/CLT/BALING/13, 15/9/66. French original and English translation [Mandingue, Peul, Tamasheq, Songhay-Zarma, **Hausa**, Kanuri].

VYČICHL, W. Sprachliche Beziehungen zwischen Ägypten und Afrika. In: Neue afrikanistische Studien, ed. J. Lukas. Hamburg, 1966, 265–72.

*VILLIERS, A. Noms vernaculaires [Tamacheq et **Haoussa**] de quelques animaux de l'Aïr. Notes afr. IFAN, 40, 1948, 23–35.

VON ESSEN, O. Implosive Verschlusslaute im **Hausa**. Afr. u. Übersee, 45, 4, 1962, 285–91.

WÄNGLER, H. H. Singen und Sprechen in einer Tonsprache (**Hausa**). Z. f. Phonetik, 11, 1, 1958, 23–35.

—— 1963. Zur Tonologie des **Hausa**. Pp. 187. Berlin: Akademie-Verlag (Schr. z. Phonetik, Sprachwiss. u. Kommunikationsforschung, 6). [Reviewed in J.A.L., 4, 1, 1965, 73–5; Bull. S.O.A.S., 28, 3, 1965, 669–70.]

—— Über die Funktion der Tone im **Hausa**. Z.f. Phonetik, 16, 1/3, 1963, 231–40, bibl.

*WESTERMANN, D. H. A standard **Hausa** dictionary [Review of G. P. Bargery's Hausa dictionary]. Africa, 7, 3, 1934, 371–4.

WOLFF, H. Sub-system typologies and area linguistics. Anth. Ling., 1, 7, 1959, 1–88, [incl. **Hausa**].
YUSHMANOV, N. V. 1937. Stroi yazyka **Hausa**. Pp. 38. Leningrad: Inst. Orient. Stud.
ZHURKOVSKIY, B. V. Ideofony kak chast' rechi v afrikanskikh yazykakh [Ideophones as a part of speech in African languages (based on **Hausa**)]. Narody Azii i Afriki [Moscow], 6, 1966, 114–16.
ZIMA, P. Some remarks on loanwords in modern **Hausa**. Archiv. Orientální [Prague], 32, 4, 1964, 522–8.
—— On syntactic alternation of verbal forms in **Hausa**. Mitt. Inst. Orientforschung [Berlin], 13, 2, 1967, 188–98.
—— **Hausa** in West Africa: remarks on contemporary role and functions. In: Language problems of developing nations, Fishman, J. A., et al. New York, 1968, 365–77.
—— A contribution to the analysis of verbal forms in a WNW **Hausa** dialect. Archiv. Orientální, 37, 1969, 199–213.
—— Quelques remarques sur le vocalisme d'un parler **haoussa**. Acta Universitatis Carolinae —Phonetica Pragensia 2, 1970.

2. OTHER LANGUAGES

FÉDRY, J. Syntagmes de détermination en **dangaléat**. J.W.A.L., 6, 1, 1969, 5–19.
*GUERPILLON, M. Les langues dits **Kotoko**, Ét. camerounaises, 1, 23/24, 1948, 23–30, carte.
JUNGRAITHMAYR, H. Vokalharmonie im **Tangale**. Z. Phonetik u. allg. Sprachwiss., 10, 2, 1957, 144–52.
—— Beobachtungen zur tschadohamitischen Sprache der **Jegu** (und **Jonkor**) von Abu Telfan (République de Tchad). Afr. u. Übersee, 45, 1/2, 1961, 95–123.
—— Die Sprache der **Jegu** im zentralen Sudan und ihre Stellung innerhalb der tschadohamitischen Sprachen. Wiener Z.f.d. Kunde d. Morgenlandes, 59/60, 1963/4, 44–51.
—— Specimens of the **Pa'a** ('**Afa**') and **Warja** languages with notes on the tribes of Ningi Chiefdom (Bauchi Province, Northern Nigeria). Afr. u. Übersee, 50, 3, 1967, 194–205.
—— A brief note on certain characteristics of '**West Chadic**' languages. J.W.A.L., 4, 2, 1967, 57–8.
—— [See also H. Jungraithmayr's articles listed under Section VIII.]
LUKAS, J. Tschadohamitische Sprachproben aus Nordnigerien (**Karekare**-und **Bolanci**-Texte). In: Neue Afrikanistische Studien, ed. J. Lukas. Hamburg, 1966, 173–207.
—— Nunation in afrikanischen Sprachen. Anthropos, 63, 1968, 97–114 [incl. **Bade, Ngizin, Bolanci, Muzgu, Masana**].
—— Tonpermeable und tonimpermeable Konsonanten im **Bolanci** (Nordnigerien). In: Ethnological and Linguistic Studies in honour of N. J. van Warmelo. Ethnological Publications, 52, 1969, 133–8.
—— Das Verbum im **Bade** (nordnigeria). Afr. u. Übersee, 53, 1970.
LUKAS, RENATE. Das nomen im **Băde** (Nord-nigerien). Afr. u. Übersee, 51, 2, 1968, 91–116; 3, 198–224.
MIGEOD, F. W. H. Ngala and its dead language. J. Roy. Anthrop. Inst., 52, 1922, 230–41 [**Kotoko?**].
NEWMAN, P. A brief note on the **Maha** language. J.W.A.L., 2, 1, 1965, 57–8.
SOLKEN, H. Untersuchungen über die sprachliche Stellung der einstigen **So** von Bornu. Anthropos, 53, 5, 6, 1958, 877–900.
*VON DUISBURG, A. Überreste der **So**-Sprache. Mitt. Sem. orient. Spr., 7 (3), 1914, 39–45. [Text with German translation.]
WOLFF, H. Sub-system typologies and area linguistics. Anth. Ling., 1, 7, 1959, 1–88 [incl. **Kanakuru**].

SECTION XI

KANURI

*BAILEY, T. G. **Kanuri** vocabulary: English-Kanuri and Kanuri-English. J. Roy, Asiat. Soc., 1911, 315–64.

*BARTH, HEINRICH. Schreiben an Prof. Lepsius (über die Beziehungen der **Kanuri-** und Teda-Sprachen). Z. allg. Erdkde., 2, 1854, 372–4, 384–7.
C *BENTON, P. A. 1911. **Kanuri** readings, including facsimiles of MSS, transliteration, translation . . . English–Kanuri vocabulary. . . . Pp. 123. O.U.P.
G ——— 1917. Primer of **Kanuri** grammar (translated and revised from the German of A. von Duisburg). Pp. 130. O.U.P.
*ELLISON, R. E. 1937. An English-**Kanuri** sentence book. Pp. 120. London: Crown Agents.
GREENBERG, J. H. Linguistic evidence for the influence of the **Kanuri** on the Hausa. J. Afr. Hist., 1, 2, 1960, 205–12.
HABRASZEWSKI, T. **Kanuri**—language and people—in the 'travel-book' ('Siyahetname') of Evliya Celebi. Africana Bull. [Warsaw], 6, 1967, 59–66.
HAIR, P. E. H. Early **Kanuri** vocabularies (1670–1820). J.W.A.L., 6, 1, 1969, 27–9.
KIRK-GREENE, A. H. M. The linguistic statistics of Northern Nigeria: a tentative presentation. A.L.R., 6, 1967, 75–101 [incl. **Kanuri**].
*KLAPROTH, H. J. 1826. Essai sur la langue du Bornou, suivi des vocabulaires du Begharmi, du Mandara et de Tombouctou. Pp. 42. Paris.
*KOELLE, S. W. 1853. Dialogues in English and Bornu languages. London.
*——— 1854. Grammar of the Bornu or **Kanuri** language. Pp. xix+326. London: C.M.H.
*——— 1854. African native literature; or proverbs, tales, fables, and historical fragments in the **Kanuri** or Bornu language, to which are added a translation of the above and a Kanuri-English vocabulary. Pp. xv+434. London: C.M.H.
——— 1968. African native literature, with introduction by David Dalby. Graz, Akad. Druck-u. Verlagsanstalt, in assoc. with Afr. Language Review, 1968. Pp. xii+xv+434. (Proverbs, tales, etc. in Kanuri and English and a Kanuri-English vocabulary. 1st ed. 1854.)
LEBEUF, J.-P. et RODINSON, MAXIME. Les mosquées de Fort-Lamy (manuscrit **kanouri** avec traduction). Bull. IFAN, 14, 3, 1952, 970–4.
*LUKAS, J. Genesis der Verbalformen im **Kanuri** und Teda. Wiener Z. Kunde Morgenlandes, 34, 1/2, 1927, 87–104.
*——— Transition und Intransition im **Kanuri**. Wiener Z. Kunde Morgenlandes, 35, 3/4, 1928, 213–41.
*——— **Kanuri**-Texte. Mitt. Sem. orient. Spr., 32 (3), 1929, 41–92, i–xxx.
*——— Lautlehre der **Badawi-Kanuri** in Bornu. Z. Eingeb.-Spr., 25, 1, 1934, 3–29.
*——— Aus der Literatur der **Badawi-Kanuri** in Bornu. Z. Eingeb-Spr., 26, 1, 1935, 35–56; 2, 133–50.
*——— Sprichwörter, Aussprüche und Rätsel der **Kanuri**. Z. Eingeb.-Spr., 28, 3, 1938, 161–74.
*——— Aus dem Leben der **Kanuri** ihre grossen Tage, ihre Wohnung. Z. Eingeb.-Spr., 29, 3, 1939, 161–88.
*——— Fabeln der **Kanuri**. Z. Eingeb.-Spr., 30, 3, 1940, 161–81; 4, 273–95.
——— Umrisse einer ostsaharanischen Sprachgruppe. Afr. u. Übersee, 36, 1/2, 1952, 3–8.
——— 1967. A study of the **Kanuri** language: grammar and vocabulary. Reprint (1st ed. 1937). Pp. xvii+253. London: Dawsons for Int. Afr. Inst.
*MIGEOD, F. W. H. The language of the **Manga**. Man, 24, 46, 1924, 60–61.
*NOEL, P. 1923. Petit manuel français-**kanouri**. Pp. 130, bibliog. Paris: Geuthner.
*——— Note sur les noms de captifs en pays **Kanouri**. Rev. Ethnog. et Trad. populaires, 5, 1924, 368–72.
*NORRIS, E. 1853. Grammar of the Bornu or **Kanuri** language with dialogues, translations, and vocabulary. Pp. 101. London.
*PATTERSON, J. R. 1926. **Kanuri** songs. Pp. viii+32. Lagos: Govt. Printer.
*POUX-CRANSAC, GERMAINE. Tage Rabebe, chanson de Rabah. J. Soc. Afr. 7, 2, 1937, 173–87.
*PRIETZE, R. Die spezifischen Verstärkungsadverbien im Hausa und **Kanuri**. Mitt. Sem. orient. Spr., 11 (3), 1908, 307–17.
*——— Bornulieder. Mitt. Sem. orient. Spr., 17 (3), 1914, 134–260.
*——— Bornusprichwörter. Mitt. Sem. orient. Spr., 18 (3), 1915, 85–172.
*——— Bornu-Texte (mit MS. in arabischer Schrift). Mitt. Sem. orient. Spr., 33 (3), 1930, 82–159, i–xxxii. [In Manga dialect, with translation and notes.]

*RICHARDSON, J. 1847. Sentences for the purpose of conversation in the Arabic, **Kanuri**, called Bornuese, and Sudanese languages in Arabic characters. London: Foreign Office.

UNESCO. Rapport final sur la réunion d'un groupe d'experts pour l'unification des alphabets des langues nationales, Bamako, 28 fév.–5 mars, 1966. UNESCO/CLT/BALING/13, 15/9/66. French original and English translation [Mandingue, Peul, Tamasheq, Songhay-Zarma, Hausa, **Kanuri**].

*VON DUISBURG, A. 1913. Grundriss der **Kanuri**-Sprache in Bornu. Pp. 185. Berlin: G. Reimer (Arch. Studium dtsch. Kolonialspr. 15).

*—— Untersuchungen über die Bedeutung einiger Bornu-Namen. Anthropos, 26, 3/4, 1931, 563–8.

*WARD, IDA C. Some notes on the pronunciation of the **Kanuri** language of West Africa. Bull. S.O.A.S., 4, 1, 1926, 139–46.

WOLFF, H. Sub-system typologies and area linguistics. Anth. Ling., 1, 7, 1959, 1–88, [incl. **Kanuri**].

SECTION XII

CREOLES AND PIDGINS

Compiler: Ian F. Hancock

GENERAL

BERRY, J. Pidgins and creoles in Africa. In: Symposium on Multilingualism, Brazzaville, 1962. CCTA/CSA publication No. 87, 219–225.

—— Pidgins and creoles in Africa. In: Current trends in linguistics, Vol. 7, Linguistics in Sub-Saharan Africa, ed. Thomas A. Sebeok. Bloomington: Indiana University, 1970.

SPENCER, J. (ed.) 1970. The English language in West Africa. London: Longmans.

1. SIERRA LEONE KRIO (English-derived creole)

BERRY, J. Creole as a language. West Africa, 2207, Sept. 1959, p. 745.

—— The origins of Krio vocabulary. Sierra Leone Stud., 12, 1959, 298–307.

—— English loanwords and adaptations in Sierra Leone Krio. Creole Language Studies, 2, 1961, 1–16.

—— A note on the prosodic structure of Krio (Sierra Leone). I.J.A.L., 36, 2, 1970.

—— A note on Krio tones. A.L.S., 11, 1970, 60–3.

BRADSHAW, A. T. von S. A list of Yoruba words in Krio. S.L.L.R., 5, 1966, 61–71.

COLE, A. 1955. A pocket grammar and dictionary of Krio. Pp. 113. London.

*COLE, E. T. The Sierra Leone vernacular. In: Sierra Leone Weekly News, Freetown, Nov. 3rd, 1888.

*CRABBIT (pseud.) The Krio or Creeo language. In: The Daily Guardian, Freetown, Oct. 18th, 1939.

*CRONISE, F., and WARD, H. 1903. Cunnie Rabbit, Mr. Spider and the other beef. (38 tales in Krio.) London and New York.

DECKER, T. Three Krio poems. S.L.L.R., 3, 1964, 32–4.

—— Julius Caesar in Krio. S.L.L.R., 4, 1965, 64–78.

—— Udat di kiap fit; a Krio adaptation of *As you like it*. S.L.L.R., 5, 1966, 50–60.

DEIGHTON, F. C. 1957. Vernacular botanical vocabulary for Sierra Leone. London: Crown Agents for Govt. of Sierre Leone. Krio vocabulary, pp. 86–92.

DWYER, D., and KOROMA, A. 1969. A brief sketch of Krio. Pp. 19 (mimeo). Freetown: Peace Corps in Sierra Leone.

HANCOCK, I. F. English-derived creoles of the Atlantic area. A.L.R., 8, 1969.

—— West Africa and the Atlantic creoles. In: The English language in West Africa, ed. J. Spencer. London: Longmans, 1970.

JONES, E. The potentialities of Krio as a literary language. Sierra Leone Stud., N.S.9, 1957, 40–8.
—— Some English fossils in Krio. Sierra Leone Stud., N.S. 12, 1959, 295–7.
—— Mid-nineteenth century evidences of a Sierra Leone patois. S.L.L.R., 1, 1962, 19–26.
—— Krio in Sierra Leone journalism. S.L.L.R., 3, 1964, 24–31.
—— Some tense, mood and aspect markers in Krio. A.L.R., 7, 1968, 86–9.
—— Krio: an English-based language of Sierra Leone. In: The English language in West Africa, ed. J. Spencer. London: Longmans, 1970.
*MIGEOD, F. Sierra Leonese. In: The languages of West Africa. London: Kegan Paul, 1911 and 1933, 252–5.
SPITZER, L. Creole attitudes towards Krio: an historical survey. S.L.L.R., 5, 1966, 39–49.
THOMPSON, R. A Caribbean sister for Krio. Sierra Leone Studies, June, 1962, 227–32.
TURNER, L. 1964. An anthology of Krio folklore and literature. Chicago (mimeo).
—— 1965. Krio texts, with grammatical notes and translations in English. Pp. 115. Chicago (mimeo).
*WEST AFRICA. Sierra Leone Creo. West Africa, 31, 1564, Jan. 1947, 62–3.
WILSON, J. et al. 1964. Introductory Krio language training manual. Pp. iii+227. Bloomington Indiana University. Sierra Leone Peace Corps Project.

2. PIDGIN ENGLISH (NIGERIA, CAMEROONS, FERNANDO PO, LIBERIA)

ANNAN, B. The situation of Pidgin English in West Africa. University of Leeds, Phonetics Dept. Report 2, 1969, 18–28.
*ANON. 1945? Petite grammaire Pidgin, suivie d'un lexique français-Pidgin. Pp. 26.
CASSIDY, F. Toward the recovery of early English-African pidgin. In: Symposium on Multilingualism, Brazzaville, 1962. CCTA/CSA publication No. 87, 267–77.
CHRISTOPHERSEN, P. Some special West African English words. Eng. Studs., 34, 1953, 282–91.
—— A note on the words 'dash' and 'juju' in West African English. Eng. Studs., 40, 1959, 115–18.
D'AZEVEDO, W. L. 1967. Some terms from Liberian English. Pp. 74. United States Peace Corps in Libera.
DWYER, D., and SMITH, D. c. 1966. An introduction to West African Pidgin English. Pp. vi+572. East Lansing: Michigan State University Press.
FORDE, D. (ed.). 1954. Efik traders of Old Calabar. (Text of a Pidgin English diary written between 1785–1788). Pp. xiii+166. London: O.U.P. for Int. Afr. Inst.
*GRADE, P. Das Negerenglisch an der Westküste von Afrika. Anglia, 14, 1892, 362–93.
*HENRICI, E. Westafrikanisches Negerenglisch. Anglia, 20, 1898, 397–403.
*HERSKOVITS, M. Tales in Pidgin English from Nigeria. Journal of American Folklore, 44, 1931, 448–66.
*HUTTER, F. Das Küstenenglisch. In: Wanderung und Forschung im Nord Hinterland von Kamerun. Braunschweig, 1902, 60–4.
KISOB, J. A. A live language: 'Pidgin English'. Abbia, 1, 1963, 25–31.
MAFENI, B. Some aspects of the phonetics of Nigerian Pidgin. M.Litt. dissertation (unpublished). Univ. of Edinburgh, 1955.
—— Nigerian Pidgin. In: The English language in West Africa, ed. J. Spencer. London: Longmans, 1970.
*MANN, A. (n.d., c. 1880) Negerenglisch. Lagos.
MAYR, A. A pidgin english nyelvről. Egyetemes philologiai közlöny 12, 141 [Discussion of Cameroons Pidgin English in Hungarian].
*MARIANO DE ZARCO, R. P. 1938. Dialecto inglés-africano o broken-english de la Colonia española del Golfo de Guinea: Epitome de la gramática seguido del vocabulario español-inglés y inglés-español. 2nd edition, Turnhout.
*MERRICK, G. Notes on Hausa and Pidgin English. J. Afr. Soc., 8, 1908, 303–7.

SCHNEIDER, G. 1961. Cameroons Creole dictionary. Pp. 258. Bamenda, (mimeo.).
—— 1963. First steps in Wes-Kos. Pp. vii+81. Hartford: Hartford Seminary Foundation, Studies in Linguistics 6, (mimeo.).
—— 1965. A preliminary glossary, English Pidgin-English. (Wes-Kos.) Pp. v+69. Athens, Ohio: Center for International Studies. (mimeo.).
—— 1965. Pidgin English proverbs. Pp. ii+46. Athens, Ohio: African Studies Center, Michigan State Univ. African language, monograph 6.
—— West African Pidgin English—an overview: phonology, morphology. Journ. of English Linguistics, 1, 1967, 49–56.
—— 1967. West African Pidgin English—an historical overview. Pp. 24. Ohio University. (Papers in Internat. Studs., 8).
TATE TEBO, M. A lingua franca for Cameroon. Abbia, 3, 1963, 1963, 190–1.
*VON HAGEN, G. 1913. Kurzes Handbuch für Neger-Englisch an der West Küste Afrikas unter besonderer Berücksichtigung von Kamerun. Pp. 68. Berlin.

3. PORTUGUESE CREOLES

(a) Northern (SENEGAL, GUINEA, CAPE VERDE)

*BRITO, A. DE P. Apontamentos para a grammatica do Crioulo que se falla na Ilha de S. Thiago de Cabo Verde. Bol. Soc. Geographia, Lisbon, 7, 10, 1887, 612–69.
BRUCH, J. Das Suffix des Portugiesischen 'Crioulo'. In: Portgual-Festschrift der Universität Köln, 1940.
CHATAIGNER, A. Le créole portugais du Sénégal: Observations et textes. J.A.L., 2, 1, 1963, 44–71.
*DE BARROS, F. Lingua creola da Guiné Portuguesa e do archipelago de Cabo Verde. Revista do Estudos Livres (Lisbon, 1885–6).
DE CARVALHO, J. G. H. Le vocalisme atone des parlers créoles du Cap Vert. 9ème congresso internacional de linguística românica, Univ. of Lisbon, 1915. Acts, vol. 3, 1962, 3–12.
—— Sincronica e discronia nos sistemas vocálismos do crioulo caboverdiano. Misc-hom. Martinet 196, 43–67.
DO ESPÍRITO SANTO, J. Nomes vernáculos de algumas plantas da Guiné Portuguesa. Junta de Investigações do Ultramar, Lisbon, 1963.
FERREIRA, M. Comentários em torno do bilingualismo Cabo-Verdiano. In: Colóquios Cabo-Verdianos, Estudios de Ciências Politicas e Sociais 22, Junta de Investigações do Ultramar. Lisbon, 1959, 53–8.
*LEITE DE VASCONCELOS, J. Dialectos crioulos portugueses de África. Revista Lusitana, 5, 1897–9, 241–61.
*SCHUCHARDT, H. Beiträge zur Kenntnis des kreolischen Romanisch II: Zum Negerportugiesischen Senegambiens. Zeitschr. für Rom. Phil. 12, 1888, 301–12.
*—— Beiträge zur Kenntnis des kreolischen Romanisch III: Zum negerportugiesischen der Kapverden. Zeitschr. für Rom. Phil. 12, 1888, 312–22.
TEIXEIRA DA MOTA, A. O problema do português e do creoulo. Guiné Portuguesa [Lisbon], 1, 1954, 227–33.
VALKHOFF, M. 1966. Studies in Portuguese and Creole. Pp. xi+282. Johannesburg: Witwatersrand Univ. Press.
WILSON, W. A. A. 1962. The Crioulo of Guiné. Pp. x+49. Johannesburg: Witwatersrand Univ. Press. [Reviewed in J.A.L., 4, 1, 1965, 76–7].

(b) Southern (ANNOBON, SÃO TOMÉ, PRINCIPE)

BARRENA, N. 1957. Gramatica annobonesa. Pp. 95. Madrid: Instituto de Estudios Africanos.
*COELHO, A. 1881. Os dialectos românicos ou neolatinos na África. Asia e América. Lisbon.
DE ALMEIDA, A. Sobre a terminologia anatómica no crioulo de S. Tomé e Príncipe. Portugal. Anais da Junta de Investigações Coloniais. [Lisbon], 1958, 51–61.

Do Espírito Santo, J. Nomes crioulos e vernáculos de algumas plantas de S. Tomé e Príncipe. Bol. cult Guiné. port., 24, 93, 1969, 193–211.
*Negreiros, A. O dialecto de S. Thomé, In: Historia etnográfia da Ilha de S. Thomé. Lisbon, 1895, 303–69.
*—— Etnográfia de S. Tomé e outros elementos linguísticos, In: Anuário commercial, industrial e agrícola da Província de S. Tomé e Príncipe, 1928.
*Schuchardt, H. Kreolische Studien I: Über das Negerportugiesische von S. Thomé. Sitzungsberichte der k.k. Akademie der Wissenschaften zu Wien, 101, 1882, 889–917.
*—— Kreolische Studien VII: Über das Negerportugiesische von Annobom. Sitzungsberichte der k.k. Akademie der Wissenschaften zu Wien, 116, 1888, 193–226.
*Vila, I. 1891. Elementos de la gramática Ambú o de Annobón. Madrid.

4. WEST AFRICAN PIDGIN FRENCH

Calvet, M. et Dumont, P. Le français au Sénégal. Interférences du wolof dans le français des élèves Sénégalais. Bull. IFAN, 31 (B), 1, 1969, 239–63.
*Delafosse, M. Petit-Nègre. In: Vocabulaires comparatifs. Paris, 1904, 263–5.
—— Parlers négro-européens de la Guinée. In: Les langues du monde, A. Meillet de M. Cohen. Bordeaux, 1960, 504–6.
Flutre, L. De quelques termes usités aux XVIIe et XVIIIe siècles sur les côtes de l'Afrique occidentale, et qui ont passé dans les récits des voyageurs français du temps. Etymologica (Tübingen), 1958, 209–38.
—— De quelques termes de la langue commerciale utilisée sur les côtes de l'Afrique occidentale aux XVIIe et XVIIIe siècles, d'après les recits de voyages du temps. Revue de Linguistique Romane, 25, 1961, 274–89.
Mauny, R. 1952. Glossaire des expressions et termes locaux employés dans l'Ouest africain. Dakar: IFAN Catalogues IX.
Metz: Mission Catholique. 1939. Catéchisme en français-pidgin. Pp. 125.
Vonrospach, J. Le français populaire d'Abidjan. Sommaire du VIIIe congrès de la Soc. Ling. de l'Afrique Occidentale. Abidjan: Inst. Ling. Appl., Université d'Abidjan, 1969, 36–9.

INDEX

Abacama see Bachama
Abadira see Lala
Abam-Ohaffia: Igbo 90
Abawa see Nupe
Abbey, Abe, Abɛ 78
Abe: Baule 81
Abegoŋ see Egon
Abewa see Ebe
Abigi, Abiji see Ari
Abo-Igbo: Sobo 89
Abonwa see Abure
Abouré see Abure
Abri, Abribi, Abrinya, Abriwi 50, 53, 54
Abron, Abrong, Abroŋ see Brong
Abure 77
Abutu see Afutu
Aɓi: Musgu 166
Achifanchi: Kamuku 103
Achifawa, Achipawa 104
Accra see Gã²
Aculo, Acülo see Awuna¹
Ada¹: Igbo 90
Ada² see Jaba
Adamat see Dyamate
Adangbe, Adangme 82, 91
Adele 98, 99–100
Adiukru see Adyukru
Adja see Aja
Adjolo see Awuna¹
Adjoukrou, Adjukru see Adyukru
Adoma see Kelawa
Adun: Mbembe¹ 116
Adya see Aja
Adyakatye see Kakanda
Adyoukrou, Adyukru 11, 20, 21, 23–24
Afade: Kotoko² 165
Afema: Anyi 80
Afiteng see Boritsũ
Afudu: Tangale 164
Afuno see Hausa
Afutu: Guang 81
Agalati see Ebe
Agari see Kahugu
Agatu: Idoma 140
Agbado: Sobo 89
Agbanyito see Guang
Agbengau, Agbenyao: Baule 81
Age 127
Agie see Ngi
Agni see Anyi
Ago see Ahlõ
Agola see Badyara
Agona see Agwa
Agua see Metyibo

Aguro see Kagoro
Agwa 78
Agwɔlɔk, Agwɔt see Kagoro
Ahanta: Anyi 80
Ahizi 49, 78
Ahlõ 97, 98
Aholio see Morwa
Ahoulan see Awuna¹
Aizi, Aïzi see Ahizi
Aja: Ewe 83
Ajam see Ejagham
Ajer see Azer
Ajio see Kaje
Ajitora see Longuda
Ajomora see Jomoro
Ajukru see Adyukru
Akan 57, 78–82, 90, 92
Akanda¹ see Aworo
Akanda² see Kakanda
Akapless see Abure
Akasele see Kasele
Akem: Twi 79
Akiulo see Awuna¹
Akoko: Yoruba 85
Akonto see Mbembe²
Akpa see Jukun
Akpafu 97
Akpana see Logba¹
Akpɛdɛ see Kpelle
Akposo see Kposo
Aku see Yoruba
Akuapem see Akwapem
Akurmi see Kurama
Akuut see Birom
Akwamu: Twi 79
Akwapem, Akwapim: Twi 79
Akweŋko: Mbembe² 142
Akye 78
Akye-Kotoko see Bode
Akyem see Akem
Ala see Wala
Alada see Gũ
Aladian, Aladyã, Aladyan, Alagian 76
Alante see Balante
Alege see Gayi
Alladian see Aladian
Amampa see Bulom
Amanrehia see Nzima
Amanya see Nzima
Amap: Jarawa 107
Amrehia see Nzima
Ana see Yoruba
Anago see Yoruba
Anang: Ibibio 133
Andone: Bete 49

Andone-Ibeno: Ibibio 133
Andoni 134, 137
Angan see Kamantan
Angas, Angass 138
Angonu see Ngonu
Anhaqui see Bidyogo
A'nima see Lamba
Animere: Tem 70
Anirago see Kahugu
Ankulu see Ikulu
Ankwe 138
Anlo see Awuna²
Anno see Nganu
Anpika see Bolewa
Anta see Ahanta
Anufo¹, Anufɔ: Anyi 80
Anufo² (Cakosi): Anyi 80
Anum: Guang 82
Anupe, Anupecwayi, Anuperi see Nupe
Anyaki see Bidyogo
Anyang: Ekoi 114
Anyanga, Anyaŋa: Guang 81
Anyi 79–80
Anyun see Banyun
Aŋlo, Aŋwona see Awuna²
Aŋwõnwi see Aowin
Aowin: Anyi 80
Apa see Jukun
Apafo, Apafu see Akpafu
Aploni, Aploniyo see Nzima
Apollonia see Nzima
Appa see Jukun, Tiv, Yergum
Arago: Idoma 140
Aregwe see Irigwe
Ari 78
Aro: Igbo 90
Arringeu see Pongo
Arun see Adun
Asante, Ashanti: Twi 79, 93
Ashingini see Shingini
Asoko see Nzima
Asolio see Morwa
Assaye see Safwi
Assumbo: Ekoi 114
Asulio see Morwa
Asuŋliatʃaŋ see Dschang
Aswanik see Soninke
Ataka: Katab 104
Atchi see Akye
Atemnɛ see Temne
Aten see Ganawuri
Atissa: Ijo 121
Atiʃeraak see Kachichere
Atobu: Akye 78
Atrugbu see Nyangbo

INDEX

Atsam, Atsama see Chawai
Atshi see Akye
Attaka see Ataka
Attié see Akye
Atwi see Twi
Atyap see Katab
Atyɛ see Akye
Atyoti: Guang 81
Auci, *Auchi*: Kukuruku 88
Aulo, Aulopo see Abri
Avaɗe see Afade
Avatime 96, 98–99
Avikam 76–77
Awa see Nzima
Awieso see Oso
Awõhĕ see Konyagi
Aworo: Yoruba 85
Awuna¹: Kasena 61
Awuna²: Ewe 83, 84
Awutu see Afutu
Axus see Balante
Ayan see Basari
Ayigbe see Ewe
Ayu 107
Azen see Konyagi
Azer: Soninke 32
Azjer see Azer
Azumu see Kurama

Ba: Dan 40
Baasa see Bassa
Băbara see Bamana²
Babadjou 129
Babal: Mbum 147
Babir, Babɪr see Babur
Babouantou 129
Babur: Bura 153
Babute, Babuti see Vute
Bacama, *Bachama*: Bata 139, 155, 166, 161
Badawa: Jar 115
Bade 163, 174–5
Badebo see Palipo
Badyar, *Badyara*, Badyaranke, Badyaraŋkɛ, Badyare 16
Badzumbo 114 n.
Bafang 129, 130
Bafinge 132
Bafoussam 129
Bafu see Akpafu
Bafumbum see Fungom
Bafut 127, 128
Baga 13–14, 37
Baga Fore 14
Bagam 129
Bagbala see Sisala
Bagbɔ see Tafi
Bago: Tem 70
Bahauʃe see Hausa
Baibai see Jukun
Baïnouk see Banyun

Baïot see Bayot
Bajama: Mumuye 139
Baju see Kaje
Bakɔbɔnya, Bakɔpɔ see Twi
Bakou 129
Bakpelɛ(nya) see Likpe
Bakulŭ: Jar 115
Bakwe, Bakwo 49
Balant, Balanta, *Balante* 15
Balda 158 n.
Baleko: Bete 48
Balessing 129
Balɛ see Santrokofi
Bali¹ (ŋgaa ka) 122–3
Bali²: Yendang 139
Bali³ (ndaɢam) 150, 151
Balu see Lome
Bamana,¹ Bamanaŋkɛ see Bambara¹
Bamana²: Senufo 55
Bambara¹ 33, 34, 42
Bambara² see Bamana²
Bambara³ see Dyimini
Bambaro see Bomberawa
Bameka 129
Bamekon see Kom
Bamendjou 129
Bameta see Menemo
Ba-mɛmbila see Mambila
Bamileke 128–31
Bamougoum 129
Bamoum, Bamum, Bamun 130, 131–2
Bana¹ 130
Bana² see Mundang
Bana(na): Masa, Musei 167
Banda see Ligbi
Bandara see Nafana
Bandi 39, 42
Bandjoum, Bandjoun 129
Bangangte 129–30
Bangawa, Bangi: Dakakari 103
Bangwa¹, Baŋwa: Dan 40
Bangwa² 129
Banhun see Banyun
Bankalawa: Jar 115
(Ba)nkulu see Ikulu
Bankwet 130
Bansaw, Banso see Nsaw
Bansoa 129
Banugba see Logba²
Banyoŋa see Bali¹
Banyuk, Banyun, Banyung, Banyuŋka 15
Baoule see Baule
Bara: Bolewa 163
Barain, Baraïn, *Barein* 169
Barba see Bargu
Barboe: Bakwe 50
Bareshe see Reshe
Bargu, Bariba 70, 74

Barka see Baga
Barobo: Grebo 50
Baron see Ron
Barracin see Serer
Basar, Basari 17
Baso, *Bassa* 51
Bassa-Kaduna 103 n.
Bassa-Komo: Kamuku 103
Bassa-Nge: Nupe 86
Bassari see Tobote
Basua: Boki 115
Bata 115, 160–1
Batonnun see Bargu
Batragbo, Batrugbu see Nyangbo
Batta see Bata
Bauchi see Baushi
Baule 80–81
Baushi: Kamuku 103
Bavũnɛ see Akpafu
Bawuri(nya) see Bowili
Bayikpe see Ewe
Bayot, Bayotte: Dyola 17
Beafada see Biafada
Beba Befang 132
Bedde, Bede see Bade
Bedjola see Biafada
Befunya see Akpafu
Belaka: Mbum 147
Belante see Balante
Bema see Moba
Bemba, Bembra see Mossi
Bemuma see Twi
Bendega: Boki 115
Benigbe see Ewe
Berba¹: Gurma 68
Berba² see Bargu
Bergit: Mubi² 169
Beri: Guang 82
Berom see Birom
Besema see Bachama
Bete¹, Betegbo 48–49
Bete²: Boki 115
Betye: Anyi 80
Bɛdere, Bɛdrɛ see Adele
Bɛɛge: Musgu 166
Bɛɛlɛ see Kwaa
Bergit see Bergit
Betãmmadibɛ, Betammaribe see Somba
Biafada, Biafar 16, 19, 27
Bidoyo, Bidyogo 16
Bidyola see Biafada
Bijago, Bijougot see Bidyogo
Bikom see Kom
Bilauun see Kanakuru
Bimba see Gurma
Bimoba see Moba
Bindiga see Bendega
Bini 87, 88, 90, 92
Binik see Binye
Binna: Lala 111

Binumba *see* Gurma
Binye: Baule 81
Binyinu *see* Kasena
Biotu *see* Sobo
Bira *see* Igbira Igu
Birgit *see* Bergit
Biri *see* Igbira Igu
Birifo¹ *see* Gan¹
Birifo², Birifor 53, 66
Birom, Biroom 106
Birra *see* Pura
Bisa, Bisagwe, Bisano *see* Busa
Bisi *see* Piti
Bitare 113
Bitshamba *see* Tobote
Biyan *see* Basari
Biyobe *see* Soruba
Biʒagɔ *see* Bidyogo
Bırsa *see* Bata
Ble: Dyula 35
Bliss: Dyola 17
Bloho: Dan 40
Blu *see* Twi
B'Moba *see* Moba
Bobo 60
Bobo Fï, Fing, Finng 40, 60
Bobono: Bete 49
Bobwa: Bete 49
Bode: Akye 78
Bodo *see* Hwane
Bodon: Tem 70
Bodoro *see* Padogho
Boeni: Tenda 17
Boezonyo *see* Grebo
Boga: Tera 157
Bogo *see* Ahlõ
Bogung *see* Bargu
Bohum *see* Burum²
Boki 114–15, 120–1
Boko¹, Bokoberu, Boko Bussawa, Bokolawa *see* Busa
Boko² *see* Woko
Bokra: Bete 49
Bokwe: Bakwe 50
Bola 16
Bolawa, Bolea, Bolenchi, *Bolewa* 157, 163
Bolokwe, Bolokwɛ̃: Bakwe 50
Bolom *see* Bulom
Bombarawa: Jar 115
Bome, Bomo¹: Bulom 12
Bomo²: Baule 81
Bonda, *Bonna*: Baule 81
Bono *see* Brong
Borada *see* Lefana
Borgawa, Borgu *see* Bargu
Boritsũ 114
Borlawa *see* Bolewa
Boso: Guang 82
Bouamou *see* Nienege
Bouddouma *see* Buduma

Boudoukwa: Bakwe 49
Boumpé *see* Mende
Bourrah *see* Bura
Boussance *see* Busa
Bowili 97
Bowli¹ *see* Baule
Bowli² *see* Ewe
Bozo: Soninke 32
Bɔɔ *see* Gbunde
Brame *see* Bola
Brass: Ijɔ 121
Brassa *see* Balante
Briama: Loma 38
Brignan, Brinya *see* Avikam
Brissa *see* Anufo
Brong, Brɔŋ: Guang 82
Brusa, Brussa *see* Anufo
Bua *see* Hona
Buburi *see* Adyukru
Bubutubi *see* Ewe
Budduma *see* Buduma
Budjago *see* Bidyogo
Buduma 116, 175–6
Buëm *see* Lefana
Bufu *see* Bafut
Bugago *see* Bidyogo
Bugoŋ *see* Egon
Buguli, Buguri: Grusi 63
Buile, Builsa *see* Kanjaga
Bujawa: Jarawa 107
Bukra *see* Bokra
Bukurmi *see* Kuramɛ
Bulahai *see* Matakam
Bulama *see* Bola
Bulanda *see* Balante
Bulea *see* Kanjaga
Buləm, Bullom, Bullun *see* Bulom
Bulo *see* Kanjaga
Bulom 12–13, 20–23
Bulse *see* Bobo Fï
Bulufai *see* Lamba
Bulug, Bulugu *see* Kanjaga
Bulyama *see* Briama
Bum¹: Bome 12–13
Bum² 123
Bungnu 143
Bunu: Yoruba 85
Bura¹: Kasena 60
Bura² 153, 160–1
Buram, Burama *see* Bola
Buressya *see* Anufo
Burom *see* Brong
Burra *see* Bura²
Burrikem *see* Widekum
Burrum *see* Burum²
Buru *see* Degha
Burum¹ *see* Brong
Burum² 106
Busa, Busagwe, Busanchi, Busano, Busanse 41
Butawa 108

Bute *see* Vute
BuxıdIm *see* Margi
Buzi *see* Loma
Bwa *see* Bobo
Bwanda *see* Bonna
Bwareba *see* Bachama
Bwidebo: Grebo 50
Byetri *see* Metyibo
'Bete *see* Bata
'Bidyo 168

Cabrai, Cabre *see* Kabre
Cado *see* Habe
Cakosi: Anyi 80
Cala, Cãla: Tem 69
Camba¹ *see* Sisala
Camba² *see* Kasele
Can *see* Jukun
Cansi *see* Kasele
Caŋborəŋ *see* Ncumuru
Carabane: Dyola 17
Cassanga, Cassangue *see* Kassanga
Cemba *see* Tobote
Cɛ *see* Kasele
Chala *see* Ron
Chamba¹ *see* Tobote
Chamba² 149–50
Chamba Daka 150
Chamo 108
Chang *see* Dshang
Chawai, Chawe, Chawi 106, 108, 109, 111
Cheke 156
Chibbak, Chibbok, Chibbuk: Margi 154
Chilila *see* Dakakari
Chokobawa: Jarawa 107
Chokosi *see* Cakosi
Cimiaŋ *see* Tshimiang
Cogniagui *see* Konyagi
Commendi *see* Manya
Conhague *see* Konyagi
Copowa *see* Konkomba
Cotokoli *see* Tem
Coulailai *see* Kulele

Dã *see* Dan
Daa: Kotoko² 165
Daba 158–9
Dabu *see* Adyukru
Dadia: Tula 112
Dadyessu: Baule 81
Dafe, Dafing: Dyula 35
Dagaaba, Dagaao, Dagare, *Dagari*, Dagarti, Dagati, Dagatsi 66
Dagbamba¹, Dagbambe, Dagbane, *Dagomba* 64, 71–75
Dagbamba² *see* Mamprusi
Daho: Dan 40

INDEX

Dahoméen see Fɔ̃
Daka see Chamba Daka
Dakakari, Dakarawa, Dakarchi 103
Dakuya: Bete 49
Dama see Boki
Dan 39–40
Danda, Dandawa see Dendi
Dangaleat 168, 176
Daŋmeli see Adangme
Dari 167
Date see Late
Dawari see Dagari
De 51, 52
Debe see Sisala
Degha, Deɣa: Grusi 62
Deforo see Kurumba
Delo: Tem 69
Dendi: Songhai 46, 47 n.
Deŋ: Gola 12
Dera see Kanakuru
Dewĕmā, Dewoi see De
Dei see Kissi
Dekərici see Dakakari
Diakanke see Dyakanka
Dian see Dyan
Dibo: Nupe 86
Dida: Bete 48
Difu see Boritsũ
Dikpaŋkpamdi see Konkomba
Dima see Chamba
Ding-ding: Mumuye 139
Diŋi, Diŋyim, Dɩŋa see Chamba
Diola see Dyola
Dioula see Dyula
Dipo see Kweni
Ditamaba see Somba
Djallonke see Dyalonke
Djedji see Fɔ̃
Djerma see Zarma
Djimini see Dyimini
Djola see Biafada
Djongor see Jongor
Do see De
Doayo: Namci 149
Dogohe, Doghosie, Doghossie, Doɣosye: Senufo 57; Lobi 60
Dogõ, Dogom, Dogon, 60–61
Dokhobe see Doghosie
Doma see Jaba
Domar Buzi see Loma
Domawa see Kelawa
Dompago: Tem 69
Doŋɔi see De
Dorhossie see Doghosie
Dɔ wud̯u: Kru 51
Drebo, Drɛbo: Gweabo 50
Drewin see Neyo
Dschang, Dshang 128–9, 131
Dschubu see Jibu
Duhu: Margi 154

Dui: Duru 148
Duka, Dukanchi, Dukawa 102
Dunu see Bata
Dupa: Namci 149
Durru, Duru 148–9
Dyabarma see Zarma
Dyabe: Anyi 80
Dyaɣa, Dyaka, Dyakanka: Dyula 35
Dyakanke see Soninke
Dyalonke: Susu 36
Dyamate: Dyola 17
Dyamu, Dyamuru see Degha
Dyangirte: Bambara[1] 34
Dyan, Dyane, Dyanu, Dyā: Lobi 59
Dyarisso: Soninke 32
Dyarma see Zarma
Dyawara: Soninke 32
Dye: Gurma 68
Dyéguèmé see Serer
Dyembaren, Dyembering see Karones
Dyerma see Zarma
Dyimini: Senufo 56
Dyoba see Serer
Dyokereu see Dyula
Dyola 17
Dyolof see Wolof
Dyoma see Degha
Dyomande see Mau, Konya
Dyoula, Dyula, Dyulaŋke 33, 35
Dza see Jen

Ebe: Nupe 86
Ebrié see Kyama
Edda see Ada
Edo see Bini
Efik 133, 134–7
Egba: Yoruba 85
Egbɔte bɔ see Kebu
Egbura see Igbira
Egola mie see Gola
Eggon, Egon 107, 109
Egu see Igbira Igu
Egun see Gũ
Ehabe see Kakanda
Ehwe, Eibe see Ewe
Ejagam, Ejagham, EjaGam, Ejam: Ekoi 114
Eket: Ibibio 133
Eki see Bunu
Ekiti: Yoruba 85
Ekoi, Ekɔi, Ekwe 114
Elomay, Elunay see Banyun
Embeliŋga see Kanakuru
Enyong: Ibibio 133
Epit see Piti
Eple see Kwaya
Eregba 113
Erohwa: Sobo 89

Esa, Esã see Ishan
Eshupun see Oshopong
Esimbi see Age
Etaŋ ekom see Kom
Etien see Ganawuri
Etkyɛ̃ see Kentu
Evadi see Kambari
Evalwe see Afema
Eve, Evegbe see Ewe
Evhro: Sobo 89
Ewe 83–84, 90–94
Ewutre, Ewuture see Metyibo
Ezam see Ejagham
Ezi nupe see Nupe

Ɛbono see Brong
Ɛdo see Bini
Ɛgba see Egba
Ɛrohwa see Erohwa
Ɛtepe see Nedi
(Ɛ)tsaso see Babadjou

Fakara: Dakakari 103
Fali 151–2, 154, 156, 158, 159
Fante, Fanti: Twi 70, 90
Febe see Dyula
Fefe see Bafang
Fela see Bassa
Felata see Fulani
Feloup, Felupe see Flup
Fetu see Afutu
Fɛ'ɛfɛ see Bafang
Fika, Fikankayen see Bolewa
Filani see Fulani
Filham see Flup
Fiteriya see Hona
Floup, Flup: Dyola 17
Fogny see Fony
Folo[1] see Minya
Folo[2]: Senufo 56, 72
Fon see Fɔ̃
Fony: Dyola 17
Fore see Baga Fore
Foro see Folo[2]
Foulbéré: Fulani 19
Fɔ̃, Fɔ̃gbe: Ewe 84
Fra[1]: Kasena 61
Fra[2], Frafra[1] see Kusasi
Frafra[2] see Nankanse
Friesco, Friesko see Kwaya
Fu see Bafut
Fuga: Kukuruku 88
Ful, Fula, Fulani, Fulata, Fulɓe 18–19, 24–30, 64
Fula: Fulani 19, 26
Fulsap see Bafoussam
Fulse see Kurumba
Fulup see Flup
Fungom 123–4, 125
Fusaŋ, Fusap see Bafoussam
Fut see Bafut

INDEX

Gã¹ *see* Gan²
Gã² 82–83, 91, 92
Gaanda *see* Ganda
Gabi *see* Nkami
Gabin: Tera 157
Gadyaga *see* Soninke
Gagu: Kweni 40
Gain¹ *see* Gan²
Gain², Gaingbe *see* Gẽ²
Galebagla *see* Sisala
Galim: Vute 145
Gallinas *see* Vai
Gamawa *see* Ngamo
Gamargu, *Gamergu*: Mandara 159
Gambo *see* Nafana
Gan¹: Kweni 40
Gan²: Lobi 59
Ganagana *see* Dibo
Ganawuri 105
Ganda: Tera 157
Gane *see* Gan²
Gangan *see* Gyenguen
Ganne *see* Gan¹
Gaouar, *Gawar*: Daba 159
Gapershi *see* Kasena
Gara *see* Nganu
Gayegi: Gbari 86
Gayi: Boki 115
Gbã *see* Gagu
Gbagbang *see* Jukun
Gban *see* Gagu
Gbanda *see* Avikam
Gbandara *see* Nafana
Gbande, Gbandɛ, Gbandi *see* Bandi
Gbanian, Gbanje, Gbanya, Gbanyan, Gbanyang *see* Guang
Gbari 86
Gbato: Senufo 58
Gbe¹: Bakwe 49
Gbe²: Bobo 60
Gbedde: Yoruba 85
Gbeinngn *see* Gan¹
Gbẽ *see* Turuka
Gbɛize *see* Kpelle
Gbɛŋu *see* Gan¹
Gbɛrɛsɛ *see* Kpelle
Gbɔtɛ *see* Kebu
Gbɪnna *see* Binna
Gboare *see* Bachama
Gboati *see* Bata
Gboode *see* Gbunde
Gbɔ *see* Bassa
Gbunde, Gbundɛ: Loma 38
Gbwolo, Gbwɔlo: Gweabo 50
Ge: Mano, Dan 39
Gengle: Yendang 139
Gere 39–40, 49
Gerze *see* Kpelle
Gɛ *see* Ge

Gẽ¹ *see* Gã²
Gẽ²: Ewe 83, 84
Gibi *see* Gi gban
Gibo: Bete 49
Gidar 160
Gien *see* Tchien
Gi gban: Bassa 51
Gihi, Gii *see* Kissi
Gimini *see* Dyimini
Gindiri *see* Pyem
Gio *see* Dan
Girga, Girganke: Azer 32
Gisi *see* Kissi
Gisiga: Daba 158
Gisima: Loma 38
Gizi, Gizima¹ *see* Kissi
Gizima² *see* Gisima
Gme *see* Dgame
Go *see* Godye
Goali *see* Gbari
Gobwa: Bete 48
Godia, *Godye*: Bete 48
Goemai *see* Ankwe
Gola¹ 11, 20–24
Gola² *see* Badyara
Gola³: Mumuye 139
Gomoa: Guang 82
Gon *see* Ngere
Gouin: Lobi 59
Goun *see* Gũ
Gourma, Gourmantche *see* Gurma
Gouro *see* Kweni
Gourounsi *see* Grusi
Gɔbla: Gola 11
Grafi, Grafil *see* Bamileke
Grand Béréby *see* Abri
Grassfield *see* Bamileke
Grebo 50, 51–54
Grusi, Grussi 61–63
Gũ, Gũgbe: Ewe 84
Guang 81–82, 91, 92
Gude, Gudi: Bata 155
Gudu: Bata 155, 160, 161
Gudur 157
Guere *see* Ngere, Gere
Guerzé *see* Kpelle
Guibono: Bete 49
Guin, Guingbe *see* Gẽ²
Guissiga *see* Gisiga
Gujuguju *see* Cheke
Gula *see* Gola¹
Gulfei: Kotoko²
Gungawa *see* Reshe
Gunje: Kari 147
Gupa *see* Kupa
Gura *see* Nzima
Gure 108, 110
Gurense, Gureŋa *see* Nankanse
Guresha *see* Kanjaga
Guriŋa *see* Nankanse

Gurma 66–68, 73
Gurmake *see* Mossi
Gurmana 104
Gurmancɛ, Gurmantche *see* Gurma
Gurna: Angas 138
Guro, Gurumbo *see* Kweni
Gurumsi, Gurunsi *see* Grusi
Gwa 77
Gwai: Musgu 166
Gwalakwe *see* Gulfei
Gwali *see* Gbari
Gwanje: Mandara 151
Gwaŋ *see* Guang
Gwari *see* Gbari
Gwaza *see* Gwoza
Gwazum *see* Ngizim
Gweabo 50
Gwoza 158
Gyassale: Baule 81
Gyenguen: Gbari 86
Gyo *see* Dan

χəəfa' *see* Bafang
χəəkuu *see* Bakou
χəlabuunʃa: Bafang 129
χəlafa' *see* Bafang
χö pa papwantu *see* Babouantou

Habbe, *Habe*, Haɓe 61; *see also* Songhai
Ham, Hʌm *see* Jaba
Handa: Lala 111
Hausa, Hausaawaa 162, 169, 170–4
Higi, Hiji 156, 160, 161
Hima: Igbira 87
Hina¹, Hinna: Tera 157, 161
Hina²: Daba 159
Hissala *see* Sisala
Hoho: Musei 167
Holma: Bata 155
Hombeɓe *see* Habe
Hona: Tera 157, 161
Horo *see* Twabo
(H)ɔllɔm: Musei 167
Huã *see* Ewe
Hudu: Ewe 84
Huela *see* Hwela
Huene *see* Hona
Hulɔ *see* Mende
Hune *see* Duka
Hunna *see* Hina¹
Hurɔ *see* Mende
Huve, Huviya *see* Bura
Hwãle, *Hwane*: Bakwe 50
Hwela *see* Vai 36
Hwile, Hwĩne *see* Hwane
Hyabe *see* Kakanda

Ibara *see* Bassa-Nge
Ibibio 133–7

Ibie-Okpepe: Kukuruku 88
Ibilo: Kukuruku 88
Ibo, Iɓo *see* Igbo
Idafan *see* Irigwe
Idoma 140
Ife, Ifɛ: Yoruba 84
Igabo *see* Isoko
Igala, Igara[1]: Yoruba 85
Igara[2]: Igbira 87
Igbira, Igbirra 87
Igbiri *see* Gure
Igbo 89–94
Igbona: Yoruba 85
Igu: Igbira 87
Igumale: Idoma 140
Ihage, Ihaja *see* Kassanga
Ihima *see* Hima
Ijaw *see* Ijo
Ijebu: Yoruba 85
Ijesha, Ijeʃa: Yoruba 85
Ijoh, Ijɔ 121–2
Ika[1]: Igbo 90
Ika[2] *see* Igu
Ikolu, *Ikulu* 105
Ikpɔsɔ *see* Kposo
Ila: Yoruba 85
Ima *see* Ewe
Imbana: Mundang 146
Ina *see* Hina[2]
Ingwe, Ingwo *see* Ngwoi
Irapwe: Abri 50
Irigwe, Irregwe 105
Isa, *Ishan* 38
Ishekiri *see* Jekri
Isiema *see* Turuka
Isoko: Sobo 89
Issala *see* Sisala
Isu-ama: Igbo 90
Isu-item: Igbo 90
Ito: Ibibio 134
Itsekiri *see* Jekri
Itumbuzo: Ibibio 134
Iwerri *see* Jekri
Iworo: Yoruba 85
Iyala 116
Iyirikum *see* Widekum
Izare *see* Mbembe[2]

Jaba 105, 108–10
Jabo: Grebo 50, 52
Jagjage *see* Tangale
Jaku: Jar 115
Jalonca, Jalonke *see* Dyalonke
Jampalam, Jamphalam: Mandara 159
Janji: Chawai 107
Jar 115, 116
Jarawa: Jar 115
Jasing, Jassing: Mundang 145
Jekiri, *Jekri*: Yoruba 85
Jemjem *see* Suga

Jen 139
Jene kine *see* Songhai
Jeŋ: Bata 135, 160
Jera: Tera 157
Jerawa 107
Jerra, Jɛrra *see* Jera
Jibawa *see* Jibu
Jibə: Jukun 140
Jibu: Jukun 140
Jimini *see* Dyimini
Jinda *see* Kamuku
Jirai *see* Zumu
Jiri *see* Vere
Jivo: Bete 48
Jola *see* Dyola
Jolof *see* Wolof
Jomoro: Anyi 80
Jompre *see* Kutev
Jongor 168, 176
Jukon, Jukū, Jukum, *Jukun* 124, 140–1
Jumu: Yoruba 85

Kabiema, Kabieto, *Kabre*, Kabrema, Kabure, Kabye: Tem 69
Ka-ce sensa *see* Krachi
Kachichere: Katab 104
Kadara: Katab 105
Kadjagse *see* Kajakse
Kadle: Senufo 57
Kado[1] *see* Habe
Kado[2]: Dari 167
Kafibele, Kafige, Kafugulo: Senufo 58
Kafolo: Senufo 58
Kaga *see* Dyula
Kagbana *see* Guang
Kagoma: Katab 105
Kagoro[1]: Bambara[1] 34
Kagoro[2]: Katab 104, 108–9
Kagu *see* Kahugu
Kaho: Dan 40
Kahugu: Gure 108–11
Kajaakisee, Kajagise, *Kajakse*: Mubi[2] 169
Kaje: Katab 105, 108–10
Kakaa *see* Kuri
Kakaba *see* Bungnu
Kakanda: Nupe 86
Kakhumu *see* Higi
Kakono: Senufo 56
Kalabari: Ijo 121
Kali *see* Kari
Kalongo: Bambara[1] 34
Kalum: Baga 14
Kalunka *see* Kalongo
Kama[1]: Kissi 12
Kama[2] *see* Karaboro, Tiefo
Kamantan: Katab 104
Kambali, *Kambari*, Kamberawa, Kamberchi, 102

Kamberi Beri-Beri: Busa 41
Kambon, Kambosi *see* Twi
Kamburwama: Mandara 159
Kamkam *see* Bungnu
Kamuku 102–3
Kamun *see* Higi
Kana *see* Ogoni
Kanakura, *Kanakuru* 164, 175
Kandere *see* Kadle
Kanɛma *see* Avatime
Kanga Ble *see* Tagwana
Kanga Bono: Kweni 40
Kangye: Gbari 86
Kanjaga: Grusi 62, 72, 74
Kanyop *see* Mandyak
Kapsiki: Higi 156
Kapugu *see* Kahugu
Karaboro: Senufo 56
Karang, Karang-ma *see* Angas
Kare *see* Kari
Karekare 163, 174
Kari 147
Karo *see* Vai
Karoma *see* Karaboro
Karones: Dyola 17
Kasele: Gurma 67, 72, 74
Kasem *see* Kasena
Kasembele: Senufo 58
Kasena, Kasene, Kasina, Kasomse, Kason, Kassena, Kassouna, Kassuna, Kasuna: Grusi 61
Kassanga 15
Kassembele *see* Kasembele
Kasso, Kassonke *see* Khasonke
Katab 104, 108–10
Katawa *see* Igbira
Katiba *see* Kabre
Ke *see* Jukun
Keaka: Ekoi 114
Kebe: Bete 49
Kebu 101
Kedeanɛ, Kedemɔnye *see* Avatime
Kegem *see* Sin
Kelawa, Kellini: Dakarkari 103
Kemai *see* Ankwe
Kenga *see* Kyenga
Kenji *see* Kamuku
Kentu 143
Kepere *see* Pere
Kera 146, 147
Kerang *see* Angas
Kerekere, Kerikeri *see* Karekare
Kete: Akye 78
Kɛra *see* Kera
Kɔbʌk *see* Chibbak
Kə-gbəri-kə *see* Kebu
Kɔpɛrɛ *see* Pere
Kɔrɛkɔrɛ *see* Karekare
Kətoba *see* Mambila

INDEX

Khasonke 25
Kiama see Kyama
Kibbo see Birom
Kibissi see Dogon
Kibo, Kibyen see Birom
Kidʒem: Kom 123
Kiefo see Tiefo
Kiegbagha, Kiembarha see Kyembagha
Kien see Tchien
Kilba 154, 161
Kilir see Pilapila
Kim, Kimi: Bulom 12
Kimbuzi see Gbunde
Kipirsi see Kasena
Kira see Siti
Kirdiwat see Ngizim
Kirim see Kim
Kisi, Kissi 12, 21
Kittim see Kim
Klao see Kru
Kloli see Krobo
Koba: Baga 14
Kobiana 15
Kobotshi see Njai
Kobou see Akye
Koboke see Tobote
Koira kine see Songhai
Kokomba see Konkomba
Kokra: Bura 153
Kolãyo, Kolam, Kolã-mbio, Kolambo, Kolamvo, Kolaŋo see Kulango
Kolbila, Kolbilari, Kolbilla: Chamba 150
Kom 123, 124
Koma: Duru 149
Komba: Grusi 67
Komboya: Mende 37
Komendi see Manya
Komono: Senufo 56, Lobi 59, Baule 81.
Konkomba: Gurma 67
Kono: Vai 36
Konosarala see Siti
Konya: Malinke 34
Konyagi, Konyaki: Tenda 17
Konyanka see Konya
Koranko: Malinke 33
Koretiba see Kabre
Koroma see Karaboro
Kossa, Kosso see Mende
Kotafon, Kotafɔ̃: Ewe 84
Kotofo see Kotopo
Kotoko¹: Akye 78
Kotoko² 165, 175, 177
Kotokoli see Tem
Kotolo: Senufo 56
Kotopo: Duru 149
Kotokori see Igbira
Kotpojo see Kotopo

Kotrahu, Kòtroku see Godye
Kottofo see Kotopo
Kotule see Tula
Koulango see Kulango
Kouranke, Kouranko see Koranko
Kouroumba see Kurumba
Kowremba see Kabre
Kɔ: Mende 37
Kɔffa: Mogum 168
Kɔimaka see Weima
Kɔkwamba see Konkomba
Kɔndo, Kɔno see Vai, Kono
Kɔŋbaa: Gola 11
Kɔŋkomba see Konkomba
Kɔɔ: Bassa 51
Kɔsɔ see Mende
Kɔtɔkɔ see Kotoko²
Kɔtta see Mogum
Kpa: Mende 37
Kpã see Jukun
Kpaimba see Turuka
Kpakpamba see Konkomba
Kpalagha, Kpalaya: Senufo 56
Kpelego see Kulango
Kpelle 37–38, 42, 45
Kper see Pere
Kpẽ see Gouin, Turuka
Kpẽjesia, Kpɛlɛ, Kpɛlɛma, Kpɛlɛŋa, Kpɛlɛse, Kpɛlɛsetini, Kpɛrɛse, Kpɛse see Kpelle
Kpilakpila see Pilapila
Kposo, Kposso 100–1
Kpuŋkpamba see Konkomba
Kra, Krã: Kru 51
Krachi: Guang 82
Krahn, Kran 50
Krao, Krawo see Kra
Krepe, Krepi see Ewe
Krim see Kim
Krobo: Gã-Adangme 82
Krobu see Akye
Kroumen, Krumen see Kru
Kru Group 48–54
Kru 51
Kudamata see Dyamate
Kudawa: Gure 108
Kugama: Yendang 139
Kukuruku 88
Kulango 58
Kulele: Senufo 57
Kumba¹ see Tangale
Kumba²: Yendang 139
Kumba Jokoi see Loma
Kumenu, Kumwenu see Komono
Kunãt, Kunante 15
Kupa, Kupanchi: Nupe 86
Kurama: Chawai 106, 108–11
Kuranke, Kuranko see Koranko
Kurarapa see Jukun
Kuri: Buduma 166

Kuria see Songhai
Kurndel see Holma
Kurobu see Akye
Kurorofa see Jukun
Kuruma, Kurumba, Kurumdo, Kurumfe: Grusi 63
Kusage, Kusale, Kusasi: Dagomba 65
Kuseki: Yendang 139
Kuseri: Kotoko 165
Kushi see Baushi
Kussasse, Kussassi see Kusasi
Kutev 114
Kuterɪŋa see Hona
Kutin, Kutinn 149
Kuturincha see Hona
Kwa see Kwadya
Kwaa 51
Kwadrewole, Kwadya: Bete 49
Kwakwa see Avikam
Kwale: Igbo 90
Kwama see Sisala
Kwana, Kwanaba see Jukun
Kwange see Kangye
Kwararafa see Jukun
Kwaya: Bete 48
Kweni 40
Kwotto see Igbira
Kyama 77
Kyan see Gbe
Kyembagha: Senufo 57
Kyenga, Kyengawa: Busa 41
Kyerepɔŋ: Guang 82
Kyilinga see Pilapila

Labang see Kotoko²
Laego see Lekon
Lãgã see Langa
Lagubi see Mambila
Lagwane see Logone
Lahu see Avikam
La-isa see Sisala
Laka see Ŋger
Lala 111
Lama, Lamba: Tem 69
Lamja: Chamba Daka 150
Lamsɔ' see Nsaw
Landogo, Landogho, Landɔyɔ see Loko
Landoma, Landouman, Landuma 14
Langa: Susu 36
Laŋ tumu see Tikar
Laru, Laruawa: Bargu 70
Late: Guang 82
Led tumu see Tikar
Lefana 97
Legba see Dompago
Legre: Bete 48
Leko, Lekon: Chamba 149
Lela, Lele¹, L'ela, L'ele: Grusi 62

INDEX

Lele[2]: Koranko 33
Lele[3] *see* Panda
Lelemi, Lɛlɛmi *see* Lefana
Lere *see* Lele[1]
Lɛte *see* Late
Lɔlo *see* Delo
Liaro: Kissi 12
Ligbi, Ligwi: Vai 36
Likpe, Likpɛlɛ 97
Lila, Lilana, *Lilawa*: Dakakari 103
Lilse *see* Lele, Kurumba
Limba 13, 23
Lindiri *see* Rindri
Liŋga *see* Kanakuru
Lo *see* Kweni
Lober: Birifo 59, 66
Lobi[1] 58–59
Lobi[2]: Dagari 66
Loble: Bete 49
Logba[1] *see* Dompago
Logba[2] 96–97
Loghoma[1] *see* Loma[1]
Loghoma[2], Logoma, *Loghon*: Kulango 58
Logone: Kotoko[2] 165
Loko 37
Lölo *see* Delo
Lolobi 98
Loma[1] 38
Loma[2] *see* Loghon
Longuda 111–12
Loomago *see* Loma[1]
Lopawa: Bargu 70
Lorhon, Loron *see* Loghon
Losso *see* Nawdam, Lamba
Lozwa: Bete 48
Lɔkɔ *see* Loko
Lɔɔma *see* Loma
Luɛn *see* Mambila
Lukö, Lukə 122
Lunamba *see* Lamba
Lyela, Lyele *see* Lele[1]

Maa *see* Mano
Maa bã: Bassa 51
Mabila *see* Mambila
Mada *see* Nunku, Egon
Madabe *see* Twi
Madaganye *see* Kotoko[2]
Madure: Baga 14
Mădyak *see* Mandyak
Magbara *see* Lamba
Magəri *see* Kotoko[2]
Magha 153
Maghavul *see* Sura
Magu: Mambila 143
Mahi: Ewe 84
Majinda *see* Kamuku
Makari: Kotoko[2] 165
Makia: Samo 41

Malɓe *see* Gulfei
Male, Malel *see* Mande
Malgwe *see* Gulfei
Mali *see* Mande
Malinke, Maliŋka, Maliŋkɛ 33–34, 42–45
Mambai *see* Mangbai
Mambere, *Mambila*, Mambilla 143–5
Mamboma, Mamboŋa *see* Bandi
Ma mia *see* Mano
Mampa: Bulom 12–13
Mampele, Mamprule, *Mamprusi*, Mampuliga, Mampulugu, &c.: Dagomba 65
Mampwa *see* Mampa
Mamzɔkoi *see* Musgu
Mana gɔbla: Gola 11
Mancagne, Mancanha *see* Mankanya
Mandaga: Senufo 56
Mandara 159, 160–1
Mande 20–33
Mandenyi *see* Mmani
Mandeŋga, Mandeŋka *see* Malinke
Mandi, Manding *see* Mande
Mandingo, Mandiŋka, &c. *see* Malinke
Mandjaque *see* Mandyak
Mandouré *see* Madure
Mandyak, Mandyako 15
Maneŋka *see* Malinke
Manganapo, Manganepo: Tem 69
Manganasise: Tem 69
Mangbai 146
Mangbara: Tem 69
Mangbei *see* Mangbai
Mani *see* Bassa
Manimo *see* Manya
Maninyaka: Malinke 53
Manjaco *see* Mandyak
Mankanya 16
Mano, Manon 39
Manta: Ekoi 114
Mantage *see* Kotoko[2]
Manya, Manyanka: Malinke 34
Manyigbe *see* Ewe
Mapodi *see* Cheke
Maranse: Songhai 46
Marba 167
Marghi, *Margi*, 154, 161; *see also* Higi
Marka, Markaŋka: Soninke 32
Masa[1] *see* Musgu
Masa[2], Masana 167, 176
Masa gbaya: Musei 167
Masasi: Bambara[1] 34
Masfeima: Mandara 159
Masiin *see* Azer

Masmaje: Mubi[2] 169
Mata: Tupuri 146
Matai *see* Gyenguen
Matakam 158, 161
Matatarwa: Egon 107
Matengala: Egon 107
Mau, Mauka: Malinke 33
Ma'u *see* Akpafu
Mã-wi *see* Mano
Mawu *see* Akpafu
Maya[1] *see* Makia
Maya[2] 154
Maxe *see* Mahi
Mayigbe *see* Ewe
Mazagwa: Mandara 159
Mbana *see* Mundang
Mbarike *see* Kutev
Mbato *see* Gwa
Mbembe[1] (Ogoja) 116
Mbembe[2] (Cameroons) 141–2
Mbere *see* Ɖger
Mbete *see* Bete[2]
Mbichi, Mbitse *see* Tiv
Mboa: Jar 115
Mboi: Lela 111
Mbouin[1] *see* Mbwin
Mbouin[2] *see* Gouin
Mbudikem *see* Widekum
Mbum 146–8
Mbwat *see* War
Mbwe, Mbwĕ *see* Gouin
Mbwin: Senufo 56
Megamaw *see* Mogamo
Megimba *see* Ngemba
Megoŋ *see* Egon
Mekaf 116, 120
Mekibo *see* Metyibo
Mel *see* Mande
Melamba 127
Mele, Melel, Melit *see* Mande
Memmi *see* Nedi
Memne: Kweni 40
Mende, Mendi 37, 42–45
Mendenyi *see* Mmani
Menemo 127
Meninka: Malinke 33
Menkiera: Grusi 62
Meta *see* Menemo
Metyibo 77
Meyobe *see* Soruba
Mebe *see* Dan
Melɛ *see* Malinke
Meli *see* Mande
Mɛnde *see* Mende
Mesona: Mano 39
Mɔbakɔ' 150
Mɔyamo *see* Mogamo
Mfantera *see* Nafana
Mgbato *see* Gwa
Mida *see* Kotoko[2]
Miir *see* Kuseri

INDEX

Mimi: Ijɔ 121
Mina *see* Gɛ̃²
Mingi *see* Ngi
Minia, Minianka: Senufo 55
Minjilo *see* Mubi²
Minya, Minyaŋka: Malinke 34
Mitaa *see* Ŋgamambo
Mɪrki *see* Margi
Mmani 13
Mmɛ 123
Mmofo *see* Degha
Moba: Gurma 67
Mofu, Mofou: Matakam 158
Mogamaw, *Mogamo*, Moghamo 126
Mogimba *see* Ngemba
Mogum 168
Moγa, Moisi *see* Mossi
Mokolle: Bargu 70
Mole *see* Mossi
Mona, Moni *see* Mwa
Monjul *see* Mubi²
Monnai *see* Bonna
Mono 146, 147
Mora 158
More *see* Mossi
Moroa *see* Morwa
Moronu: Baule 80
Moru¹ *see* Mwa
Moru²: Lobi 59
Morwa: Katab 104, 109
Mose, Mosi, *Mossi*, Moʃi 63–64, 71, 72, 74
Mouin *see* Mwa
Moundan *see* Mundang
Mousgou *see* Musgu
Mɔab, Mɔaba, Mɔba, Mɔban *see* Moba
Mɔgamu *see* Mogamo
Mɔgum *see* Mogum
Mõnõ *see* Mono
Mɔnɔ, Mɔŋgɔ *see* Fali
Mɔwa, Mɔwan *see* Moba
Mphaadə *see* Makari
Mpsakali *see* Gudur
Msirr *see* Kuseri
Mu *see* Likpe
Mubako *see* Mumbake, Bali²
Mubi¹ *see* Cheke
Mubi² 168–9, 176–7
Muffo, Muffu, Mufu *see* Mofu
Muyɔbaatɔ *see* Makari
Muleng: Bata 155
Mulwi *see* Musgu
Mumbake: Chamba 150
Mumuye 139
Munchi *see* Tiv
Mundang 145–6, 147
Munga: Jen 139
Munshi *see* Tiv
Munyɔŋa *see* Bali¹

Musei, Musey 167
Musgoi, Musgoy: Daba 158
Musgu, Musgum 166, 176
Mussoi *see* Musei
Musugeu *see* Musgoi
Muta *see* Menemo
Muturua *see* Gisiga
Muzgu, Muzugu *see* Musgu
Mvanip *see* Ndunda
Mwa, Mwɛ̃: Kweni 40
Myoru *see* Moru²

Nabdam, Nabde, Nabdug, Nabrug, Nabt, Nabte *see* Namnam
Nabe *see* Kulango
Nabwa Kru: Gweabo 50
Nafagha: Senufo 57
Nafana: Senufo 56
Nafarha *see* Nafagha
Nafunfia: Ron 138
Naga: Balante 15
Nago, Nagot *see* Yoruba
Nagumi 115
Nagwa: Kasena 61
Nalou, *Nalu* 14
Namba *see* Lamba
Nambai *see* Kulango
Nambane *see* Lamba
Namci, Namji: Duru 149
Namnam: Birifo 66
Namtchi *see* Namci
Nanerge *see* Samo
Nangba *see* Kabre
Nankane, *Nankanse* 65
Nanna Kru *see* Kra
Nanumba, Nanune: Dagomba 65
Naŋkane, Naŋkanse *see* Nankanse
Naoudam, Naoudeba, Naoudemba *see* Nawdam
Naoulou *see* Noholo
Narabuna *see* Jerawa
Natemba, Natimba: Gurma 68
Natioro, Natyoro: Senufo 57
Nawdam: Mossi 64
Nawuri, Nawuru: Guang 81
Ncumuru: Guang 82
NdaGam: Bali² 151
Ndama *see* Jukun
Ndame: Baule 81
Nde: Ekoi 114
Ndenye: Anyi 80
Ndirma *see* Kilba
Ndore *see* Tupuri
Ndoro, Ndɔrɔ 142
Ndoute: Serer 18
Ndu *see* Wiya
Ndunda: Bungnu 143
Ndyegem: Serer 18
Ndyura *see* Dyula
Ndzungle *see* Nsungli
Ndʒubʊya *see* Bangangte

Nðale *see* Mbembe²
Neabo: Kran 51
Nedi: Akye 78
Nembe: Ijɔ 121
Newo, Newole, *Neyo*: Bete 48, 49, 53, 54
Nɛya mundʒu *see* Bamendjou
Nɛya pamuŋgup *see* Bamougoum
Nɛkovibla *see* Bali²
Nfumte 141 n.
Ngadye: Akye 78
Ngamaya *see* Ngamo
Ngamgam *see* Dye
Ngamo: Bolewa 163
Ngano, *Nganu*: Baule 81
Ngaslawe 159
Nge: Baule 81
Ngemba 127
Ngembi: Tikar 125–6
Ngere: Dan 39
Ngi, Ngie 127
Ngizim, Ngizzem 164
Ngomba *see* Ngemba
Ngonu, Ngunu, Ngwa 127
Ngwala *see* Kulango
Ngwo *see* Ngonu
Ngwoi: Kamuku 103
Niaghafolo, Niarhafolo: Senufo 58
Ni boè kwidʲin: Bassa 51
Nibulu *see* Nunuma, Sisala
Niende: Gurma 68
Niene *see* Nyene
Nienegue *see* Nyenege
Nife *see* Nupe
Nigbi, Nigwi *see* Ligbi
Ni-gɔbri: Fali 151, 152
Nihiri *see* Neyo
Ni-kaŋ: Fali 151
Nimalto *see* Tangale
Nimbi *see* Nembe
Nimiah: Gweabo 50
Nimse *see* Kurumba
Ningawa 108
Ninisi *see* Samo
Ninzam 107
Niwiɛ *see* Nimiah
Njai: Bata 155
Njal: Mbum 147
Njei, Njel, Njeny *see* Njai
Nkami: Guang 82
Nki *see* Boki
Nkom *see* Kom
Nkum, Nkumm: Ekoi 114
Nkunya: Guang 82
Nkwoi *see* Ngwoi
No *see* Neyo
Nogbo: Bete 48
Noholo: Senufo 56
Non, None: Serer 18
Nono: Soninke 32

Nor see Mambila
Noua see Nwa
Noumou see Numu
Nõguraya see Longuda
Nsare see Mbembe²
Nsaw, Nso 123, 124
Nsɔya see Mande
Nsugni, Nsungli, Nsungni 123
Ntafo see Guang
Ntribu see Delo
Nufawa see Nupe
Numu: Vai 36
Nuna see Nunuma
Nungu see Rindri
Nungu-raba see Longuda
Nunku 107
Nunuma: Grusi 61–62
Nupe, Nupeci, Nupeciʒi, Nupenchi, Nupenciʒi 85–86, 91, 92, 94
Nuruma see Nunuma
Nwa, Nwã: Kweni 40
Nyabo, Nyãbo: Gweabo 50
Nyamasa: Bambara¹ 34
Nyangbo 96
Nyene: Senufo 57
Nyenege: Bobo 60
Nyidu: Kentu 143
Nyimaʃi see Tera
Nyominka: Serer 18
Nyongnepa see Mumbake
Nyonyose see Kurumba
Nyoru see Moru
Nzangi, Nzaŋe, Nzaŋyın see Njai
Nzema, Nzima: Anyi 80, 90, 92

Dahlawe see Ngaslawe
Darã see Nwa
Dbanyato see Guang
Dgaa ka see Bali¹
Dgamambo 126
Dgamaya see Ngamo
Dgame: Musei 167
Dgamo see Ngamo
Dgbanya see Guang
Dgbanye see Gbanyang
Dger: Mbum 147
Dgəzəm, Dgizim see Ngizim
Dgoga, Dgoya see Gwa
Dgomahũm: Bandjoun 129
Dgomandʒũ see Bandjoun
Dgorafo see Kulango
Dgwalkwe see Gulfei
Dka': Bafang 129
Dkɛmi see Nkami
Dkoramfo see Kulango
Dkranfo see Gã²
Dwana see Dagomba
Dwe see Bangwa

Obaŋ: Ekoi 114
Obubra: Mbembe¹ 116
Obwa: Bakwe 50
Ocan see Jukun
Odere see Adele
Odiukru see Adyukru
Ofutu see Afutu
Ogbinya: Ijɔ 121
Ogo, Ogoebi see Ahlõ
Ogoni 134, 137
Ogo uku: Igbo 90
Ohuhu-Ngwa: Igbo 90
Okene see Hima
Okii see Boki
Okpara-Agbado: Sobo 89
Okpe 89
Okpoto see Igala, Igbira, Idoma
Okranni see Gã²
Okrikan: Ijɔ 121
Okwoga: Idoma 140
Omavırre see Mambila
Omelokwe see Pya
Ondo: Yoruba 85
Onitsha: Igbo 89, 90
Ora: Kukuruku 88
Oratta-Ikweni: Igbo 90
Orepwe: Abri 50
Orri 116
Oshopong: Mbembe¹ 116
Osikom see Boki
Oso: Fungom 124
Otshi see Twi
Otukpo: Idoma 140
Otwa: Kukuruku 88
Otwi, Otwini see Twi
Ouala, Ouara see Wara
Ouassoulounke see Wasulu
Ouatchi see Watyi
Oubi see Wobe
Oule see Wule
Ouolof see Wolof
Owe: Yoruba 85
Owerri: Igbo 89
Owo¹: Yoruba 85
Owo², O'o see Akpafu
Oyo: Yoruba 84

Ɔbaŋ see Obang
Ɔkpɛlɛ(nya) see Likpe
Ɔle see Santrokofi
Ɔ-temne see Temne
Ɔwɔ see Owo¹
Ɔyɔ see Oyo

Pabir, Pabır see Babur
Padebu see Palipo
Padogo: Senufo 56; Lobi 59
Padogo, Padoko, Padokwa see Paduko
Padorho see Padogho
Paduko 160, 161
Pahn see Kran
Paiema see Pyem
Pain see Turuka
Pajade, Pajadinca see Badyara
Palaya, Palaka, Palaxa see Kpalagha
Palipo: Grebo 50
Pallaka see Kpalagha
Pama see Kulele
Pana¹: Soninke 32
Pana²: Kari 147
Panda: Igbira 87
Pani: Mbum 147
Pani Dui: Duru 148
Panõ, Panon see Pape
Pantara see Nafana
Papaire see Metyibo
Pape: Duru 149
Papei, Papel see Pepel
Pasala see Sisala
Passam: Yendang 139
Patani: Ijɔ 121
Paxala see Kulango, Siti
Payema see Pyem
Peda see Kadara
Pemawa see Pyem
Pepel 16
Pepisa: Anyi 80
Pere: Mbum 147
Pereba see Wom
Pessa, Pessi, Pessy see Kpelle
Peul, Peulh see Fulani
Peve: Dari 167
Pɛlla see Kilba
Pɛpɛl see Pepel
Pilapila 63, 68
Pio: Gola 11
Piti: Chawai 107
Pılımdi see Hina¹
Pla, Plapi, Plapo: Gweabo 50
Ponga, Pongala: Senufo 57
Pongo, Pongu: Kamuku 103
Popo see Ewe
Pori: Bakwe 49
Potou, Potu see Gwa
Pougouli see Buguli
Poular see Pular
Pugbiri see Gure
Pugu: Mumuye 139
Pular: Fulani 19, 26–28
Pulo see Fulani
Pulu pany see Sapo
Punɩrago see Kahugu
Pura: Lala 111
Pus: Musgu 166
Puthlundi 157
Pwe see Wule
Pya, Pye, Pyɛ: Bakwe 50
Pyem 138

Rabecha see Lala
Rebinawa see Jerawa
Regba see Eregba

INDEX

Reshe 101–2
Ribinawa see Jerawa
Rindri 107
Ripere see Pere
Roba: Lala 111
Ron 138
Rop: Birom 106
Rɔba see Roba
Rukuba 107
Rum see Gisiga

Sa see Sapo
Sã see Dan
Saba: Sokoro 169
Sadar see Shadal
Safwi: Anyi 80
Sako: Susu 36
Sama[1] see Wara
Sama[2], Samabu see Chamba[2]
Sama[3] see Chamba Daka
Sambila see Sembla
Sa-mia, Samia see Dan
Samina, Samitemi see Natioro
Samo 41
Samogho[1]: Soninke 32
Samogho[2], Samoyo, Samorho, Samoxo see Samo
Sãmu see Natioro
Samwi see Afema
Sanda: Temne 13
Sane see Samo
Sangawa: Jerawa 107
Sankura: Bobo 60
Sano see Samo
Santrokofi 97–98
Sanu see Samo
Sao see Kotoko[2]
Sapã, Sapo: Kran 51
Saracole, Sarakole, Sarakolle, Sarawule see Soninke
Saremde: Mossi 64
Sari: Duru 148
Sate: Yendang 139
Sãwi see Afema
Segum: Serer 18
Sembla: Samo 41
Semolika: Kukuruku 88
Sémou, Semu see Samo
Señadi: Senufo 55
Sendeye see Bamana[2]
Senoufo, Senufo 55–58, 74
Serahuli see Soninke
Serer, Serere, Serrer 17–18, 19
Sɛdɛrɛ see Adele
Sɛkɔbɔ, Sɛkɔpɔ see Twi
Sɛkpana see Logba
Sɛkpɛle see Likpe
Sɛlɛ see Santrokofi
Sɛnye: Gola 11
Sɛxwi see Safwi
Shabe see Kakanda

Shadal: Bola 16
Shakiri see Gudur
Shanga, Shangawa: Busa 41
Shawi: Kotoko[2] 165
Shekiri see Jekri
Shellengcha see Kanakuru
Sheni 108
Sherbro[1] see Bulom
Sherbro[2]: Mende 37
Shiba see Bulom
Shingini 104
Shosho see Birom
Sia see Sya
Siama: Loma 38
Sidabe see Twi
Sidianka, Sidya, Sidyanka: Malinke 34
Sifu see Akpafu
Sigila 166
Sikasso-Nyarene: Baule 32
Silmi, Silmissi: Mossi 64
Simu, Simuse see Twi
Sin, Sine-sine: Serer 18
Sinna: Higi 156
Sinugbe see Logba
Sinyigbe, Sinyigbe-sɛ see Ewe
Sisai, Sisala, Sisale: Grusi 62, 75
Sitemou, Sitemu: Baga 14
Siti, Sitigo: Grusi 62
Siwu see Akpafu
Siwuri see Bowili
Siyasɛ see Avatime
Siyikpe see Ewe
So see Kotoko[2]
Sobane: Baga 14
Sobo 88–89
Sogha see Dyula
Soghole: Dagari 66
Sõyai, Sõyɔi see Songhai
Sokoro, Sokɔrɔ 169, 176
Solamba see Soruba
Soma, Somba, Some: Gurma 67–68
Somono: Bambara[1] 34
Songhai, Songhay, Sonraïh, Sonraï 46–47
Soninke, Soniŋkɛ 31–32
Sõŋai, Sõŋoi see Songhai
Sorouba, Soruba-Kuyobe: Gurma 68
Soso, Sosso, Soussou see Susu
Sɔrkɔ, Sɔrɔgɔ see Bozo
Ssari see Sari
Ssuga see Suga
Ssugur see Sugur
Suamle: Kweni 40
Subktu: Lala 111
Suga: Vute 145
Sugur, Sukur 156–7
Sup'ide: Senufo 55
Sura 138

Susu, Sussu 36–37
Sya: Kweni 40
Syena, Syene see Senufo
Syeneye see Bamana[2]

Ʃɛkiri see Jekri
Ʃinyewole nafame see Nafana
Ʃüpamʌm see Bamun

Tabu see Abri
Tafi 96
Tafile, Tafire, Tafiri; Senufo 56
Tagba see Bamana[2]
Tagbo see Mambila
Tagbona see Tagwana
Taghdaush see Azer
Tagouana see Tagwana
Tagwa see Bamana[2]
Tagwana: Senufo 56
Takamanda see Anyang
Takemba: Gurma 68
Takpa see Nupe
Takponin see Tagwana
Talansi, Talene, Talensi, Taleŋa, Taleŋga, Talis, Tallensi 65
Tali: Kari 147
Tamaba, Tamari, Tamberma see Somba
Tamboboba see Sisala
Tambu: Lala 111
Tampele, Tampolem, Tampolema, Tampolense, Tamprusi: Grusi 62
Tang: Nsungli 123
Tangale 157, 164, 175
Tankamba see Takemba
Taŋgale see Tangale
Taolende: Mossi 64
Tapa see Nupe
Tapessi see Tiapi
Tara, Tarase see Wule[1]
Taroh see Yergum
Tayakou: Gurma 68
Tchien: Kran 50
Te see Twabo
Tebɔte see Tobote
Tegesye, Tegué, Teguessié: Kulango 58
Tem 68–70, 71–74
Temba[1]: Gurma 68
Temba[2], Tembia see Tem
Temne[1] 13, 20
Temne[2] see Tem
Tenda 16–17
Teng: Kissi 12
Tera, Terawa 157
Terebendyula see Vai
Tepo, Tewi see Twabo
Tɛgɛ: Gola 11
Tiapi: Landoma 14
Tiba: Mbum 147

INDEX

Tiebala *see* Tyebali
Tiefo: Senufo 57
Tiĕ *see* Tchien
Tigong 113, 141, 143
Tikali, *Tikar* 123, 125–6, 127
Tim *see* Tem
Timene, Timmannee, Timne *see* Temne¹
Timu *see* Tem
Tiokossi *see* Anufo²
Titʃaat *see* Kachichere
Tiv, Tivi, Tiwi 113, 116–20
Tiwirkum *see* Widekum
Tõ *see* Twi
Tobote, Tobɔte: Gurma 70, 72, 75
Toldil: Gola 11
Toma *see* Loma
Tombo, Tommo: Dogon 61
Ton, Tonawa *see* Twi
Tongbo *see* Mambila
Toodii *see* Toldil
Toram: Mubi² 169
Torbi *see* Mambila
Toro, Toroŋga, Toroŋke: Bambara¹ 34–35
Toubakaï *see* Soninke
Toucouleur *see* Fulani
Tourouka *see* Turuka
Toussia *see* Tusia
Tɔa, Tɔalɛ, Tɔali, Tɔma, Tɔoma *see* Loma
Tɔram *see* Toram
Tɔxrica *see* Bura
Tremble *see* Drebo
Tribu *see* Delo
Tsam *see* Chawai
Tsaŋ: Kom 123
Tschamba, Tschamina *see* Tobote
Tschokossi, Tsekɔhale *see* Anufo²
Tshala *see* Cala
Tshi *see* Twi
Tshimiang: Dari 167
Tsoyap *see* Bagam
Tsugu: Chamba Daka 150
Tsureshe *see* Reshe
Tuba *see* Ligbi
Tuburi *see* Tupuri
Tugun *see* Tigong
Tukulor *see* Fulani
Tukun *see* Tigong
Tula 112
Tunbe *see* Tegesye
Tung: Kissi 12
Tunjur: Mubi² 169
Tupuri 146, 147
Tura: Kweni 40
Turka, *Turuka*: Lobi 59
Tusia: Senufo 56
Tuyo: Bakwe 50

Twabo: Kran 51, 54
Twa mia *see* Loma
Twi, Twifo 79, 90–94
Tyan, Tyanse *see* Gbe
Tyap *see* Katab
Tyapi *see* Tiapi
Tyasale *see* Gyassale
Tyebali: Senufo 57
Tyefo, Tyeforo *see* Tiefo
Tyenga *see* Kyenga

Uge *see* Gayi
Ugie *see* Ngi
Ukelle, Ukɛle 116
U-luf *see* Flup
Ura: Kamuku 103
Urapang *see* Jukun
Urhobo: Sobo 88–89
Uwurinya *see* Bowili
'Usuri *see* Kuseri

Va *see* Dyula
Vaanɛroki *see* Boki
Vagala: Grusi 62
Vai 35, 43–45
Valwa *see* Afema
Vandra *see* Nafana
Vei *see* Vai
Vere, Verɛ, Verre 150–1
Vetere, Vetre *see* Metyibo
Vɛi *see* Vai
Vige, Vigue, Viguie, Vigye: Senufo 57
Voko *see* Woko
Volof *see* Wolof
Vuela *see* Hwela
Vulum: Musgu 166
Vute, Vutere 145
Vwela *see* Hwela
Vy *see* Vai

Wa *see* War
Waa *see* Bobwa
Waana: 'Bidyo 168
Wadi *see* Zumu
Wadye *see* Bobwa
Waele: Baga 14
Waga *see* Bobwa
Waja 112
Waka: Yendang 139
Wala, Wale 65
Walia *see* Masa
Walo *see* Wala
Walu *see* Ngizim
Wandala *see* Mandara
Wangara¹ *see* Mande
Wangara² *see* Dyula
Wankara *see* Dyula
Wano: Kukuruku 88
Waŋgara, Waŋkore *see* Mande
Wapā: Jukun 141

War: Nsungli 123
Wara: Senufo 57
Warri: Ijo 121
Wasulu, Wasuluŋka: Malinke 33
Watyi: Ewe 83
Wawi *see* Dida
Waya *see* Bobwa
We *see* Fungom
Wegam *see* Kugama
Wegele *see* Gengle
Weima, Weima Buzi: Loma 38
Were *see* Vere
Wɛima *see* Weima
Widekum 126–8
Wike *see* Jukun
Wiya: Nsungli 123
Wo *see* Basari
Woaba: Gurma 68
Wobe¹ *see* Dan
Wobe² *see* Bobwa
Wodyeneka: Malinke 33
Woga 156
Woko: Duru 149
Wolof 18, 19, 21–24
Wom: Chamba 149
Worye *see* Wure
Wɔlof *see* Wolof
Wudiŋ *see* Kilba
Wudir: Woga 156
Wula: Higi 156
Wule¹: Bobo 60
Wule², Wulewule: Dagari 66
Wulisi *see* Kasena
Wum 124
Wurbo: Jukun 141
Wure: Baule 81
Wurkum, Wurkun: Jukun 141; *see also* Bakulũ
Wuso *see* Oso
Wute *see* Vute
Wymar Bouzié *see* Weima

Xasoŋke *see* Khasonke
Xɪbba *see* Kilba

Yache 116
Yadre: Mossi 64
Yaffudawa *see* Afudu
Yagba: Yoruba 85
Yakɔ, Yakö *see* Lukö
Yakoko: Mumuye 139
Yakoro: Boki 115
Yakokɔ *see* Yakoko
Yakuba *see* Dan
Yakurr *see* Lukö
Yalonka, Yalunke *see* Dyalonke
Yamma: Gbari 86
Yansi, Yarse: Mossi 64
Yassing *see* Jasing
Yauri *see* Kambari
Yawaziru: Bandi 39

INDEX

Ya win: Mano 39
Yedina *see* Buduma
Yendang 139
Yere *see* Vere
Yergam, Yergum 113
Yeskwa 107
Yidda *see* Nunku
Yidena *see* Buduma
Yimbɛ *see* Limba
Yoabou, *Yoabu*: Gurma 68
Yoba *see* Pilapila
Yofo: Yendang 139
Yoko: Bete 48
Yokogbo: Bete 49
Yola¹: Biafada 16
Yola² *see* Dyola

Yom *see* Pilapila
Yonni: Temne¹ 13
Yooba, *Yoruba* 84–85, 90–94
Yukutare *see* Bitare
Yule, Yulse *see* Kasena
Yungur *see* Lala
Yungɪrba *see* Lala

Zabarma, Zabirmawa *see* Zarma
Zadye *see* Dan
Zagai *see* Wom
Zage *see* Dan
Zamangan *see* Kamantan
Zanga: Lobi 59
Zani, Zany *see* Njai
Zara *see* Sankura

Zarma 46–47
Zazere *see* Kulango
Zegbe *see* Kwaya
Zelmogbo: Bete 49
Zimba *see* Nzima
Zinna: Mumuye 139
Zlogba: Mandara 159
Zomo *see* Zumu
Zomper *see* Kutev
Zona: Senufo 57
Zugweya *see* Busa
Zumper *see* Kutev
Zumu: Bata 155, 160, 161
Zungle *see* Nsungli
Ƶitako *see* Dibo

For Product Safety Concerns and Information please contact our EU
representative GPSR@taylorandfrancis.com
Taylor & Francis Verlag GmbH, Kaufingerstraße 24, 80331 München, Germany

www.ingramcontent.com/pod-product-compliance
Lightning Source LLC
Chambersburg PA
CBHW071813300426
44116CB00009B/1296